Theatricality and the Arts

Contents

List of Illustrations   vii
Introduction: Questioning Theatricality   1
   Andrew Quick and Richard Rushton

PART 1: MULTIMEDIA

1. Staging *Night Watch*: Theatricality and Scenes of Crime in Peter Greenaway's Screen Adaption of Rembrandt's Painting   25
   Kati Röttger
2. Theatricalising Absorption and Networked Hyper-Theatricality   41
   Lisa Åkervall
3. Theatricality and Dissonance: Frictions in Contemporary Networked Performance Practices   57
   Jane Frances Dunlop
4. Meta-Theatricality, Hypermediacy and Theatricality in the Making of *Never Swim Alone*   71
   Lowell Gasoi

PART 2: PHILOSOPHY

5. Display in Human Art and the Aesthetic Lives of Animals: On the Limits of Evolutionary Aesthetics   87
   Mathew Abbott
6. Against Experience: Theatre is Not Life (Or Theatre in the Age of Third Nature)   105
   Simon Jones

7 Theatre Against Itself: Performance, Politics and the Limits
of Theatricality 125
Adrian Kear

PART 3: ART/THEATRE/PHOTOGRAPHY/SOUND

8 Between Lies and Truth Lies the Truth: Staged Mythologies in
Damien Hirst's *Treasures from the Wreck of the Unbelievable* 145
Paula Blair

9 Owning the (Female) Experience: Theatricality, Writing and
Translation in Literature, Theatre and Cinema 167
Agneszkia Piotrowska

10 Performance, Photography, Theatricality and Citationality:
Theatricality as a Mode of Performing Citation in the Still
Photographic Image 186
Allan S. Taylor

11 Music, Miles Davis and Theatricality 201
Nicholas Gebhardt and Richard Rushton

PART 4: THEATRE AND CINEMA

12 Metaphoric Theatricality: Theatricality as a Weapon of
Resistance: The Production of *Our Grand Circus* in 1973
Greece 223
Michaela Antoniou

13 Theatricalising Sci-Fi: Theatre and the Multiverse in *Mouse:
The Persistence of an Unlikely Thought* (Daniel Kitson, 2016)
and *Constellations* (Nick Payne, 2012) 239
Anna Wilson

14 The Interconnectedness between Melodrama and
Theatricality in Pedro Almodóvar's *The Skin I Live In* (2011)
and Nelson Rodrigues' *Woman without Sin* (1941) 256
Isadora Grevan

15 Popular Theatricality in Spike Lee 272
Angelos Koutsourakis

Bibliography 293
Index 307

Illustrations

Figures

1.1	Rembrandt van Rijn, *The Night Watch*, 1642, oil on canvas. Rijksmuseum, Amsterdam	26
2.1	Ryan Trecartin and Lizzie Fitch, SITE VISIT, 2014, KW Institute for Contemporary Art in Berlin	47
3.1	*Documents of the Future: Invitation to Edit*, 2017	58
7.1	She She Pop, *Testament*, 2010	138
8.1	Damien Hirst, *Treasures from the Wreck of the Unbelievable*, 2017, Palazzo Grassi, Venice	146
10.1	Ciprian Muresan, *Leap into the Void, After three Seconds*, 2004	196

Tables

8.1	Instances of *Hydra and Kali* from *Treasures from the Wreck of the Unbelievable*	160

Introduction: Questioning Theatricality

Andrew Quick and Richard Rushton

What is theatricality? For the most part, in this collection, theatricality as a term is derived from *theatrical*: that which pertains to theatre. The suffix *-ity* gives us 'the quality of', thus making theatrical mean: the quality of that which pertains to theatre. From this we can deduce that theatricality means: that which draws attention to theatre, where theatre is a zone or mode that is distinguished from 'reality' or 'real life'. If something is designated 'theatre', then it must also signify that it is different from 'real life' in some way. That which is theatre is separated from reality. The distinction between theatre and real life, however, is not at all clear cut: there is always a substantial degree of fuzziness in trying to determine where reality ends and theatre begins, or *vice versa*. One way to mark the distinction is to highlight those facets of a performance or artwork that specifically mark it as 'theatre'; that is, as not from 'real life' or part of 'real life'. By specifically marking theatre *as* theatre, one will be asserting that *this is theatre*, not real life; it is theatrical.

This distinction between theatre and real life then opens up something of a paradox of theatricality. On the one hand, for an artwork to be theatrical, it must signal that it is distinct from real life: it must reject the assumption that what it is presenting might be taken for or mistaken for real life. It must declare to its audience: 'I am theatre; I am not real'. To be theatrical, theatre must show us that it is made, that it is fabricated, and thus that it is not natural or real. In doing so, however, the aim of the theatrical artwork is not to take us away from reality. Theatricality is not a matter of escaping from reality. Rather, the aim of the theatrical artwork is to demonstrate to us – the audience – that *reality itself is fabricated*, that reality is performed, conventional, artificial. In short, one might say that the aim of the theatrical artwork is to demonstrate that reality itself is theatrical.

Why would an artwork aspire to doing this? Why would an artwork want to show us that reality itself is theatrical? Theatrical artworks do this in order to show us that reality itself is not as real as we might suppose it to be. Rather, reality itself is comprised of codes, conventions, stereotypes, illusions, fantasies, fabrications and so on, all of which can add up to a way of declaring that reality is performed: reality itself is theatrical. If artworks are trying to exhibit such things to us (the audience, the spectators), then why are they doing such things? Here, theatre actually comes close to real life: if an artwork demonstrates its theatricality, then in doing so it reminds us – or tries to convince us – that reality itself is typically composed of theatrical elements, too. By being theatrical, an artwork paradoxically brings us closer to the real. The aim of the theatrical artwork is not to take us away from the real, it wants to bring us closer to the real, even if it is to declare to us that what we thought was 'the real' is not as real as it may seem.

What about artworks that are not theatrical? If an artwork that tries to fool us or trick us into believing in the reality of its performance – by using the techniques of linear perspective, for example, or by fostering the illusion of the 'fourth wall' in a theatre performance, by giving us a 'reality-effect' or 'impression of reality' – then such a work will also be trying to convince us that reality itself is easy to believe in; that it is seamless, natural, knowable, self-contained and self-evident. Such a mode of presentation – the traditional, transparent-fourth-wall-drama – will, however, be tricking us not only into believing in the reality of its performance or depiction. It will additionally be tricking us into believing that reality itself is natural, that reality is not composed of conventions, codes, ideologies, prejudices, contradictions and so on. For many of the essays collected here, then, any performance or artwork must resist this naturalisation of reality. By proclaiming itself 'theatrical', an artwork will be undoing the naturalisation of reality itself: it will be performing a deconstruction of the real, one might say; it will be forcing us not merely to question the nature of art or performance by way of its theatricality; it will also be asking us to question the nature of reality itself.

For example, we can take Laura Mulvey's immensely influential essay on 'Visual Pleasure and Narrative Cinema' as an indicator of these kinds of concerns (Mulvey 1989a). Yes, Mulvey's essay concerns cinema, but the essay has been very influential for art and theatre scholars, too.

As is well known, in that article on the representation of women in classical Hollywood films, Mulvey argues that women are typically rendered passive, while men are active. In depicting women and men in this way, Hollywood films are merely replicating the divisions of the real world in which women are also passive and men active. Hollywood cinema, with its methods of transparency and continuity, fails to signal itself as a construction: it fails to be 'theatrical', as it were. Mulvey writes: 'During its history, the cinema seems to have evolved a particular illusion of reality' (19). Because the mainstream cinema promotes an illusion of reality, and thus fails the test of theatricality, spectators are unable to decode the distinctions with which they are presented. When spectators see women depicted as passive and men as active, they simply accept that 'that's the way things are' or 'that's what reality is'. To defer to one of Mulvey's examples, when spectators watch Grace Kelly's character, Lisa, in *Rear Window* (Alfred Hitchcock, 1954), they see her conform to the wishes and demands of the main male character, L. B. Jeffries (James Stewart). She becomes an adventurer-type by placing herself in danger and thereby assisting in the capture of the murderer, Thorwald (Raymond Burr), all so as to satisfy the fantasy that Jeffries has of her. In other words, Lisa is passive; she conforms to the wishes of the active Jeffries. *Rear Window* thus fails to offer a critique of reality; it fails to be theatrical, and in failing the test of theatricality, it also fails as a critique of the real. There are counter-examples; films that are theatrical, as it were. Take an example from non-mainstream cinema, Chantal Akerman's *Jeanne Dielman* (1975). There, much like Grace Kelly's character in *Rear Window*, Delphine Seyrig's Jeanne is passive. But Jeanne is passive to a degree that draws attention to itself: the 'illusion of reality' is undone. By undoing the illusion of reality, by showing us the ways in which reality is 'constructed', *Jeanne Dielman* exposes the truth of the reality on view: that women are passive, and that the reality of this passivity must be challenged and overturned. The commandment of theatricality is mounted: the theatricality of the artwork exposes the theatricality of reality itself. The challenge is then to change that reality (on these points, see Mulvey 1989b).

Thus is proclaimed a chief strategy of theatricality: it will allow us, as spectators, to question the constructedness of reality itself. Often this will then mean that the aim of the artwork is one of transformation. By encouraging or demanding that the spectator question the constructedness of reality, the artwork is also asking – or demanding – that the spectator then act to change that reality. Indeed, a number of the essays collected here emphasise that the spectators of an artwork must be configured in such a way as to ensure that the spectator is in some way active, that she or he is a participant in the artwork, that audience members do not merely passively spectate but instead actively participate in works of art.

Viewer and Actor

We want to work through the consequences of this definition of theatricality with particular reference to an article published in 2012 (Lavender 2012). This article, written by Andy Lavender, focuses on the distinction between passive spectating and active participation in relation to theatre performances and other artworks and forms of entertainment (a basketball match, for example). The article, generally speaking, investigates the writings of French philosopher Jacques Rancière, especially his essay on 'The Emancipated Spectator', first published in 2007 (Rancière 2009). At one point, the article in question takes one of Rancière's claims: 'Emancipation begins when we challenge the opposition between viewing and acting' (Rancière 2009, 13; Lavender 2012, 323). What is Rancière claiming here? According to Lavender, the statement is something of a commandment or rallying cry. Rancière is declaring that we must destroy the opposition between viewing and acting so that passive viewing becomes active participation. The opposition between viewing and acting is destroyed when there is no longer any passive viewing. Emancipation begins when all viewing becomes acting. It is by destroying the opposition between viewing and acting that liberation will be delivered: the spectator will be emancipated.

We can see that this logic applies to theatricality as we have described it. By being made aware that the artwork is a construction – that it is a type of theatre – the viewer will no longer be passively viewing the artwork but will be aware of the work of art as art. This awareness is a first step towards becoming an active participant. The next step is to come to the awareness that reality itself is constructed, with an additional step requiring the viewer to then reflect on reality in order to transform it. Thus is the logic of active participation delivered: the theatricality of the artwork transforms the artistic situation from one of passive absorption of the work into an active mode of transformation. In our example from Mulvey above, the subjugation of women depicted in the artwork – in *Jeanne Dielman* – will lead the spectator to demand that reality itself is transformed so that women are no longer placed in positions of subordination.

Lavender focuses on the importance of being a participant rather than an observer (321) and laments that, in his example of being part of the audience of a National Basketball Association basketball match, it is not entirely possible for the spectator to become active. Yes, the spectator here is 'non-passive', claims Lavender, but 'the main mode remains one of watching' (326). The viewer is not active in ways that will lead to the transformation of reality. Lavender's final summation is thus a negative one:

> You don't change the event, here; you merely complete it. Nor do you change yourself. Rather, you consume culture and enjoy the visual affirmation of yourself as participating consumer. In this matrix of engaged experience, the offer is of a safe, secure arrangement for redistributed spectating. The spectator is implicated, even incorporated, rather than emancipated (326).

Lavender finds examples of works of art that nearly bring us to emancipation, that nearly transform us from being passive spectators into active participants . . . but not quite. There is no question of what the goal of the emancipatory work of art must be: it must ensure that it does not produce viewers or spectators, for these are by definition passive. What it must produce are active participants. If the artwork fails to produce active participants, it will be failing the promise of emancipation. If it is not contributing to our emancipation, then it is surely ensuring our continued imprisonment, our continuing incapacity for emancipation.

And yet . . . . There is no doubt that Lavender's account of Rancière is based on a misreading.[1] What is it that Rancière means when he writes that '[e]mancipation begins when we challenge the opposition between viewing and acting'? Does he mean, as Lavender implies, that the opposition between viewing and acting must be demolished so that all viewing is transformed into acting? Or does Rancière in fact mean something else? Might he be saying that viewing and acting do not need to be opposed? Might he be saying that, if one sees an opposition between viewing and acting, then one is mistaken. There is no opposition between them. Rather, *viewing is already a form of acting*. When I am viewing an artwork or theatre performance (or basketball match), as a spectator, I am not passive. Rather, any and every form of viewing is always already a form of acting. Spectatorship is, by definition, always active. Therefore, it is not necessary for there to be an opposition between viewing and acting.

And furthermore, emancipation begins when we get rid of the opposition between viewing and acting. And we should do this not so that viewing is replaced by acting. Rather, we should do it in order to come to the realisation that the opposition between viewing and acting is a false one: viewing is always a form of acting, or action. That is what Rancière means when he writes that '[e]mancipation begins when we challenge the opposition between viewing and acting'.

If this is the case, what implications does it have for a theory of theatricality? We have so far claimed that theatricality works by affirming the constructedness of the artwork, by ensuring that the artwork is presented in a mode that signifies 'theatre', that the artwork never be confused or conflated with reality. And yet, at one and the same time, as a result of the theatrical gesture, the consequences of the artwork are supposed to have an effect on reality: the spectator is to be transformed by the theatrical event or work so that the spectator will then, in turn, perform a transformation of reality. The viewer who is presumed to not be an actor becomes an actor, is transformed into an actor by the theatrical artwork. The quest to ensure theatre's distance from reality is merely a precursor to ensuring that the theatrical work is then put in touch with reality. In fact, the work is supposed to tell us of the faults of reality, and the theatrical work exposes this reality. By showing us the difference between theatre and reality, the consequence is thus to show us that, in fact, theatre and reality are the same. What you thought was reality is not reality; rather, it is a mode of theatre. And then what has to happen? Well, if reality is theatre, then we must do away with this reality that is theatrical. It must be replaced by reality, for we do not want a reality that is theatrical.

These are not straightforward claims. First of all, we need to consider that Rancière does not endorse such arguments. On the contrary, he is critical of them. He writes, for example, of this mode of theatre – and many will have realised by now that this mode of theatre is Brechtian above all else, and it is towards Brecht that many of Rancière's criticisms are aimed – as giving us the following result: '"Good" theatre is one that uses its separated reality in order to abolish it' (2009, 7). To abolish 'it'? To abolish theatre? Or to abolish reality? Rancière clearly means that the consequences of this logic are to abolish theatre. By abolishing theatre, the distinction between theatre and reality is also abolished. Theatre is no longer 'theatre': all theatre will become fused with reality. And Rancière repeats this claim many times in his short essay. The following comments more or less give us the big picture, in which Rancière is critical of both Brecht and Artaud:

> According to the Brechtian paradigm, theatrical mediation [call this 'theatricality'] makes them [spectators] conscious of the social situation that gives rise to it and desirous of acting in order to transform it. According to Artaud's logic, it makes them abandon their position as spectators: rather than being placed in front of the spectacle, they are surrounded by the performance, drawn into the circle of action that restores their collective energy. In both cases, theatre is presented as mediation striving for its own abolition (Rancière 2009, 8).

Theatre, theatricality, in this mode, desires its own abolition. Theatre as theatrical is striving for its own abolition. When theatre is abolished, there is no longer a distinction between theatre and reality. All is reality. As Rancière puts it, '"[g]ood" theatre is one that uses its separated reality in order to abolish it' (7). (We could further emphasise Rancière's distance from Brecht. See his damning comparison between the capitulation of Galileo in Brecht's *Life of Galileo* and Brecht's own capitulation at the House Un-American Activities Committee in 1947; Rancière 2011.)

Cloud Gate

Where does this leave 'theatricality'? We are not entirely certain where this leaves the notion of theatricality, especially in relation to the modernist theories of Brecht and Artaud that Rancière is keen to bring into question. It is worth considering in more detail another example from Lavender's article, Anish Kapoor's *Cloud Gate* (2006), located in Millenium Park, near Chicago's Institute of Art. Made of mirror-polished stainless steel, the large sculpture is shaped like a bean (the work is nicknamed 'The Bean'), and its entire surface is reflective. This means that, if you stand facing this work, you will see yourself reflected in it, albeit in a distorted way, and so too will you see the people next to you reflected, as well as the sky and any clouds that might be there, and, depending on which side of the 'bean' you stand, you may see various aspects of Chicago's cityscape reflected.[2]

Can Kapoor's *Cloud Gate* be considered theatrical? From one perspective, we might consider *Cloud Gate* as a form of theatre insofar as it is clearly not a natural object. It is constructed, and it foregrounds its fabricated aspects. Additionally, by reflecting ourselves and the world back to us in a distorted fashion, the work could be said to be foregrounding the constructedness of reality, too. It can enable us to see the real world as reflected back to us in ways we had not considered before. It can give us a different perspective on the world that surrounds us. There might be another way to come at this. Lavender emphasises two properties of the work. First of all, he claims that, with *Cloud Gate*, 'you view yourself in the act of viewing' (Lavender 2012, 318). This is a key point, for *Cloud Gate* does not function like a mirror. When looking into a mirror you are typically looking at yourself – tidying your hair, putting on makeup and so on. Here, by contrast, you do not so much look at yourself as you look at the act of looking, almost as though one of the points of *Cloud Gate* is precisely for you to question what it is you are doing there, to ask yourself what the act of looking at this object amounts to. Lavender sums it up very aptly by saying that, with *Cloud Gate*, 'you view yourself in the act of viewing'. He makes a second point: *Cloud Gate* invites viewers to touch it – it is haptic – and even to walk beneath it. The bean is shaped in such a way that it forms a kind of arch which leaves viewers room to walk beneath it.

These observations of Lavender's surely bring to mind another definition of theatricality, one proposed many years ago by art historian Michael Fried. In his (in)famous article on 'Art and Objecthood', first published in 1967, one of the properties of theatrical artworks was that they are typified by the experience of 'an object in a *situation*, one that, virtually by definition *includes the beholder*' (Fried 1998b, 153). Fried wants to emphasise here that the theatrical artwork is not complete until the viewer is there to complete it. The artwork would not exist without the viewer's being there, and to that extent the beholder or viewer is part of the artwork itself. One way of putting this might be to say that the viewer has to be active, she or he has to be 'there' in front of the work for it to be considered a work. We can see all of this in play in *Cloud Gate*. The work itself is merely a reflecting surface, so one of the things that it reflects is us (or 'me'). I cannot view the artwork without also being in the artwork. Thus, the work 'includes the beholder'. But also, because the artwork will change depending on where I stand in relation to it, then by being there, I am creating what the work is: I make it become what it is at any moment. At this level, the work is once again one that 'includes the beholder'.

Fried's comments are meant as a criticism. He disapproves of theatrical works of art, or at the very least, he sees the operations of theatricality as being very much at odds with the aesthetic intentions of the modernist art of which he approves. One way to interpret his antipathy to what he calls theatrical works of art is to declare that such works do not exist 'in themselves' as works of art. Rather, they need to be completed by the people who view them. The viewer must participate in such works in order for those objects to function as works of art. We can see this in *Cloud Gate* because much of the work is composed of what is reflected in the bean's shiny surface. The work does not exist, as it were, without a person's being there to see themselves seeing it – 'you view yourself in the act of viewing', as Lavender puts it.

Some more steps are needed here. This artwork, the artwork that is theatrical, must also therefore intersect with our real lives. As we have so far seen, the aim or the logic of the theatrical work of art is that it should abolish theatre and that it should abolish the distinction between theatre and reality. By way of theatricality, the work of art becomes indistinguishable from life itself. Fried's cutting example is of one artist's sense of awe while driving down an unfinished section of the New Jersey turnpike – the artist was Tony Smith. Fried comes to the conclusion that the experience of the unfinished stretch of road gave this artist something no artwork ever had. '[T]here is no way you can frame it', Smith declared, 'you just have to experience it' (Fried 1998b, 158). The experience of the artwork is all there is. There is no object; rather, the work is produced by the spectator's experience of it. Or, more than that, it is the product of the active participant's experience of the work, for passive spectators, too, will have been done away with in this world without artworks, where everything has become art, even an unfinished section of freeway.

Fried's response might be one of saying that artworks are already artworks. We know how to approach and respond to works of art because we know they are not real. Or, to put it another way, their realness consists in their being real works of art. And their being not real – not the same as reality – gives them a specific advantage (we might see such a thing especially in the case of the deaths and murders that we have in theatre performances or films, as well as in novels and other literary works: a fictional death is ontologically different from a real death). Perhaps Herman Melville put it best: 'The people in a fiction, like the people in a play, must dress as nobody exactly dresses, talk as nobody exactly talks, act as nobody exactly acts. It is with fiction as with religion: it should present another world, and one to which we feel the tie' (Melville 2006, 187). Ultimately, this might all be a way of declaring that works of art do not need to draw attention to their constructedness: they do not need to be theatrical. If an artwork is an artwork, or if a theatre performance is a theatre performance (and so, too, for poetry, films, novels, television programmes and so on), then do we not know this already? We do not need a demonstration of a work's constructedness or theatricality: artworks are artworks, and in being artworks they stand apart from reality.

We do not believe that this is necessarily Fried's point, but it is certainly Rancière's point. He will tell us that words are merely words and that those words are not made of the same stuff as the real world out there is – or, to adopt Melville's phrasing, those words are written in ways that are not quite like what it is they describe (if they were the same as what they describe, we would not need the words). Rancière, with some complication, puts it this way:

> To dismiss the fantasies of the word made flesh and the spectator rendered active, to know that words are merely words and spectacles merely spectacles, can help us to arrive at a better understanding of how words and images, stories and performances, can change something of the world we live in (Rancière 2009, 23).

Do we need to rebel against theatre? Do we need to abolish theatre? Do we need to condemn theatre in the name of transforming reality? Rancière certainly does not think so. Rather, let us enjoy words as words, spectacles as spectacles, films as films . . . . Merely doing this, and expecting artworks to be artworks, nothing more or less, will open the door to the transformation of reality. From this perspective, spectators are always already emancipated. They are not passive, and they do not need theorists of the theatre (such as Brecht or Artaud) to show them how they should be emancipated. Spectators are always already emancipated.

There are some points of crossover in the work of Fried and Rancière. Both consider that something significant in the history of art emerged in France during the eighteenth century. For Fried, this was the establishment of the painterly goal of absorption. For Rancière, it is the emergence of a modern conception of art; what he calls the aesthetic regime of art. Indeed, to some degree both authors call upon commentaries of Chardin's or Greuze's paintings by the brothers Goncourt to make their points, although, in truth, Fried views the Goncourts negatively.[3] Rancière foregrounds the importance of writing about art – that is, the importance of critics and historians for art as such. Critics began to write about art in a new and different way in the eighteenth century, and such writing led to a new understanding of what art was or could be. All of this, ultimately, was a key ingredient in the recipe that would produce the high modernism of Malevich, Kandinsky, Pollock and others.

Rancière nevertheless questions Fried's criticisms of theatricality. He asks: is the kind of theatre Fried refers to not simply the kind of naturalist or realist theatre – a theatre of the 'invisible' fourth wall – invented in the second half of the nineteenth century, and which had by and large petered out by the middle of the twentieth? If this is 'theatre', then it is a rather narrow definition of it (see Rancière 2007, 88). And then Rancière goes further to ask of Fried: was not the quest of such a theatre one in which the distinction between theatre and 'real life' could be demolished? And if that were to occur, would not any distinction between art and life also be demolished? In short, for Rancière, is not the end point of Fried's critique much the same as that pursued by the advocates of theatricality – for Brecht, Artaud, Andy Lavender, and others? All of this leads us to declare that we have not so much answered any questions here; rather, we have merely found more questions to ask.

The Reals of Theatricality

Of course, Rancière's purpose is bent towards the transformation of reality, the change in the 'something of the world' that he sees as being the function of art. This still begs the question of what the real might be, how we can access the (unnameable) object to be transformed. It is interesting that the real is conjured up by Rancière as a *something*, a term that would appear to evade any definition or parameter. If we linger on the discipline or enterprise of theatre (something Rancière does not explore at all), we can see that theatre, configured as it is via interleaved sets of practices, always negotiates and has some relationship to the *idea* of a real. This is why philosophers such as Derrida and Lyotard repeatedly invoke theatre as a model of representation, or as a machine or apparatus that reveals how representation operates (see Derrida 1981; Lyotard 1973). Put simply, this model is based on an originary separation from and exclusion of the real (what is marked out as the auditorium and then the stage) that allows a representation of reality to take place (action on the stage itself). In short, to be real on the stage one needs to be separated from the reality of the real (whatever that might be), otherwise we would not know it as theatre. Theatre, as a site that organises time and space, is haunted by the modalities of separation – street and foyer, foyer and auditorium, seating area and stage, stage and wings and back- or off-stage – that allows the operation of theatre, theatricality, to take place.

This dynamic of (dis)placing is at the core of theatre. Indeed, it is woven into the etymology of the word: a place to behold, a viewing place, to put in place and connect the term to neighbouring words such as theory and theology. Making seen, making sense, bringing into being, placing before – these are the defining phrases that express what might be understood by the term theatrical, as well as the practices of mimesis, illusion and representation with which the theatre is more usually associated. This notion of placing, this operation via different degrees of separation, is pursued entirely to create a particular relationship between the viewed and the viewer. As such, the art and act of spectating (and here Rancière's thinking is particularly insightful) also has to be at the heart of any understanding of what we might mean by the term theatrical.

However, we are still left with the problem of what constitutes the real within the temporal spatial ordering that configures the theatrical. Yes, Rancière is correct in his privileging of an already emancipated spectator, but he barely makes mention of what is being spectated upon and reduces the complexity of what takes place in the machines, the theatres of representation, to 'words as words, films as films' and so forth. If there is a gap here in Rancière's thinking, then a quick turn to how theatre has historically negotiated the concept of the real might help us understand his configuration of emancipation more fully.

Historical narratives of theatre and theatricality, particularly those from a Western perspective, usually begin with an exploration of ritual practices, which are often cited as formations of the earliest manifestations of performance. Within the discipline of Performance Studies, the writings of Richard Schechner have led and dominated this field. Schechner, and this is a somewhat brutal reduction of his various writings, argues that the function of ritual is to transform concepts into realities, to make the abstract tangible. Ritual creates and uses performance to shore up and play with structures that make sense of a world to those who participate in its multiple events, a world that is at least constituted out of an attempt to negotiate an understanding of the past, the present and the future, an endeavour that Giorgio Agamben has called the transformation of 'unstable signifiers into stable signifiers' (Agamben 1993, 83).

Pursuing this historical trajectory further, the power of ritual declines as consequence of the enormous cultural shifts associated with modernity. As people move from the rural to the urban, as people's immediate relationship to the land and sources of food and so forth is irrevocably changed, the operations of ritual as a way of structuring meaning recedes. This is not to say that ritual disappears. The tropes of ritual are absorbed into new formations of theatrical practices. These practices, however, put the individual at the centre of experience. This is the consequence of modernity, the product of the seismic shift that produces the bourgeois subject, which, in turn, results in the practices of perspective in the arts, the creation of permanent theatres with their architectural arrangements that permit the spectator to perceive a world which is created before them. Here the world is perceived from a point of view, and the stage begins its transformation from pageant wagons and temporary spaces to the permanent buildings we know as theatres today, where we sit and watch the spectacle of a world unfolding before us. Here the spectator is seated, static, situated and separated from the place of action (the stage), far removed from the regime of participation that ritual practices previously enabled.

Alongside this transformation that is fuelled by modernity is the drive to map, to categorise, to turn experience into knowledge, to commodify and, in turn, to exploit. And at the centre of this evolution is an ever-increasing emphasis on the power and authority of sight and the visible, in order to, as Galileo commanded, measure everything and make everything measurable. Just as in painting, perspective and the power to measure become the defining aesthetic, and the reflection of a notion of subjectivity, a version of singular identity, begins to be performed on the stage. The eye is seen in direct relationship to the I of subjectivity, and this is played out both for the performer and the spectator in the theatre.

There is not enough space here to reflect on the development of the theatre as a place for seeing across the arc of modernity, but this emphasis on sight reaches its zenith with the emergence of Naturalism and Realism at the end of the nineteenth century. Zola's imperative is that art must follow the models provided by the positivist physiologist Claud Bernard and 'replace novels of pure imagination by novels of observation and experimentation' (Zola 1893, 9). Although Naturalists privileged the surface appearance of things and Realists sought the truth in a revelation of what lay in the subterranean layers below the surface, both pursue truth through a capacity to see truly.

It is no surprise, then, that, when the bourgeois subject comes under attack in the twentieth century, the dominant modes of representing bourgeois identity are also subject to a brutal assault. This is the energy that fuels the historical avant-garde (Futurists, Dadaists and Surrealists) which wanted to tear down not only the authority of bourgeois subjectivity to define human experience, but also the art forms that were seen to represent them and the intuitions that shored these forms up: the gallery, the museum and the proscenium arch theatre. As a reaction to bourgeois representation, the avant-garde's turn to notions of speed, of chance, of shock and the inner workings of the unconscious can be seen as an attempt to discover the true reality of experience: a reality that is always beyond the scope of the bourgeois mind, a reality that does not rely on sight as its foundation. It is this drive which seems to provoke Tristan Tzara's final words in his *Dada Manifesto*: 'DADA DADA DADA: – the roar of contorted pains, the interweaving of contraries and of all contradictions, freaks and irrelevancies: Life' (Gordon 1987, 51).

What is fascinating about this early part of the twentieth century is the emphasis on theatricality to somehow get to a real that could not be retrieved via what were considered bourgeois forms. This is what connects the practices and theories of Artaud and Brecht, despite their obvious ideological differences. Both figures were focused on accessing a previously obscured or ignored idea of reality. Brecht's reality was configured through a reality conjured up in an attempt to locate a reality that is arrived at via a dramaturgy of dialectics. Artaud sought his reality through locating what he called 'life itself', the antithesis of what he calls 'an imitation of life' (Artaud 1976, 167). Artaud's Theatre of Cruelty is not achieved through the pain that the performer and spectator have to endure to exceed the limits imposed by any particular representational order or an assault on the audience. Cruelty is the move beyond representation itself, a move that would annihilate representation to become a living force, an instance of life itself, or, as Artaud puts it, 'giving birth to forms' (ibid).

This giving birth to forms is not anti-theatricality. Far from it. Brecht and Artaud are practitioners in the theatre, and both focus on particular formations of theatricality to get access to their specific concept of the real. In this sense, the focus on theatricality in their endeavours is not to somehow expose the limits of the theatre, to reveal a certain concept of hollowness or the hidden operations of certain ideological formations, but rather to show how theatricality itself can lead us to some encounter with truth or reality.

Both Brecht and Artaud configure the spectator at the centre of this attempt to get access to a real that has previously been evaded or deliberately masked in other formations of theatrical presentation. Theatricality, whether it be the use of half curtains, media, songs, narrators, or the fractured physicality often invoked by Artaud, is foregrounded *in practice* as devices or processes with which the performer engages or through which the performer passes in their attempt to get at the real in the act of performing itself. The turn to theatricality is a set of practices, modalities, that enable this endeavour. Theatricality, far from revealing theatre's artificiality, becomes the playing space where the real might be sought. And at the centre of these playing spaces are spectators who give energy and bear witness to these various voyages of discovery.

Consider, for a brief moment, the work of The Wooster Group, a New York company led by director Elizabeth LeCompte, who have been making theatre since the mid-1970s, often exploring classic texts through a direct exploration of theatricality across the disciplines of theatre, film, media, music and dramatic writing. The act of self-discovery, of self-revelation is often foregrounded by LeCompte in various writings and interviews. Writing in a programme note in 1993, LeCompte invokes the mask as a theatrical device that enables the performer to discover something profound about themselves. Reflecting on what she demands from the performer, she comments: 'Actors are searching for masks of themselves – not of character. Who they are on stage is who they are on stage – period. They must be more "themselves" than in life' (Quick 2007, 274). A continuous trope in The Wooster Group's work is an explicit exploration of theatricality within the playing space of the multiple performance works that have spanned more than fifty years. These spaces, described by LeCompte as 'architectonic' always demand that a performer relinquishes a prescriptive control within the performance and forces them to be open to the dynamics of the performance, the theatricality, of the performance itself. It is in such spaces that LeCompte infers that they can be more 'themselves'. Long-term collaborator Ron Vawter puts this more succinctly in his elaboration of his performance of Vershinin in

The Wooster Group's production of *Brace Up!*, their adaption of Chekov's *Three Sisters*:

> It wasn't about my ability to impersonate or 'be' Vershinin. What was important was that I find ways of being myself, as best I could, publicly . . . It's a very difficult thing to describe . . . It's the sort of thing that still makes me want to go onto the stage because I'm still trying to figure out what it is I'm doing in front of an audience. There is no lesson to be learned, but I'm still interested in finding out who I am in front of an audience (Quick 2007, 274).

Here Vawter acknowledges that his process of finding out has to be public, in front of and in the presence of the spectator, a presence that can feed back into his endeavours. Acting is described as a doing, not as an impersonation or even as an embodiment of a character. And this process of doing always involves an encounter with the meaning-making regimes that operate within the performance space, the active dynamics of theatricality that allow theatre (and representation) to take place, those systems that turn unstable signifiers into stable signifiers. Theatricality, then, becomes the very crucible of possibility, of discovery, of making contact with the real. Far from being the object to be exposed and derided, it is the place where the very truth of our being, 'the something of the world', might be unveiled.

On Theatricality

Where does this leave us in relation to theatricality (we ask again)? As we have already stated, in this collection, theatricality as a term is derived from *theatrical*: that which pertains to theatre. And, thus, theatrical means: the quality of that which pertains to theatre. And, therefore, many of the pieces here work precisely on that: they try to identify and/or define *the quality of that which pertains to theatre*. These essays are not necessarily in accord with what we have outlined here in our introduction, and it is true to say that many of the essays here will challenge the kinds of arguments we have made. But one thing is certainly clear: these essays open up debates about how to characterise the importance of theatricality. They do so in relation to theatre, yes, but also in relation to works of art more generally, to internet art, to jazz music, to television and cinema. The range of approaches here is a marker of the importance of 'theatricality' as a theoretical term. The collection cannot deliver any definitive definition of theatricality. Rather, what we hope to offer is a continuation of debates in and around the term theatricality.

* * *

Theatricality and the Arts begins with a section on 'Multimedia'. The chapters in this section offer a series of reflections on theatricality as that term pertains to a range of performances and objects that cannot be easily grouped in terms of traditional media. These approaches break down the barriers between different media and offer conjunctions of art, film, internet art, as well as theatre. Kati Röttger discusses the art of Rembrandt, especially via the re-workings of *The Night Watch* taken up several years ago by filmmaker Peter Greenaway. Röttger carefully challenges Michael Fried's conceptions of anti-theatricality and, with great deftness, traces a notion of theatricality as 'staging'. One of the achievements of Greenaway's *Nightwatching* is to engage in a process of staging Rembrandt's *The Night Watch*, while maintaining an approach that resides somewhere between film, theatre and painting.

In her chapter on 'Theatricalising Absorption', Lisa Åkervall turns Fried's distinction between absorption and theatricality inside out, especially as that distinction is elaborated in Fried's 1980 book on *Absorption and Theatricality*. Examining a number of recent internet artworks – via YouTube, Snapchat and elsewhere – Åkervall argues that we have entered an era in which absorption need no longer be posited as the opposite of theatricality. Rather, what is at stake today is our increasingly being absorbed by theatricality. In short, modes that a writer like Fried or Denis Diderot might once have posited as purely theatrical no longer function in a theatrical way; rather, they encourage and function by virtue of states of absorption. Jane Frances Dunlop, in a chapter on 'Theatricality and Dissonance', looks at some aspects of contemporary 'networked performances'; that is, performances that unfold live via interconnected, collaborative screens from (more or less) anywhere in the world. Dunlop stresses the importance of dissonance in such performances, linking the dissonance of performance with what Jacques Rancière has called the 'dissensus' or 'disagreement' central to democratic processes. The dissonance of networked performances, so Dunlop argues, opens up the possibility of new terrains of signification, a potential transformation of the ways in which we experience and understand the world. Lowell Gasoi, in a final contribution from this section of the book, reflects on his own production of David MacIvor's 1991 play, *New Swim Alone*. One of the characters in Gasoi's production, rather than being played by a 'real live actor', was instead played by a projected character constructed out of elements filmed before the production. These elements were then integrated into the play's 'live' performances. Gasoi uses this premise as a way of reflecting on notions of meta-theatre and intermediality, thus complicating the ways in which theatre and theatricality blur the boundaries between live theatre and its non-living, pre-filmed ghost.

In the book's second section, 'Philosophy', three authors provide accounts of theatricality from philosophical perspectives, broadly speaking. Mathew Abbott, in a fascinating and somewhat curious way, asks the question of how human artworks are different from the kinds of artworks – or 'displays' – that can be attributed to animals. In an argument that to some extent defends Michael Fried's anti-theatrical claims, Abbott states that, unlike animals, humans are capable of deception. 'Deception', in the way in which Abbott frames it, is a human concept, and if a human being approaches a work of art, then they will be affronted if the artwork is deceptive in one way or another. Working from Kant's *Critique of Judgment*, Abbott reflects on the difference between a birdsong, on the one hand, and, on the other, the human imitation of a birdsong that is intended to deceive; that is, an imitated birdsong, the intention of which is to make its listeners believe that it is the song of a 'real' bird. Abbott argues that these are distinctions that matter for human beings, and ultimately such factors make human artworks markedly different from the aesthetic performances of animals.

Next, in a provocative piece titled 'Against Experience', Simon Jones defends the messiness of traditional theatre spaces, the spaces of bodies and objects and performers and audience members. He does so in order to emphasise the relationality of such experiences, for theatre spaces open up a series of relations, between performers themselves, between audience members jammed into their seats, between performers and audiences, between the action of the performance and the space occupied by spectators, and so on. In elaborating his claims, Jones relies on arguments put forward by German philosopher Martin Heidegger, especially in his seminar on *Mindfulness*, while also offering an examination of a theatre performance called *Real Magic*, staged in 2017 by Forced Entertainment. The final chapter in this section of the book is by Adrian Kear. In 'Theatre

Against Itself', Kear proposes the term *theatricalisation* as the process of making something into a scene; namely, the staging of something. To this extent, theatre acts as a framing device, and thus – in ways that are similar to the claims we have made above – theatre cuts something out of reality to enframe it as 'theatre'. Kear reflects on Shakespeare's *King Lear* – especially on Stanley Cavell's famous interpretation of that play – as well as Donald Trump's hair and a recent reworking of *King Lear* by She She Pop.

In the book's next section, 'Art/Theatre/Photography/Sound', Paula Blair first of all offers an account of Damien Hirst's 2017 exhibition *Treasures from the Wreck of the Unbelievable*. At stake here is the question of artistic intention: how are we supposed to respond to an exhibition that so brazenly tries to pass itself off as true and genuine historical archaeology, while even the most superficial of background checks will tell us that this is a fabrication? To some degree, Blair tries to chart an answer by way of a series of arguments concerning the relationship between theatricality and veracity. In the kind of theatre constructed by Hirst, she asks, what is true, and how can we verify such truths? And then, what are the consequences of the fakery and falsity on display here?

Agnieszka Piotrowska, in her chapter on 'Owning the (Female) Experience', characterises theatricality in terms of that which disrupts the mundane. Where spectacle is a matter of sustaining the dominant ideology, argues Piotrowska – and to do so she is enlisting Rancière and Guy Debord, as well as providing an excellent discussion of Brecht's *Verfremdungseffekt* – theatricality intervenes in order to provide a disruption to any 'normal' routine. Theatricality therefore brings with it the possibility of changing the world. These concepts are discussed by way of three fictional works: Olga Tokarczuk's novel *Flights* (originally published in 2007); Julia Kristeva's novel *Teresa my Love* (2008); and Piotrowska's own adaptations of Stanley Makuwe's play *Finding Temeraire*, both as a theatre production (which premiered in 2017) and as a film, *Repented* (directed by Piotrowska and released in 2019).

Allan S. Taylor then provides a sustained discussion of photography, with a focus on the concepts of theatricality and citationality. Taylor's approach is inspired by French philosopher Jacques Derrida, and he uses Derrida's concept of *différance* to chart the delay or deferral that occurs between the object of a photograph and the photograph itself – the distinction between the object that *is photographed* and the object that *is a photograph*. This *différance* opens up the space of theatricality in photography, a play of differences which, so Taylor argues, leads to a doubled alienation of the body. Three related photographic works are brought to bear on this argument: Yves Klein's *Leap into the Void* (1960); and two reworkings of Klein's photograph, one by Yasamusa Morimura and another by Ciprian Muresan.

Finally, in this section, Nicholas Gebhardt and Richard Rushton offer some reflections on the play between theatricality and absorption in the musical performances of jazz trumpeter Miles Davis. The authors focus on several recordings of the classic jazz standard, 'My Funny Valentine', as recorded by different Davis jazz bands between 1956 and 1965. They argue that Davis's performances are vehemently anti-theatrical, characterised most emphatically by his gesture of turning his back on his audience. As a result, Davis's goal at this point of his career, it is argued, was to reach some sort of complete absorption in the music he and his bands were making.

The book's final section, 'Theatre and Cinema', examines theatre and film works, often in conjunction. Michaela Antoniou's remarkable chapter focuses on the historical significance of the 1973 production, performed in Greece, of *Our Grand Circus*. Antoniou articulates a concept of *metaphoric theatricality,* whereby an obvious, 'social' meaning is doubled by a metaphorical one. This metaphoric theatricality was used, so Antoniou argues, as a very specific political weapon in 1973, insofar as *Our Grand Circus* brought forth a critique of the prevailing political situation – a critique of the ruling Military Junta. Antoniou suggests that the public's support for *Our Grand Circus* played a part in the eventual overthrowing of the Junta in 1974.

Anna Wilson examines the interface between science fiction and theatre. Wilson argues that science fiction is much more commonly the domain of cinema and written fiction, and that it poses specific difficulties for live performance. Out of this, Wilson examines the specificity of theatre and the question of how producing sci-fi on the stage is a matter of 'making into theatre'. The chapter also focuses on conceptions of the 'multiverse', a notion first formulated by Hugh Everett in 1957. Wilson does this by way of a close analysis of two stage productions: Daniel Kitson's 2016 staging of *Mouse* and *Constellations*, written by Nick Payne (2012).

Isadora Grevan writes across theatre and cinema, the former by way of Nelson Rodrigues's *Woman Without Sin* (1941) and the latter in Pedro Almodóvar's *The Skin I Live In* (2011). For the central characters in these narratives, what is at stake is a mode of 'manipulating performance' while in states of captivity. One way to put this is to declare that by being fake – by being theatrical – the characters in these fictions manage to free themselves from captivity. Grevan thus offers an impressive and detailed defence of the conceptions of theatricality as they are proposed by the plots and characters of these fictions.

Finally, Angelos Koutsourakis offers an account of popular theatricality in the films of Spike Lee – in *School Daze* (1988), *Do the Right Thing* (1989), *Bamboozled* (2000) and *Chi-Raq* (2015). Koutsourakis's conception of popular theatricality is taken from a variety of sources, chiefly from Noël Burch's discussions of early cinema and 'attractions', from the theatre of Meyerhold and the cinema of Eisenstein, and elsewhere. Koutsourakis argues that Lee's films, defined in many ways by his hyperbolic style, engage techniques that aspire to an aesthetic of *popular theatricality* which combines entertainment with political critique.

* Some words of thanks are in order. Some of the essays here were originally presented as part of a symposium held at Lancaster University in 2017. The symposium was held as part of a research project on 'Theatricality and Interrelations Between Art, Theatre and Cinema', which was funded by the Arts and Humanities Research Council in the United Kingdom during 2017–18. Special thanks go to Professor Sir Christopher Frayling for being a central part of all of these activities.

Notes

1. Indeed, several authors in this collection take up Rancière's arguments from *The Emancipated Spectator* (see Dunlop, Piotrowska, Taylor and Wilson). We, as editors, have not been prescriptive in this respect, and the interpretations of Rancière that appear on the following pages must stand on their own.
2. There exists an excellent Wikipedia page for *Cloud Gate*: https://en.wikipedia.org/wiki/Cloud_Gate
3. Indeed, we are simplifying here, as Fried is very much opposed to the Goncourts' 'optical' assessment of Greuze (see Fried 1980, 8), whereas Rancière marks the importance of the Goncourts' endorsement of opticality for the history of modern art (Rancière 2007, 80).

Part 1
Multimedia

1

Staging *Night Watch*: Theatricality and Scenes of Crime in Peter Greenaway's Screen Adaption of Rembrandt's Painting

Kati Röttger

Introduction

In 2007, the British artist and filmmaker Peter Greenaway launched the film *Nightwatching* as part of a larger project of the same title that he created for the year-long 2006 celebration of Rembrandt's 400th birthday in the Netherlands. That project included an opera, an installation and in 2008 a sequel to *Nightwatching*, a film called *Rembrandt's J'accuse*. As the title of the project implies, it departs from Rembrandt's prestigious painting *The Night Watch*. That painting is prominently displayed in the Rijksmuseum Amsterdam as the most famous of the Dutch Golden Age paintings, a piece of heritage estimated in 2011 at about 500 Million Euro, which has, moreover, turned into the most precious tourist attraction in the Netherlands.

Having been commissioned around 1639 to Rembrandt van Rijn by the Amsterdam shooting company, the painting was originally titled *Militia Company of District II under the Command of Captain Frans Banninck Cocq* and also known as *The Shooting Company of Frans Banning Cocq and Willem van Ruytenburch, Ready to March*. It was completed in 1642, at the peak of the Dutch Golden Age.

It depicts the eponymous company moving out, led by Captain Frans Banning Cocq (dressed in black, with a red sash) and his lieutenant,

Fig. 1.1: Rembrandt van Rijn, *The Night Watch*, 1642, oil on canvas. Rijksmuseum, Amsterdam.

Willem van Ruytenburch (dressed in yellow, with a white sash). It is difficult to pinpoint the exact reasons for the fame and glory that the painting has achieved. But what is mostly mentioned is its enormous size (11.91 ft X 14.34 ft), the theatrical use of light and shadow (in the mode of so-called tenebrism) and the perception of motion in what would have traditionally been a static military group portrait at that time.

Where others preferably saw might and honour in Rembrandt's celebration year, Greenaway was confronting the audience (and Dutch art history scholars) with a veritable provocation. Instead of praising the painting for being an honourable portrait of the Militia Company, the film posits a conspiracy to murder within the musketeer regiment of Frans Banning Cocq and Willem van Ruytenburch. It suggests that Rembrandt may have immortalised an accusation by depicting a subtle allegory in his group portrait of the regiment, subverting what was to have been a highly prestigious commission for both painter and subject. This is literally laid out in the sequel *Rembrandt's J'accuse*, by providing a detailed analysis of the compositional elements of the painting. The scene of crime is located in the here and now of the Netherlands, because the accusation is also directed at the current Dutch authorities: at the beginning, we see a police car arriving with emergency lights in front of the Rijksmuseum, today. In the very centre of the vanishing point in the middle of the museum's front arises the head of Peter Greenaway, saying: 'This is the Rijksmuseum, in Amsterdam, Holland. The home of the prime collection of Dutch painting. The Rijksmuseum is currently the scene of a shooting'. The camera zooms in on the fragment of the painting where a gun is firing a bullet. We see the painting placed on a stage, surrounded by the very figures which appear on the painting, embodied by actors, the same as Rembrandt 'himself', asking: 'Where does the bullet go?' Adding: 'I accuse you, gentlemen, of murder!' At the end, Greenaway's talking head is followed up by a camera, again filming the front of the Rijksmuseum, this time during night fall, while the police car is crossing the scene with the sirens on, and we hear Greenaway saying: 'A man is murdered. The relevant authorities should investigate'.

In the following I do not want to judge the quality of *Nightwatching* as a film. In fact, a fierce debate about this topic has taken place, accusing it on the one hand of being a dead loss as narrative cinema (Qinn 2010, *Independent*) and on the other hand praising it as a creative response to Rembrandt's famous painting (Povoledo 2008, *New York Times*). While it would certainly be worth following the lines of these arguments, my interest is focused on the claim that the film gets to the heart of the matter of theatricality and the arts. To explore this argument, I will firstly lay out the concept of theatricality on which I am relying and then underpin this concept with an analysis of the compositional elements of the film. In a second step, referring to the picture theory of W. J. T. Mitchell, I will reveal that the scene of the crime is not only a narrative clue that Greenway uses to unveil the image. It will also demonstrate the specific relationship between theatricality and crime at stake when medial surfaces – the pages of books, the surfaces of paintings, the latest video gadget – are 'under suspicion' (Groys 2012) for harbouring a secret, sub-medial realm whence the plots themselves are thought to have emerged. Ultimately, I want to determine to what extent theatricality is a matter of intermediality. In that sense, Greenaway's work does challenge observers to engage visually and rigorously with what is on the screen and to undo themselves from what he calls their visual illiteracy.

The Complications of the Concept of Theatricality

For over twenty years, theatricality has been widely and controversially discussed in Theatre and Performance Studies and has gained a prominent place as analytical concept in scholarly discourse (Schramm 2017, Münz 1998, Féral 2002b, Davis and Postlewait 2003). There is no space here to delve into the complex history of the concept, but it is certainly necessary to discuss some of the complications that the concept is calling up, before adapting it to the analysis of Greenaway's cinematographic project.

The simplest assumption seems to be that theatricality is a question concerning theatre. In a phenomenological approach, the question concerning theatre aims at taking apart the structures that constitute theatre. The cohesion or correlation of these structures is what we call theatricality. In other words, theatricality means those elements that constitute theatre. In that sense, theatricality is a way to define or perceive a certain attitude, moment, situation, object, or area (such as politics) and so on, *as* theatre.

But this simple assumption contains challenging complications. It concerns firstly the notion of theatre itself. Josette Féral even goes so far as to claim that the recently prominent emergence of the term theatricality is related to an increasing dissolution of the specificity of theatre:

> The emergence of theatricality in areas tangentially related to the theater seems to have as a corollary the dissolution of the limits between genres, and of the formal distinctions between practices, from dance-theater to multi-media arts, including happenings, performance, and new technologies. The specificity of theater is more and more difficult to define. To the extent that the spectacular and the theatrical acquired new forms, the theater, suddenly decentred, was obliged to redefine itself. From that time on, its specificity was no longer evident (2002b, 94).

But at the same time, the complications emerge out of a controversial understanding of the term. In many cases, theatre is identified with a classical notion of drama (see, for example, Szondi 1987).

Theatricality in a Dramatic Mode

This identification of theatre and drama at the same time generates a contradictory tension between the two, which is caused by a certain hierarchy between the textual and the visual. For the traditional understanding of drama, as long as the *mise-en-scène* is determined by the formal structure of the dramatic text, theatre as medium has to comply with the fictional logics of action, time and space according to the poetic laws of drama, creating a supreme illusion of reality which denies the act of staging and enables the spectator to feel pity or to identify with the characters involved in the plot. Theatre in that case is appreciated when it 'disappears' as medium behind the surface of the depicted action loyal to the textual source of the drama. On the other hand, as soon as an awareness of the visual, theatrical construction of the actions on stage arises, it is associated with fake and betrayal. This understanding of theatre and, consequently, theatricality, as mimicking and faking reality goes along with a long historical tradition of anti-theatrical prejudice (Barish 1981). When, for instance, referring to politics, adjectives such as 'illusory, deceptive, exaggerated, artificial, or affected' stand in for the theatrical, as well as 'acts and practices of role-playing, illusion, false appearance, masquerade, façade, and impersonation' (Davis and Postlewait 2003, 4). 'The theatre', in this sense, Davis and Postlewait explain further, 'conceals or masks an inner emptiness, a deficiency or absence of that to which it refers' (2003, 5).

The dramatic notion of theatre is most prominently called up in Michael Fried's influential book *Absorption and Theatricality: Painting and Beholder in the Age of Diderot* (1980). As the title suggests, Fried draws a clear separating line between the concepts of absorption and theatricality. To do so, he refers to Diderot's considerations on the fourth wall. Fried's main account concerns the status of the beholder. By introducing the notions of absorption and theatricality into art historical discourse, he aims to define two different modes of perception. The (literally called) 'dramatic conception of painting' (108) produces absorption, while theatricality points to a conscious presentation of the painting to the beholder, the exhibiting to the public gaze and, therefore, to exaggeration. In defending the anti-theatrical tradition, Fried tears apart drama and theatre, praising the illusionary effect of the one and blaming the exposing effect of the other. Hence, absorption is an effect of the dramatic concept to guarantee dramatic illusion, 'dependent for its successful realization upon the establishment of the supreme fiction of the beholder's nonexistence' (108). Only by means of 'the complete absorption of a figure or group of figures in various actions, activities, and states of minds [. . .] the painter was able to establish the fiction of the aloneness of the figures' (108–9) – which means that the painting's figures are depicted as if they ignore the fact that they are being looked at. They are positioned behind a transparent fourth wall which separates them from the world of the beholder (for a more extensive critique of these points, see Röttger 2010). In this, the value (or appreciation) of a painting is dependent on the neglect of the medium which is bringing it forth. To establish the fiction that no one is standing before the canvas at the same time includes beholding by neglecting it as well as the canvas. This iconoclastic attitude is justified by the anti-theatrical discourse on literature and the textual dominance of drama that organises stage depictions according to the poetic laws for creating an illusion. By transferring the discourse on theatre and drama to the realm of the arts, Fried repeats its intrinsic value judgments: good painting (absorptive) versus bad painting (theatrical), measured in moral terms as a disdain of pure pretention (Fried 1980, 5).[1]

Theatricality in an Epistemic Mode

Over the last three decades, the focus in Theatre Studies has shifted from drama to performance, from the dominance of the drama-text to the material and medial conditions of what is staged and/or performed (Lehmann 1999). Against this background, the notion of theatre (and with this, theatricality) has to be conceived from a different perspective. Although the Greek word *theatron*, which means theatre, has undergone a complex process of semantic evolution over the course of history, in the current scholarly debate we find a quite common definition as the 'discord happening in front of the eyes of a crowd' (Marciniak 2007, 287), or a gathering of people, audience, or place to watch. This, in turn, is derived from the Greek verb *theásthai* which means 'to watch' or 'to look at' (Balme 2007, Gadamer 2013). Against this background, the structural condition of theatre could be described in very broad terms, as an event of seeing and being seen in the here and now, or the constellation of performing and spectating in one and the same moment. Deriving from this structural conditioning of theatre, theatricality (aiming at taking apart the structures that constitute theatre) in the broadest sense means to take apart the structures that condition the dynamics of the relationship of seeing and being seen (performing and spectating) as they unfold in a certain space and time, on a material or metaphorical stage, however constituted. Josette Féral on her terms defines theatricality in a similar mode, but much more specifically:

> [Theatricality] is a process of looking at or being looked at. It is an act initiated in one of two possible spaces: either that of the actor or that of the spectator. In both cases, this act creates a cleft in the quotidian that becomes the space of the other, the space in which the other has a place. Without such a cleft, the quotidian remains intact, precluding the possibility of theatricality, much less of theater itself (Féral 2002b, 97).

Departing from the assumption that theatre in this relational sense – as well as in a material and metaphorical sense, the notion of stage – always produces relationships of observation, I agree with Elizabeth Burns (1972) that theatricality in the first instance is a mode of perception. But as such, it also serves as an epistemic category, a mode of thought (recognition). In *Karneval des Denkens* (1996), Helmar Schramm extensively proves that the notion of theatricality in line with the baroque metaphor *theatrum mundi* includes the meaning of worldview, a certain perspective on the world. Schramm detects an analogy between the localisation of an ideal observer in the representational space of knowledge and science and the time-spatial organisation of seeing, acting and speaking in the history of European forms of theatre. According to this correlation, theatricality offers a perspective of questioning historically evolved world pictures (Schramm 2017, xvii). This close correlation between theatricality and awareness or states of knowledge supports the epistemic quality of theatricality. As such, theatricality operates on the two sides of the coin called theatre: dramatic illusion and the materiality of what is staged, fiction and reality. Thus, I understand theatricality as a notion that represents neither disguise or deception, nor exposition to a gaze, but rather a negotiation of the chiasm between both sides in relation to what we call reality, truth, authenticity, by questioning the illusionary totality of a dramatic conception, and with this a worldview as conceived as truth or nature. It enables the beholder to acquire an awareness of the relationship between truth and deception, between reality and a fiction-under-construction.

Theatricality as an epistemic mode inserts a gap between the beholder and that what is beheld, a gap that establishes a relationship with alterity, thus regulating and deregulating relations of perception: either by referring to the very status as beholder by opening up another perspective, an outsider's perspective, or by referring to the status of the beheld that 'breaks out of the frame' when it is considered to be theatrical. The pivotal point is the relationship of truth and illusion within the economy of epistemic objects, for theatricality suspends the basic constituents of the belief in perception, the 'deep-seated set of mute "opinions" implicated in our lives' (as Merleau-Ponty [1968] states). Theatricality creates the effect of spectatorship and is at work on the ever unstable and shifting border between fact and fiction, envisioning cultural acts as theatre or adapting the basic structures of theatrical settings (sceneries) to define cultural dynamics and epistemological shifts, to envision new perspectives on the world. Thus, theatricality is always functional at the borderline of the beholder's perspective: it is at work on the blind spot. This means it calls into question the simple transmission of visual information by the bodily eye and therefore the self-understanding of the observer. 'This destabilizing identity' – to adopt W. J. T. Mitchell's approach (1994, 57) – is also a phenomenological issue in so far as the transaction between the perceived and the perceiver is activated by the structural effects of multistability; that is, the shifting of figure and ground, the switching of aspects. The moment of switching from one to the other can be defined as the moment in-between, an unstable moment that enhances both – the one and the other – and which negates a clear decision or demarcation.

Theatricality and Mediality

To understand the effect of theatricality in Peter Greenaway's *Nightwatching*, in a last step, it is important to connect this destabilising effect of theatricality to the issue of media difference and media identity, and to concentrate on the transactions between media, the mediated and the observers that are activated by the internal structural effects of multistability. In doing so, I will argue for a performance analysis that takes into consideration the whole ensemble of relations between media and between those phenomena that are brought to light by media: the interplay of seeing and speaking, of sounds and images, of words and things, the visible and the audible. I depart form a very broad definition of medium, considering it as the middle state, something intermediate in itself. Defined as such, we can say that everything we perceive we perceive by media, our eyes, our ears, technical apparatuses and so on. Media are constituted by transmissions that result in, but which are also the consequence of, our perceptions. Epistemologically speaking, media also open up and transmit perspectives on the world. This aspect is marked by a paradox: while media intervene in our perception of the world, they remain aesthetically neutral. The problem is that we are able to observe a medium only when it appears in a visible or audible figure, as a form (for example, image or word) that is constituted by another medium (such as colour or voice).[2]

Media open up and stage perspectives on the world. When we recognize that everything that is given to people is given in perception, and when communication and cognition is given in media, then we see that the mediality of all things given necessitates this perspective. Media, with their potentiality of differentiation and transmission, cannot be considered individually in so far as they fundamentally enter into relationships with each other. This holds good primarily for theatre and theatricality, as far as theatricality works as an epistemic mode.[3] When a perspective of theatricality is opened up, an intermedial event not only appears to be identical with the media that constitute it, but it also opens up and stages perspectives on the media by way of breaking up or cutting through their aesthetic neutrality. In the moment when one medium stages another (for instance, the actor's body staging the text), it becomes an epistemic object, an epistemological object. This is the pre-condition for the perspectivity that is implied. The slower the movement of the transmission is carried out, the more stable is the aesthetic neutrality of the media that are involved and, hence, the illusionist or homogeneous effect of the performed (an effect that is more and more often seen as immediacy). I would like to call this process, following W. J. T. Mitchell, the 'Vortex-Effect' (Mitchell 1994, 75). The Vortex represents the multistability effect of intermedial performance that 'takes the beholder into the game' (ibid.) and at the same time does not neglect the historical impact of his or her perspective and of the medial conventions that are shaping it. All these operations, I want to add, take place between the visible and the invisible. And it is the impact of the gaze, the decision of the beholder, which decides what counts as (invisible) medium and what counts as its (visible) form, and thus shifts between figure and ground.[4]

Nightwatching, the Film[5]

In the case of *Nightwatching*, Greenaway applies theatricality to unfold a process of intermedial transmissions which happen in between painting, film and theatre; transmissions closely interwoven with the plot of the film. Greenaway's website gives the following account of the plot:

> In 1654 the Dutch painter Rembrandt awakes from a dream of blindness in his marital bed in Amsterdam, to remember the year 1642, and his most celebrated work later to be known as the *Nightwatch*. He was then at the height of his powers, his career and his wealth and as a consequence commissioned by the Amsterdam Musketeer's Militia to paint their group portrait, 31 amateur soldiers of the Amsterdam Home Guard on parade. At the insistence of his pregnant wife Saskia, anxious to create a secure future for their longed-for, unborn child, he finally agrees to accept the commission [...]
>
> From the retrospective standpoint of 1654 [...], Rembrandt recalls his preparations for the *Nightwatch* [...] Suddenly there is a death. The sympathetic captain of the Militia is shot dead at musket practice. It is pronounced an accident. There is a new commanding officer backed by new family members and associates. The commission is re-ordered [...]
>
> Rembrandt begins the preparatory drawings of the 31 sitters of the group portrait, only to become gradually disenchanted with their arrogance and their hypocrisy, their unashamed lust and greed [...] Rembrandt investigates the apparent murder, uncovering more corroborating evidence. Rembrandt very confidently imagines he can build his accusation of murder against the conspiring soldier-merchants into the painting they have commissioned. He collects all the information he needs to make the entire painting an indictment for those who have eyes to see.
>
> And then his moment of great good fortune changes. He confidently, even arrogantly, unveils the finished *Nightwatch* [...] The painted conspirators understand the message and recoil from his accusation. The reaction of the sitters proves their discomfort and guilt, and they seek at once to try to destroy Rembrandt because they dare not destroy the painting which is already being acclaimed

a significant work. They start to create the financial and social circumstances for his descent into penury [...]

Moving between 1654 and 1642 [. . .] the blackmailed Rembrandt is obliged to make humiliating concessions. [... T]he finished painting is hung in its appointed place in the Amsterdam Militia Headquarters, on a court occasion where the Militia painting commissioners are seeking preferment. There they plan Rembrandt's blinding, the blinding that Rembrandt continues to dream about in 1654, a blinding that is in fact no dream but a reality.

Based on analytical proofs detected in the painting itself by literally taking it apart, the film is telling on the one hand the speculative story of a crime, which never has been proven officially; hence, 'it is time to re-open the case'. On the other hand, this investigation is combined with a recounting of biographical facts of Rembrandt's life. While wealthy and popular when he started to paint *The Nightwatch* in 1642, Rembrandt thereafter descended into poverty and disrepute: this was one of the miracles that raised Greenaway's suspicions and inspired the story.

Preparing the Intermedial Event

But how is this story depicted? In the mode of theatricality, Greenaway opens up an epistemic perspective on watching, more precisely watching the night, by confronting the beholder of the film with the dark eye of the vortex of intermediality. Things are set into movement from the beginning of the film onwards. The presentation calls up the blind eye, or the invisibility of the medium, which unveils itself only if watched and staged by another medium. To do so, in his introduction to the film, Greenaway literally installs an empty stage on the screen, which, in the manner of the painting, is dominated by darkness (some of the militias move by briefly, we see and hear a gunshot fired). Out of this darkness arises a white, closed curtain placed in the centre of the filmic image. We see and hear some tumultuous acts of violence behind the curtain, in the mode of a shadow play; flashes of torches pass the eye of the beholder. Suddenly, the curtain opens, framed by a draped dark theatre curtain, and Rembrandt (Martin Freeman), dressed in a white nightgown, is thrown through the curtain, on a wooden floor beneath the curtained stage. The curtain opens, and out of the 'dark nothing', the open curtain reveals the shutters (to be recognized by their historic costumes) entering the stage. The static picture comes to life, the figures enter the stage, released out of the dark as if leaving the black hole of the sub-medial realm of the painting and, along with this, the dark camera-eye of the film-medium itself.

The shutters overpower Rembrandt, blind him with a torch and leave him on the ground. For a second, the beholder again is confronted with a filmic image that sets into motion an intermedial processing: while a sparingly lightened empty 'travelling stage' framed by the open white curtain (which at the same time appears to be a bed) forms the vantage point of the darkened image, Rembrandt is lying on the wooden floorboards in front of this 'stage'. What we see here is a meta-picture of a stage on a stage, with the figure of a naked Rembrandt in the dark at the centre, standing up, turning his back towards the audience, looking to the stage on the stage, meanwhile prolonging the beholder's gaze, shouting repeatedly: 'I am blind! I am blind!' Then, sitting on the bed, he says: 'Miles and miles and miles of painted darkness. Emptiness, darkness', while the screen itself is shrouded in total darkness for a second. Only when Hendrickje appears is Rembrandt released from his fear of blindness: 'A nightmare', he tells her. 'This night, I was looking into the darkness, without ending, I was watching darkness, I was watching the night, I was nightwatching'. Darkness, thus, is not only depicted here as a condition of seeing, but also as a medium of light, and with this as a condition for the recognition of a medium by being staged by another.

This very witty reflection on and staging of the mystery of darkness as condition for the configuration of (inter)medial transmissions is directly followed up by a short discourse on another facet of an intermedial interplay: the interplay between media and the senses as 'inter-sensory entity' (Merleau-Ponty 1968, 370), like a veritable short phenomenological lesson by Merleau-Ponty on the kinaesthetic perception of art and the theory of colour.

Both Rembrandt and Hendrijckje are still depicted in the dark, in the shadow of dimmed light scarcely reflected by the whiteness of the curtain, still sitting centre stage, in front of the 'bed'. Rembrandt starts a completely different dialogue, screwing his eyes with his fingers: 'Can I, in fact, see you, Hendrickje, red-bloodied Hendrickje, as I know, I know your blood is red, do I remember your eyes are blue? I suspect your piss is yellow?! How do you describe colour?' While the lights come up and he is dressing himself, he goes on: 'Describe the colour of red, Hendrickje, to a blind man' (the lighting turns slightly red). Hendrickje: 'You just said;

the colour of blood!' Rembrandt: 'Your red is thick, to touch, [. . .] red is touchable'. Hendrickje: 'And it's warm'. Rembrandt: 'What is yellow?' (the lighting turns yellow). Hendrickje (while opening the blinds, letting sunlight in): 'The sun? Yellow smells, it is a smelling colour'. Rembrandt: 'Yellow is thinner than red, it is more transparent, yellow moves. Red is toughly, becomes solid. Yellow always moves, yellow could be a liquid. A new bear, piss!' (he pisses, his back turned to the beholder, in a chamber pot he places on the bed). 'Doesn't smell so ugly'.

This prelude to the film prepares spectators for being alert to the intermedial event that is awaiting them over the next two hours, by removing all figures that are depicted in the painting from the canvas and awakening them to cinematographic life. It is a matter of theatricality in two connected ways: the depicted stage literally refers to the theatre played in the scene, but moreover it opens up a theoretical scene which challenges the beholder to understand how the image that appears on screen or canvas is constructed.

Scene of the Crime

While most of the film is staged like a theatre play in a dramatic mode in terms of role-playing, fictionalising Rembrandt's loves and life and a dramaturgy of suspense, the visuals are held in the in-between of stage, film-image and painting. This is most prominently at stake when the painting is presented to the Musketeers. Again, we are confronted with the intermedial ingredients described above: watching the *Night Watch* in terms of 'night watching' mirrors the invisibility of the medium (film, camera obscura) by way of staging the transposition of one into the other. We see the enormous painting staged on a stage. In front of it, at the edge of the stage, directed towards the painting, are the Musketeers in a row, firing a bullet with the gun. The camera zooms in on the painting, on cadet Jan Visser Cornelissen and Clais van Cruisbergen. Then, the painting comes to life: all figures step out of it, onto the stage, while the painting in the background remains intact. Both, the painted and the acted Musketeers look directly into the eye of the beholder. 'Isn't it curious', Rembrandt says, stepping towards the edge of the stage, 'that a painting is normally silent. But we will give to this painting, this picture, this image . . . sound!' We hear drums, voices, while the figures in the painting switch in between freezing and moving. When the camera zooms in on

Rembrandt's head, we hear him say: 'There is, of course, another sound'. One of the Musketeers moves centre stage and directs his gun towards the audience. We hear a shout of 'Fire!' and he fires a noisy shot at them. From here on, the talking head of Rembrandt opens up the scene of the crime by delivering a careful analysis of the painting, starting by saying: 'I accuse you, gentlemen, of murder!'

To understand how this crime not only unfolds on the narrative level of the film (telling the reasons for the accusation of the powerful musketeer regiment of murder), but also on an epistemic level to conceive theatricality at work, in the following I will reflect on W. J. T. Mitchell's canonical article 'The Pictorial Turn' (1994). 'To "see" the crime', W. J. T. Mitchell wrote to illuminate the kernel of his *Picture Theory*, 'we need to remove the figures from the stage and examine the stage itself, the space of vision and recognition, the very ground which allows the figures to appear' (1994, 31). Mitchell here brings in the meta-picture of the stage to install what he calls a theoretical scene, 'a scene of greeting between Subjects – between the speaking and the seeing subject, the ideologist and the iconologist' (1994, 30). The two subjects to whom he refers are Erwin Panofsky and Louis Althusser, both authors of different scenes of greetings. While Panofsky sketches the scene of a man who removes his hat towards someone else to perform the man's recognition of another person as a scene that lays the ground for his theory of iconology, Althusser designs the scene of a man who knocks on a door to be heard at the other side of it by someone else. Both scenes, the scene of hearing and the scene of seeing, not only deliver two different descriptions of the constitution of subjectivity (to be recognized), but they both also at the same time intend to define a theoretical scene of knowledge, more precisely two constitutive theoretical scenes of science: 'What we learn from these greetings', Mitchell explains, 'is that the *temptation to science*, understood as the panoptic surveillance and mastery of the object/"other" (individual or image) is the "crime" imbedded in these scenes' (1994, 30). By asking each to greet and recognize and greet itself in the other, they are confronted with the hidden motivations 'behind' (or in the sub-medial spaces) of each scene. The clue of this staged encounter of ideology and iconology is Mitchell's claim to 'give up the notion of a metalanguage or discourse that could control the understanding of pictures and to explore the way pictures attempt to present themselves' (1994, 24). What he, on the contrary, is aiming for is the 'construction of the human subject as a being constituted by *both* language and image' (1994, 24, italics mine).

In that sense, Mitchell's challenge is certainly not far from Greenaway's attempt, as staged in *Nightwatching*, to undo the beholders from what he calls their visual illiteracy. Mitchell accuses both Panofsky and Althusser of being blind to their constructions of supposed scenes of naturalness by following a dramatic concept that is dominated by the 'logos' which is language. And he directly hints at Panofsky's legacy followed by Michael Fried, in a way that is worth quoting at length:

> There are plenty of reasons to accept the naturalness of the scene of greeting as a starting place for the explanation of painting. The silent, visual encounter of the gesture of raising that hat, the motif of 'gesturality' as such may be simply inevitable as a basic example, since it captures one of the central features of Western history painting, the language of the human body as a vehicle for narrative, dramatic, and allegorical signification. We might also look forward to Michael Fried's accounts of gesture in modern painting and sculpture to reinforce the sense of Panofsky's scene as inevitable and natural. But suppose we resisted these natural inevitabilities and question the scene itself? (1994, 26)

In the given context, I cannot delve into the six arguments that in the following are brought forth by Mitchell to underpin the necessity of resistance against Panofsky's iconological model of 'bourgeois civility' (1994, 26). What is important here is that, without mentioning the term theatricality, Mitchell constructs a highly theatrical scene to prove the ideology behind the surface of the fictional greeting that enforces iconology, a scene he calls a 'recognition scene' (1994, 30). By removing the figures of conventional greeting from the stages, he presents the empty stage so as to enable us to detect the scene of crime (in a manner very similar to Greenaway's removal of the figures from the painting that allow us to see the night). Under this condition, '[i]conology recognises itself as an ideology, that is, as a system of naturalization, a homogenizing discourse' (1994, 30) that claims the universalising truth of illusionistic and figurative painting. And 'ideology recognizes itself as an iconology, a putative scene, not just the object of a science. It makes this discovery most simply be re-cognizing and acknowledging its origins (etymological and historical) as a "scene of ideas" in which ideas are understood as images' (1994, 30). This re-cognition, I want to insist, needs a mode of perception that serves as an epistemic category, as an attitude of theatricality.

I do not know if Greenaway read Mitchell's text. But Greenaway's fierce plea to get rid of the hierarchy between text and image is well known. In *Nightwatching*, he blames the crime as a sort of a double operation between ideology and iconology. He rips the painting apart by implanting a theatrical perspective, to unveil the hidden ideology of the Dutch power elite and to destroy the naturalising gesture of the painting, breaking through its closed medial surface. Naturalising also, because the newness of the painting in the seventeenth century was exactly praised for the gesture of absorption that Rembrandt introduced for the first time in portrait painting. Fried would call this naturalising gesture absorption. But he himself struggled with the fact that 'the concept of absorption is not one that we can apply systematically to the art of the past'. And yet he does concede that, 'supremely, Rembrandt come(s) at once to mind – those states and activities are rendered with an intensity and a persuasiveness never subsequently surpassed' (1980, 43). The reason might be the already mentioned limits of this concept.

In the end, we cannot know whether Greenaway's accusation is true. But this is exactly the work of theatricality. It confronts us with the question of the relationship between truth and illusion within the economy of epistemic objects, because it suspends the basic constituents of the belief in perception, the deep-seated set of mute opinions implicated in our lives.

Notes

1. Interestingly enough, Fried later tried to revisit his concept, admitting: 'My earlier presentation of Diderot's views was incomplete' (Fried 1980, 131). He introduced a 'secondary or pastoral concept' that we nowadays would call immersion, one that does not deny the beholder, but 'transforms and redeems the estrangement of the beholder' (132).
2. See also Sibylle Krämer: 'Media work like window-panes: the more transparent they are, the better they fulfil their tasks' (in Krämer 1998, 73–74). Quotes are translated from German by Matteus Borowski.
3. For a more extensive approach to intermedial performance analysis (focused on the performance *Forever Godard* by I. Bauertsima), see Röttger 2013.
4. I would like to refer here to Ludwig Wittgenstein's idea of the 'aspect' to which he points by using the example of the 'Duck-Rabbit', a drawing that, depending on the aspect of looking, can be recognized as the image of either a duck or a rabbit (Wittgenstein 2009). See also Mitchell 1994, 49–57, about the duck-rabbit drawing as meta-picture.
5. See inclusive the credits of the film: https://www.luperpediafoundation.com/nightwatching (accessed 8 May 2019).

2

Theatricalising Absorption and Networked Hyper-Theatricality

Lisa Åkervall

About halfway through Season Four of the HBO series *The Sopranos*, mob boss Tony has an excessive home cinema installed in the pool house behind his suburban New Jersey McMansion. The gratuitousness of the installation and Tony's self-satisfaction with it act as a kind of medium-reflexive comic relief. The home theatre testifies to the indulgent dream of privatised televisual absorption at the dawn of the twenty-first century, even as it unmasks the crass material infrastructure behind this experience of immersion. Its oversized screen, a panoply of speakers and two rows of gaudy easy chairs lend movie magic to Tony's home screenings of classic films on VHS tape. When his wife Carmela later throws him out of their house, this temple of media excess even becomes his home: Tony sleeps, eats and has heartfelt conversations with his children by the glow of the popcorn machine.

Tony's home theatre tells us something about the state of theatricality and absorption in contemporary media cultures. Its fabulous material accoutrements suggest that, before the spectacle of today's consumerist media cultures, aesthetic absorption may, in fact, be synonymous with self-absorption. Tony stands in as an ironic double for home viewers indulging in the arts of so-called 'quality TV', a style of self-consciously absorbed spectatorship inaugurated by *The Sopranos* and carried on in later series from the critically acclaimed realism of *The Wire* to the more recent big-budget spectacle of *Game of Thrones*. If this absorption delivers to its viewers an experience of complete immersion in the moving image, it does not do so without a certain 'theatre', an infrastructure of physical and conceptual elements necessary to producing the proper frame of mind for this experience. For the chuckling spectators of *The Sopranos*, the sheer boorishness of Tony's indulgence in this theatre of absorption threatens to deconstruct their own indulgent absorption at the altar of quality TV. In other words, this episode of *The Sopranos* theatricalises absorption.

This theatricalisation of absorption in *The Sopranos* is typical of a changed relationship between work and audience, and absorption and theatricality in contemporary moving image cultures that other scholars and I have termed postcinema (see Shaviro 2010; Denson et al., 2016; Åkervall 2015; Hediger et al., 2016; Hagener et al., 2017). In this essay I probe the history of theatricalised absorption in moving image cultures and analyse why it is particularly pronounced in postcinema. Starting with a review of literature on theatricality, absorption and media – thinking about absorption and theatricality in painting (and sculpture) with Michael Fried and theatricality and absorption in cinema with Tom Gunning, Richard Rushton and others – this essay proceeds to investigate the changed relationship between absorption and theatricality in postcinema in two key examples, Ryan Trecartin and Lizzy Fitch's video installation *SITE VISIT* from 2014, and in somewhat greater detail Hannah McPherson's snapchat horror-thriller *Sickhouse* from 2016. Based on this discussion, I will show how postcinematic media cultures cast new light on theatricality and absorption, alongside more general changes in aesthetic experience.

Theories of Theatricality and Absorption

The most celebrated reflection on theatricality and absorption comes from Fried's reflections on painting (and sculpture). In his critique of Minimal Art, 'Art and Objecthood' from 1967, Fried memorably distinguishes theatricality from absorption (perhaps we should rather say he launches an attack against theatricality through a defence of absorption), positing that these two forms of address stand in opposition to one another. He understands theatricality as a mode in which beholders are directly addressed and that act of addressing, as such, is foregrounded and exposed. Fried casts aspersions on theatricality, arguing that art should 'de-theatricalize beholding' (Fried 1998b). For him, absorption implies the opposite of theatricality. Whereas Minimal Art – or 'literalist art', as he calls it and which he despises – is in his view theatrical, he sees modern art – or, at least the modern art which he champions – as non- or anti-theatrical. Fried also calls the modern artwork *introverted*, concerned with itself, as it does not explicitly draw attention to the fact that it is being looked at, saying 'here I am' (see Rushton 2007). This non- or anti-theatrical tendency of modern art that Fried values is something that he sees coming to an end with minimal art in the 1960s.

In another context, namely when he is thinking about French paintings of the eighteenth century, Fried continues his thoughts on absorption and theatricality. He examines a number of paintings in which we see characters who are so fully absorbed by their tasks that they seem to entirely ignore the presence of the beholder (Fried 1980). He analyses, for example, Jean-Baptiste-Siméon Chardin's Le Dessinateur from 1759, which shows a painter at work, turning his back to the beholder and seemingly ignoring her. Fried is particularly interested by a paradox in the effect that Chardin's painting has on its beholder: although (or perhaps even *because*) the beholder is excluded from the world of the painting, she feels herself to be part of its world. The self-absorption of the depicted world as an enclosed, hermetic space does not lead to an alienation of the beholder but instead facilitates her absorption. The beholder is equally absorbed by the painting, as the painter depicted in it is by his act of painting.

Theatricality in Cinema?

In his essay 'Early, Classical and Modern Cinema: Absorption and Theatricality', Rushton convincingly argues that Fried's concept of absorption is essential for the analysis of the cinema and its spectator (Rushton 2004). The absorptive intensification in modern painting that Fried describes recalls the situation with which the cinema confronts its spectators, as the setting of two separated worlds – that of the spectator and that of the fictional world depicted. The correspondence, of course, is not exact. As Rushton suggests, the distinction between absorption and theatricality in cinema echoes the distinction between voyeurism and exhibitionism that inspired passionate debate in film theory. In this reading, voyeurism is absorptive, whereas exhibitionism is theatrical. The situation of the cinematic spectator sitting before the screen conjures up that of the observer of Le Dessinateur: the key mode of spectatorial address is absorption. Classical Hollywood Cinema and its invisibility of the means of production exemplify cinema's absorptive core. Although the cinematic spectator knows about the illusion and the fictionality of the filmic world, she allows herself to be absorbed by that world. This might mean that, however hard one tries, within the medium and the dispositive of cinema, theatricality is always destined to fail. One might even suggest that the famous accounts of imaginary identification in cinema put forth by Christian Metz, Jean-Louis Baudry, Laura Mulvey and others are expositions on its absorptive core.

Cinema, however, is not only a medium for the continued manifestation of absorption. If Fried calls our attention to those moments in painting and the history of art when a singular theatre of absorption can be opened up, then cinema – the child of spectacle, a medium of industry, the carrier of what Miriam Hansen calls 'vernacular modernism' – also provides a theatre of its own for scrutinising the contours of absorption in an era of new mechanised visions and automated sounds (Hansen 1999). Sprung from psycho-technical technologies for probing the powers of sensation to witness not only moments but also micro-moments, early pioneers such as Etienne-Jules Marey, Albert Londe, Edweard Muybridge and Hugo Münsterberg used the emerging techniques of the moving image to objectify attention and thereby probe the absorptive powers of the image (Holl 2002, 137–58). Perhaps it was this early orientation within the techniques of the moving image that embedded within the history of cinema and its development not only a spectacular power for absorbing the attention of the masses but also a peculiar attention to what it is to be absorbed by a moving image. This comprises a counter-history of absorption and theatricality, or what I call 'theatricalised absorption' in cinema. This mode particularly comes to the fore at moments of medial and technical transition, when something about the medium and its modes of spectatorship invites both immersion and alienation. In film historical analysis, these moments of theatricalised absorption are often staged strictly in terms of their theatrical aspects, which is to say the modes in which the audience or spectator finds herself disembedded from the experience of absorption by modes of address that call attention to the fact of the exhibition. As Gunning's complex and nuanced account of the 'cinema of attractions' hints at, the cinema of attractions seemed to pair obscene theatricality with the prospect of disembedding absorption. If the 1902 short *Uncle Josh at the Picture Show* solicits a culture of attractions by calling attention to the way in which a naïve country rube mistakes cinema for real life, its lambasting requires of its audience – not entirely unlike the quality TV viewers of Tony Soprano's home theatre – a certain ability to recognize the exquisite absorption induced by cinematic projections. Just as the absorption of Uncle Josh and Tony require a certain temple-like theatre for its production, the theatrical effects that these works elicit rest on the conceit of absorbed spectatorship. This relationship between theatricality and absorption is given literal embodiment in the short silent comedy film by James Williamson's *The Big Swallow* from 1901, in which a man being filmed swallows the camera that is taking his picture. Using trick film and extreme close-ups *The Big Swallow* theatricalises an act of corporeal absorption, as the protagonist's mouth swallows – or absorbs – the photographic camera itself. The mouth is here an entry point into a process of digestion that culminates in the absorption into another body. In this way, already in the cinema of attractions we encounter an early form of theatricalised absorption.

In Godard's cinema of political modernism, by acts of looking into the camera and even showcasing the camera, the cinematic illusion itself is theatricalised. Indeed, so it seems, Godard defies cinema's absorptive and illusionist tendencies, which he wants to expose (see Rodowick 1994, xii–xiv). When we see the characters in his films looking into the camera, or when we even see the camera itself, a kind of theatricalisation takes place, which opposes the absorptive tendencies of cinema and tries to ignore the fourth wall. We could say that Godard is trying to theatricalise cinematic production. Here theatricality is reintroduced to question – if not thwart – the film medium's illusionistic powers and burst its deceptive surfaces of absorption. In a cinema of political modernism, laying bare film's processes of production becomes an anti-illusionistic and anti-absorptive performance.

From *The Sopranos* to *SITE VISIT*: Theatricality in Television and Postcinema

Contemporary moving image cultures continue to investigate the relations between absorption and theatricality, but according to conditions that elsewhere, following Steven Shaviro, I have termed postcinema. This term, postcinema, refers not necessarily or only to digital or networked media that is no longer celluloid-based, even though, in practice, most postcinematic media is reliant, in part or in whole, on digital means for its production and exhibition. Postcinema instead designates cultures of the moving image that take place in the technological and economic norms that follow the high eras of classical cinema and the network era of American television, which maintain a parasitic relationship to the characteristics of these earlier media (rather than breaking entirely with their norms), but explore them within an emerging set of medial, economic and aesthetic affordances. Postcinema refers to film, television, and streaming media conceived through networked cultures of production and consumption, which themselves are linked to global economic markets driven by neoliberal imperatives, but which for various reasons – such as intellectual property laws that encourage the recycling of earlier franchises, or marketing strategies that, as with Tony's home theatre market nostalgia for earlier media in contemporary products, continue to repurpose or recall earlier media cultures. Kevin B. Lee's wry take on the Transformers franchise in *Transformers: The Premake*, for instance, displays a number of these features, showcasing how a 1980s film and television franchise is assembled globally today, drawing together networks of global producers, political imperatives and audiences that mirror the current world economic dynamics.[1] Variants on these networks and economic imperatives are also at work in the kinds of global art networks described by David Joselit in *After Art*. His suggestion that we think about contemporary art not in terms of medium but instead in terms of their circulation in heterogeneous networks, characterised by relays across formats, offers conceptual kin to postcinema.

A characteristic feature of postcinema that inflects its inquiry into absorption and theatricality is its tendency towards a kind of reflexive doubling and exaggeration of medial conditions that generate sounds and images in today's media cultures. In the sphere of sound recording, sampling, remix cultures and autotune thematise the production of sound and act as self-conscious elements in its consumption (see Åkervall 2015). In the ironic storylines of TV series such as *South Park* or the often much more 'straight' storylines of contemporary reality TV shows such as *Keeping up with the Kardashians*, the status of the moving image itself and its suspect positioning within broader media cultures often emerge as a topic or theme. In the case of the latter, the status of the work is not necessarily problematised in the series itself, but often through a maelstrom of secondary works (paparazzi photos, tabloids, tweets, product lines, Kim Kardashian's published book of selfies and so on) that thematise the production of the world of the series. While classical cinematic and televisual content persists, alongside it a growing body of postcinematic works thematise its reworking within emerging networked media cultures. If *Uncle Josh at the Picture Show* and *The Big Swallow* pioneered a theatricalisation of absorption, and if the Brechtian techniques of Jean-Luc Godard's films of the 1960s pioneered theatricalised production and its conditions, more recent postcinematic works theatricalise both absorption and production, paired with a hyper-theatricality that affects both the performances depicted and the exhibition of the work itself. This hyper-theatricality exists alongside an inflation of attention to the techniques of image production and an almost perverse fascination with the cultures of absorption, particularly as they reflect back on the self-absorbed, self-satisfied stars themselves.

Trecartin's and Lizzie Fitch's installation *SITE VISIT* from 2014, curated by Ellen Blumenstein and Klaus Biesenbach at KW Institute for Contemporary Art in Berlin, is an extraordinary exercise in hyper-theatricality in which the networks of *After Art* and postcinema converge. With *SITE VISIT*, Trecartin and Fitch, who were adolescents when *The Sopranos*, that early avatar of so-called 'quality TV', made its way around American cable networks, have one-upped Tony. As much posttelevisual as postcinematic, the installation recalled the above-mentioned home theatre of Tony Soprano, now brought to such an exaggerated embodiment

Fig. 2.1: Ryan Trecartin and Lizzie Fitch, SITE VISIT, 2014, KW Institute for Contemporary Art in Berlin.

as to surrender all appeals to realism and descend from the comical to the grotesque.

In lieu of Tony's four easy chairs and classic movies playing on VHS, Trecartin and Fitch presented dozens of chairs seemingly randomly distributed in space, all beckoning visitors to become spectators absorbed by 360 degrees of high-resolution digital video projections of hyperactive performers, often with high-pitched voices. The walls were packed with screens and loudspeakers. The videos were shot in the harsh glow of high-definition digital video, and the performances depicted were best characterised as fuelled by narcissistic chains of recursion, such as self-humiliation, self-curation and self-reference. SITE VISIT obscenely exaggerated Tony's theatre of absorption with the performative excess characteristic of a later generation of theatrically self-absorbed TV stars based in New Jersey, such as *The Jersey Shore*, *Jerseylicious* and *The Real Housewives of New Jersey*. Like those shows, the installation absorbed its audiences in its hyper-theatricality, even as it theatricalised a spectacle of excessive absorption, for example, with gratuitous lights and vibrating mechanisms installed in easy chairs, where visitors were encouraged to sit down while taking in the spectacle.

In *SITE VISIT*, theatricality and absorption are no longer even conceivable as opposites. The theatre does not produce absorption, nor does theatricality detract from absorption, but theatres of production are the object of audience absorption – as well as of a performer's self-absorption. The resulting absorptive hyper-theatricality owes as much to reality television as it does to cinema. The frenetic, low-resolution quality of *SITE VISIT*'s videos reminds us of YouTube videos and Instagram feeds, the onscreen performances of the characters entail strategies of self-display mimicking the theatricality of reality TV. Like other art and installation work by Trecartin and Fitch, *SITE VISIT* also offers a funhouse-mirror reflection of contemporary youth and reality TV cultures where the display of theatricality is a way of life – we might call it the MTV's *Jackass* and *Keeping up with the Kardashians* generation.

Following the spillage gestured towards by Joselit in *After Art*, or displayed in the endless marketing of the Kardashians across platforms, Trecartin and Fitch's hyper-theatricality included a spectacular genesis of publicity that seemed to enter into the show itself. For example, recent works by Trecartin and Fitch quickly take on a second and third life on Instagram and social media, which includes social media commentaries on the coverage of their works.

This second- and third-generation theatricalisation, a marginal aspect of *SITE VISIT*, found a more extreme expression a year later at the same gallery when DIS, a collective of young designers and media professionals a few years younger than Trecartin and Fitch, curated the 2015 Berlin Biennale. DIS and its preoccupation with so-called post-internet art, its modes of irony, low-fi mediation and self-reflexivity turned the Berlin Biennale into a hyper-theatrical artifact of the media and markets responsible for its production. Consider, for example, the massive statue of the singer Rihanna by Colombian artist Juan Sebastián Peláez staged in front of KW, which Rihanna came to visit and took a selfie in front of, for the single most viral image of the entire exhibition.

Which was 'the work' – the statue, the endless series of selfies in front of the statue, Rihanna's own selfie in front of the Rihanna statue, or the influx of visitors that followed her posting of the statue? It could be argued that none of these by themselves were the work; rather, the networks of relays across these platforms – constantly reflecting back upon itself, producing exaggerations of a caricature, injected into the heart of a fine arts exhibition – were the work. This widening of the realm of theatricality exemplifies a point that Joselit makes in *After Art*, that we are moving beyond traditional notions of the medium in art in favour of a concern for the format and the population – namely, the institutional regulatory mechanisms, the communities of collectors and markets, and the bodies of works, which define the networks in which art comes to function (see Joselit 2012).

Hannah McPherson's *Sickhouse*

As the spillage from work to network is reincorporated back into the work itself, absorptive hyper-theatricality gives way to networked hyper-theatricality. In recent years the postcinematic project that most concertedly developed this networked hyper-theatricality was Hannah McPherson's horror-thriller *Sickhouse*, produced by Indigenous Media and released on the teen-and tween-oriented instant video- and photo-messaging app Snapchat in 2016. *Sickhouse* took postcinematic hyper-theatricality from the somewhat precious enclosed spaces of galleries and their global networks of buzz to the sprawling, unpredictable tangle of apps and platforms and the affected forms of address of the Snapchat generation. *Sickhouse* does not invent new digital forms but instead innovates existing cinematic forms (in this case, the protocols of the 1999 found-footage horror film *The Blair Witch Project*) for twenty-first-century networks. Like the original which it adapts with admirable shamelessness, *Sickhouse* is set in a forest and follows a group of friends who set out to find a haunted cabin in the woods. *Sickhouse*'s setting, its style of filmmaking relying on shaky cameras, and its mode of address involving characters talking straight into the lens recall the *The Blair Witch Project* and the web-series *lonelygirl15*. But in an era of selfies, snapchats and camera phones, reality itself is increasingly *Blair Witch*-like, and *Sickhouse* simply draws out themes of a world that's already running like the poorly lit low-budget horror films of an earlier era. The hokey absorption that animated the 1990s low-budget film (itself a spin on 1970s poorly lit low-budget horror films) gives way to the fully ubiquitous hyper-absorption of YouTube, reality TV and app-based algorithmic filters that saturate contemporary culture with that very same aesthetics of low-budget horror. (In a fairly symptomatic reversal, however, the low-lighting of 1970s and 1990s horror today seems switched by the saturated excess of lighting produced in part by the automated sensors of contemporary digital media.)

This remediation of earlier cultural forms is one of the sources of the networked hyper-theatricality on display in *Sickhouse*. *The Blair Witch Project* was already an experiment in excessive theatricality in its own right: as a transmedia film, it structured its effects around theatricalising the narrative possibilities of working across media. *The Blair Witch Project* presented itself as a found-footage film consisting of material shot by film students who allegedly disappeared in the woods near Burkittsville in Maryland during their filming of a supposed documentary about the Blair Witch, and it addressed its audience with the pretence of authenticity. From its inception, the story theatricalised the evidentiary status that attended the proliferation of home video footage – small video cameras equipped with miniature screens so that everyone could suddenly make their own movies – and the peculiar forms of address related to home video aesthetics. Part of the innovation of *The Blair Witch Project* was also to move beyond the frame of amateur found-footage to include a wider apparatus. *The Blair Witch Project* was among the first major films to use the internet, in the form of a website for the film featuring a number of fake interviews, police reports, as well as photographs of the supposedly missing students, of whose found footage the film claims to be made. These sites online became a way of expanding the narrative into new spaces, while also serving as primary mechanisms to promote the film. In this way, *The Blair Witch Project* spearheaded the use of networked forms of theatricality.

In characteristic postcinematic fashion, *Sickhouse* redoubles and transforms the dynamics at work in *The Blair Witch Project*. While the general storyline of the scary cabin-in-the-woods remains pretty much the same from the found-footage original to the *Snapchat* remake, the execution incorporates contemporary social media platforms and protocols that provide a kind of real-time generation of the buzz, transmedial circulation and cross-media stitching together of stories that *Blair Witch* spent months building. The excessive theatricality that built to a crescendo in the marketing and exhibition of *The Blair Witch Project* is the constant companion of a socially networked film that permits commenting functions in real time and thereby accelerates its theatrical effects.

Sickhouse was shot on a number of iPhones, distributed through the social media app Snapchat and is best watched on a smartphone. McPherson's film not only explicitly targets reception on smartphones and via social media apps, but also theatricalises our relationship and our hyper-theatrical forms of address to digital screens, devices and apps. *Sickhouse* follows Andrea, who picks up her cousin Taylor from LAX airport and lets her take over her social media account, as they plan for a camping weekend in the woods of Southern California with two social-media-obsessed friends. All clips address the audience directly and are posted live to Andrea's Snapchat account. Paradoxically, within the protocols of twenty-first-century media users, this framing also enhances the feeling of authenticity necessary for its reality effects and its distribution on Snapchat. This, too, is part of a networked hyper-theatricality, where the media and apps themselves seem to enter centre stage and take on a theatricality of their own. The directorial choice of not uploading any footage due to supposedly too poor reception for hours at a time further enhanced the theatrical effects of the film, while also allowing the director to (invisibly) edit the material before uploading it.

The manner in which the film constructs a narrative across platforms enhances its networked hyper-theatricality: for instance, Andrea is played by YouTube celebrity Andrea Russett, who plays herself, as do the online celebrities Sean O'Donnell and Lukas Gag, while newcomer Laine Neil plays Andrea's Cousin Taylor. Thus, while the movie takes place on Snapchat and is screened on Snapchat, it is already enlisting a set of conventions, audiences and expectations developed around Andrea's

YouTube channel, as well as its parasitic projection into other social media, such as Twitter and Facebook, where her fans follow, comment on and elaborate on the short, sketchy story snippets.

Even though *The Blair Witch Project* had already chosen a direct form of address, in *Sickhouse* we can see a peculiar perspective and camera angle that directly relates the film to a twenty-first-century media aesthetic: one that is focused on the self and its theatricality. The film incorporates a more self-centred perspective typical not only of smaller screens but also of the peculiarities of their users. Both *The Blair Witch Project* and *Sickhouse* are filmed with shaky hand-held cameras, but while *The Blair Witch Project*'s camera focuses both on and away from its characters, *Sickhouse*'s camera predominantly focuses on the characters themselves, who are addressing their audience in typical video-blog style. *Sickhouse*'s actors were in fact instructed to interact with the iPhones used for the shoot in a way in which they would normally when using Snapchat privately: addressing the camera face on and talking straight into it. This hyper-theatricality of self (inspired by an aesthetics of reality TV, with its penchant for melodramatic confessionals and self-reveals) is enhanced by a theatrical foregrounding of media, as the film explores different functions of Snapchat along the self-centred camera angle, such as writing and drawing on the screen, as well as adding funny faces to the characters depicted. In this Snapchat-specific way, the screen itself is theatricalised and becomes part of the narrative in a novel way in *Sickhouse*. No longer just an interface between film and viewer, a recording and displaying surface, *Sickhouse* becomes a writing pad.

As clips forming the *Sickhouse* storyline were posted online, they invited real-time commentary, generating new audiences that became part of the network of performance. To ensure credibility among its live-audience, *Sickhouse* not only showed clips of the search for the haunted house but added a number of clips showing the characters going about their daily activities, such as eating, chatting and driving in a car. Here the live-ness of television gives way to the real-time-ness of digital media. The fact that events unfolded in quasi-simultaneity effectively enfolded observers into the event, with commentary functions even giving the illusion of participation. This fractal spreading of the performance network took the blurring of reality and cinematic fiction characteristic of *The Blair Witch Project* and made it integral to the real-time production of a postcinematic event that does not distinguish between production and reception, author and audience.

After *Sickhouse* was released on Snapchat, it took its followers-turned-spectators a while before they realised that they had watched a movie, believing themselves to have participated in a real-time event. Because the social media app Snapchat is commonly used for sharing photos and videos from one's daily life with friends and peers, Russett's followers were encouraged to take what they saw for reality. The use of supporting actors who also were internet celebrities further enabled the story to spread across platforms and develop a large following made up of fans of the various cast members. And indeed, some of Russett's followers were unaware of her being cast as an actress playing in a film and did not see the snippets they found online as the aesthetic experiment across media platforms that they are, but instead mistook them for reality. This became evident as a number of followers started to interact with Russett's Twitter and Instagram accounts to find out whether the events shown on Snapchat were actually taking place and whether Russett and her friends were harmed.

This imbrication of fiction and reality directly plays into the question of the evidentiary status of digital images. Already with the proliferation of images in the 1990s, the status and evidentiary value of the moving image came into question. Incidents such as the police beating of Rodney King in Los Angeles and its airing on national television unleashed new debates about the reliability of amateur video and how factors such as race and class shaped the interpretation of these unsanctioned amateur-produced images. Debates over the veracity of the video immediately became embroiled in uncertainty about the evidentiary value of non-professional eyewitness movies. In her book *After Uniqueness*, Erika Balsom discusses the ambivalence of digital and video reproduction and the complicated place that the copy inhabits in contemporary cultures between excitement over possibilities of reproduction and anxieties about ownership and authenticity (see Balsom 2017).

The Blair Witch Project contributed to the wider 1990s debates over the proliferation of screens and moving images as well as the authenticity of video by adapting amateur video footage to tell a new kind of horror story, wherein the suspense derived from the uncertainty of the footage and its production. The apparatus and the screen endowed the footage with uncanny, suspenseful qualities. The film played on this changed evidentiary status of the image and its networks, successfully blurring the lines between fact and fiction, and its transmedia narrative was used to enhance this blurring and to charge the film with authenticity. The uncertainty of found video footage was joined with the uncertainty of the internet, where media circulated with no real ability to track its origin or prove its veracity. By exploiting the multiplication of outlets and screens that marked 1990s media cultures, the narrative and aesthetic of the film related to its suspense between screen cultures – its blurring of their binary lines and oppositions, as well as the opening up of experiences and stories in that in-between space. This technique (which Henry Jenkins would later associate with spreadable media) was unusual at the time and played on the ambiguity of the reality status of the material shown: is it a documentary (see Jenkins, Ford and Green 2013)? Or a fake documentary? Audiences tried to determine the truthfulness of the events and did so in discussions in online chat rooms, which offered a sort of free advertisement for the film. This resulted not only in narrative success, but also in financial and institutional record-making: *The Blair Witch Project* grossed nearly 250 million USD, making it the financially most successful indie film of all time. *The Blair Witch Project* embodies the institutional possibilities of production opened up by video, which allowed entities outside the studio system to produce an international blockbuster that pivoted around suspending the familiar narrative and media norms of established screen cultures.

Sickhouse updated the techniques of *The Blair Witch Project* for the conditions of reality and the evidentiary in an age of social media. Whereas already *The Blair Witch Project* was set up as a theatrical transmedia project, *Sickhouse* developed in a much more unconventional manner. It took both theatricality and transmedia storytelling to the next level, as it migrated from Snapchat to Instagram and Twitter. Already using viral media as its starting point for distribution (via Russett's Snapchat account), the film did not control the liking and sharing that subsequently took place across various Twitter and Instagram accounts. What we are therefore dealing with here is not just theatrical and transmedia, but networked hyper-theatricality paired with trans-author storytelling, as over the course of this migration we see a transformation not only of content, but also of authorship and authors, and therefore stages for theatricality. The film's narrative had taken on a life of its own. Furthermore, *Sickhouse* exists in different lengths and formats. Its first version was shot in real time on Snapchat between 29 April and 3 May 2016, as a series of ten-second-long snaps uploaded to Andrea Russett's Snapchat account. This is notable because it shows how the change to different screens and the accommodating of content to new platforms generates new possibilities in terms of length, cut, exhibition, formats and forms of address. This process, which started appearing around another digital format, the DVD, is taking on new scales online. Whereas Andrea's 500,000 plus followers received updates every time a clip was uploaded to Snapchat, they were not explicitly told that the bits and pieces of video they were receiving were snippets of a movie. In that way, they watched the film in a hyper-distracted way, one snap at a time, unsure about the evidentiary or fictional status of the images. The material was live for twenty-four hours and then disappeared. The posts by Andrea Russett were seen over 100 million times on Snapchat over its first five days. The snap format had a strong effect on the evidentiary status of the image, by introducing constant pauses, cuts and suspense, while taking into account the shorter attention spans associated with mobile media platforms and exploring these as affordances for the unfolding of a narrative.

The second version of *Sickhouse* was released on Vimeo as a sixty-eight-minute-long feature film later that year. The feature version was composed of the Snapchat snaps but edited with the unused footage from the shoot in order to assemble enough material to create a feature-length film. This more durable version of the film that was released on the online streaming platform Vimeo – while tied to a more classical form of absorption which we might associate with cinematic and other moving-image media experience – is, notably, also designed to be watched on a smartphone. Having been shot on and for smartphones, incorporating the typical smartphone aesthetics into its narrative, this version of *Sickhouse* approached the length of a feature film and in that way thwarted the moving images usually produced for Snapchat as it exceeded the compact form that these usually take. However, due to the limited length of the clips that can be uploaded to Snapchat, the filming was chronological, and clips were uploaded in real time. This is a kind of film production very different from what one would normally see.

As *Sickhouse* enacts a networked hyper-theatricality specific to the emerging formats, environments and methods of distribution characteristic of contemporary digital cultures, it also offers a reflection on those cultures and their conditions. No longer tied to theatrical exhibition, much less a contemplative engagement with a discrete aesthetic object, postcinematic absorption involves an experience of cognizing across apps, platforms and interfaces. It is this spanning of platforms and frames in the space of moments that makes *Sickhouse* so interesting for our reflections on theatricality and absorption. It shows how, for today's screen cultures, theatricality and absorption are increasingly articulated across entities, in the spaces, gaps and leaps from one platform to another. This loosens the poles between theatricality and absorption affirmed by Fried and challenged by Godard and others. Absorption and theatricality appear less related to the specific qualities of the self-contained mind of a self-possessing individual and more as variable features of the medial conditions responsible for their precise ratios. Networked hyper-theatricality suggests that absorption is what the word itself always suggested: an experience of dissolution that can only reflect the object and conditions of its own dispersion, breakdown and redistribution outside the self. Whether this redistribution reveals itself is not a contradiction to the absorption but a reflection of its particular condition. Far from being poles or opposites, networked hyper-theatricality suggests that from its inception absorption was always the self-concealing expression of a very particular theatricality, one whose play is increasingly the subject of media experience.

Notes

1. See Kevin B. Lee, *Transformers: The Premake*, https://vimeo.com/94101046, and Åkervall 2020.

3

Theatricality and Dissonance: Frictions in Contemporary Networked Performance Practices

Jane Frances Dunlop

It is hot at Gasworks, a small gallery in southwest London, and it is busy. The space on the street is filled with people drinking; it is a muggy May evening in 2017. This is the opening of *Hollow Tongues*, a virtual-reality installation and performance from (Play)ground-less. In the foyer, a rendered landscape plays on a monitor beside a desk where someone hands out beers. Nearby, there are thick curtains leading into a room that is plush deep pink and dark red. The room has velvet curtains around the walls and a thick carpet. At the door, there are white cloth boots to put over one's shoes before entering. The sound of voices fills the room: the soundscape is being created live by the four artists and streamed into the space. Four artists are performing. Sarah Bayliss, María Angélica Madero, Ninna Bohn Pedersen and Belén Zahera trade VR objects and text within the virtual space that they have created for the purpose of performing together from four different cities in as many countries. There is a jar of candies near the door and pillows on the ground; people sit listening and sucking candies as they watch others take their turns with one of the Oculus Rifts. Inside the Oculus, the rendered landscape shows a tongue that seems to jitter as it turns before it all goes black and the landscape changes.

A few months later, I am tired, and it is the middle of the night as I sit in front of my computer. The green halo of Zoom screensharing outlines the screen, and instantly my desktop is mirrored on a monitor in Melbourne and San Francisco. I am performing as part of *Documents of the Future: Invitation to Edit*. Beside me on stage, and in the gallery, is the projection of a Google Doc. Images drop in, and words appear in different colours from different cursors. The document is being edited by artists located elsewhere, by numbers of the audience who sit with laptops and phones open as they watch. We are all together taking part in making something of this digital place. I am next to them, in three places at once: it is midday Sunday, 9 September, and I am on stage in Melbourne at the Australian Centre for Moving Images, as part of Channels, a festival of experimental video works. It is the evening of Saturday, 8 September, and I am part of the performance installation at CTRL+SHFT Collective, a gallery space in San Francisco, USA. It is very early in the morning in London, where I sit bringing up videos and speaking softly to the camera as my performance unfurls on my screen. The event is many screens, mirroring many desktops. The artists who participate and perform get entangled with the audiences who are present and shifting about the document. It is unruly, contained by screens but messy and too much within them. I perform for an hour and then go to sleep.

This chapter focuses on how the 'back-and-forth' relations that occur via the internet – a technology with almost complete ubiquity in the contemporary social landscape – matter for performances and performative art practices. I will consider these two works in order to think about what is happening when internet-mediated relation is performed. It is, so I will argue, the theatricality of both these works that lends a broader critical relevance to them. 'Theatricality', as work by performance scholars such

Fig. 3.1: *Documents of the Future: Invitation to Edit*, 2017.

as Tracy Davis and Thomas Postlewait (2003), Marvin Carlson (2002) and Josette Féral (1982) have demonstrated, does not simply reference spectacle in theatre but is a concept that accounts for a process – both in artistic performance and within social life – wherein the construction of performance *as* performance is visible to its spectators. It is a concept that brings attention to the relation between spectator and the performer (or object, event, space). My focus is on that process within performances that make use of the internet and specifically on how theatricality assists in generating what I term 'dissonance', the affective consequence of how emotional and technological politics become imbricated. Dissonance emphasises the inharmonious or discordant. It implies an imperfection that aligns both with the noise and friction of technological communication (Chun 2016, Galloway 2012, Mejias, 2013) and with the various ways in which (near) failure characterises performances (Carlson 2002, Bailes 2011, Stein 1988), as well as our experiences of relation. This chapter investigates why and how that dissonance is valuable as a tactic for understanding and approaching the relations mediated by the internet.

Theatricality is a kind of performance noise: it both confirms and exposes the conventions through which a performance operates. Building on this, my use of theatricality will provide a means of understanding the dissonance of relations produced in the sites and shared moments instantiated through internet-situated performances. By internet-situated performance, I mean performances that unfold in meaningful ways on the internet and are also sustained through the internet. Dissonance can be understood as one approach to what Donna Haraway, with reference to the work of Marilyn Strathern, terms the 'muddles and tangles' that productively trouble attempts to create universalised perspectives (Haraway 1988, 2016; Strathern 2004). Strathern and Haraway are among the feminist scholars whose approach to knowledge-making and understanding inform my own work both philosophically and artistically. They draw attention to the tensions that belie a universal perspective and call for a productive engagement with those tensions. Their emphasis on the 'muddled' or 'tangled' is an acknowledgement of the difficulties that come with resisting a universalising perspective. In a sympathetic theoretical move, Anna Lowenhaupt Tsing's *Frictions: An Ethnography of Global Connection* argues for friction as a critical strategy for nuancing universals (2011, 6). Acknowledging that universals have a value in research, Tsing's book uses friction to provide a theory for situating those universals: these 'engaged universals' are complicated by attending to the frictions between macro and micro contexts that universalising concepts often erase. Here, I use friction primarily to describe technological difficulties. However, the artworks I consider and create as well as the critical propositions I make are a consequence of entangled social and technological systems. For this reason, Tsing's use – the friction between different conceptual scales and research paradigms – provides nuisance to both technological rendered friction as well as to the tensions of theatricality. These frictions underwrite my artistic research, an example of which is part of the case-studies I discuss here. These frictions, and their possibilities, are also the bedrock of my epistemological agenda: I begin and end with them, in my artwork and in my research.

Theatricality

Theatricality brings to the stage frictions to trouble the notion of 'frictionless user experiences'. It occurs in artworks that remind us that there are frictions, some that we experience and some that are invisible to us as consequence of our privilege. And, in return, these works provide a means for clarifying why the spectatorial emphasis of theatricality continues to be a vital artistic tactic. The artworks that are the focus of this chapter amplify the digital operations that mediate our relationships. Both works not only make use of the tropes of networked communication tools but also invite the audience into them. They spectacularise the now ubiquitous and often mundane processes that mediate our relationships and, thus, turn our attention back to those processes. They evoke a theatricality that relies on an exchange between the spectator and the spectacle, a friction that shows both operations as well as the intersubjective agreement as to what those operations are.

Both the artworks I discuss here are products of the internet. They are occurring online, are supported by networked processes that enable them to manifest something between multiple geographic locations, with various actors affecting what occurs. They are products of the internet, and they are products of their time. Both make use of the networked communication processes that abound around us, the ease with which these tools mediate us and with which we access them. Artists involved in each have extrapolated from their lives, not just their collaborative processes but also the ways in which they conduct their relationships with friends, family, lovers. At ACMI, the audiences bring their own computers and participate. At Gasworks, the audience is asked to stay off the internet so that the VR can load faster. These works respond to and occur within the technical and social processes of the internet. At each, the spectators understand the context; the relationships that are staged within them and the technologies that mediate them. They are artefacts of contemporary digital ubiquity, postdigital in the sense that these tools are present and ordinary aspects of daily life (Chun 2016, Berry 2014, Berry and Dieter 2015). *Hollow Tongues* and *Documents of the Future* are reflective of the persistence of the internet as a communication tool and its widespread adoption as a central facet of life throughout vast areas of the world.

In this chapter, I will argue that theatricality can be approached as a kind of performance friction, produced by something comparable to the glitch or noise of technologies that draws our attention to malfunctions and near or real failures. I propose dissonance as an (aesthetic and) affective quality that is the consequence of an imbrication of technological and emotional frictions specific to digital ubiquity. Following this, I contend that theatricality provides an artistic context and support for what I term dissonance. The emphasis on relation and the conventions within the frame of the theatrical are extrapolated into the interactions and systems that are the basis of interface functions. Through theatricality, the internet communications processes brought onstage by these performances provide valuable insights into the ways in which relation and sociality are enabled through these technological processes.

My use of theatricality develops from theoretisations of the term as they are rooted in theatre and performance studies. As a quality of performance, a focus on theatricality enables critical assessment of what happens, since these artistic modes begin to take on, and take place within, networked communication. Whereas performativity brings attention to the generative possibilities of performance, theatricality focuses on the relational implications. Drawing from the work of key Performance Studies scholars (Carlson 2002, Davis 2003, Féral 1982, Foster 2002), as well as social anthropologic approaches (Goffman 1959, Burns 1972), the definition of theatricality that I propose – and that I am working with throughout – relies on two interwoven aspects:

(1) An engagement with – such as a reiteration or intentional/'artistic' deviation – with established conventions that a performance reproduces. The 'failure' to make invisible and the resulting visibility of

these codes (be it socially reified codes or generic conventions) suggests an awareness or volition in their reiteration that differentiates theatricality's 'performing' from performativity's 'doing'.
(2) The presence of a spectator who experiences, evaluates and reflects on a performance's engagement with 'conventions'.

Central to theatricality is its ability to mark a moment where a performance is seen to be functioning as a performance, a quality that can be attributed to artwork and social performances alike. Theatricality is a concept that highlights the spectator, the audience, the beholder as a person who enters a relation with an artwork. It foregrounds the agency that a person (the spectator, the audience, the beholder) has within the meaning that is made from a work of art, meaning that is contingent on and a consequence of the relation between a person who sees a work and an artwork. In the theatre, this weighting of the audience-performer relation offers a conceptual framework for understanding performance as a practice of social relation. Similarly, noise – in the context of technological communication – is a result of the imperfections of a connection, a failure to perform as expected. It confirms that there is a connection being made between two parties, even if that relation struggles or fails to occur seamlessly. The awareness of being inside a system of relation, be it a digital communication operating through the internet or the performer-spectator relation of performance, is what connects theatricality with dissonance here.

Tracy Davis, in 'Theatricality and Civil Society', argues that the historical usage of the term is significant for linking theatre and spectating to the way in which intersubjectivity is experienced in the public sphere. Davis argues that spectatorship rehearses an ethically responsible relation to the other, its ability to 'bring into being self-possession of a critical stance' (Davis 2003, 153). This 'self-possession of a critical stance' is integral to how theatricality reflects my aim of articulating the critical possibilities of relation and subjectivity that unite theatricality and dissonance. It is a quality that is associated with the spectatorial experience of a performance, a quality that relies on the viewer's evaluation of a given work. When thinking through a visibility or attention to the emotional and technological politics of internet communication, theatricality provides a tactic for understanding these systems as intertwined. It foregrounds a relational experience, relying on the presence of both performers and audiences to feel the work's working.

In highlighting processes of construction, it provides a means for locating the effects of performance in the ongoing exchange between the various positions that the work enables. Theatricality's historical association with a failure to produce perfect representations (Bailes 2011, 7; Davis 2003, 139), and the emphasis on the theatrical frame that it creates, aligns productively with glitch, noise and friction in digital technologies. By bringing audiences into the sites of performance, an 'invitation to edit' the performing document or an immersive virtual environment within an immersive installation, these works necessitate an awareness of the performances as performances. As Davis writes, '[t]he actor is always conscious of being on stage: it is the audience who occasionally forgets this, and in doing so may believe that the actor is more (or less) than he is' (Davis 2003, 139). Here, the theatrical nature of these works and the position of the audiences within each are a means of positioning technology as an actor. The layers of mediation and intermediality create an intense consciousness of being onstage, a being onstage which– in these works – is synonymous with being on the internet. Each work stretches to find a sense of being together within and despite the digital tools that they use, an experience that mirrors a sense of the connectivity and distance that characterise internet communication more broadly.

Dissonance

In *Off the Network* (2013), a study of the political and social value of sites defined in opposition to networks such as the internet, Ulises A. Mejias argues that we need to understand that noise communicates presence (2013, 17). This 'noise as presence' underscores difference, communicating 'alternative subjectivities' (16–17). Similarly, the theatrical communicates presence within the theatre as the spectator accounts for their evaluating position. This is, as I will discuss later, where the critical possibilities of theatricality are located. The attention of presence enables evaluation and reflection. Through the attention to relation present in theatricality, these artworks make it possible to see more clearly how the technological functions of internet communication become metonymically related to the emotional and affective experiences that they mediate. Relation, as network connection and as affective experience, is always subject to imperfection and irritations. This emphasises how we are performing our relationships through these technologies; it highlights the conventions and assumptions with which systems operate and foregrounds the necessary give-and-take of spectator-performer relations.

In *Hollow Tongues* ([Play]ground-less), the audience is invited to step into the moments shared by the four artists within the virtual site where these artists meet from their various international locations.[1] This happens in various ways, in the sound installation of the room and in the virtual environment of the Oculus. However, in none of them is there a sense that this relation is false because it is performed between multiple places. Their distance from us, from each other, does not undermine the fact of their being 'together'. It is the ability of the work to create this together, a together that feels nervous as the performers pull together from different time zones and a person waits anxiously for their turn, which makes the work interesting. It is a nervousness that Gertrude Stein first found in the theatre: the sense of emotional times out of sync between audience and performer (Stein 1988, 95). A similar nervous friction is present in *Documents of the Future*: the document unfolds so quickly, and from so many points. It is impossible to see it all at once, to understand all the threads that are running through it or to know all the voices present. Still, the audience is invited to jump in at any point and to participate in the flow, to navigate it in their own way. The document offers cohesion as much as it demonstrates the fractal nature of mediated relation. The presence of two artists on stage, the monitors displaying their desktops where they participate in the document, underlines this. Like the feedback sounds of tongues licking microphones in *Hollow Tongues*, the physical presence of live bodies creating the work and their entanglement with the devices that mediate them is central. It is a performance, but one that brings with it the dissonance of internet-mediated relation. The theatricality of the performance operates along the line between the artistic performance and the social performance that instantiates it.

The unreality of the rendered space, the eerie blue commander centre glow, the tactility of the noise of voices and licking, the many bodies present and contributing to the artworks, the confused and dispersed sites create as well as complicate the sense of being together in *Hollow Tongues* and *Documents of the Future*. The affect is complex as it strains across geographical distance and technological difficulty. 'Together' can be temporary and intense, a generous affect caught in the accumulated frictions that characterise dissonance. The frictions and abrasions of relation can take many forms. A feeling of together is the result of their accumulations, the tensions between points of relations and the feelings that collect in them.

It is produced through the performance friction that renders both conventions and audience-performer relations visible in their (mal)functionality. The together that occurs in the sites and the shared moments that are formed and reformed through these artistic practices demonstrate the functions of relation. Dissonance marks the strain between relationships and network connections that brings unease and instability into these processes of relation. It allows the unease of imperfect understanding to be paralleled by (and entangled with) the epistemological possibilities and perspectives that these artistic practices index.

These instances serve as a reminder that technological and emotional difficulties are produced with inconsistent impacts: who feels friction, and why is it not evenly distributed? Focusing on the dissonance of together in internet-situated contexts becomes a means of understanding both the impact of contemporary mediating technologies as well as broader social abrasions of relation: the dissonance of together online highlights other frictions of relation. When artists make use of this dissonance, they reposition this tension as a means of understanding the present and generating complex futures. The social and technological strains or stresses of friction mark the instances when the actual exceeds the imagined: as a system (be it a network or cultural narratives of meaning) comes in contact with the practical specificities of the world, it rubs. The tensions created, between the expectations or lack thereof, by a performance's (in)ability to reproduce theatrical conventions, confirm a work as performance while also troubling the category.

Dissonance is a term that addresses the already occurring ruptures of experience and perspective as they intersect at the point of an artwork or performance. As many artists and theorists have shown, anyone who is not white, cisgendered and straight-presenting runs the risk of the technical difficulties that result from inbuilt assumptions in technologies' cultural models (Blas and Gaboury 2016, Chan 2014, Chun 2009, Russell 2012, 2020). Thinking theatricality into digital ubiquity, it is possible to understand how systems position us spectators and how artworks entangled within these systems draw our attention nearer to their functions. It is the failure to become really real that makes theatre theatrical: for digital communications, the same is true. The promises of frictionless user experience are a promise that the systems that move information will never be seen. When we see them, we are made subject to the internet's objecthood: we see it, see ourselves in relation to it. It is then that we can understand the frictions as affect.

Documents of the Future: Invitation to Edit and *Hollow Tongues* both capture the frictions of social and technological processes that mark collective efforts: the strain of systems in moments that, as Wendy H. K. Chun writes, '*our media matter most when they seem not to matter at all*, that is, when they have moved from the new to the habitual' (Chun 2016, 1; emphasis in original). Technologies and cultures develop together, each strand solving and creating problems for the other, and each the product of a 'collective effort'. Performance – and its ability to move between the social and the artistic – enables us to critically consider how the increasing ubiquity of internet communications contributes to how relationships are performed in the twenty-first century. They are performances that aim, and both succeed and fail, to create a shared space between multiple locations. They extend the utopian promise of global connectivity into performances where bodies and technologies are crammed together in glitchy real-fake spaces that test the limits of that promise's possibilities. In *Hollow Tongues*, this is apparent as the network and the equipment available strain to hold the performance that occurs. The work overburdens the space, there are too many people, and on the network, there is too much information. In doing so, the work makes apparent the frame within and for which it performs, as something that is both disrupting and disrupted by the performance. It is a theatrical effort to create a site of collaborative unity within a virtual space, one that plays absurdity into both its use of performance and visual art as well as in its relationship to technology.

In the promotional image for *Documents of the Future*, a Google Doc reads: 'Less like an object, more like the weather'. The doc is open on a desktop (my desktop), alongside an image of Pavarotti in a microwave and the video of a cylindrical cloud. The performing document is 'more like the weather': it is changeable and ongoing. It is not still or settled, nor safe. Prior to the performance, the artists officially involved decided that the document would be archived periodically in case someone entered the document and erased it all. This potential risk underlines the intimacy of the document and of the desktops that are shown across the stage. These are private spaces, usually used to collect and consider our thoughts before sending them out in more formal ways. Social media theorist Nathan Jurgenson proposes the term 'augmented reality' for addressing the disintegrating difference between on/offline (Jurgenson 2011). He argues that it is necessary to move beyond the dichotomy of on-line and off-line space – what he calls digital dualism, the belief that on- and off-line are separate spaces – into critical considerations of how we live in augmented reality, when distinction is no longer relevant, useful, or even readily apparent. Artistic interventions and engagements with the internet reflect the intimacies of our social exchanges and the frictions that they produce. Theatricality here is both artistic consequence as well as strategy for bolstering these frictions. It is a means for extending the unpleasant, annoying, or inconsequential effects of these frictions, in ways that draw our attention back towards the things we always already know and experience within digital ubiquity.

In contrast to *Hollow Tongues*, the staging of *Documents of the Future: Invitation to Edit* emphasises its digitality. Cool blue light fills the stage at ACMI, a stage that has monitors placed around a large projection screen and multiple people sitting at laptops. The stage is sterile and dark, in contrast to the overabundance of information and images that are unspooling on the screens. Each monitor mirrors a desktop: different perspectives of the document are visible, as are the two artists downstage (Nikki Lam and Katie Paine) who are contributing live. In the video documentation of the performance, more screens are visible in the audience, as people take photos and contribute to the document themselves. The performances overlap, different voices coming from the performances that overlay the document. Around the fifty-five-minute mark, Caroline Sinders begins to explain that she is leading a tutorial on being a social media break-up coordinator. With a slowly rising volume, my voice begins to drown out her instructions. Instead of the clearly detailed emotional and technical processes that are the centre of Sinders's work, there is a fast torrent of abstract language as I talk about trees and the past and the future. Sinders moves between a direct-to-camera 'camgirl'-style address and her desktop. 'Now, I will return to sharing my desktop' cuts through the feedback noises, sounds of typing and my rapid speech. Instead of seeking unity, these works make use of the friction of relation as it is paralleled by the tensions of digital mediations. The mediating effects of contemporary digital technologies are just one way in which our interactions with one another are subject to cultural and social frames. It is the multiplicity of these frames – and the ability to understand digital technology not only as a perhaps newer and evolving frame, but also as nonetheless implicated in a broader fabric of mediation by material and conceptual processes – that is essential.

Conclusion

In the theatre, theatricality is most present in the moments when a performance oversteps its bounds and, as it does, the audience members begin to reflexively evaluate that overstepping. In life, it is present in the moments where our participation and reiterations of social norms are visible. In both cases, it relies on an exchange between the performer and the spectator. Theatricality occurs between the spectator and the work, and it is inherently importantly relational: as Davis writes, theatricality is the 'way we experience intersubjectivity in the public sphere' (2003, 127). Theatricality, when it occurs, underlines a collective participation in world imagining. It reveals the collectively held conceits through which an imaginary – the fictional world of a performance or our notions of a public – is held. Dissonance is an effect that is bolstered by theatricality; it runs parallel to the relation that theatricality names, to the emphasis that exhorts the beholder. Through theatricality, the spectator pulls an artwork into position within the world. They are affected and affecting, and they are able to evaluate and understand how this work has come to be. When a thing is theatrical, its spectacle shows; it becomes impossible to forget that it is made of stuff that means to pull on our attention.

Art, particularly performance, is always responding to the context in which it is made: performance as an art form is imbricated with the ways in which social relations are enacted publicly. The mediation of relation, through emotion and various cultural frames, here becomes interwoven with technologies, enabling artworks that are implicated not only in the technical or social specificities of a contemporary moment but also in the mutually constituting relation of these different specificities. Tracking the response of artists to digital forms tracks the ways in which technologies become entangled (or are already entangled). It is an acknowledgement of the always already political nature of technologies; always already implicated in the systems through which society functions. Technologies shape the world, as much as they are shaped by it, and our containment is often an exercise in catching up. Over the period of writing, this has been borne out by the EU General Data Protection Regulation 2018 coming into effect (Burgess 2018); by the presence of Mark Zuckerberg at hearings in the USA and Europe that interrogate corporate responsibility in this new context (Madrigal 2018, Stone 2018) and by the continued critiques of social media networks such as Facebook (Burrington 2015,

Cadwalladr 2019).[2] Artworks situated on the internet provide a double service of capturing mediated relation within a specific moment, as well as interrogating and making strange its processes in ways that enable critical perspective.

It is in the centrality of the spectator that theatricality returns to alterity, the intersubjective relation as generative of knowledge. The political importance of the spectatorial experience that Davis articulates as key to theatricality is not dissimilar from what Jacques Rancière refers to as 'dissensus'. In his book *The Emancipated Spectator* (2009), Rancière defines dissensus as an expansive kind of social disagreement that shifts 'perception and signification', examples of which can be found between spectators as well as between spectators and artists in their understandings of the meaning of a work: dissensus 'means that every situation can be cracked open from the inside, reconfigured in a different regime of perception and signification' (2009, 49; see also Rancière 2004, 84). He argues that this dissensus is key to the political possibility afforded to the subjectivity of an 'emancipated spectator': spectators are able to construct their own meaning, constructed from an artwork's relation to their given context and existing knowledge (Rancière 2009, 49). However, Rancière's emancipated spectator is only one articulation of the counter-construction of knowledge and meaning that operates in the arts, particularly in performance. If, as Davis argues, theatricality is the moment of critical distance, what she refers to as 'enabling effects of active dissociation' that 'bring into being the self-possession of a critical stance' (Davis 2003, 153), then applying this dissociation to the ways in which social life is immersed in digital culture enables us to take a critical stance on how we are currently reassembling the social.

This chapter was a very contemporary exercise: it is about the practices of relations that occur in the technologies of a specific moment. As such, the objects of my analyses move into the past very quickly. However, my intention has been to focus on the apparatuses of relations as much as – more so, even – than the particularities of technologies. For this reason, I hope to be able to both give an account of a particular moment in the evolving response of artistic practices to the internet while also providing a framework for engaging more broadly with the imbrications of artworks, technologies and social practice. I have focused on what occurs at the intersection of the 'in process' qualities of performance and technologies. It is through the interwoven frictions of performance and digital technology, of practices of relation with the frames that mediate them, that I have aimed to define internet-situated art. At one point, in the script for *Hollow Tongues*, the artists say:

> And yet, no-thing always turns out to be something.
> So let us pretend, for a moment,
> that we can touch, that we can meet,
> even knowing that the pronoun we will also disappear,
> that we will disappear in the future.

In this fragment, the will to be sharing space is a shared space that the artists and their audience occupy, even as it disappears. The text references the trading of pronouns – I, you, we – that indicates intersubjective relation (see, for example, Benveniste 1971). We are all in a moment together, a virtual site within the gallery site that is framed by the aurality of four bodies performing with technologies together. Vitally, the aim here has never been to resolve that friction. Friction is present in all our current practices of relation, in all the ways that our current practices of relation are always already performing the social into its future iterations.

Notes

1. For more detail, see https://www.ninnabohnpedersen.com/Hollow-Tongues (last accessed 20 September 2023).
2. As this chapter was prepared for publication in 2022, any experience or understanding of being together on the internet was dramatically reconstituted by the global COVID-19 pandemic.

4

Meta-Theatricality, Hypermediacy and Theatricality in the Making of *Never Swim Alone*

Lowell Gasoi

I am sitting in the dark of a little theatre in Hudson, Quebec. It is opening night, a feeling and an experience I know all too well: the nerves, the adrenaline, the culmination of a journey and the slight feeling of sick at the back of the throat. This is a moment that encapsulates a year-long, practice-led research project that explores questions around hypermediacy, intermediality and theatricality that have seldom been addressed with the intimacy and experience of embodied knowledge.

The play I choose as a means to examine these questions is *Never Swim Alone* (1991), written by one of Canadian theatre's most celebrated playwrights, Daniel MacIvor. Throughout the 1990s, MacIvor, often working alongside director Daniel Brooks, wrote and performed a series of one-man plays, including *Wild Abandon* (1990), *See Bob Run* (1990), *House* (1996), *Here Lies Henry* (1997) and *Monster* (1998). The plays had a unique meta-theatricality that became the hallmark of MacIvor's work. As Mary Ann Frese Witt argues, this meta-awareness reflects the theatricality of the world back onto its audience (Witt 2014, 14), and I believe onto the players as well. In *Never Swim Alone*, this meta-theatricality is described by critic and scholar Carol Bolt as a play in which characters 'seem to believe their audience will actually help' (Bolt; in MacIvor 1993, 8). This chapter seeks to interrogate how technological mediation, the integration of intermediality, might intersect with that sense of theatricality.

Back in the theatre, my eyes flicker back and forth from the two actors on stage to my laptop screen, filled with video clips, controls and monitors that represent one of the three characters in this play. I sit here, in plain view of this audience and of the two live actors on stage, my fingers hovering over the computer keyboard, prepared to launch my element of this performance: a pre-recorded, projected player to match wits with those two actors on stage. I have guided these two actors through this play as their director. As video-maker, I have guided this third character, their virtual acting partner, capturing her performance, virtually slicing it up, and now I propose to project it, in concert with the live action, as a fellow performer. The play's successes and failures, its challenges and processes have led to a belief that the initiation of this sequence of projected images seeks to test: that digital media can exhibit a theatricality just as relevant as a live performer. The two live characters, Frank and Bill, begin the first lines of the play: 'Hello. Good to see you. Glad you could come'. And the screens – the four spread dramatically across the stage space to give this projected character the ability to move around and interact with the live players, as well as the screen in front of me on my laptop – all come to life… somehow.

This scene opens the door to questions about the growing use of intermedial theatre. Can the idea of meta-theatre, a theatrical awareness that blurs the mediation of the theatrical frame, be a means to interrogate this practice? Meta-theatre is a revelatory concept, a form of theatre that lays bare the artifice and thereby invites new engagement with the presentation of the story on stage. How can performers, directors, designers and scholars be more engaged in a critical and informed reflection of their processes and, particularly, their relationship to intermedial elements? In a multi-screened world where technological mediations and representations have infiltrated not just the theatre but our culture, politics and practices more widely, how do we map that network of concepts such as intermedial theatre, meta-theatricality and hypermediacy, and ultimately the idea of mediation in theatricality?

Never Swim Alone offers its particular idea of theatricality in a rumination on male rivalry, consumerism and the perils of being the 'first man': the first to the top, the first across the metaphysical finish line that divides winners from losers. Two men, played in my production by Aaron George (as Frank) and Alex Goldrich (as Bill), engage in a metaphorical boxing match, gauging their superiority over one another, through everything from their height, romantic and family relationships, financial successes, to the size of… well, you get the idea. These rounds are judged by the Referee, performed by Paula Jean Hixson, an enigmatic woman in a swimsuit, halfway between Goddess and ghost, who we slowly discover represents the trauma of a past incident that haunts both men. As boys, visiting the beach 'all day every day' in the summer of their youth, they swam against each other in a race 'to the point', failing to notice that the girl they were trying to impress had fallen behind and drowned. The Referee, as both judge and embodiment of this memory, could be imagined as existing on a different temporal plane than the men, and so I chose to place her on a different medium as well. The meta-theatrical nature of the play, as well as the final moments that suggest a Buddhist-like cycle of repetition of this same story and competition, allowed me to imagine this iteration of *Never Swim Alone* to be a version wherein the Referee would be technologically remediated. I made the decision to capture Paula's performance of the Referee, place it on video, manipulate it through editing and project it, by using VJ software, onto the stage alongside Frank and Bill. The play just became intermedial meta-theatre.

Intermedial Meta-Theatre and Hypermediacy

Freda Chapple and Chiel Kattenbelt define intermedial theatre as 'the incorporation of digital technology into theatre practice, and the presence of other media within theatre productions' (Chapple and Kattenbelt 2006, 11). It is to both of those definitions that this research speaks. In *Never Swim Alone*, we have the presence of video onstage, the presence of the operator and the technology visible in the theatre. More than this, my examination of intermediality sought to go beyond the moment of performance. I believe it should encompass the processes that lead to the performance, what Patrice Pavis suggests is a vital method for studying theatre-making, a holistic examination of the entire practice of incorporating digital technology into the cycle of conception, creation and reception (Pavis 2018, 223–24). For me, and for scholars like Pavis and David Saltz, this is what makes the research process in producing an intermedial work so rewarding that attention can be given to the entire process, and not just the moment of encounter with an audience. Chapple and Kattenbelt further expand on intermediality as 'a self-conscious reflexivity that displays the devices of performance in performance' (2006, 11). This indicates to me that the practice of incorporating various digital mediations into live performance is somehow linked to a revealing of the process of that mediation, a theatrical process of seeing (Weber 2004, 3). It also suggests that intermediality and hypermediacy have a kinship that is worth exploring, as suggested by the work of Andy Lavender on *Jet Lag* (Lavender 2006, 57) and by Aristita I. Albacan (2016) in discussing the work of Robert Lepage.

As part of the double logic suggested by Jay Bolter and Richard Grusin in their book *Remediation: Understanding New Media* (2003), hypermediacy involves revelling in the act of mediation. Bolter and Grusin argue that the ways in which we relate to so-called old media (live performance might be placed here) and new media (video-mapped projection) and the ways in which they relate to each other are governed by the logic of transparent immediacy and hypermediacy. Transparent immediacy is the attempt to erase all signs of mediation, the photographically perfect computer-generated image (Bolter and Grusin 2003, 11–15). A useful recent example of the aspiration to transparent immediacy are the attempts to create the totally life-like Gollum in Peter Jackson's *Lord of the Rings* films (2001–3). Hypermediacy is the opposite yet related idea, the revealing of the process of mediation, showing the green-screen, seeing the video operator in the house rather than hidden away in a booth. Bolter and Grusin tend towards the aesthetic implications of these ideas, and yet I argue that the link to meta-theatricality can offer a wider frame than the examination of creative production, both live and recorded. Lavender, in examining what he calls hypermedial theatre, including *D.A.V.E.*, a production that uses the body of a live actor as a screen for an intermedial character, states that 'the virtual can be thought of in terms of presence [...] the actual and the virtual are simultaneously in play' (64), a multiplication that he also studies in terms of the pleasure it brings to an audience.

What about the term meta-theatre? The whole notion of 'meta' has become a little murky with its dissipation into popular cultural parlance. The ironically self-referential is often the most common definition, and it now generally tends towards the cynical. It is the cheeky mug to the camera, or the constant references to political realities as reality television, as Debord (1995) already warned decades ago, a world composed of self-aware spectacle. Here in 2019, as I write, with a reality TV star in the White House, it is not difficult to imagine the implications of meta-theatre in the political and cultural realms. In the theatre, however, the meta has more specific connotations. Lionel Abel has coined the term meta-theatre, and while it has been used to describe a lot of postmodern or postdramatic plays, it is not quite as simple as the play-within-a-play of *Hamlet*, or the self-referential shenanigans in Tom Stoppard's *Rosencrantz and Guildenstern are Dead* (1967). According to Abel, meta-theatre is a play that captures a moment that is already dramatised (Abel 2003, 60). In other words, the play understands that it is a play, and that awareness allows the players on the stage to engage with each other and the audience in a highly reflexive manner, a property of intermediality as well. The action, and more particularly the characters, in such a play are too large to be contained by the play's structure (62), and so they leak out, blurring the lines between the staged reality, what I refer to as the story space, and the material reality of the theatrical event, or the stage space.

Many of MacIvor's characters exhibit this largeness, this pre-dramatic existence. In the foreword to *2 Plays*, Carol Bolt imagines Victor, the main character in MacIvor's 1996 play, *House*, as having rented the theatre (the stage space) that night to tell his story (to create a story space) (Bolt; in MacIvor 1993, 8). In my production of *Never Swim Alone*, the Referee herself is both the memory of a young girl and an iconic judge, able to decide how the two men, Frank and Bill, will square off against one another. Frank and Bill themselves lean towards the iconic: they wear precise uniforms, described in their dialogue as 'White shirts. Blue suits. Silk ties. Black shoes. Black socks' (MacIvor 1993, 19). They speak in a type of ritualised patter throughout the play, for instance, in this sequence (26–27):

> *Bill*: I know this guy better than he knows himself.
> *Frank*: And that's what makes it sad
> *Bill*: But sad as it is, it's true
> *Frank & Bill*: and the truth of it is:
> *Frank*: And this is much
> *Bill*: much
> *Frank & Bill*: much more
> *Frank*: than something as simple as
> *Bill*: his bum leg
> *Frank*: his trick knee
> *Bill*: his weak wrist
> *Frank*: his slipped disc

And these rituals extend into the dramatic invocation of the Referee character herself, which in the original play text involves the two men lifting a sheet from the sleeping form of the girl. In our production, this is reimagined as the synchronised launching of a computer programme. Abel imagines these characters as if they had already existed in a theatrical mode before their stories are captured and set down by the playwright

(MacIvor 1993, 60). In MacIvor's *House*, for instance, Victor is a character, even when he is negotiating the imagined rental of the actual, physical theatre in which the play is mounted. The theatricalisation of his existence is complete. He can move from stage space to story space, as if no boundary existed, just as he does during the play when he leaves the stage and comments on the architecture of the theatre or the drinks at the bar (38–39). In *Never Swim Alone*, the Referee – both arbiter and Lisa the drowned girl, both here and then, both memory and reality – moves through stage and story space like a ghost and a real woman. It is not unreasonable then to imagine that she is also capable of challenging the boundaries of mediation, bringing the recorded, the technologically mediated, into conversation with the live, with the theatrical.

In my discussions with MacIvor in the spring of 2014, during the course of preparing for this research project, he shied away from the term meta-theatre, perhaps not wishing to define his work too simply. MacIvor's work, I believe, is indeed more subtle and complex than some of the traditional notions of direct address, Brechtian wall-breaking, shifts in style or tone, all present in much of what we think of as meta-theatrical work. When I suggested to him that this makes his work appropriate for the exploration of intermediality, he became excited by the idea and offered his blessing for the research project, something that, to my knowledge, had not been previously attempted with any production of his work.

Much of the research on intermedial theatre, as in the case of Lavender (2006), is concerned with audience reception and tends to background the longer process of creation. Rand Hazou touches on questions of authenticity and credibility in his examination of the work of Mnouchkine and her Theatre du Soleil (2011, 298–99), and while this chapter cannot delve too deeply into Hazou's argument, the question of how intermedial representations come to represent a species of truth, or at least, a credible source, within the imagined world of the theatre is significant. What I think is unique about my take on mediated performance and live, co-temporal action is a focus on the actors' and creators' role and relationship to the hypermediated events of recording, editing, rehearsal and performance. The virtue of practice-led research brings my own experiences as video-director, play-director, my intimacy with my actors, all these elements into an embodied knowledge that I feel is not always present in research on intermedial practice and on meta-theatre. Coming as I was from a theatre background, but with a research agenda based in Media Studies, I felt there was something new that I might add to this conversation.

What began to emerge from this work was a clear connection between the idea of hypermediacy, grounded in Media Studies, and that of the theatre-based concept of meta-theatricality. Canadian researcher and theatre-maker Jenn Stephenson has pointed this out, stating in a blog article about hypermediacy in 2017: 'By displacing theatrical conventions in support of mimetic representation and drawing our attention explicitly to those conventions, the effect of metatheatricality is the same [as that of hypermediacy]' (Stephenson 2017). In other words, an awareness, even a celebration, of the artifice inherent in meta-theatrical works exhibits a kinship with hypermediacy in that both display the technologies of theatricality, while seemingly suggesting that there is something underneath the artifice that is being revealed. These ideas, hypermediacy and meta-theatricality, demonstrate a performative relationship between the mediated and the 'real' even within the overall fantasy of a theatrical production. In this manner, we can see the potential for theatricality itself, as Weber suggests (2004), to act as a medium and to embrace and implicate other media in the process of remediation.

The Referee's existence in a distinct technological medium, and the possibility that we explored in rehearsal, that she has been a part of this recurrent replaying of this competition and its traumatic result over and over again, all give her extraordinary theatrical power. The theatrical decision we made in the final production was to include a brief onstage prologue where the actors playing Frank and Bill silently argue over how their Referee will appear in this iteration of their ritual: will she appear as a live person; will she appear on the screens which they dutifully arrange around the stage? The implication is that the existence of this Referee questions the conception of Peggy Phelan as performance being 'representation without reproduction' (Phelan 2003, 146). A technologically mediated character is, in some sense, eminently reproducible, and yet her projection into the space, her manipulation by the live operator/performer blurs that line. She is something new, in both the technological and the theatrical sense.

On the Beach, in the Editing Room and in the Studio

My research collaborators offered some fascinating insights into these processes, and if I am to present an argument about the need for further exploration of theatricality as it impacts on the processes of working within this network of live, meta-theatrical and mediated performances, I must turn my attention to our collective experiences.

One of the first questions that Paula asked me when we started talking about the filming of this project was: 'Are you planning to shoot the whole play in one shot?' While she shared that her apprehension stemmed from being able to remember all the lines (not something generally expected of film performers), my concern was with what I might be able to capture and what would be missed if I tried to treat the filming process as the capture of a theatrical performance on another medium. I chose not to include the future live actors in the process of shooting the video performance with Paula. Instead, my assistant and I read lines for her, trying to offer as vague and undirected a reading as possible. Paula was asked to play with her own memory of past performance (she had been involved in an original live production that we created together more than a decade before), and her imagination of the potential future performance in relation with yet unknown scene partners. I sought her performance as something divorced from the live as much as possible, as part of the experiment in examining these processes as discretely as I could. I recognized, as did Paula, that her separation from the other actors made her performance much more challenging. We did try to shoot mostly in sequence, and we did shoot long sequences of the play in single shots, but we did not shoot the whole play in one take.

If all Paula knew was that I was doing a film adaptation of *Never Swim Alone* and that her scenes were being shot separately from the other actors, she could easily make the shift in her technique and presence to that of 'film actress'. Forcing her, and myself, to reframe the process as one that stands in relationship to the live performance happening at an unspecified later date, with unspecified performance partners, made her performance something undefined. But there were a number of ways in which I tried to mark it as either video or live performance, such as the curious mix of techniques applied during the filming process. All the trappings of video production were present: camera, sync sound, full costumes and an on-location set, an actual beach near my home. By removing the elements of theatricality from the video performance space that might be present on a soundstage, I was trying to question the kind of technique that Paula might apply to her performance. Paula told me that the experience was not particularly theatrical for her, since she was not involved in any of the rehearsals or working with other actors, something she considered as endemic to the theatrical mode of working. While I tried to work with Paula in what I would describe as a theatrical mode, it is interesting to consider that my efforts may not have translated to Paula, partly because the 'stage' was so obviously absent.

Whether this process was more or less theatrical is a question that harkens back to hypermediacy. If the trappings of mediation are present and foregrounded, then according to Bolter and Grusin's double logic, a more immediate engagement with the moment might be possible (2003, 9). Paula, as an experienced film and theatre actress, did not seem to feel that the lack of large-scale equipment and a crew of make-up people, production assistants and gaffers made a difference to her relationship with the camera. As a much less experienced video-maker, I felt that the video camera, the extra sound recording device, clapping and shot-stating, even the speaking of the words 'action' and 'cut', provided a sense of hypermediacy for me. The simple act of looking at the video camera screen and Paula's live performance echoed the experience I would later seek to create, both in the rehearsal room and in the theatre.

From the video space, I move into the rehearsal studio, a curious environment. I would argue that it is almost always a multiplicity of representations, making it a site of hypermediacy. In rehearsal, we acknowledge the Potemkin reality: markings on the floor represent set pieces and stage dimensions; a stick represents the prop sword that we will wield in the final production; stage managers read stage directions and scenic transitions, and we accept them as real. Even the well-established act of calling for a 'line' when a performer forgets the next piece of dialogue is a practice that represents a reality where performers are expected to stay 'in the moment', while reaching out from the story space to the rehearsal space.

As the rehearsal space is slowly transformed by means of rehearsal props, set mock-ups, and costume bits and pieces into a representation of the final performance space, the representation of that representation of the director's and designer's visions of the play is realised. According to Bolter and Grusin, 'the logic of hypermediacy acknowledges multiple acts of representation and makes them visible' (2003, 33). The actors, director, designers and technicians have engaged in a hypermediated practice, bringing the mediation to the foreground of the entire team's consciousness.

If we acknowledge that theatre is always a hypermediated practice, then how do technologies such as projections and mediated characters accept their own theatricality? As David Saltz discusses in his work at the Interactive Performance Laboratory, the integration of technology and its timing during the rehearsal process is crucial (Saltz 2001, 120–21). I did not wish for Alex and Aaron, as my live actors, to have any access to the Referee as a presence beyond mediation. I wanted their relationship to be defined by that of the screen performance only. I was looking to bring the practice of hypermediacy into the rehearsal process from day one. The actors would need to integrate their perceptions of each other and the stage space with the screen space occupied by the digitally rendered Referee on her digitally rendered beach.

To increase that sense of hypermediacy, I pushed the actors to have a constant, meta-theatrical awareness of my presence as a video operator/performer, to be aware of the screens and to be aware of their own knowledge that they have created this character. This direction created a lot of tension in the rehearsal room, as the actors, Aaron in particular, struggled to try to understand who they were and with whom they were actually playing the scenes. We sought an understanding of how the meta-theatrical and hypermediated elements worked in terms of dramatic choices and how to work with the mediated image, although we barely scratched the surface of such a complex process.

It was the rehearsal room, and the early technical rehearsals that allowed me to breathe once again. As I worked with the video clips of the Referee and brought them into the space of the theatre, a real conversation was happening between this potential future performance and Paula's recorded performance. It was not a question of simply poring through the hours of footage I had taken over the five days we shot, but rather a dynamic back and forth that allowed Paula's performance to determine the shape of the video structure, as well as the theatrical vision. Once I began to take my laptop and projector to the theatre for a couple of test projection sessions, I also discovered that the architecture of the theatre re-engaged that conversation. The breaking up of the stage area into distinct screens would allow me to theatrically block or create stage movement for Paula, just as I would for the live actors. A further metaphorical space was available to me above the main stage, a discovery I only made during my second visit to the theatre, which forced a complete rethinking of the placement of images and video clips. And so back and forth I went, a process that I realised was answering the questions I sought to address.

Playing with Light

Digitally mediating a character places this creation in terms of David Saltz's taxonomy of live and mediated theatre articulations as 'dramatic media' with possible elements of 'virtual puppetry' (Saltz 2001, 126), since I, as video performer, was in fact controlling the bits and pieces of video performance that played alongside Aaron and Alex. My attempt here is to begin to break down the live/mediated binary entirely and to stop looking at the two practices as separate pieces willed to live together by clever designers and techno-geek directors. A key question emerged: how do intermedial techniques reveal something about the truth in *Never Swim Alone*? From the moment MacIvor's characters enter the stage space and greet their audience, the ritualistic and heightened story space that they create is evident in its theatricality. This is particularly apparent in the moment of 'creation' of the Referee, the girl resurrected by Frank and Bill to judge and ultimately work through their past trauma. In the original play, it is ritualistic, almost religious in its stage direction (Frank and Bill lift a sheet to reveal the character under it, and she 'awakens'). In our production, the two men synchronise their computers, launching their Referee almost as an app. Immediately, however, audience and actors are aware, due to my presence in the house as video operator, that this is just an empty ritual, and the Referee is another performer whose presence slides from mediated absence to screen presence, to present technology, to live operator. It is a rich soup.

At several points during the process, I asked Aaron and Alex what they thought the Referee was. I admit that I was looking for an answer about her materiality that might speak to the theatricality, the mediation of a digital performance. Instead, Alex called her 'a manifestation of the natural laws that govern this place'. The place to which Alex was referring seemed to blur between the stage and story space. Despite my initial concerns that her mediation would somehow distance her from the live moment in a way that could not be reconciled, the performance rather added a further dimension to the meta-theatricality of the story space, by inviting an encounter with the stage space. As Stephenson (2017) suggests, meta-theatre offers a unique insight into the construction of theatrical truth and convention within an intermedial play.

What's Next?

Enjoying some drinks after a particularly gruelling rehearsal for the show with Alex and Aaron, I am prodding them a little to talk about the experience, how they are reacting to Paula's performance, now being projected onto the back wall of our rehearsal space and manipulated through the mapping software by my hands. Aaron is struggling with the whole experience, much more so than Alex. As I am trying to get him to think about the mediation of her performance, he hits me with a surprising request. Could I ask Paula to come into town, maybe even a week or so after the run of the play, and have one performance with them all live in the room together? It would not even have to be before an audience, he explains, as Alex looks a bit stricken. Why would you want that, I ask? What value would it bring for you? For closure, he says.

What is it that Aaron is seeking when he requests Paula's presence for a 'closure' performance? I wonder if this is not a manifestation of theatrical convention that can be challenged by intermediality. Connecting the language of Media Studies and Performance Studies can be a productive way to reassess the methodology of intermedial theatre creation. To push beyond representational relationships between actors, characters, mediated performances and the play space and stage space can allow us as theatre practitioners to consider how we are engaging in the process of mediation as we articulate pieces of the creation process together.

Alex Goldrich's contention that Paula's mediated performance was natural in some sense is a function of the hypermediated environment which we created from day one, and that environment is both metatheatrical stage space and story space. To create and see plays that explore these emerging relationships in both form and content is how the practice stays relevant. While there are increasing numbers of multimedia spectaculars that push the form beyond known boundaries, it is through more intimate plays that the spectacle can be given less focus and the network of actor/character/mediation/story can be explored more closely and lovingly.

The actors with whom I created *Never Swim Alone* were talented, well-trained and experienced performers, and yet their highly differentiated approaches to bridging the practice of intermedial theatre – that is, how Alex and Aaron understood the mediated character as both the perfect actor and a complete hack, how Paula performed on camera with some attempts at understanding that projection within a live event was the ultimate destination for that performance; their divergent responses ranging from utter confusion, over dogged persistence, to a retreat to long-established patterns of theatre and film-making – indicate that a paradigm of training and a discourse of practice has yet to emerge for what has very quickly become ubiquitous. And if artists themselves are not quite there yet with a shared and embodied knowledge of these practices, we are potentially building a castle on shifting sands.

And perhaps that is exactly what artists should be doing, but, as scholars and educators, we must continue to examine the relationship between theatricality, intermediality and hypermediacy through a sustained interrogation of the entire process. Meta-theatrical plays like *Never Swim Alone* offer a rich source for that exploration.

Part 2
Philosophy

5

Display in Human Art and the Aesthetic Lives of Animals: On the Limits of Evolutionary Aesthetics

Mathew Abbott

In *The Art Instinct: Beauty, Pleasure, and Human Evolution*, Denis Dutton presents evolutionary biological accounts of the origins of our aesthetic practices and of art's significance in human life. Positioning his contribution as an alternative to the 'hermetic discourse that deadens so much of the humanities' (Dutton 2009, 1), Dutton wants to show how the pressures of natural and sexual selection have produced *Homo sapiens* as a 'species obsessed with creating artistic experiences' (3). His approach is grounded in a fact that should be of interest to all aestheticians: 'The universality of art and artistic behaviors, their spontaneous appearance everywhere across the globe and through recorded human history' (30). Although Stephen Davies is more sceptical than Dutton about the plausibility and explanatory power of evolutionary approaches to art, in *The Artful Species* he also makes a case for a link between art and evolution, on the basis of the universality of art and aesthetic experience in human life. As he acknowledges, aesthetic responsiveness is 'universal among humans', and if 'art' is understood reasonably broadly, then art making is found in all human cultures, and almost every human being appreciates 'one or another kind of art'. This is 'suggestive of a link between evolution and both art and aesthetics' (Davies 2012, 7). Archaeological, ethnographic and anthropological evidence provides powerful support for the idea that human beings have always and everywhere engaged in practices recognizable as artistic; this indicates that these practices may be part of our biological inheritance.

The more difficult question is not whether there is a link between art and human evolution, but what kind of link there is, and what this can tell us about the former. Dutton makes some strong claims here. He purports to do so without denying the 'cultural character' (Dutton 2009, 31) of our aesthetic practices, but he has a way of underspecifying the role of culture, to the point of rendering opaque the contributions it makes. Note the language he uses when trying to describe the relationship between biology and culture: he speaks of the 'human impulses and drives that underlie our culture' (9); he speaks of 'emotional human responses' that are 'revealed in basic, prerational longings and desires' (34); he writes of how the arts 'in all their glory are no more remote from evolved features of the human mind and personality than an oak is remote from the soil and subterranean waters that nourish and sustain it' (3). These spatial metaphors set up biology as a kind of ground or base. Dutton takes himself to be revealing the fundamentals of our aesthetic practices, features of human biology that subsist beneath the reach of culture. (As Matthew Rampley characterises the picture: 'Modern cultures and societies are just a *veneer* laid over much older mental instincts'; Rampley 2017, 25; my emphasis). This makes it difficult for him to get a grip on the cultural aspects of our aesthetic practices, which inevitably appear as making superficial contributions to something whose real source lies deeper in the human psyche.

This paper argues that narrowly naturalistic approaches to art, such as Dutton's, give little insight into the normative structure of our aesthetic practices, because they cannot account for the role played in them by rationality. That argument proceeds in the following way. First, the paper outlines Dutton's attempt to explain human aesthetic behaviours by highlighting parallels between them and animal displays. After pointing out problems with the scientific basis of Dutton's claims, the paper considers philosophical issues with his account. It invokes three stories on the role of display in human art and the aesthetic lives of animals: a passage from Immanuel Kant's *Critique of Judgment* about a nightingale song faked by a landlord for his unwitting guests; a passage from Charles Darwin's *Descent of Man* about the delight that peacocks take in their displays; and a passage from the art historian Michael Fried's *Absorption and Theatricality* on the problem of display in eighteenth-century French painting. I argue that the stories bring out profound differences in our aesthetic responses to nature and to human art. Aesthetic display is central to the aesthetic lives of many animals, but only for rational ones does that very fact become problematic, such that it can present to artists as something to be neutralised (and such that we can ask after its origins in our biology). The paper concludes by turning to Terry Pinkard's interpretation of

G. W. F. Hegel, showing how it can help us make sense of the complications that rationality introduces into our aesthetic lives.

While previous evolutionary psychological theories of art and evolution tended to emphasise natural selection, the novelty of Dutton's work consists in his attempt at giving a philosophical account of the impact of sexual selection on our artistic practices. He sets up his account with reference to Darwin's 1860 letter to the American botanist Asa Gray, sent one year after the publication of *The Origin of Species* as the biologist worked through problems raised by his theory of the evolution of species through natural selection. As Darwin wrote to Gray (with some facetiousness): 'The sight of a feather in a peacock's tail, whenever I gaze at it, makes me sick!'[1] Peacock tails present a problem for aspects of the theory outlined in *The Origin of Species* because it is difficult to explain them as adaptations through natural selection. The tails are large and therefore extremely 'costly' for the birds to produce, using up valuable calories. The size and weight of them make agile movement more difficult. Their bright colours and conspicuous patterns may make it easier for predators to spot the birds. From the perspective of *Origin*, opulent ornaments like peacock tails should never have evolved.

The solution – first outlined by Darwin in *The Descent of Man* in 1871 – is the theory of evolution through sexual selection. Animals evolve not only features that improve their chances of surviving, but also ones that make them attractive to potential mates. Superb plumage, imposing antler sets, thick manes, complex songs, powerful calls, impressive dances and the like all emerge out of sexual selection in this way. Or rather in two ways, as Darwin identified: some features (such as antlers) equip animals to compete for mates in combat; other features function ornamentally as attractions in themselves. In both cases, the idea is that animals sporting these features are more likely to reproduce and, therefore, more likely to pass heritable features on to their offspring, creating a positive feedback loop, as the animals who prefer such features pass on those preferences (see Darwin 2004, 243).

The case of ornaments presents some difficulties, however, because it seems to require that evolutionary biology explain why certain features are preferred by potential mates. Darwin had no qualms about framing his account of this in aesthetic terms. 'When we behold a male bird elaborately displaying his graceful plumes or splendid colours before the female', he writes, 'it is impossible to doubt that she admires the beauty of her male partner' (Darwin 2004, 115). Darwin even makes explicit links between the aesthetic sensibilities of birds and humans, as when he writes that birds 'appear to be the most aesthetic of all animals, excepting of course man, and they have nearly the same taste for the beautiful as we have' (Darwin 2004, 408). These kinds of assertions would prove unsatisfactory to many of those taking up his theory (see Jones and Ratterman 2009). From some modern perspectives, Darwin was anthropomorphising when he argued that peahens 'appreciate' their mates, having 'rendered the peacock the most splendid of living birds' through their 'continued preference of the most beautiful males' (Darwin 2004, 487). The most influential developments of Darwin's theory give another explanation: animals are attracted to ornaments because they signal health and genetic fitness. Here the costliness and unwieldiness of such features are an explicit part of the story. A plume of especially large and bright tail feathers, for example, supposedly demonstrates that the peacock endowed with these ornaments is strong enough to survive with them, even while paying the substantial costs of doing so; hence the attraction that they produce in peahens seeking to maximise the fitness of the offspring which she will produce with him. In other words, these kinds of accounts allow the evolutionary biologist not simply to accept that certain traits may evolve in spite of handicapping survival, but to explain how they evolve precisely because of how they handicap it (on this point, see Zahavi 1975, cf. Zahavi and Zahavi 1997).

That is the basis of Dutton's inferences to human practices. He argues that, although language has obvious adaptive benefits, a good deal of our life with it extends beyond its applications to matters of everyday survival. He mentions vocabulary size, joke-making and appreciation, the competent use of metaphors and narrative skill, all of which are 'noticed and prized by human beings as direct signals and displays of mental quality' (Dutton 2009, 149). He links this to the cave paintings of Lascaux and Chauvet, Swabian animal carvings, ancient necklaces and the use of cosmetic ochre, Pleistocene flutes and jewellery, and the tattoos on Ice Man, the 5,300-year-old mummy found in the Tyrol (149–50). The principle in all these cases is supposedly the same as with animal displays: our artistic practices are costly investments which we have been hardwired to make by sexual selection. As Catherine Wilson writes, on this account artistic production is 'a form of "creative intelligence" that was selected for in human males by human females . . . ' (Wilson 2016, 245).

Although Dutton does not use the term, it appears that he wants to follow Geoffrey Miller (whom he cites repeatedly, and who himself is developing an idea from Richard Dawkins [1989]) in taking artworks to be part of the 'extended phenotype' of the human organism: 'a genetically evolved, species-specific artefact constructed outside the individual's body, but very much in the service of the individual's genes' (Miller 2001a; cf. Miller 2001b). On this kind of account, the most powerful analogy for artworks in the lives of animals is probably the bowerbird's court, an artefact constructed by the male bird for the purpose of display – and which, on 'good genes' accounts, must be a means of signalling his fitness. Hence Dutton's points about the role of 'costliness and waste' in art (Dutton 2009, 156): it follows from his picture that works of art will frequently be made of 'rare or expensive materials'; they should take a lot of time to make, or it should take a lot to learn the skills required to make them; they will tend to be 'remote from any possible use'; and they should require 'special intellectual or creative effort to create' (Dutton 2009, 157). Because artistic talent is unevenly distributed and the relevant skills costly to refine, those who flaunt such skills by creating fine artworks are making themselves more attractive, by showing that they had the capacity, time and resources to develop them. By combining this account of the role of sexual selection in our artistic practices with his account of the role of natural selection in our aesthetic preferences, Dutton believes that he is making progress towards a 'complete theory of the origin of the arts' (152).

Although I will turn to the philosophical issues presently, the problems with the account are not only philosophical: Dutton is passing off some contentious scientific claims as uncontroversial. As Wilson argues, four things would have to follow if the claim that art is an adaptation from sexual selection were true:

> First, it would have to be the case that some male humans had more artistic talent and more propensity to display it than others in human prehistory. Second, these qualities would have had to be heritable to a significant extent. Third, females would have had to prefer artistic males as mates for these qualities, not on account of some qualities associated with them. Fourth, the preferences would have had to be effective in determining mating success and the number of offspring (Wilson 2016, 246).

In principle, longitudinal studies could examine evidence for the first three conditions, provided it were possible to disaggregate artistic talent from other potentially attractive features. But finding support for the fourth may be impossible, as we simply do not know which features won out most often in Pleistocene sexual sorting. Artistic talent and achievement may have played a role, of course, but other criteria could have prevailed here, and for the account to hold in its strongest form, it has to be artistic ability that is selected for, not the benefits (such as status) that artistry might bring. As Davies points out, the account underplays domestic art, a great deal of which has been produced by women (it is less prominent in the archaeological record, but women's art has typically not been made from the most durable materials; see Davies 2012, 125–26). Miller claims as evidence for his theory the fact that human history provides many more examples of successful male artists than female ones, but this could be explained by the limited opportunities available to women (the issue is complicated by the fact that humans have relatively low sexual dimorphism). And the difficulties do not just pertain to the application of results from evolutionary biology to human practices: although Dutton does not mention them, there are controversies in biology about the role of sexual selection in animal ornamentation, where the handicap theory has been the subject of serious debate, and where there is disagreement about the connection between mate choice and offspring fitness (on these issues see Byers and Waits 2006; cf., Prokop et al. 2012; Prum 2012, 2017).

Even if we reject some of its stronger claims and oversimplifications, however, aspects of the account deserve to be taken seriously. If we consider the costs involved in producing art, the fact that aesthetic behaviours are universal in human life provides *prima facie* evidence for the claim that they were adaptive: if they did not grant evolutionary benefits of some sort or other, how should we explain their emergence in all human cultures? As Davies argues, we cannot deny the 'central premise of Evolutionary Psychology': that 'we have inherited (some) ways of thinking and perceiving, emotions, personalities, and values because those behaviors and attributes promoted the survival and reproduction of our distant forebears ...'. (Davies 2012, 42). While it is hard to assess claims about the specific adaptive origins of art (see, for example, Rampley 2017, 9), we 'do not need to settle that issue [...] before we can conclude that art behaviors' are 'relevant to the biological imperatives and interest that affect us as a species' (Dutton 2009, 119). However we explain animal ornaments, it is easy to be struck by the parallels between them and human artworks, and between the behaviours of animals such as peacocks and our practices with art, especially regarding display and evaluation. But we are back to the difficult question: what should we make of the parallels? As I will argue, regardless of the extent of empirical support for the claim that art is an adaptation from sexual selection, important aspects of this problem are not empirically tractable.

The ornithologist and evolutionary aesthetician Richard Prum brings out something important when he argues that natural selection arises from 'external forces in nature [...] acting on the organism', while sexual selection comes out of 'real choices' (Prum 2017, 25, 6). The agency inherent in sexual selection is internal to organisms; hence, Prum claims that it involves animal decisions and even autonomy. It is natural to speak of animal choices in this context. How else should we describe what the peahen is doing when she passes up one male in favour of another? And it is natural to refer to the subjective experiences of cognitively sophisticated animals when speaking of such choices. If a peahen selects a male because of the appearance of his tail, we often presume that this is connected to an affective state, one we might describe in terms of attraction, desire, liking, fondness, pleasure and so on (see Davies 2012, 13). Although it is easy to see how it could become so, there is nothing necessarily anthropomorphising or misleading about language of this kind. Much like Darwin, however, Prum deliberately uses the language of aesthetics in developing his account of sexual selection, arguing that 'many animals share with humans the capacity for aesthetic agency [...] participating in process[es] of aesthetic expression, evaluation, judgment, and change' (Prum 2013, 813).

Davies calls for caution here. He characterises the argument on which Prum and Darwin seem to be relying as follows: 'The female bird selects her mate because his appearance is pleasurable to contemplate. To experience pleasure in the contemplation of appearances is to respond to beauty. Therefore, hers must be an aesthetic response' (Davies 2012, 14). Davies takes issue with the second premise; he thinks it is a mistake to assume that 'this looks good to me' is equivalent to 'this looks beautiful to me'. If there is a danger of anthropomorphism in these contexts, however, a certain anthropocentrism must be an equal and opposite danger. For what would really be achieved if we were to follow Davies's recommendation and call these kinds of affective states in animals responding to appearances 'proto-aesthetic' (Davies 2012, 10), rather than aesthetic, except the drawing of a boundary of unclear semantic substance between human and non-human forms of responsiveness? And although the term 'beauty' takes on heavy conceptual baggage in the context of philosophical aesthetics, neither Darwin nor Prum require the claim that animals engage in disinterested aesthetic contemplation in the classically Kantian sense. In fact, they are using 'beauty' and related terms in ways that non-philosophers often do. This does not mean there are not substantive differences between the aesthetic lives of animals and humans; it is simply that terminological boundaries are unlikely to help us make sense of them (see Rampley 2017, 31). For that we will need to attend to the differences between responding aesthetically to nature and to human art, and what they show about the significance of display in these contexts.

Consider this passage from Kant's *Critique of Judgment*:

> What is more highly extolled by poets than the bewitchingly beautiful song of the nightingale, in a lonely stand of bushes, on a still summer evening, under the gentle light of the moon? Yet there have been examples in which, where no such songbird was to be found, some jolly landlord has tricked the guests staying with him, to their complete satisfaction, by hiding in a bush a mischievous lad who knew how to imitate this song (with a reed or pipe in his mouth) just like nature. But as soon as one becomes aware that it is a trick, no one would long endure listening to this song, previously taken to be so charming; and the same is true with every other songbird (Kant 2000, §42, 303).

Crucial to Kant's story is the transition in attitude which he claims that the guests will inevitably experience because of their discovery. Why does their realisation that the song they had been appreciating is an imitation of a real nightingale cause such disappointment? Although aestheticians have tried to draw analogies with forgery in human art, the problem cannot simply be about deception, because the discovery of the deceit involved in such a clever parlour trick could obviously delight the guests and not disappoint them (see Muelder Eaton 2004; cf. Dutton 2009, 189). Nor could the discovery merely give the lie to a perception of skilled performance, for the youth must obviously be an accomplished player, and a skill like his would take serious time and work to cultivate.

Instead, we can read the story as bringing out a difference between our aesthetic appreciation of nature and of human art. It is important to the disappointment that the imitation is intended to produce a particular response in an unknowing audience, an effect that is quashed when the audience gets that knowledge. When we appreciate the song of a real bird, it is (at least in part) because the sound is not *for* us. To borrow some language from John Stuart Mill, we might say that part of the charm of birdsong is that it is not something directly 'heard' but rather *overheard*, as though we are listening in on something that, unlike human musical performance, was not intended for our ears (see Moran 2018). As this section of the third critique makes clear, this is part of the relevance of Kant's understanding of nature's appeal: we do not merely appreciate nature for its form (in the mode of what Kant calls 'free beauty'), but also for being the kind of thing it is. In the case of the nightingale, the guests appreciated how the song appeared to be sung without regard for them. That is what is destroyed by the discovery: even though the sound undergoes no change in form, the imitation is disappointing to the guests – even becoming intolerable, as Kant claims [*niemand kann es lange aushalten*] – because it was self-consciously *meant* all along and meant to work on them in a particular way. The guests see it had designs on them.

Consider now this discussion of bird displays in Darwin's *Descent*:

> Ornaments of all kinds [...] are sedulously displayed by the males, and apparently serve to excite, attract, or fascinate the females. But the males will sometimes display their ornaments, when not in the presence of the females [...] as may be noticed with the peacock; this latter bird, however, evidently wishes for a spectator of some kind, and, as I have often seen, will shew off his finery before poultry, or even pigs. All naturalists who have closely attended to the habits of birds, whether in a state of nature or under confinement, are unanimously of opinion that the males take delight in displaying their beauty (Darwin 2004, 444).

Set aside the empirical questions raised by the opining of Darwin and the naturalists. Can we not see ourselves entertaining the thought that a displaying bird is taking delight in itself? And could we not be charmed by a display that we take to be self-delighting? It may seem difficult to square that with the Kantian insight that we delight in the unselfconsciousness of bird displays. For if the difference between appreciating the song of a real nightingale and a faked one is that, in the latter case, we cannot get past the knowledge that the song is performed self-consciously, this may seem to imply that we cannot delight in birdsong when we take the bird to be taking delight in itself. It will be a problem for our Kantian insight about birdsong if it comes at the price of forcing us to accept this. It will be a further problem if it also has the corollary that we cannot delight in bird displays when they *are* 'for' us in the broad sense of being directed at us. After all, it is easy to imagine a case where a peacock displays not for poultry or pigs but for a human audience, fanning out his tail before us (and perhaps with a kind of delight in himself). Why deny that we could find that charming?

Now consider this passage from *Absorption and Theatricality*, where Michael Fried is discussing Denis Diderot's conception of the problems facing painting in France in the late eighteenth century:

> The problems [...] suggest that simply disregarding the beholder was not enough. It was necessary to obliviate him, to deny his presence, to establish positively insofar as that could be done that he had not been taken into account. And Diderot seems clearly to have felt that there was in principle no more efficacious means to that end than to take as subject matter the deeds and sufferings of conscious agents who were, to say the least, fully capable of evincing awareness of the beholder, and then to forestall or extinguish all traces of such awareness in and through the dramatic representations of those deeds and sufferings. [...] Diderot's conception of painting rested ultimately upon the supreme fiction that the beholder did not exist, that he was not really there, standing before the canvas (Fried 1980, 103).

The problems that Diderot considered to be facing painting emerged out of the issue of display. They pertained to the potential for inauthenticity – or what Diderot called 'theatricality' – engendered by the fact that paintings are made to be exhibited before audiences. This was the grounds for both his distaste for the mannered rococo and his support of painters such as Jean-Baptiste-Siméon Chardin and Jean-Baptiste Greuze, whom he praised for how their masterful depictions of subjects completely absorbed in their activities helped establish the 'supreme fiction' that the painting was not created for beholding. By depicting absorbed figures, so Diderot argued, these painters were able to neutralise theatricality, because the figures' absorption gave viewers the sense that they were looking at somebody unaware of them. For Diderot, the task that these painters faced was to depict absorption convincingly, such that the subjects of the paintings betrayed nothing contrived or staged; if they were suffering, they could not be 'grimacing'; if they were frozen in rapture or entrancement, then they should nevertheless not be *posing* for us (see Fried 1980, 97–100).

Thus, we have three stories about the issue of display in aesthetic experience. There is Kant's story, in which the discovery that what was taken as an animal display actually consists of a human imitation destroys its appeal. There is Darwin's story, in which animals such as peacocks delight in their displays, which they are apparently willing to perform for just about anyone. And there is Fried and Diderot's story, in which the need to neutralise the problem of display becomes a determining force in the development of eighteenth-century French painting (eventually, for Fried, becoming the founding problem of modernism). Even as they highlight the importance of display in the aesthetic lives of both animals and humans, the stories bring out significant differences between them. Note how, in Darwin's story, the bird does not just delight in itself (in the way in which an animal stretching in the sun might delight in its own embodiment), but delights in itself *displaying*, showing not only a kind of self-awareness, but also an awareness of the other (the audience for whom he displays). But note, too, how peculiar it would be to disparage the bird for being manipulative, for having designs on us in the way in which Kant's roguish youth did, or for being theatrical in Diderot's sense. Discovering that a bird we are admiring is a hologram or automaton will quash the aesthetic appeal emerging from our sense that it was part of nature, but the same would not be true of discovering that a real peacock is displaying for us. It may even make it more charming. For part of what is appealing about animals is that they do not play the fraught recognitive games that humans play. (It may be telling that Davies never broaches this in his account of the aesthetic appeals of animals; see Davies 2012, 65–85). Even if we take them to have an awareness of audience, that will not set in motion problems of authenticity (birds may pose but could never be *poseurs*). Think here of the aesthetic category of 'naturalness', which can take on such importance in human aesthetic contexts. Diderot can praise anti-theatrical painters for the naturalness of their depictions, but we would not praise a peacock for the naturalness of his display, even though his being natural is crucial to its charm. This is a way of understanding Kant's claim – which would probably have been congenial to Diderot – that the successful artwork 'looks to us like nature' (Kant 2000, §45, 306), by which he means something like 'appearing uncontrived'. There is no paradox in saying that nature cannot be natural in this way, that only the artificial can achieve (or fail to achieve) naturalness.

Issues such as these go missing from narrowly naturalistic accounts. Dutton and Miller claim that the true function of art consists in the display of talent, intelligence and refined skills, but the display of ability is far from always sufficient for successful artworks and performances. In many contexts, to say that an artist is engaged in mere display is to censure them. Think of the jazz player who uses her solo to show how adroit an instrumentalist she is, bringing little else to the music; think of the neo-classical painter whose work is stilted and lifeless, despite or because of his considerable technical accomplishments; think of the Hollywood blockbuster that ends up a mere vehicle for deploying special effects. In such cases, the notion that the art is being used as a device for the display of skill and technique is precisely what is wrong, as the abilities in question – no matter how impressive – start becoming ingratiating (hence Kant's claims about genius as the capacity – and it is crucial that he regards it as a kind of natural gift – to go beyond technical formulas; Kant 2000, §46). Here is another difference between the aesthetic lives of animals and humans. It is difficult to imagine an animal faulting a display for being contrived, laboured, sycophantic, or saccharine: the work of a panderer, manipulator, or mere technician.

Although it may require widening the account beyond sexual selection, it would of course be possible to develop evolutionary psychological explanations for why we find certain forms of aesthetic display galling. In their recent work *The Elephant in the Brain*, Kevin Simler and Robin Hanson account for our dislike of braggarts by arguing that it is part of our 'forager aversion to dominance' (Simler and Hanson 2018, 55). A theory such as this could quite easily be extended to cover the kinds of aesthetic behaviours to which I am referring here: perhaps we censure artists engaged in them because we are really just bristling at their ploys at establishing dominance by showing off their abilities. If the critique of narrow Naturalism I am developing holds good, however, it should also apply to accounts such as this. As with Dutton and Miller's claims about our aesthetic behaviours, Hanson and Simler want to claim something much stronger than that our social behaviours are instantiated in our biology, or that evolutionarily acquired biological drives play a role in social life. They give causal priority to our biology, even appearing to grant it special ontological status as what is 'really going on' underneath our social interactions (Simler and Hanson 2018, 5, 100). Even if we grant that our aversion to braggarts may have evolutionary origins, reducing the complex recognitive backs and forths that are the stuff of human social life to biology in this way leaves us with paltry insight into them. As with Dutton and Miller's remarks about art, this lack of insight into social life is itself significant, calling out for explanation (for a useful account of the limitations of evolutionary psychological approaches to literature, see Kramnick 2011). The one I will offer below is that important features of human life – those emerging out of rational self-consciousness – are just not visible for narrow Naturalism.

Although I have been invoking Kant, it is less in Kant than in Hegel that we find the most promising way of accounting philosophically for the kinds of differences that I am tracking. That is because Hegel has a more plausible, powerful and indeed naturalistic way of understanding rationality. If Kant understands it as a special endowment that sets us apart from mere nature – with the familiar problems that it entails – for Hegel rationality should be conceived not as a property that separates us from animality but as constitutive of our particular way of being animal. In his account, human animals are distinctive on earth because of their particular mode of responsiveness to reason. While animals can be said to act for reasons – they have reason to seek food, to flee from predators, to display to conspecifics and so on – only rational animals are responsive to them *as* reasons. Living in the space of reasons means seeking justification, to each other and to ourselves. Yet, our reasons are not disconnected from our biological needs, and the ends we pursue – food, shelter, perhaps aesthetic satisfaction, even loving relationships – cannot be understood without reference to them. Hence, Pinkard's claim that Hegel's Naturalism should be understood as turning on a 'transformative' rather than 'additive' conception of rationality (Pinkard 2017, 11). The additive account takes rationality as a 'special sort of module', giving human beings the ability 'to *monitor* and *regulate*' the beliefs that they form on the basis of their perceptions and the acts they perform because of their desires (see Boyle 2016, 528). It therefore takes the perceptual capacities and conative activities of rational animals as no different in kind from the perceptual capacities and conative activities of non-rational animals. The transformative account, by contrast, takes rationality to transform animal perception and conation: it is not the mere capacity to monitor the rational standing of our animal perceptions and desires, but extends all the way out into our perceiving and desiring, changing how we see and feel. The transformative conception can help us make sense, not only of the continuities and differences between the aesthetic lives of animals and humans, but also of how differences can emerge out of those very continuities.

If rationality does not absolve humans from being animal but changes the ways in which we are, then it is not that rationality allows us to transcend our instincts. It is that, at some point in our development out of early childhood, we establish a kind of relation to our instincts that is not found (as far as we know) in the rest of nature (on these points, see Macbeth 2014, Tomasello 1999, Kern and Moll 2017). It is not the relation of a detached subject that monitors its drives and resists (sometimes) the pull of instinct, trying (somehow) to be more rational than animal. For Hegel, the relation of the human being to its animal nature is a relation of *Aufhebung* or sublation: as we enter rational life, we do not overcome or leave behind our drives but raise them up, cancelling them in their original form while preserving them in another. Like all animals, we are driven by the instincts that our species has acquired through blind evolutionary processes. Unlike animals with very limited cognitive capacities – such as the bee, to which Heidegger refers in the *Fundamental Concepts of Metaphysics* and which continues to suck honey even after its abdomen has been removed (Heidegger 1995, §59) – we are not driven blindly by those instincts. In this we are like great apes, dogs and birds, whose sophisticated cognitive capacities allow them to be *responsive* to their perceptions and conations, by re-evaluating courses of behaviour in particular environmental contexts, making real choices about how to act. Unlike these cognitively sophisticated but unselfconscious animals, however, we *understand* and *interpret* our perceptions and conations, actualising our drives and biological capacities such that they are *meaningful* to us. And we do that collectively, in concepts, speech and action, by extending forms of *recognition* to other rational agents, interpreting their standing in our world. Rational self-consciousness is a 'reflexive complication' of animal life, turning animals into interpreters of themselves and interpreters of each other (and who interpret themselves by interpreting each other). Pinkard writes:

> We are self-conscious, self-interpreting animals, natural creatures whose 'non-naturalness' is not a metaphysical difference (as that, say, between spiritual and physical 'stuff') or the exercise of a special form of causality. Rather, our status as *geistig*, as 'minded' creatures, is a status we 'give' to ourselves in the sense that it is a practical achievement (Pinkard 2012, 18).

Because it means that we take them as the self-conscious acts of other rational animals, this distinctive capacity is why we respond to works of human art differently from how we respond to aesthetic features in nature (on this point, see Pippin 2014, 57–58). It means that it is natural to ask of artworks questions such as the following: *Am I right to feel moved by this work? Was its author just trying to produce an effect on me? Or have they achieved something more significant? How did they achieve it? And what are they trying to say?* It would make little sense to ask such questions in response to a stretch of birdsong, because birds are not like us in those respects that give these questions purchase in the human context. That does not render animal displays aesthetically insignificant; it gives them a different kind of significance, such that they are appealing, partly because there is no question of their having self-conscious designs on us. We delight in birdsong's being *not about us*, not simply because we are not conspecifics, but because animal displays do not have to bear the pressures that rationality brings into our aesthetic lives. (Note that these complications would still be in play in cases where a human artist is unaware of having an audience – say, if we chanced across a flautist practicing in the woods, without alerting him. It follows from the claim that rationality transforms our capacities that his playing could be manipulative, affected, maudlin, or whatever, regardless of whether he knows he has an audience – which is not to deny that awareness of audience can and often does affect performances.) Thus, we can be charmed by a peacock's self-delighting display – such that there is no question of finding anything affected or contrived in it – but we may have second thoughts about such displays in human art. And there is no tension between Kant's claim that discovering what we took to be birdsong was really a human imitation will undermine its aesthetic appeal and the claim that a real nightingale may be aware of itself displaying before an audience. Animals charm in that they are not regarding us as rational beings are regarding each other. Nature's beauty delights in seeming gratuitous: given, but not given *to* us.

As in cases of Batesian mimicry – where harmless species evolve to appear like aposematic ones, taking the benefits of seeming dangerous without incurring the costs of developing a self-defence system – animals can sometimes fake signals. Part of the point of handicap theory is to explain costly ornaments on the grounds that the fitness that they signal is impossible to fake, because the investments required to produce them have to be genuine (see Miller 2008, 215). But the question whether an animal signal is fake is empirical. The kinds of worries that have their home in the context of human aesthetic display – including worries about theatricality, contrivance, inauthenticity and the like – cannot be resolved empirically. That is why the aesthetic judgments of rational animals have a particular kind of contentiousness. There is no natural scientific means of confirming whether they are good or not, no empirical method for settling the disagreements that they provoke (compare this with the issue of forgery, which is an empirical one: it may be controversial whether a painting was forged, but that there is a fact of the matter about whether it was is uncontroversial; it is telling that Dutton wants to read Kant's remark about nightingales in terms of the question of forgery; see Dutton 2009, 189). To the extent that they can be resolved, it will be in the space of reasons, for they are the kinds of worries that (only) rational animals have about (only) rational animals. There is no reason to think that natural science will never explain the origins of rationality. But narrowly empirical forms of Naturalism cannot get traction on the normative features that this capacity engenders in our lives because they are only open to view from the midst of it.

As is typical of narrow naturalists, Dutton is hostile to rationalist accounts of human motivation, emphasising instead the role of evolved affective propensities in our aesthetic lives. Despite this hostility, he ends up accepting key aspects of the additive account of rationality that have played such a powerful role in the history of rationalist thought. After a discussion of Thorstein Veblen's theory of conspicuous consumption, Dutton tries to counter the qualm that his account of innate tendencies will force us to accept that human beings are doomed to follow irrational instincts, such as the propensity to be awed by expensive materials. He starts by attacking Kant's view of the distinction between beauty and finery but concludes by conceding that he was right that 'the experience of art is a practice of contemplation – in it, we need not be slave to our innate proclivities, our passions' (Dutton 2009, 162). Like the additive theorist, Dutton conceives of innate preferences as 'prerational', and so he has to take them as standing in tension with our intellectual powers, powers that may nevertheless be strong enough to override those preferences. That explains why he sets up biology as the ground or base of culture, struggling to make intelligible the contributions of the latter; it is why he is so focused on what is going on 'beneath' our conscious engagements with art, trying to reveal biological truths lying under the veil of culture. Only if we conceive of rationality in a more expansively naturalistic way – taking into account the reflexive complications that it introduces – can we begin to make sense of how our aesthetic practices come out of our animal lives transformed by self-consciousness.

That a display is moving is not sufficient for it succeeding because we can be moved despite ourselves. But this is not the result of a contest between instinct and intellect; being moved by art does not mean having our responsiveness to reasons overridden. Reasons *are* moving (even though not all of them are good). When I find a work dishonest or manipulative – 'theatrical', in Michael Fried's terms – it is not because my rationality is acting as overseer, checking a base emotional response. It is because I (think I) have *seen* something inauthentic in it, perceiving a feature a non-rational animal could not perceive. It is because I (claim to) have felt a failure in it, something only a rational animal could have felt. To argue that gaining substantial insight into the normative structure of our aesthetic practices requires going beyond narrow Naturalism is not to claim that art is 'beyond the reach of evolution' (Dutton 2009, 2). On the contrary, art is part of how we negotiate our problematic status as rational, self-conscious animals, part of how we make sense of being instinctual creatures alive in the space of reasons.

We have seen that, according to Fried's account, eighteenth-century French painting was responding to pressures of theatricality, with artists such as Chardin championed by Diderot for how they negated the fact that their works were meant to be displayed and beheld. We can interpret this moment in French painting in terms of a struggle with self-consciousness, as artists faced problems engendered by a new sort of awareness of art and audience (and the audience's awareness of that very awareness). But the question arises: why then and there? What was it about emerging modernity that forced the hands of artists in this way? If Fried is right – and if the problematic Naturalism I have been developing here should be granted any weight – it would give credence to Hegel's idea that the struggle for recognition in human life unfolds historically, with particular inflections of it emerging at particular times (on this, see Pippin 2014, 83–95). It may also give credence to some more controversial Hegelian ideas about the consequences of the notion of the autonomy of self-conscious animals that starts to take hold in modernity. For another way of interpreting the problem that Diderot's favoured painters met is what to do with art in the face of the discovery of the freedom and equality of all rational animals. After all, to manipulate such an animal is not just to deceive but to wrong it: to use it as a mere means to an end.[2]

Notes

1. Charles Darwin, 'To Asa Gray', 3 April 1860 (available at https://www.darwinproject.ac.uk/letter/DCP-LETT-2743.xml).
2. I would like to thank Robert Arculus, Thomas Battersby, Kael McCormack-Skewes, Emilie Owens, Richard Prum and Winfried Menninghaus for their suggestions and critical comments on earlier drafts of this manuscript. I would also like to thank the audiences at *Engaging the Contemporary* (University of Malta), the conference of the *Society for European Philosophy* (Essex University), *Theatricality and the Arts* (Whitechapel Gallery) and the 2019 conference of the *Australian Hegel Society* for helpful comments and questions.

6
Against Experience: Theatre is Not Life (or Theatre in the Age of Third Nature)

Simon Jones

In this chapter, I want to sketch out in two parts how theatre as an art form can respond to our contemporary predicament – what I am calling Third Nature (see Jones 2018). It proposes in general terms why theatre is *the* art to resist the hegemonic forces of global techno-capital with their increasing emphasis on 'the experience economy' (see Pine and Gilmore 1999). By implication, I take some issues with current forms of participatory or immersive performance, as well as with the enthusiastic incorporation of new technologies into performance as means of offering new insights into being human or (maybe) becoming post-human. In doing so, I silently acknowledge those that have gone before, such as Claire Bishop's critique of Bourriaud's Relational Aesthetics (see Bishop 2004), or Jen Harvie's analysis of artistic co-production as labour (see Harvie 2013), or Adam Alston's recent re-thinking of immersive theatre 'where a more fundamental gap exists in immersive theatre that is filled through a particular form of audience productivity: the objectification of experience as art' (Alston 2016, 7). To help me build my definition of Third Nature, I use Martin Heidegger's *Mindfulness* as foundation, particularly his thoughts on 'The Epoch of the Completion of Modernity' and read it in part against his earlier essay on 'The Origin of the Work of Art'. For me, Heidegger succinctly critiques making art in the modern age, the twentieth century, and eerily describes our millennium's cultures as what he calls modernity's completion. In so doing, he offers a very powerful and comprehensive understanding of the current phase of capital with its techno-cultural-economic assemblages, which goes beyond a simply phenomenological or materialist understanding of the impact of technologies upon cultures and the possibilities of an aesthetic response. With this as philosophical underpinning, I then go on to argue, using Forced Entertainment's recent show *Real Magic*, for theatre's decisive resistance to experience and the terms of its apparently liberatory aesthetics as eulogised by Josephine Machon in her analysis of immersive theatre as 'an artistic form that encourages the rehumanised and resensitised in an individual experience [...] *because* it encourages and celebrates [a] feeling of "aliveness"' (Machon 2013, 143 original emphasis).

Part One: Living in the Moment (or) The Completion of Modernity

In Third Nature, as I am defining it, we live amongst ready-to-hand technologies in a process of rapid convergence. As such, our cultures valorise the affects of immediacy and instant gratification, ravelling up duration, indeed, smoothing out the many chronologies of being alive into one universal world clock and collapsing space from its cragginess and haeccity into an infinitely smooth virtuality. These affects enhance the currency and ubiquity of digital interactivity and shareability in order to accelerate the liquidity of capital, where goods and services are being supplanted by organised 'experiences': in effect, a profound process of exteriorisation is underway in the so-called 'experience economy'. Clearly, the 2020–22 crisis of the global Coronavirus pandemic accelerated this process to some degree, atomising individuals and families into their isolated households, dependent on internet platforms for their social interaction, shopping and work. Within days, fundamental behaviours, such as the commute or night out, were replaced by the two-dimensional space of the video call or Zoom meeting. Sharing times has become synchronous events; school classes have become asynchronous tasks. The spatio-temporal somatics, delineating work and play, individual and group, have suddenly been affectively disembodied and effectively rendered down to the flat screen, the tinny audio, the download speed of a universalised, amorphous online event. What is disturbing about this enforced acceleration towards Third Nature is not only the concurrent epidemic of mental ill-health or the cruel exposure of the precarity of so many people's lives, but also the comparative ease with which large sections of the population, particularly those in high-value occupations, have adapted to or even embraced the move online. Third Nature was, in essence, already well underway before the pandemic struck.

It is no surprise, then, that theatre as an industry was both the first and, as I write (in 2020), will probably be the last to emerge from this crisis. The extent to which theatre as an art form has been most vulnerable to disruption by COVID-induced lockdowns equally demonstrates its inherent resistance to Third Nature, thence the digital work-arounds obliged by social-distancing and remote working. Indeed, beforehand, theatre had responded to the apparently inevitable logic of Third Nature by reinvigorating the spectacular, the immersive and participatory, riffing off video-gaming, often incorporating new technologies. This is partly why theatre had persisted in the pre-pandemic digital age: because it had already been in an evolutionary race with technology's zeal to capture and commodify, always running ahead of each new platform's claim to higher resolution and greater fidelity. This calls to mind Guy Debord's warnings from the 1960s about the pervasive and deadly effect of the assemblage of capital with technologies to engineer mass-consumption: 'The spectacle in its generality is a concrete inversion of life, and, as such, the autonomous movement of non-life' (Debord 1995, 12). However, there was a paradoxical doubleness at play in this issue for theatre-makers, now working *amongst* the readiness-to-hand of smart technology, in that the drive to explore the transformative potentialities of these technologies runs up against the role of the performer as both agent and flesh, and the performance as both event and lived. In essence, this reinstates the foundation of theatre as a gathering of persons in the here and now of the performance. In effect, theatre-makers found themselves both proselytising on behalf of a post-human techno-future *and* claiming a Luddite-like resistance grounded in the origins of theatre as an artform. Indeed, despite this ambiguous role, theatre has always been an early adopter of new technologies, and as such it should have been well placed to both actualise their potential and critique their impact when COVID-19 struck. However, the pandemic has posed an existential threat to theatre as both an art form and an industry, precisely because of what predicates theatre – the face-to-face encounter of the theatre set-up. Thus, at this critical moment for theatre *as theatre*, it is even more crucial that we understand theatre's unique role in critiquing the particular assemblage of Third Nature, which renders life as living and commodifies it as experience.

I have argued elsewhere (see Giddens and Jones 2009) that, if an artist is genuinely open to collaborating with others working in different media, this inevitably leads to a deconstructive practice wherein that which each media cannot express effectively discloses the discontinuity in our everyday perception. These gaps are normally masked by the brain's desire to produce a continuous account (I might say – a fiction) of our being in the world, whereas, in fact, so much of how we experience is learnt through a combination of physical development and acculturation: so, what we inherit from the genome – our first nature – encounters what we acquire through interacting with the world – our second nature. Here, I figure *nature* as a general process whereby the individual embodies knowledge and techniques through establishing behaviours that are reinforced by exchanging information with the environment in ever more predictable circuits of feedback. Firstly, the child's own body is its environment, and instinctive, inherited systems encourage the learning of how to coordinate hand to mouth, to see, to walk and to talk. Secondly, the world enlarges to include multifarious objects beyond what is simply *there*, and techniques develop which involve the body interacting with specific external technologies, such as bicycle, pen, mobile, or PC. With every acquisition, the initial encounter is always profoundly disturbing: the knowledge always appears first as nonsense or the technique as ungraspable. Then we master it: what was outside becomes part of the inside of being, to such an extent that its strangeness is forgotten; it becomes as one with us: the trick is embodied as second nature. Here, theatre as an essentially mixed-media art form has the potential to intervene by using those very senses and technologies, or rather by using the gaps between them, upon which our knowledges and techniques are grounded, against themselves, to reveal them as fundamentally other. I have called this deconstructive potential in theatre *de-second-naturing*.

However, in what way is Third Nature paradigmatically novel? And how is that novelty particularly pernicious to human life? Even before the acceleration forced by the pandemic, scholars have described the profound transformations through which we are living as posthuman (see Braidotti 2013 and Hayles 1999, or Max Tegmark's recent *Life 3.0* [2017], which sees humanity's very survival challenged by artificial intelligence); but I think it is better understood as *third nature*: a paradigm shift in the human-event occasioned by the development of complex, integrated and networked technologies, assemblages of robotic and digital machines, which have wholly exteriorised what previously – in the realm of second nature – was experienced as *the relation between* embodied and disembodied knowledges. Robots do more accurately and enduringly what humans do; computers think faster and more comprehensively than humans think; digital archives remember all that we have forgotten. Of course, my anthropomorphisation masks the actual non-congruence of these technological assemblages, in the same way that second-naturing internalises the fundamental strangeness of older technologies, their non-humanness. As Heidegger points out in his example of the broken hammer in *Being and Time*, the wood-worker only notices the tool in their hands when it fails to function in the way they expect: it becomes alien once more in its failure. And for Heidegger, this failure of technology marks a more crucial point where the artwork leaves mere functionality behind and emerges in its own right:

> In fabricating equipment – e. g., an axe – stone is used, and used up. It disappears into usefulness. The material is all the better and more suitable the less it resists vanishing in the equipmental being of the equipment. By contrast the [artwork], in setting up a world, does not cause the material to disappear, but rather causes it to come forth for the very first time and to come into the open region of the work's world (Heidegger 1978, 171).

To this extent, all technologies extend the capacity of the human, so second nature is already a move towards the non-(or post-)human, or rather a troubling of the very notion of what it means to be human, as Steven Mulhall writes of Heidegger's ontology of *Da-sein* as *a being whose being is an issue for it* (1996, 14). What marks Third Nature as paradigmatic is the ubiquity and capacity of these techno-assemblages to perform functions and store and correlate data. Through their ever-readiness-to-hand, their locative and interactive capacities, the so-called smart technologies of handheld devices, networked to big-data cloud-technology, have shifted the everyday ways in which we acquire and use knowledges and techniques. They not only offer us the experience of an augmented reality, but their apparent instantaneous reply embeds the illusion of immediacy; that is, a knowledge apparently without a channel of communication – literally a new kind of embodied knowing, personified in what Marc Prensky has described as 'the digital native' (see Prensky 2001). Here, this techno-assemblage stores and deploys the bulk of (human) knowledge *outside the person*, thus relieving them of the (evolutionary) necessity to embody it – that is, *to know it* for themselves. As such, their readiness-to-hand and their storage and transactional capacities make them obvious go-to tools in a global pandemic. With the urgency of life and society under threat forcing us faster along a direction of travel, we reach for them as naturally as we would for a knife and fork.

From a phenomenological as well as political perspective, the externalisation of these functions and knowledges in what I am calling Third Nature fulfils what Heidegger had predicted in the 1930s would be 'The Completion of Modernity'. This was to be achieved when human life was rendered into that which is producible – that is, reproducible, representable, commodifiable, exchangeable. In *Mindfulness* (2006), Heidegger first makes the link to technology: 'The rational animal has become subject and has developed reason into "history", whose sway coincides with the sway of technicity' (2006, 21). This first move relocates the perspective from which the human event in its totality is to be understood: here to align the human as a subject from the point of view of the scientific and (so say) rational and empirical gaze; in effect, to reduce the human to that which is observable, measurable and so comparable: to *depersonalise* what it means to be human. This echoes Edmund Husserl's critique of the natural sciences for claiming 'a transcendental feat to cognition' whereby the scientist could place themselves in a transcendent objectivity making nature, including humankind, a subject to be observed as if from the outside (Husserl 1964, 30–31). For Husserl and his student Heidegger, this fallacy of transcendental thinking obtains wherever knowledge is predicated on a subject-object relation. The implications of this move are too momentous to be fully handled here; suffice it to say that the individual can no longer be understood on their own terms, but only by way of a group, species, community or data-set. What is more, this process is interwoven with the development of technology in general and specifically those technologies which are able to maximise the measurement and comparability of the individual in relation to that communal dataset, to such an extent that a confusion grows between so-called rational, human, machinic and market behaviours. This begins another process of what might be called *reverse anthropomorphisation* whereby we increasingly think of ourselves in relation to the attributes and capacities of and language used to describe technology: take, for instance, the way that memory is now commonly described as if we were computers.

Thinking of the future of culture from the 1930s onwards, Heidegger then applies this twinned process of subjectification and technicalisation to 'Art in the Epoch of Completeness of Modernity'. This results in a valorisation of that which is *producible*: '[I]n its pleasantness, art is an unconditionally organised delivery of makability of beings unto machination' (2006, 23), which he defines as 'the accordance of everything with *producibility*, indeed in such a way that the unceasing, unconditioned reckoning of everything is pre-directed' (2006, 12). So, for Heidegger, the rational force of subjectivising the human leads to the replacement of art's capacity to actualise the issues for Being with a super-objective, already determined in advance; to produce everything in life as representable, thence commodifiable:

> What art brings forth is [...] not works in being-historical sense that inaugurate a clearing of be-ing – the be-ing in which beings first have to be grounded. What art brings forth are 'installations' (form of *organizing* beings): 'poems' are 'declarations'; they are 'appeals' in the sense of *calling out* what already exists in the domain of the all-directing and all-securing public. Word, sound and image are means for structuring, stirring, rousing and assembling masses, in short, they are means of organizing (2006, 23–24).

For Heidegger, this strips art of its decisive function both to penetrate the surface of existence and to actualise novel ways of being (more of this later) and reduces it to organising what is already apparent and commonly understood to have value. This would inevitably lead to art which ...

> ...no longer search[es] 'behind' or 'above' beings, not even feeling 'emptiness', but searching and finding exclusively and maximally, what in the enactment of the machinational is 'liveable', and as such can be incorporated into one's 'own' 'life' – which is shaped by the masses – and thus to foster this as what is solely valid and assuring (2006, 26).

Note the pejorative speech-marks around 'own' and 'life'. The purpose of this form of art-making is to organise reassurance for the greatest good of the largest mass of individuals – what politicians of all creeds like to call 'the people', a purpose all the more pressing during a pandemic. Furthermore, this process of making, or – in Heidegger's terms – this machination replaces life with what is liveable; and the individual's capacity and freedom to assert their own response to such artwork is rendered down to a process of assimilation and mimicry: our life becomes not our own, so much so that 'sharing the sway of technicity and "history", art undertakes the organizing of beings whose being is decided upon in advance as machination' (2006, 27). Notwithstanding COVID-19, for us today, the authenticity of each person's life is lost in the exchange of images and activities of 'living' in the experience economy that literally use up the (available) time of one's life. Here I am reminded of Andy Warhol's injunction in his philosophical work *From A to B and Back Again* (2007) that everything is work, including fun, or these days 'COVID-secure measures': in other words, all aspects of our existence are reduced to that which can be (re-)produced. To this extent, Heidegger predicted that the fundamental inter-relation of technology, capital and self in the modern age would pose a profound threat to the individual's capacity to (in everyday words) 'be most her/himself':

> Metaphysically, the sway of 'culture' is the same as the sway of 'technicity'. Culture is the technicity of 'history' – culture is the manner in which 'historical' reckoning with values and 'historical' production of goods arrange themselves and so spread the forgottenness of being (2006, 147).

Consider the Selfie as a contemporary example of how machination works to organise art-making in the images which we produce of ourselves along with smart technologies, and with which we develop an extended performative culture of the Self by way of cloud data-storage and social-media sharing. The self is seen from the point of view that s/he could never occupy her/himself, that of the equipment: our embodied projective seeing is reduced to the capture of the camera's two-dimensional lens: that which can be *re-presented rather than felt*. In Heidegger's terms, this set-up organises or pre-directs us to see our self *as these lifeless images*: we perform them. The apparently immediate retrieval of the image appears to behave like a mirror, as if we were in the same time as our image: however, this image appears out of the techno-archive in an entirely different time, discontinuous with our own. We repress this strangeness and uncanniness in our second-naturing of this techno-assemblage – smart device/selfie-stick/cloud-archive as instant gratification and freedom of choice, made available by the co-production of pro-sumption and its global circulation through social media. However, in Third Nature, this leads to a terrible reversal of Heidegger's ontology of technology, whereby, instead of second-naturing and so embodying the technology we use, it is *our own nature that disappears into the technology's uses of us*: the techno-archive, in remembering us, forgets our distinctive Being. Of this reverse anthropomorphisation, Amelia Jones writes: 'We don't know how to exist anymore without imagining ourselves as a picture' (Jones 2006, xvii).

Hence, from the perspective of Heidegger's analysis of modernity, the development of the experience economy leads, in actuality, to a degradation of living, as what was once life is rendered down into experiences and bundled up together as bucket lists: quite literally one's life as activities to tick off before one dies. So much so that, for Heidegger, art's function is reduced to the organisation of these experiences and the maximisation of their value in terms of exchangeability: an economy of experience masquerades as life, replacing authentic existence with that which is *effective*: the virtual supplants the actual.

> This relation at the end brings itself in the whole to predominance as machination, wherein the *effective* counts as the actual and this in turn as beings and as the 'living' in a broad sense to which 'live-experience' remains subordinated (Heidegger 2006, 284; emphasis added).

Into this techno-capital assemblage, theatre has (often unwittingly) played its part through the ubiquity of performativity as a concept. Coupled with the force of machination and producibility, the impact of performativity (unintended by those such as Judith Butler who promulgated the term and sought to emphasise its libertarian potentialities) is to estrange us actively from life by organising it into a series of performances of part-selves. This returns performativity to something much closer to its precursor in Foucault's idea of discipline. The attributes of these part-selves, or life-styles or life-choices, are always determined in advance by the techno-capital assemblage: only that which can be produced, commodified, represented can be validated as identity, as experience, as *life*. Thus, the self becomes a problem of representation, and specifically in terms of that everyday presentation of self – one of performativity: one's effectiveness *as role-play*, as employee, as parent, as tourist, a set of normative roles to perform, demographically organised by big-data-sets into multiple-choice tick-boxes: the Turing Test reversed where it is not the machine that appears to be human, but the human who performs like a machine. In Third Nature, if the computer says yes, we are approved *as human*: we match the predetermined list. For Heidegger, this technological relation would be yet another instance of the individual's relation to the mass, as outlined here in the earlier *Being and Time*:

> In these modes [of averageness] one's way of Being is that of inauthenticity and failure to stand by one's Self. [. . .] The Self of everyday Dasein is the *they-self*, which we distinguish from the *authentic Self* – that is, from the Self which has been taken hold of in its own way. [. . .] *Proximally*, it is not 'I', in the sense of my own Self, that 'am', but rather the Others, whose way is that of 'they'. In terms of 'they', and *as* the 'they', I am 'given' proximally to 'myself' (Heidegger 1962, 167).

Paradoxically, it is the machine's very machinic-ness in its objectively approving the individual that assures the self that it is human. In effect, we no longer decide on the person in their own right *as a person*, judging their actions against the law in the given circumstances: the individual can only be approved as behaving appropriately in terms of normative sets of predetermined attributes and actions, *decided on in advance*. In this way, procedures of approval replace judgement as the decisive act which transforms individuals' lives. Here, it is easy to see how many practices of participatory, immersive or environmental theatre and performance are uncritical expressions of this techno-capital assemblage: for example, in critiquing performance company Punchdrunk – the internationally recognized British pioneers of participatory and immersive theatre, known for their large-scale works which occupy non-theatre spaces, Adam Alston draws compelling parallels between their aesthetic and 'neoliberal value [. . .] implicit in frameworks for immersion and productive participation'. He claims that 'exclusion and exclusivity are tied into entrepreneurial values that are both asked and expected of [Punchdrunk's] participating audiences' (Alston 2016, 141). Helen Nicholson, too, makes a link between 'this form of aesthetic participation [and the] commodified experience economy': 'they share the same affective pull, fostered by similar dramaturgical devices, and [. . .] this seduction requires a new political vigilance' (Nicholson 2013, 116). My vigilance is less concerned with the explicit resonances between neoliberalism and participatory work, as has been fiercely critiqued by Jen Harvie who sees such audience-participants as 'workers [. . .] rendered, in many ways, insecure, deskilled and alienated' (Harvie 2013, 44), and more with the false ideology of participatory ethics. Patricia Reed has succinctly identified for me the most troubling aspect of co-production in such artworks, as having '[a] direct correlation with virtuous normativity, and with (unsituated) natural law discourses: a conflation that strips the subject of any self-authorizing force beyond the external decree of norms, and indeed the law itself' (Reed 2012, 27–28). This normativity limits the expressive and imaginative potential of the participants: they must perform the part-selves determined for them in advance by the *artrepreneurs* who still run the show. As an aesthetic experience, it closely models other experiences sold as ground-breaking, innovative, challenging and thrilling, such as theme-park rides and video-games. And it is precisely the force or 'sway' (as Heidegger would have understood it) of this normativity that must be accurately reproduced/re-performed in the experiencing of the experience, that prevents this kind of theatre from ever achieving 'the full sentience of the human body' claimed by Machon (2013, 80), along with 'a personal abandonment of everyday boundaries' (28). Indeed, in the event, these boundaries are effectively reinforced by such theatre precisely because of its requirement that 'the audience-immersant is *always* fundamentally complicit' (98; original emphasis): under the collective, mutual, disciplinary gaze, the participant is obliged to perform the normative role in order to secure and earn approval. An even more pernicious aspect of this approval is its fundamental conjugation *as the future perfect*, when life cannot be lived in the present because it will already have been lived in the data yet to be archived as experience and experienced as archive. This knowing in advance how one is expected to perform one's self amounts to a doomed attempt to forestall one's own death. It marks the apogee of modernity's completion: one cannot die because all experience is producible as depersonalised and disembodied procedures, thence endlessly reproducible as performances of living. Therefore, if performativity is widely accepted across many fields as a key indicator of worth, if not the truth of living (see Jon MacKenzie's account in *Perform or Else*; 2001), in Part Two, I want to outline why counter-intuitively *the theatrical* remains stubbornly suspect and, as such, has suffered so much during the pandemic: not so much a ghost in the machine of Third Nature, rather a wetware clot in its pristine software, a slowness in its picnolepsy, an (actual) now-here in its (virtual) no-where.

Part Two: Theatre's Being-Historical

For Heidegger, art (I might say 'culture') colludes in the processes of producibility as mass entertainment, validating normative lifestyles, reinforcing the already known, oscillating between re-assuring and pacifying and their structural twins – terrorising and anesthetising. Now, I turn to what he envisaged as the possibilities of resisting these forces *in the quest for being-historical* and how that might be used to understand better the way in which theatre as an art form itself resists Third Nature. For Heidegger, being-historical preserves knowing as an unending undertaking and so postpones the moment and comfort of having arrived at knowledge; as such, it is profoundly deconstructive and deterritorialising, as well as radically solitary, as Heidegger would have put it – most *owned by Da-sein*. This means that it cannot be communicated, cannot enter an exchange, nor become part of modernity's life experiences; and so, it offers a radical model of life opposed to living as experience. Often written as a series of aphoristic statements, grouped under similar titles, *Mindfulness* repeatedly returns to the first principles of thinking – or, in Heidegger's terms, knowing-awareness, recursively accumulating meaning over 300 pages. Here are several aphorisms that today read like soundbites, laying out the self-deconstructing, contradictory and incommunicable nature of being-historical:

- *a-sein* means taking over the distress of the grounding of the truth of be-ing – it is the beginning of a history that has no 'history' (2006, 17).
- The keenest threat to be-ing is understandability (78).
- *Da-sein* is incomparable, and it admits no perspective within which it could still be lodged as something familiar (288).
- *Da-sein* forestalls all mania for explanation (288).
- *Da-sein* is not demonstrable. It can never be shown and exhibited as an object, just as little in terms of 'lived-experience' (289).

Hence, if being-historical is ontologically opposed to modernity's producibility and processes of exteriorisation and commodification, how can it provide the basis for resistance? More specifically, how might this resistance relate to theatre? When critiquing Artaud's attempt to flee representation, Derrida describes theatre as 'neither a book nor a work, but an energy, and in this sense it is the only art of life' (Derrida 1978, 247); but I have implied that, by adopting new technologies, strategies of interactivity and co-production, theatre risks being co-opted, wittingly or otherwise, into these general processes of Third Nature. I want to suggest that Heidegger's percolating definition of being-historical maps so closely onto his earlier description of the artwork in the essay 'The Origin of the Work of Art', that art becomes the event most likely to disclose the fullest possibilities of being-historical: what life could become, were it not for the everyday. And I argue, by extension, that theatre resists Third Nature in the way in which it actualises being-historical's thinking *more originally*.

Firstly, I want to compare Heidegger's definitions of being-historical with that of the artwork. Being-historical happens in a self-deconstructing zone, what Heidegger calls *the ab-ground*, out of the everyday – a clearing which is fundamentally in-between all the other forces of life. In this in-between, thinking can work in the most unimpeded and original manner:

> To [*Da-sein*'s] swaying belongs the originary onefold of the 'in-the-midst of' and 'amongst' (the temporal-spatial *clearing*) [...] within which the trajectories of strife and countering cross among themselves and radiate unimpairably in the clearing in all directions (Heidegger 2006, 285–86; original emphasis).

This thinking is driven particularly by one's will to analyse ceaselessly the conditions of life, to think what it is possible to think: that is, to follow a path towards becoming most clearly and unconstrainedly oneself in radical thought, without falling into selfishness or avoiding the circumstances of where one finds oneself:

> This 'will' is the will to be-ing, en-owned by be-ing itself unto what is ownmost to this will. This 'will' is not autocratic self-seeking and exertion; the 'will' here means the ardour, the grounding-attunement of persevering in the destiny of acquiescing to the distress of the ab-ground (Heidegger 2006, 52).

Now here is his definition of the artwork from the essay 'The Origin of the Work of Art':

> Preserving the work means standing within the openness of beings that happens in the work. This 'standing-within' of preservation, however, is a knowing. [...] He who truly knows beings knows what he wills to do in the midst of them. [...] [T]he essence of *Existenz* is out-standing standing-within the essential sunderance of the clearing of beings (Heidegger 1978, 192; original emphasis).

Here, the artwork becomes the in-between of being-historical in its holding open the relationship between its participants, in the case of theatre

– its performers – auditor-spectators with the flesh of both as ur-medium. In effect, it sustains this relationship as its own particular standing-within, its own particular eventhood, so actualising being-historical as out of the everyday, explicitly *as not life*. And as this unique out-standing in-between, the work is a non-place that offers its participants the greatest possibility to explore their humanity: '[A] work is in actual effect as a work only when we remove ourselves from our commonplace routine and move into what is disclosed by the work, so as to bring our own essence itself to take a stand in the truth of beings' (Heidegger 1978, 199).

Of course, the fundamental set-up of theatre materialises this ontology of being in-between in a particularly intense way, since it foregrounds not only its eventness, its happening in that time and in a certain place; but also the manner of its mixing of persons, their fleshes and histories, their desires and prospects. It does this through an intensification, not of one particular relation between a material, its expressing by means of a single object, and the solitary viewer, as in Heidegger's chosen example of the relationship of viewer to painting, but by compounding the sensations of *the relation between relations*. One fundamental in-between, that of different kinds of material, each with their own means and media, such as the visual, the sonic or somatic, their own middles that meddle each in their own curious ways, is compounded furiously in the 'heat' of the event with another in-between, that of the gathering of persons, each aware of the others *as persons* each in their own right. In the theatre-event, we put ourselves forth in this doubled sense: *into the midst of various middles amongst others*. In this respect, theatre literally incarnates what Heidegger describes as being-historical's ceaseless return to and deconstruction of first principles in its un-grounding grounding; and in doing so, it makes its participants most vulnerable, as 'the only art of life', to the ravages of a virus, actualising Artaud's iconic metaphor of theatre as plague.

For Heidegger, this being in-between that is inaugurated in the artwork, between one human and another, always provokes in its remorseless re-thinking three crucial relationships: what matters most between one people and another – in essence, what it is that constitutes the community or the polis; secondly, between the (human) world and the (material) earth – in essence, how humans relate to nature as both animals and animators, and, in contradiction to that manipulation, how the natural environment appears *in its own right* before us; and thirdly, between the (human) world and the (ideal or possible) super-human or gods – in essence, how the compromises of our socialisation and material existence reach out to the limits of our imagination and will. It mirrors the unrelenting deconstructive force of being-historical:

> *The rising and enowning meet in the be-ing-historically dis-sociating ex-position*. [...] *The en-owning* is the ground as the ab-ground of clearing, the struggle that struggles in the countering of god and man with the strife between earth and world (Heidegger 2006, 72–73; original emphasis).

These relationships are opened out within being-historical in yet another crucially distinct manner: not in order to arrive at a resolution, as that would be a purely political function, but to sustain them as compossible differences. This is precisely echoed in his definition of the artwork, where the in-between, in allowing each participant to appear as their ownmost selves with their ownmost wills, again provokes what he calls 'strife' where 'opponents raise each other into the self-assertion of their essential natures [...] each opponent carries the other beyond itself' (Heidegger 1978, 174); similarly, not to reach agreement, but to force differences to appear as most clearly distinct:

> In setting up a world and setting forth the earth, the work is an instigating of [...] strife. This does not happen so that the work should at the same time settle and put an end to strife by an insipid argument, but so that the strife may remain a strife. [...] It is because the strife arrives at its high point in the simplicity of intimacy that the unity of the work comes about in the instigation of strife (Heidegger 1978, 175).

Clearly, theatre's fundamental predicate of the face-to-face encounter of performer with auditor-spectator, complicated within the drama by the face-to-face between performer-characters, automatically actualises this irreconcilable otherness in-between ourselves, which, for Heidegger, preserves the strife, and for others – such as Emmanuel Levinas – exposes the infinite responsibility that the one bears to the other (see Levinas 1998). Because Heidegger focuses primarily on painting and the solitary viewer in 'The Origin of the Work of Art', his earlier essay says little about how preserving this in-between is enacted in the artwork. However, in *Mindfulness*, two critical aspects to being-historical, concerning an approach to developing and sustaining this un-grounding grounding, offer us a way to think towards a methodology. Typically, this is a non-method method that projects being-historical forth along an absolutely non-teleological vector: 'The be-ing-historical question of being "has" no "method" for "investigating" the being of beings as well as beings themselves. Rather, the be-ing-historical questioning "of" be-ing *is* a pathway and only this' (Heidegger 2006, 308; original emphasis).

Furthermore, this non-method must be wilfully sustained by a radical not-knowing, which actively, rather than haphazardly, un-knows; and it is only through this perverse and wayward un-knowing that one can maintain oneself amongst the inter-relations which animate one's own being-historical:

> Errancy is that within which a particular interpretation of be-ing must err, which erring alone truly traverses the clearing of refusal – traverses in accord with the clearing of what is lighted up. The fundamental consequence of errancy as the sway of the truth of be-ing is that any being that enters into and stays within the openness and can possibly preserve this openness, simultaneously resides in 'un-truth' (Heidegger 2006, 229).

This actively residing in un-truth through a remorselessly wilful waywardness, a deliberate straying from the known method, a revelling in the potentiality of error, when applied to theatre, gives it in the open eventness of theatre's face-to-face preserving-encountering a decisive priority over other art forms. Heidegger goes further in *Mindfulness* to characterise this non-method as *a crossing* the in-between: 'Be-ing-historical enleaping into the *crossing*. The grounding of the historical uniqueness of the crossing' (Heidegger 2006, 359, original emphasis). Again, he foregrounds the absolute specificity for the individual in their own experiencing of being-historical and carefully goes on to exclude from this action any sense of dialogic or dialectical relation which might suggest a coming to terms, some form of communication or community:

> Hence the crossing [e. g., from *a* past to *a* future, through *a* history] is never a mediation, but the de-cision that can ground itself unto that for the sake of which the decision decides to be that which is to be grounded. Reckoned 'historically', crossing into the suddenness of the rupture of what cannot be mediated is a leap into 'the nothing' (Heidegger 2006, 358).

This captures brilliantly the ineffable sense in which any artwork establishes finally and in the instance of its own actualising its own truth on its own terms. However, in the heat of the theatre-event, these crossings do leap into the nothing between the one and the other, as much as one is called by that other to be most oneself, and in so doing recall Herbert Blau's definition of theatre as a gathering of the asocial: 'For we simply do not know, in any reliable – no less ideal or accountable – sense, *who is there* nor, in the absence of the classical subject, *where to look*' (Blau 1990, 355). Indeed, in materialising the in-between of in-betweens, the relation of relations, theatre's non-method works by crossing across in-between its media and persons, as if phase-transitioning between solid, liquid, gas, sensing synaesthetically, seeing in hearing, hearing in seeing. Heidegger identifies crossings-across the relations of being-historical as how any one being approaches Be-ing in general. It is not possible to arrive at a description of what it means *to be historically*: only to live through a series of crossings-across, the specific issues of living can give us a sense of what our lives might become. Theatre, at its most energising and provocative, maintains these crossings-across as its way of sustaining not-knowing; the problem is posed in performance from the multiple perspectives of all those involved in the event: the artists who instigate the set-up call out to the auditor-spectators who gather. They, too, play their part since their responses are not answers, as in solutions to the problem posed: they hold open the work's eventness, holographically, as an infinitely complex manifolding of crossings-across the in-betweens of media and persons present. In preserving the performance's spaciousness, they *live along with* what it is possible to think and do *as if life, but not life* – in-between actual and potential. So, the performance does not say what is to be done, in a historical or political sense: rather, it unsettles what it is possible to do and does what is possible to think there-then in that opening out of being-historical.

Whilst Heidegger does prioritise in *Mindfulness* what he describes as 'the serenity of the mastery of [philosophy's] imageless knowing-awareness' (Heidegger 2006, 42) over art's imageful materialising, it is theatre that most acutely models and enacts being-historical's ontological foundation as 'the decision [that] decides to be that which is to be grounded' (2006, 358) – that is, 'the beginning of a history that has no "history"' (2006, 17). This is because theatre, in being amongst and witnessing all these crossings-across, is the art form predicated on decisiveness: amongst the tumult of performing with its unavoidable irreversibility, its unremitting call to act – which is precisely the attribute that the audience-spectator pays to experience, at the crossings-across this being-historical is *the performer acting*, making a decision to act, even if that decision is to suspend all decisions. This decisiveness draws us through theatre, energises it and essentialises it as an art: in the instance of a decision taken and witnessed by an audience, theatre appears *as theatre*, most its self, its ownmost being-historical.

Take as a wonderful example of this decisiveness at work in theatre's being-historical the show by Forced Entertainment, *Real Magic*, which I experienced at Arnolfini Bristol at its British premiere in February 2017, as part of the In Between Time Festival of Live Art and Intrigue. Three performers appear on an oblong of green floor-cloth in front of fluorescent tubes on vertical stands, dressed variously in a loose suit or evening gown or a large chicken costume, complete with headpiece. They appear to be trapped in a TV game-show routine, asked to guess what word is in the head of their fellow performer; however, from the myriad possibilities of what that word could be, it soon becomes clear that there are only three – algebra, caravan and sausage. They variously take turns to play the host, the contestant and the thinker of the word, sometimes exchanging pieces of clothing or a wig. The host uses a microphone. The patter, question and answer are brief, basically generic of any one of a number of game-shows: they are repeated with (I recall) very little (if any) variation, except for which of the three words is held up on a hand-written cardboard sign and the contestant's guess. Three or four times in the incessant repetition there is a short break to dance a chicken dance. This spare and pared-down routine quickly focuses the audience's attention on the action of trying to guess the word; although, through changing roles, each performer gets to hold up each of the three signs on multiple occasions, no contestant ever answers with any one of the correct, possible options.

At a political level, *Real Magic* could be read as a critique of neoliberalism: life is reduced to a TV format, a game-show, in which the answers are rigged, even though the question is impossible to answer in any event – what word of all possible words in the English language has the contestant chosen? And yet they as performers and we as audience still want someone to answer correctly, to win – whatever the prize is, we will never know. And despite the frustration of realising through the multiple iterations of the cheesy, shallow patter, that no performer is going to answer correctly – algebra... caravan... sausage – our desire for them to win only builds through the ninety-minute performance. At this historical-critical moment, this is a metaphor for how capitalism holds out the promise of success, by degrading the complexity of living and masking in mere entertainment the fact that the odds are stacked against us exponentially. The absurdity of this degradation of our lives is enacted through the chicken costumes, which work variously through the long duration of the show, sometimes charming, sometimes kitsch, sometimes sinister: we are partly mesmerised by the repetition and bland expectation as any other spectacle of false ideology would operate.

However, there is something both more profound and more human at work here, something that exposes *Real Magic*'s opening out of a being-historical amongst us that night in the Arnolfini, which resists the very impoverishment of the routine in which we are trapped as 'experience'. It is precisely how we hang on the possibility of difference in the endless play of repetition in the suspended moments of witnessing the performer *decide how* to answer what word. In that action, all possibility of acting is opened out, as each repeat ushers in (absolute) difference in potentiality, and then holds it in-between us and the performers: even though we may only want one of three correct answers, the moment before the answer is given suspends all possibility in which the show could go anywhere, take any course. Indeed, these moments in *Real Magic* show how far we have fallen from the decisiveness of Hamlet's 'to be or not to be', an absolute human agency over the very existence of the ontological self, to a neoliberal, late-capitalist simulacrum, actualised in Forced Entertainment's utterly *inconsequential* decision-making – 'which word am I thinking?' This hollowing out – indeed, desecration – of all agency, of the complexities and plenitude of life, is both cruel mockery and coruscating critique of the contemporary condition, which the vast majority of human beings endured in the current phase of techno-capital, even before the COVID-19 pandemic struck. As a degradation of both being and its theatrical quotidian – theatre emptied of its potential to model decisiveness, this about-to-answer actually exposes radical deciding-to-act as *the possibility of* revolution, abandonment, love in the perversity of its then-not-taking that action, its brutal disregard of its audience's will and willingness to action, to decisiveness, to life. Only theatre as an art form can actualise this crucial aspect of being-historical – the will deciding to act, which alone can realise the possibility of what it means to be human.

In this persistent and ontologically necessary unsettling and undoing, inherent in the crossings-across the voids in-between, *Real Magic* and – beyond that instance – theatre refuse to complete the experience of life as that which can be produced. And so, as an art form it best approaches 'the brink of the ab-ground' upon which being-historical so tremulously stands. And through the concreteness of its compossible images, incarnated in the presence of/amongst the wills of others, *Real Magic* actualises an aesthetic response to Third Nature, which says something more about theatre: that at its heart it embodies *knowing more originally as being-historical* because *its very performing is an issue for it*, as Heidegger's Da-sein is a being *whose being is an issue for it*. Indeed, this obligation to return to what constitutes theatre *as theatre* drives every performance tradition and even more closely aligns theatre with Heidegger's sense of mindfulness as a relentless undoing of foundations in constantly returning to the most ontological principles of thinking be-ing, which he realised in the very writing of *Mindfulness* as a collection of returns to beginnings. For theatre, every new generation of performers must go back to those foundations, or rather, must re-build those foundations *as if for the first time and now amongst the techno-capital assemblages of our third nature:* an even more pressing task as theatre as art form and industry reconstructs itself out of the pandemic. Now more than before, theatre must continue to challenge modernity's completion of experience as reproducible procedures leading towards a so-called better, more productive life, by exploring its fundamental relationship to its own Third Nature – as perpetual unsettling reinvention in the promise of what's to come.

7

Theatre Against Itself: Performance, Politics and the Limits of Theatricality

Adrian Kear

Staging Theatricality

With the world stage increasingly dominated by images and events which seem self-knowingly staged, artificial, or even fake, it would appear timely to return to the question of *theatricality* as a way of thinking about the relationship between politics and aesthetics.[1] The term theatricality might be understood to be operating here as both a discursive formation and a conceptual apparatus – as a problem to be thought through and a critical framework to enable such thinking. In common-sense terms, when 'theatricality' is invoked as a description of a behaviour, an activity, or an event – whether in everyday social practice or public political discourse – it is more often than not to account for a sense of contrivance or stagey-ness – a certain 'mode of excess' (Brooks 1976, ix; cited in Davis and Postlewait 2003, 21) – which appears calculated, deliberate and self-evidently over the top. Here, theatricality is used dismissively as an indication of a lack of credibility or seriousness, a mere extension of the theatrical world of exaggeration, pretence and downright silliness associated with the theatre as such. In other words, the conventional deployment of the term theatricality carries within it an implicit *anti*-theatrical sentiment – as being unworthy of further thought rather than requiring it.

A similar trajectory is evident in the development of theatricality as a critical concept, at least in art theory. Michael Fried, for example, both characterises theatricality as a fixed, over-determined relation antithetical to genuine aesthetic experience and as simply signifying 'a nothing, an emptiness, a void'. In the process he appears to reduce *theatre* – as the cultural form and practice directly associated with the production of theatricality – to 'an empty term' – a critical void and philosophical nothing – 'whose role it is to set up a system founded on the opposition between itself and another term' (Krauss 1987, 62–63; cited in McGillivray 2009, 105). Such a negative conception of theatricality – and of theatre as a negative construct – seems to pervade the *anti-theatrical* discourse of theatricality in its various forms.

But how, then, does *theatre* think through theatricality? Does it offer a material counterpoint to this logic or simply internalise its terms? Given that theatricality is a discourse arising from outside of the theatre – whether a common-sense anti-theatricality or from the elevated perspective of the visual arts – what would it mean to think theatricality from the point of view of theatre? If theatre and theatricality are always yoked together as seemingly coterminous or coextensive, how might they be thought of as existing in tension with one another?

The *Oxford English Dictionary* asserts their co-dependency in defining theatricality as 'the quality or character of being theatrical' while regarding theatrical as 'connected to the theatre or stage'. This 'cluster of concepts', as theatre historian Tracy C. Davis casts them, therefore appears to rely on theatre as its foundational term (Davis 2003, 127). Whilst the dictionary definitions appear to move seamlessly from theatre, over the theatrical, to theatricality as an expanding field of terms, Davis is at pains to demonstrate that their historical emergence indicates that they mean rather different things. She argues that the terms should be prised apart in order to account for a 'crucial distinction between *the theatrical* and *theatricality*' (128), a distinction which hinges not on staging or intention but on spectatorship and reception. Put simply, Davis argues that the spectator '*creates theatricality*' through the activity of looking (141); through the *theatricalisation*, so to speak, of what they see, as if it were a scene appearing before them, for them to see. This logic of active looking, she proposes, is integral to the appearance of theatricality, whether in the specifically designated space of the theatre or on the broader public stage of which it is part.

Before continuing with Davis's argument about theatricality's 'considerable importance for understanding public life' (131), it is worth pausing to acknowledge the introduction of my own term to this cluster of concepts: *theatricalisation*. By this, I mean the process of turning people and actions into figures within a scene, whether or not they regard themselves as on display, performing, or otherwise being there to be seen. Theatricalisation operates through the framing or re-framing of material as theatrical, irrespective of its being explicitly staged as such, constituting a *seeing as* mode of perception which produces theatricality as its effect. Theatricalisation serves as a key dynamic of power; a constitutive structure of representation rendering observable, knowable and controllable that which otherwise simply appears to be present. It turns presence into representation, into a formalised configuration of relations of power, knowledge and visibility. It is, in other words, a political and aesthetic apparatus which produces the idea of otherness and situates the spectator as its presumed subject.

Accordingly, to examine the relationship between theatricality and theatricalisation is to open up a *political* question. It is to question the politics of representation and to see theatricality as primarily a political operation. But what has any of this have to do with *theatre*? What is the relationship between theatre and theatricality when thought of as a question of politics? How is theatre implicated in the dynamics of desire and the political production of otherness? And how can theatre, rather than being a critical and aesthetic void, operate as a space in which the process of theatricalisation and the production of theatricality can be explicated and challenged as well as reproduced? What are the grounds – and the limits – of its political claim? This chapter seeks to investigate these questions directly, arguing that theatre operates as a space in which the process of theatricalisation and the production of theatricality can be explicated and challenged, as well as reproduced; with theatre functioning as the specific aesthetic form and political site through which the limits of theatricality may be examined and exposed.

The argument forwarded here thereby seeks to reverse – or at least to question – the logic of extension implied by the *OED* definition of theatricality as emanating from theatre and the theatrical. It will suggest, rather, that the institution of theatre emerged as a site in which to limit and contain generalised theatricality and might be seen to provide a way of knowing and showing the political effects of the aesthetic framing and visual construction of otherness. Hence, the question is not really chicken and egg – which came first, theatre or theatricality? – but rather one of critical position and investigation. How does theatre frame, expose and delimit theatricality? How does theatre think through the problem of generalised theatricality, as well as through theatricality's visual production of alterity?

Such a shift in emphasis reflects an interdisciplinary commitment to interrogating performance as both a specific cultural practice (call it *theatre*, in this instance), and an important social process (here characterised as *theatricalisation*). In this vein, cultural archaeologist Yann-Pierre Montelle argues that 'theatricality' should be regarded primarily as the social process governing the construction of the gaze and the production of otherness, 'as the paradigm out of which the institution of the theatre emerged' (2009, 2). Theatre, for Montelle, operates as the site of the formalisation of theatricality, providing a structured and sanctioned space for its practice and regulation through the development of specific codes and conventions. Theatre, then, provides a way of knowing and regulating the modes of seeing and showing attendant on the production of theatricality as a form of appearing to one another.

For philosopher Samuel Weber, 'theatre and theatricality emerge as names for an alternative' way of knowing and understanding human beings and social behaviours to the Western conceptual tradition of thinking based on 'a certain notion of identity, reflexivity and subjectivity' (Weber 2004, 2). He suggests that theatre emerges as a practice which troubles the security of ontological categories and the distinctive boundaries of self and other, dislocating and disorienting 'the Western dream of self-identity' by always appearing only to disappear and re-appear somewhere else, often *as* something else. Theatre as such therefore needs to be thought of not only as a place and a taking place – an event explicitly staged in a cave or *theatron* and directed towards assembled spectators – but as a *medium* whose slipperiness and irreducibility troubles conceptual clarity and any uniform definition of reality. Weber suggests that theatrical thinking 'haunts and taunts' the philosophical project of rendering transparent by offering a kind of dirty materialist resistance to its logic (7). Hence Plato sought to ostracise theatre from the domain of knowledge, characterising theatricality as an artificially constructed chimera designed to hold its spectators in thrall, through a fixed relation of domination rather than as an investigative space designed to enable thinking and self-realisation. Platonic *anti-theatricality* seeks not only to reduce theatre to a primarily mimetic activity – a barely credible game of play and imitation – but to tie theatre and theatricality together in order to constrain their operation. For Weber, theatre as medium will always seek to elude and escape this tethering, refusing to be fixed either ontologically (as a form or place) or ideologically (as a specific spectatorial relation or way of seeing). Yet, what the cultural historian Jonas Barish famously called 'the anti-theatrical prejudice' – 'the ancient distrust of the stage' as duplicitous and deforming (1981, 3) – continues to over-determine our thinking about theatre and performance.

In many ways, common-sense notions of theatricality as either frivolous fakery or dangerous excess rely on this tradition of diminishing theatre's claim to philosophical and political seriousness, and theatre itself has often been inclined to incorporate anti-theatricality into its aesthetic codes and historical conventions. Consider, for example, how the emergence of Naturalism and Realism in the theatre of the late nineteenth century was predicated on the repudiation of the overtly theatrical in order to appear authentically real, seeking in the process to produce an anti-theatrical theatre that attempted to 'render the theatrical medium absolutely transparent' and to banish the stain of theatricality from the theatre as such (Williams 2001, 285). Contrastingly, the Renaissance re-animation of the theatre as a significant cultural form and social practice was connected to a renewed understanding of theatricality as an organising principle for society. As theatre historian Thomas Postlewait argues, playwrights 'often used the theatre to attack the theatrical' and to expose the 'inherent theatricality' of the 'performance of power' through critically re-directing and creatively re-imagining the power of performance (2003, 100–16). In this context, theatre emerges as a specific, even specialised, way of knowing theatricality and questioning the process of theatricalisation – and perhaps even of opening up ways of contesting its grip on the social formation.

We will return to these questions through a case-study investigation and contemporary theatrical reading of Shakespeare's *King Lear* (1606) in order to analyse further how theatre thinks through theatricality and attempts to differentiate itself from it politically. Before doing so, however, it is worth returning to Davis's conception of theatricality as being produced through critically engaged spectatorship. Drawing on an etymological understanding of the theatre as a seeing place – *theatron* – where spectators gather to engage in the emotional participation of watching something take place as performance, Davis argues that the spectator's process of theatricalisation is actively involved in the construction and formalisation of the event they see (2003, 141). Historicising this development of the concept of theatricality in the context of the Enlightenment and the French Revolution, Davis suggests that the operation of national-popular democratic society is dependent on a self-reflexive, 'volitional spectatorship' that enables the adoption of 'a critical stance toward an episode in the public sphere' (145). While this may include watching a theatre event, it is not limited to it, as theatricality is produced by the spectator choosing to see something as a scene taking place before them, through their participation in a practice of theatricalisation. Davis is careful to point out that such a conception of theatricality might function as a highly racialised and 'masculinized form of viewing, a gender specific kind of participation in civil society' (146), which seeks to reassert the gaze of the spectator as the locus of power and arbiter of meaning. Yet, at the same time, she argues that such spectators are aware 'of their own acting' – an awareness that might challenge their pre-existing 'sense of themselves' (148). In other words, the operation of theatricality might serve to disrupt and disturb the gaze as well as reaffirm it, destabilising the security of the subject position that it otherwise brings into effect.

The question of whether theatricality necessarily operates as mode of transgression, or as a form of normalisation thereby appears as something of a false opposition. As Josette Féral points out, theatricality has 'no autonomous existence' or definite essence but is 'graspable only as a process' – as the continuous interplay between repetition and difference which both produces possibility and circumscribes its limits (Féral 2002a, 12). Theatricality, then, appears as both normative *and* transgressive. It appears in the moment of crossing a boundary which simultaneously reaffirms its presence; in the movement between the opening up of a question and its recuperation into the existing logics of representation. While it might be seen to destabilise the boundaries of the subject, it nonetheless continues to constitute them, reproducing relations of power as well as appearing to contest them. So, if theatricality is neither one thing nor the other, but rather a mode of recognition of their interpenetration, how might it be useful as a way of 'understanding public life', as Davis suggests, as well as the spectatorial dynamics of subject formation? How might it open up the theatre of politics as well as the frame of the political?

On Populist Theatricality; or, Staging Donald Trump's Hair

In his critical exposition of 'The Populist Temptation', Slavoj Žižek makes recourse to one of his signature jokes to explain the recent re-ascendance of the populist right in Western democratic societies. Commenting on that subject of much conjecture and speculation, Donald Trump's hair, Žižek notes: 'When a man wears a wig, he usually tries to make it look like his real hair. Trump achieved the opposite; he made his real hair look like a wig; and maybe this reversal provides a succinct formulation of the Trump phenomenon' (2017, 260). The joke, like most good ones, is really rather familiar. In concert with the characterisation of the populism it implies, it seems to trade on a certain anti-theatrical logic, re-inscribing the binary between the real/authentic and the mimetic/inauthentic through exposing the theatricality of the inversion of their terms. The fact that Trump's hair appears fake – even if, apparently, it is not – somehow indexes the fakery of his political showmanship, the self-evident inauthentic stagey-ness of which must surely be seen to undermine itself. And yet it does not; and the various parodies that seek to draw attention to the lack of seriousness or credibility of Trump as a political figure fall foul of their own anti-theatrical, binary thinking. Thus, for Žižek, performing his own critical reversal of the apparent priority of the real over the imaginary, the joke reveals the populist distortion of the boundary between them: 'At the most elementary level', he writes, Trump 'is not trying to sell is his crazy ideological fictions as a reality – what he is trying to sell us is his own vulgar reality as a beautiful dream' (Žižek 2017, 260). In this respect, it is not surprising that, following Alain Badiou's characterisation of the emergence of Trump as 'symptom of global capitalism', Žižek sees right-wing populism as appealing to the rhetorical ground of working-class dispossession and disenchantment in order 'to prevent the dispossessed from defending themselves' (273). Žižek presents the populist 'slide into vulgar simplification and personalized aggressiveness' (241) embodied by Trump as a mask concealing yet revealing the true face of neo-liberal capitalism; but the very logic of mask and face, mimetic construct and theatrical falsehood is left in place. This effectively allows the populist turn to be derided as an *intentional* manipulation – a theatrical sleight of hand or ideological conjuring trick – which *pretends* in order to persuade its audience of its own claims to truthfulness.

Something important is missing from this analysis; something apparent in the misunderstanding of theatricality demonstrated in the discussion of Trump's hair as real/fake. Populist theatricality is not a joke. If it is regarded simply as an attempt to deceive – as theatrical in the most directly vulgar sense – we will continue to miss its most important ideological operation: the capacity to play with indeterminacy, the variability of meaning, to disconnect and re-articulate what Stuart Hall calls 'the multi-accentuality of signs in discourse', so that they can be combined differently in order to produce popular consent to an increasingly privatised, personalised and authoritarian mode of address (Hall 1988, 140). The point that Žižek misses about Trump's hair – and about the Trump phenomenon, by extension – is that any attempt to limit the consideration of its theatricality to inverting the binaries of real/fake, authentic/inauthentic does not go far enough in examining its operation and effects. Rather, it reproduces and sustains them. For if, as Volosinov argues, 'everything that belongs to ideology has a semiotic value' (cited in Hall 1988, 140) – even the floating signifier of Trump's hair – we need to understand how these signs are articulated to one another in constructing the populist project.

An important starting point would seem to be the recognition that theatricality, as Erika Fischer-Lichte argues, destabilises the hierarchal organisation of signifier/signified by producing 'a shift of dominance in the semiotic function' in which particular signs appear as 'signs of signs' (1995, 88). At least partially emptied of their signifying value, they become mobile, malleable and ontologically indistinct. While this theatrical emptying of their referential content might appear to render them void, and thereby also appears to void the concept of theatricality as having any explanatory purchase or critical power, it simultaneously makes visible the fundamental emptiness of the sign as only ever subject to the play of signification. The demonstrable theatricality of the sign thereby makes whatever it signifies appear as empty or void, pointing to its apparently arbitrary, ideological construction. Hence, the self-evident theatricality of Trump – and Trump's hair – appears to void any claim to authenticity, even though it is actually real (isn't it, really?). Yet, as I have been trying to argue, it is important not to stop here. To do so would leave the concept of theatricality once again in the position primarily constructed by its anti-theatrical art critics, such as Fried, as simply signifying 'a nothing, and emptiness, a void'; rendering theatre 'an empty term whose role it is to set up a system founded upon the opposition between itself and another term' (Krauss 1987, 62–63). More importantly, it would be to leave the discussion of theatricality (and Trump, and of politics) at the level of what it is rather than what it *does*.

As Elisabeth Burns points out, theatricality is not an inherent property or quality of things, people, practices, or objects; it is rather a historically and culturally constructed 'mode of perception' which serves to 'frame' these through specific 'rhetorical and authenticating conventions' and discursive practices (1972, 1). Hence, as a 'mode of perception', theatricality requires and is produced by the activity of the spectator, albeit under historically and culturally constructed conditions of spectatorship. Accordingly, Josette Féral argues that 'theatricality is the result of an act of recognition on the part of the spectator' – an act of seeing that opens the gaps in the current regime of representation and produces theatricality as the effect of 'making a disjunction in systems of signification' (2002a, 10). In this respect, theatricality emerges as the result of perceptual and critical operation which disturbs the distinction between reality and representation, by recognizing their interpenetration and co-constitution. As such, its appearance might be seen to offer the spectator a 'critical lens' through which to gain a purchase on 'how, and why, we act' (Nield 2014, 556), as well as an optic through which to interrogate our own ideological production as a desiring subject. Although Féral, like Davis, tends to assume the subject as pre-existing the theatrical relation rather than being constituted by it, she usefully makes the connection between spectatorship and the construction of alterity. In her succinct formulation, 'theatricality cannot be, it must be for someone. In other words, it is for the Other' (Féral 1982, 178).

The relation between the theatricality produced by the performer yet addressed to the Other – remembering that, in Lacanian terms, desire is often manifested theatrically as desire for the Other, as desire for the Other's desire – is crucial in attempting to understand the populist political claim. As we have seen, it is insufficient to attempt to essentialise theatricality as a critical operation that opens up a cleavage in the ideological social formation and enables us to see its disjunction, as Féral suggests. For theatricality is also at play in covering up this gap, by, as Michael Taussig puts it, suturing 'the real and the really made-up' (Taussig 1993, 86). Theatricality, as such, is not necessarily resistive or contestatory; it is as much inscribed in the construction of the regime of representation as in any apparent moment of its destabilisation. Put simply, theatricality, as Trump shows and knows all too well, is as much a space of ideological investment and semiotic volatility as it is anything else; and, in being addressed to the desire of the Other, it effectively resides in the construction of a range of subject-spectator positions rather than in the credibility of its address. Accordingly, the examination of the populist political project should not be reduced to questions of intentionality, in/authenticity and the 'voiding' of affect; it must return to the dynamics of spectatorship as the site of the political production of the subject.

In order to move this analysis forward, I want to give critical consideration to how theatre as the specific space dedicated to the task of making theatricality appear, and as the specific historical practice developed to produce a way of knowing theatricality and understanding its effects, might be approached as offering a useful mode of critique of the generalised theatricality and vulgar theatricalisations of the emergent authoritarian populist moment. In order to do so, I want to turn to philosopher Stanley Cavell's reading of *King Lear* (1967), and specifically to his argument that theatre, in its materiality as a place and practice, offers a limit to theatricality as an otherwise apparently 'diaphanous' medium by forcing its revelation as a political operation (Weber 2004, 7). In particular, I want to examine Cavell's claim that, with *King Lear*, theatre extends an invitation to its audience to try to stop theatricalising. In other words, I want to see if this argument might be reanimated and deployed in order to turn theatre against itself – or more precisely, against the theatre that has apparently already separated itself from the specificities of theatre as such: generalised theatricality. Can theatre offer resistance to theatricality? Or is it indelibly implicated in its construction and operation? How might theatre be thought of as exposing the dynamics of theatricalisation and as serving as a limit point to generalised theatricality? What are the limits of its political claim?

Staging Theatricality: Trump/Lear

But what has *King Lear* got to do with populist politics, or, for that matter, with Donald Trump's hair? Some of the connections might already be found ghosting the brief commentary on the conceptualisation of theatricality offered already, not least the idea that theatricality constitutes a void space, a semiotic emptiness: a nothing. 'Nothing? Nothing. Nothing will come of nothing. Speak again'. Cordelia's famous refusal to engage Lear's self-regarding question – 'Which of you, my daughters, shall we say, does love us most?' – effectively operates as a refusal to enter the theatricality of the love test set-up in Act 1 Scene 1 as an overtly performed display of obedience to his all-encompassing patriarchal, authoritarian power. Sam Mendes's 2014 production of the play for the Royal National Theatre makes this point very clear. Antony Ward's stage design demonstrates how Lear, played as an ageing autocrat by Simon Russell Beale, constructs a theatre of his own within the theatre in which the play takes place – a meta-theatrical court theatre in which everyone and everything appears before him as subject to his gaze and acts in accordance with his desire. Cordelia's 'nothing, my Lord' in response to his attenuation of the obligations of intergenerational exchange to the dynamics of a property transaction – 'What can you say to gain a third more opulent than your sisters?' – is a refusal to *pretend*; a refusal to act according to the conventions of the theatre set-up, staged for Lear's spectatorial pleasure entirely from his own perspective. Her refusal to adhere to his authorial direction – 'Mend thy speech a little lest you mar your fortunes' – is both a refusal to play the game and a refusal to act the part: a refusal to appear to him as he would have her appear, a refusal of his *theatricalisation*. Cordelia's 'nothing' empties Lear's drama of succession of its manifest content in order to draw attention to its theatrical construction, exposing, so writes Peggy Phelan, 'the utter emptiness of the ceremony and his demand for love' (Phelan 2005, 25). Her refusal to pretend is, as Cavell points out, itself already doubled – she refuses to pretend to love him because she actually does, whereas her sisters can pretend because they know how to act as if they do, even if they do not. In other words, she refuses to *act*. Cordelia protests with the line 'I cannot heave her heart into my mouth', not only because this would void her love and turn it into an empty signifier, but also because to do so would be to accept Lear's theatricalisation of her as Other than herself, as only existing for him in his imaginary relation, not in her specificity. In Mendes's staging, the dynamics of this scene are explicitly sexualised: Regan's (Anna Maxwell Martin) coquettish acting-up to Lear's demands earns her a slap on the behind from her over-excited, boundary-crossing father; the demonstrable inappropriateness of this situates Cordelia's (Olivia Vinall) subsequent refusal to perform as a rejection of the sexualisation of their relation at the very moment of her selecting a husband. It is clear from this that Lear's theatricalisations serve to maintain his sense of retaining ownership of his possessions – including his daughters and his kingdom – even after he has given them away, effectively reducing his view of inter-personal relations to relations of property and power that sustain his subjective sovereignty.

There are some obvious points of comparison between Lear's court theatrics and descent into the role of player King and Trump's highly personalised and increasingly privatised approach to government and the construction of authoritarian populism. Of course, there has been the uncomfortably nepotistic promotion of immediate family members, notably of Trump's daughter Ivanka and her husband, Jared Kushner, to positions of delegated responsibility; the awkward resonance of the inaugural cabinet meeting in which the newly appointed office-holders were required to attest their love for, and acquiescence to, the president, alongside their willingness to serve; and the impetuous banishments and exclusions directed at those who fail to please. But more importantly, what Žižek euphemistically calls Trump's 'vulgarity' – his racism, homophobia, misogyny and unbounded objectification of women, including his daughter – which might otherwise be termed his consistent *theatricalisation of otherness*, so it only appears within a property relation and a logic of self-extension, seem straight out of the Learean repertoire of reduction and misrecognition in order to render otherness obedient, observable and owned. In this respect, the mode of excess of authoritarian populist theatricality might be not only its vulgarity, but also its construction of what Edward Said terms 'a closed field, a theatrical stage', already tied to a specific mode of cultural production (Said 1978, 63). And perhaps that mode of cultural production is inimical to the construction and operation of racist, sexist and proprietorial discourses and power relations. For Said, accordingly, 'the notion of theatricality designates a particularly Western style of thought' whose operation is coextensive with a colonial regime of representation which delimits and circumscribes the appearance of the Other within the logic of the stage. Theatricality, in other words, plays an integral part of the perceptual production and configuration of an apparatus of alterity rather than simply providing the grounds of its recognition.

Returning to *King Lear* for the moment, or at least to Cavell's reading of it – the complexity of which is so rich that there is insufficient space to do it justice here – it is worth recalling that the play demonstrates how the theatricalisation of others produces a refusal to acknowledge what is in plain sight: the reality of other people existing in and for themselves, and not only within the perceptual economy and epistemic violence of the construction of Otherness. For Cavell, theatricalisation serves as an avoidance of recognition, of mutuality; the avoidance of being seen as well as seeing. It is subjectivation without relation, without *love*; without the encumbrance of having to appear to other people as another person and without the need to recognize the specificity of their personhood. As such, Cavell suggests, theatricalisation has to stop; and it is theatre, as the material space of seeing and being seen by other people – on stage and in the auditorium – which 'gives us the chance to stop' (1967, 334). In other words, the specific conditions of theatre enable the manifestation of the material relations of seeing through which we come to recognize the dynamics of theatricality and to acknowledge alterity as the concrete reality of other people. As such, theatre's exposition and exposure of theatricality can be seen to limit and critique theatricalisation more generally. As Phelan points out, theatre 'exploits theatricality in order to defeat', delimit and deconstruct its operation (2005, 23). Accordingly, for Cavell, *King Lear* represents theatre against itself – or against the over-extension of theatricality as a way of seeing – and presents a way of knowing its effects: 'Tragedy has moved into the world, and with it the world becomes theatrical' (1967, 344).

Re-Staging *King Lear*: She She Pop's *Testament* (2010)

She She Pop's *Testament* – itself a version of *King Lear* – might offer a contemporary, postdramatic example of theatre working against itself, or at least with an awareness of the apparatus of theatricality that it seeks to both expose and exploit. The piece was made and performed by members of the experimental theatre company in conjunction with their real-life fathers, who, rather than being represented by trained actors as if they were characters, were very much present on stage themselves. Although clearly 'playing a part' – occupying performance personae demonstrably mediated by the stage environment and at least in part produced by the theatrical apparatus – they nonetheless appeared as themselves rather than as fictional figures. In other words, they performed as themselves rather than as actors pretending to be someone else; and, as a result, they both presented and represented themselves while fully acknowledging the artificially constructed reality of the theatrical staging and scene. Their awareness of themselves performing while performing as themselves is consistent with the work of the other performers in the company, who likewise eschew pretence in favour of recognizing their own and each other's presence – as well as the presence of the audience. This dual emphasis on performing rather than acting and on recognizing the specificity of the theatre event as engendering a self-aware mode of spectating is a hallmark of much postdramatic theatre. As Hans-Thies Lehmann observes, the postdramatic 'strategy of refusal' of pretending reverses the privileging of the fictive reality of the world of the drama over the theatrical reality of the world of the stage in order to re-animate and re-envisage their inter-relation. In doing so, it tends to embrace overt theatricality as tacit acknowledgement of the reality of theatrical situation and formal disruption of the apparently illusionistic conventions governing the construction of dramatic fiction. This enables the performers to inhabit the stage rather than simply inhabiting their role, thereby drawing attention to the reality of performing and the reality of performance over and above any

Fig. 7.1: She She Pop, *Testament*, 2010.

fictional reality being performed. Accordingly, performers often address the audience directly – not as characters, as per the aside – but as people sharing the same space and time, co-present in the theatre event and therefore included in the process of its composition (Lehmann 2006, 90, 109).

In *Testament*, the performer's theatrical relation to the audience is first and foremost mediated through their material relation to one another. They are, after all, relatives: real fathers and daughters (and, in the version at the Barbican Centre, London, one son) occupying the stage in order to stage the grounds of their relation as a means of opening up the question of parental love, filial obligation, intergenerational exchange and the sustaining of personal dignity. Using the text of *King Lear* as a pretext, or perhaps an urtext underlying the construction of their own, the company seek to investigate the age-old problem of the shift in responsibility between parents and children as they become elderly and infirm, examining how the distribution of property and the dissipation of authority are subsidiary to the need for recognition and the renewal of respect above and beyond the bonds of duty. In responding to Shakespeare's play, rather than simply re-staging it, She She Pop and their fathers make *Testament* an exploration of familial love and the ethics of care within as well as through a theatrical framework. The company members put themselves and their fathers on stage – under conditions of explicit theatricality – in order interrogate their own theatricalisation of (and by) the paternal relation. In other words, they use the theatre to both frame and challenge the theatricality of their lived experience, making it available to be seen under explicitly theatrical conditions so as to explicate its perceptual dynamics.

At the outset of the show, one by one, the regular company performers enter stage left, wearing faux Renaissance ruffs, and approach stage centre to introduce their fathers to the audience by telling us how we might gain their respect. Behind them, stage left, a projector screen displays the title page of Shakespeare's play, in German. Once the introductions are complete, the text scrolls down to make visible the stage direction 'Enter King Lear', which a performer highlights in red ink. A trumpet sound is indicated in the text, and so a trumpet is indeed played to mark the entrance of each Lear/father onto the stage. One by one, they take up their positions on the row of three armchair thrones aligned stage right and look at the performer-daughter/son who has announced them. The last is in fact the trumpeter, who, by announcing his own entrance as he had the others, destabilises any sense of a formal, fixed signification of hierarchy. The fathers stand to switch on the cameras in front of their chairs that then project their faces into cardboard picture frames hung at the back of the stage, behind their children. Although they appear in a dominant, central position, we see their seeing – they are both looked at and looking. Their presence there, on stage, is shown to be mediated – literally framed – by the theatricality of the performance taking place. In other words, even in this postdramatic performance presence is always crosscut by representation; there is no 'authentic' presence without a form of mediation. The theatrical set-up of this scene draws attention to the fact that the fathers are presented as much as simply present; they are visibly staged and framed by an apparatus drawn to the attention of the audience, rather than rendered invisible. As a result, we become aware of our own implication in the theatricalising of these figures, how our looking at them in this context is part of their production in and as the *mise-en-scène*.

Not surprisingly, then, the theatricality of both the audience's encounter with these figures and the always already mediated form of their relation to one another is underscored by the show's turn to popular song as the people on stage sing: 'And so I stand in line until you think you have the time to spend an evening with me . . . ' The concluding lyric is, of course, the key: 'And then I go and spoil it all by saying something stupid like I love you'. As the performers read from the text of Act 1 Scene 1, it becomes clear that Cordelia's 'nothing' is here rendered as 'something stupid like I love you'. The theatricality of the postdramatic performance is thereby used to explicate the theatrical context of the dramatic text without emptying it of its resonance entirely. Accordingly, the text becomes the ground of negotiation between the fathers and their children, and the theatrical occasion turns into an opportunity to investigate the dynamic of intergenerational exchange and the desire for mutual recognition. For example, one of the fathers offers a lecture-exposition deconstructing the false logic of Lear's seemingly self-interested reasoning; while one of the children responds with a calculation of care costs that questions the notion of inheritance entirely. This is expounded further in a visual demonstration of the impossibility of moving the professor father's books from his three-storey house in Frankfurt to his daughter's two-bedroom apartment in Berlin – showing that they would take up the totality of the floor space and leave no room for living. Here, Regan and Goneril's forced reduction of Lear's entourage of a hundred knights is given a contemporary manifestation, enabling us to understand the problem of accommodation as an enduring, everyday phenomenon. Once again, the dramatic and the theatrical are shown to be inter-animating and mutually deconstructing, with the reality-effects of the performers' seemingly authentic presence ghosting and being ghosted by the reality of representation.

Conclusion: Endlessly Re-Thinking Theatricality

She She Pop and their fathers' *Testament* draws attention to the limits of attempting to separate *reality* and *theatricality* as if they were opposing terms. It exposes such logic as being overly reductive and simplistic, and counter to the knowledge that theatre itself makes available: that the real and the really made-up are always co-constituting and inter-dependent. Rather than seeing theatricality as artificial and inauthentic, as per the popular and critical anti-theatrical discourses that would dismiss it as having any significance as a way of knowing, seeing and thinking; or as necessarily politically disruptive and destabilising, showing the gap between the real and the represented (Féral); or as exposing the unavoidable emptiness of signification (Fischer-Lichte) and the fictive processes of ideological construction (Žižek); theatre demonstrates the operation of theatricality as a medium – as consisting in neither one thing nor the other, but as the mode of their co-appearance and inter-relation – which redefines the boundaries between subject and object, self and other, presence and representation (Weber 2004, 29). As such, theatre emerges as the material space in which the apparatus of theatricality is rendered tangible and distinct. Theatre thinks through theatricality in order to make its operation visible, to force its dynamics to appear: not simply as theatre, but as a mode of theatre-thinking that challenges and critiques the regime of representation which it nonetheless contributes to and sustains. In this respect, theatre which thinks through theatricality is also theatre which appears to think against itself. Yet, in doing so, it also thinks against the grain of the generalised theatricality and politics of theatricalisation that it renders visible, calls into question and seeks to redress.

At the end of *Testament*, one of the father-daughter pairings reprise 'Somethin' Stupid' as a duet sung face to face rather than across the space of stage. Although it is tempting to see this as a concluding moment of recognition in which they acknowledge their love for one another as a relation without mediation – without theatricality – it is important to acknowledge that this relation is as theatrically mediated as everything else on stage. How could it not be? If theatre makes theatricality appear, it also inevitably theatricalises and re-theatricalises the very grounds of its appearance. As the duet progresses, the other performers frame it for the audience through taking apart the set and unravelling the text, refracting the performance through its own dismantling. They end up forming a beautifully composed heap of bodies on the stage – an image, no less – which the duet singers join as the song fades along with the lights. The show stops; the theatre ends, as it must. But does the logic of theatricality ever stop, as Cavell argues it too surely should? The final image suggests that, while theatre might appear to produce this demand in itself, its very nature *as theatre* necessarily theatricalises it all the same.

Performances Discussed

King Lear, dir. Sam Mendes, Royal National Theatre, London, UK, 23 January – 28 May 2014. For full production information and background materials, including cast list and programme, see http://ntlive.nationaltheatre.org.uk/productions/44084-king-lear. For a clip of the scene discussed in the essay (part of Act 1, Scene 1), see https://youtu.be/L_womZ_BE0Q

**Testament, She She Pop and their Fathers, Barbican Centre, London, UK, 3–7 June 2014. For full production and touring information and a video trailer of the work, see http://www.sheshepop.de/en/productions/archive/testament.html

Notes

1. An earlier version of this chapter was published as 'How Does Theatre Think Through Theatricality?' in M. Bleeker, A. Kear, J. Kelleher and H. Roms (eds), *Thinking Through Theatre and Performance*, London: Methuen/Bloomsbury, 2019, 296–310. Reproduced by permission.

Part 3

Art/Theatre/Photography/Sound

8

Between Lies and Truth Lies the Truth: Staged Mythologies in Damien Hirst's *Treasures from the Wreck of the Unbelievable*

Paula Blair

As visitors approached the threshold to the first gallery room of British artist and collector Damien Hirst's 2017 exhibition *Treasures from the Wreck of the Unbelievable*, they were greeted with the text, in block capitals above the door, BETWEEN LIES AND TRUTH LIES THE TRUTH, indicating that all may not be as it seemed. From 9 April to 3 December, the show was displayed across the Punta della Dogana, Venice's former customs house, and the Palazzo Grassi, a former private family palace constructed at the height of the former city-state's vast empire built on marine voyaging and trade (Crowley 2011, 3). Today these expansive venues are largely owned and operated as exhibition sites by the foundation established by French billionaire and art collector François Pinault. From these few details setting the scene, it can already be discerned that some trickery and much excess was involved in staging the show's elaborate tangle of truth and lies, history and myth. In analysing various steps and approaches towards that staging, I aim in this chapter to begin performing the untangling needed to show where truth may in fact lie.

The exhibition texts and paratexts claim that *Treasures from the Wreck of the Unbelievable* comprised a vast array of 2,000-year-old coral-encrusted sculptures depicting ancient-world myths first discovered in the Indian Ocean in 2008 and contemporary replicas and like-themed additions made of bronze, Carrera marble, black granite (gabbro), precious stones and metals, as well as photographic and videographic documentation of the discovery and recovery processes. The exhibits apparently lend credence to the myth of their existence, their collection by a freed slave called Cif Amotan II, and their transportation on the fated ship, the *Apistos*.

The exhibition's staging lies well beyond the confines of its time and space. Hinting at this spillage in several pieces displayed outside the venues, it seeps into film culture and cyberspace, with a film sharing the exhibition's title (which was viewable on Netflix from January 2017 to December 2019) played so straight that it would do a young Luis Buñuel proud, and plants on websites designed to convince anyone curious enough to search for the *Apistos* or Amotan, but too pressed for time or too easily satisfied to probe further at details and dates. Notably, many are geared towards tourism.[1]

While it is often the Roman names for gods used throughout the exhibition, the trails back to ancient Greece, polytheism and cultural exchange in the *Treasures* works is significant in the early twenty-first century, when nationalism, separatism and anxieties around migration seem to be experiencing increases globally, as is the denial of science and the platforming of opinions based on assumptions and untruths. The more recent dominance of ancient Rome, in turn, led to the prevalence of Roman myths and legends, which are largely adapted from the earlier Greek stories that formed early understandings of the earth and its inhabitants through

Fig. 8.1: Damien Hirst, *Treasures from the Wreck of the Unbelievable*, 2017, Palazzo Grassi, Venice.

allegory – that is, until monotheism in the form of Christianity rose and served to establish the divine right of the single (male) saviour head of state and empire (Scott 2016, 325). The first records of the classical myths of ancient Greece are found in the poems attributed to Homer and Hesiod, written in the eighth to seventh centuries BCE (March 2009, 1). When the new art form of tragic drama emerged in Athens in the late sixth century BCE, the myths were adapted and brought to life in dramatisations. As Jenny March points out, given their explorations of all facets of the human condition – 'how human life is, how death is, the way in which mortals relate to other mortals and to the everlasting gods' – they have never stopped being a source of inspiration for storytelling and creative expression (2009, 10–11). Indeed, life, death, science and religion are the fundamental concerns of Hirst's body of work.

Eventually understood to itself be founded on myth, the exhibition received polarised responses. Reportedly some visitors and film viewers were angered by, they felt, being led to believe, only to find that they had been lied to (Halperin 2018). In his rumination on the nature of truth and myth, Paul Veyne posits that '[m]yth is truthful, but figuratively so. It is not historical truth mixed with lies; it is a high philosophical teaching that is entirely true, on the condition that, instead of taking it literally, one sees it an allegory' (1988, 62). To reiterate the show's threshold text: the truth lies – exists, is situated and fibs – between lies and truth. Lies are dressed as truths, but truths also masquerade (where more appropriate than in Venice?) as lies; they perform one another and everything in between. We each make truths from the information we access. With the understanding that the coral-covered artefacts and their replicas are simulacra – copies without an original – my investigation takes me to the areas wherein lie masked truths, and the performative ways in which they emerge in the works. I show this by identifying the extent of fabrication, or staging, in the show's scenography, texts and an example of an exhibit that stages and is key to untangling the show's exchange between truth and lies, history and myth.

Setting the Scene

Treasures was curated by Elena Geuna, the former director of Sotheby's who in 2012–13 also curated the *Freedom Not Genius* exhibition of Hirst's extensive Murderme collection of works by other artists. Throughout the

Venice show's run, Geuna performed a series of interviews and curator-led tours in which she plays the part of mediator and narrator. In an interview with Judith Benhamou-Huet posted to YouTube three days before the exhibition's opening, Geuna firstly describes it as a 'wonderful adventure' shaped around Cif Amotan, his collection and the sinking of 'his incredible boat, the *Apistos*'. When disrupted out of a rehearsed narrative about how the hundred works are being resurfaced near the waters of Venice and pressed about Hirst's involvement, she becomes ambiguous, stating:

> Damien Hirst could have financed the excavation project. Damien Hirst could have conceived the project. Damien Hirst could have been the artist. It's up to you and up to each one of us to ask the question once we visit the exhibition in looking at these wonderful corals, and the span of the dimension could go from six, seven metres high in Punta della Dogana, which is the customs house, to the more intimate in scale Palazzo Grassi, the last Patrician palace on the Grand Canal, where we will have the treasure, the real treasure that have been pull [sic] from the sea, or have been created by Damien Hirst.

When pressed further about how recent so much of the work looks, Geuna asserts:

> The source of inspiration is definitely mythological from antiquities and the making could have been recent. I think that what Damien here would like to do is to provoke question [sic], and is for us to looking [sic] at the beauty of this object to wonder, is it the past being reinvented to give us a vision of the future?[2]

Videos of guided tours show Geuna going into deeper detail on the Amotan story, telling the version beginning with a golden foetal monkey (listed as *The Sadness* in the exhibition guide), claimed to be found in 2008 by fishing crews working off the East African coast, as enacted in the mockumentary. This then led to the excavation, Hirst's involvement and the finds being attached to the Amotan story.[3] Another video shot during the same talk (and published on 31 May 2017) shows gallery director Martin Bethenod explaining that Hirst began making works for the project 'nearly ten years ago' and first entered into discussions with the galleries in 2013, already with the title of *Treasures from the Wreck of the Unbelievable* and ideas around the art collector and works being raised from the seabed in mind. Speaking in Dogana, Bethenod explains that, as the customs house, every import and export in and out of Venice had to be processed through this building, 'and so it made such a perfect sense [*sic*] with every object coming from the sea' for the exhibition to be sited there as well as in the Palazzo Grassi, which has been used to house substantial art collections since the eighteenth century. Furthermore, Bethenod points out that the paired venues have also exhibited historical collections and archaeological finds in recent years.[4]

These videos show the performative side to marketing a product (the exhibition) and brand (Hirst). The Amotan story and the mystery of what caused the boat to sink (Geuna lists sea monsters, a tempest and a crash as possibilities), as well as the ambiguity around Hirst's roles as financer/collector/facilitator/creator build the mystery and raise questions, while the venues' histories and previous exhibitions of unquestionable artefacts add plausibility. Together, these approaches build curiosity for potential international paying visitors. That the talks were given in English and circulated online extends this reach. This was an exhibition and a marketing campaign aimed largely at tourist footfall in a city where tourism has for many years been its main trade, which until 2020 more than doubled its population annually.

Another element of the exhibition's scenery and paratextual extensions in publicity materials and catalogues that simultaneously validate and cast doubt on its stories is the underwater photography by Christoph Gerigk. In 2001, Gerigk was awarded third prize in the Science and Technology category of the annual World Press Photo competition for his coverage of the European Institute of Underwater Archaeology's (IEASM) excavations in Aboukir Bay, approximately fifteen miles northeast of Alexandria, Egypt. His continued documentation of the institute's long-term 'Sunken Civilisations' project led by marine archaeologist Franck Goddio earned him second prize in the same competition and category the following year.[5]

More recently, the findings yielded from these sub-aqua excavations significant for their discovery of the sunken port cities of Thonis-Herakleion, Canopus, Menouthis and Naukratis – lost for so long that they were thought to be mythical – led to major international exhibitions. From September 2015 to January (extended to March) 2016, the Arab World Institute, Paris, presented *Osiris, Sunken Mysteries of Egypt*, comprising around 250 artefacts from the digs which began in the late 1990s, in addition to around forty borrowed from the museums of Cairo and

Alexandria. Framed around the Mysteries of Osiris, the ceremonial rites of the Egyptian deity, visitors were encouraged to participate in an imagined re-enactment of celebratory processions along the River Nile, while also exploring the submerged cities in environments designed by scenographers Sylvain Roca and Nicolas Groult.[6] Rather than being invited to simply see the artefacts, visitors were engaged in performing these dual roles as underwater archaeologists and participants in ancient cultural traditions. Not quite as performative but no less spectacular in design and scope was *Sunken Cities: Egypt's Lost Worlds* at the British Museum, London, from 19 May to 27 November 2016. The first exhibition there to focus on marine archaeology, it involved around 300 artefacts which, similarly to *Treasures*, ranged dimensionally from coins and jewellery to enormous statues weighing six tons.[7] As well as the monumental nature of many of the works, the exhibition's theatricality was heightened by audio installations, videos and lighting arrangements.

Finding and showing these artefacts has recovered cities such as Thonis-Herakleion from the realm of myth. Not only do they resituate what once was a major Mediterranean trading port in history, but the artefacts also provide evidence for its mixed cultural life. Particularly significant is an inscribed stele which confirms that Thonis and Herakleion (named for the Greek hero Herakles) were not separate Egyptian and Greek cities but were in fact one large Greco-Egyptian city with its inhabitants sharing gods and exchanging artistic processes and styles (Sooke 2016). Several reviewers point out that this is no more prominent than in the statue of the deified Ptolemaic Egyptian queen Arsinoe II. As James Pickford describes, '[t]he figure adopts a dignified pose seen in Egyptian statuary [that is, with the left leg forward, a stance denoting power and grace] and is fashioned from local granite. But the artful folds of the delicate garment that she wears are typical of Greek sculpture'. He also quotes exhibition curator Aurelia Masson-Bergoff as saying that 'the discoveries "have completely transformed our understanding of interaction between these great civilisations in the late first millennium"' (Pickford 2015). The finds strongly indicate that socio-cultural histories are more entwined than many biased historians working in the eighteenth and nineteenth centuries would have us believe.

London and Paris, like Venice, are international hubs for tourism, art and culture capable of, in turn, marketing Egypt as a tourist destination to their galleries' patrons.[8] As early as 2000, the potential for tourism of showing these unearthed markers of our ancient ancestors was already being realised. Lost for over a millennium, the findings from the IEASM digs provide growing indicators that ancient Greeks participated in cultural exchanges and lived in mixed communities instead of solely claiming foreign land for their empire's outposts. Rather than this knowledge and how it could impact today's culture and society, it is the money to be made from international tourism that attracts sustained financial backing for continuing excavation and research at the sites. Writing for *The Guardian* around the time of initial discoveries, Brian Whitaker states: 'Archaeology in Egypt has become increasingly influenced by politics and showbusiness. Mindful of its beneficial effect on the tourist industry, government ministers often become directly involved in projects, while major discoveries are carefully stage-managed and invariably televised' (2000). Egypt has since experienced increasing terrorist activity which has affected its numbers of visitors and means that perhaps the works are safer and can entice holiday-makers back if shown internationally. This scale of stage-management was itself stage-managed and is one of many theatrical elements of Hirst's similarly-themed Venice show the year after the British Museum's. It too incorporated media interest around the finds into the fabric of its mythology, using the weight and verisimilitude of Gerigk as not just any underwater photographer, but as one recognized in prize culture for his journalistic documenting of real-world excavations.

In his images of Goddio's team and their findings, Gerigk went beyond purely observational documentation of the events as they happened. With high-key lighting cutting through pollution and the clouding caused by disturbances to the seabed (which are largely absent from the *Treasures* images), Gerigk's framings of giant bronze and stone deities, kings and pharaohs, emerging from the silt into long-lost light or looking up to the surface as schools of fish swim by, possess a dramatic aesthetic that befits the significance of their recovery. Such posing and framing of the artefacts in photographs recurs throughout *Treasures* as indexical markers of their discovery and recovery, which is staged much more elaborately in the accompanying documentary clips screened in both exhibition venues and the feature-length film released on Netflix more than a month after the exhibition's close. Although it was categorised on the streaming site as mockumentary, the film apparently intends to invite an audience unfamiliar with the exhibition to suspend disbelief. It holds back clues revealing the story's fabrication until its closing minutes, when it finally includes long, static shots held for brief durations of coral-covered Disney figures and busts replicating known celebrities such as Rihanna (*Aten*) and Pharrell Williams (*Unknown Pharaoh*). Conversely, whichever route exhibition visitors took, it was never long before they encountered an unsubtle reference to contemporary popular culture being posed or performed within the sculptures.

Often, what is referenced from film culture are characters whose presences and actions rely on special effects in one way or another. These include the Harryhausen-inspired figures discussed later, actor John Hurt's prosthetic make-up in *The Elephant Man* (dir. David Lynch, 1980) recreated in the *Proteus* sculpture, or 'Bruce' the animatronic shark from *Jaws* (dir. Steven Spielberg, 1975) about to catch its favourite meal of a perceived-to-be-sexually-available young woman in *Andromeda and the Sea Monster*. Each example embodies the meeting of ancient and contemporary myths and dramatisations, some of which, as is the case with *The Elephant Man*, are rooted in real-life stories and indicate that the ancient myths provided ways of understanding natural phenomena before the development of the sciences.[9] Such mythologised truths form the basis of the photographic and videographic works that lent verisimilitude as part of the scenery in *Treasures*. While the physical sculptures were real presences in the galleries, the camera-based works mounted around them reinforced the idea that these objects really had been submerged and photographed underwater – and many were, but more likely in special-effects water tanks and protected areas off the Kenyan coast rather than further out in the Indian Ocean.[10]

Gerigk's IEASM photography gave the global public access to the institute's excavations for nearly twenty years prior to the Hirst show, which used that grounding in established reality to indicate to visitors that there was no disbelief to suspend. The presence of the images and Gerigk's name in the exhibition credits (Corry 2017, 71) – should anyone consult them and look him up, the assumption being that most people will not – lends credence to the show's truth claims. Gerigk's work, then, is both process and part of the scenography – literally writing the scene with images of an imagined past for the exhibition items and perpetuating the mystification of their existence. The impression given and largely taken was that the exhibited pieces were collaborations across space, place and time: they were created by ancient-world artists, moved by a freed slave who became an art collector, sunken and damaged in a shipwreck, added to by oceanic life-forms, recovered by marine archaeologists and exhibited to the world by Hirst and the Pinault Foundation. This is the *Treasures* creation myth. As with the performances of the curator and gallery director, the photographs provide as much evidence contrary to the myth as they do to support it. Gerigk's images from the IEASM digs show that, apart from the layers of sand, silt and dead shells that were cleaned off with relative ease, no life-forms had made the artefacts – many of which were far over 2,000 years old – their homes. The photos also show just how dark and murky the bay's shallow waters are. While the 45-metre depth had low visibility, due largely to pollution, the main basin of the Indian Ocean has an average depth of over 3,700 metres. It simply is not feasible to light the ocean floor – particularly for *Hydra* and *Kali*, to be discussed below, which the film claims were discovered in a trench – as brightly and with such clarity as the items appear without special/visual effects facilitation.

It is also relevant to bear in mind the further behind-the-scenes labour of the production-line-like set-up at Hirst's company, Science Ltd, and the outsourcing of casting or carving his sculptures to mould-makers such as the Clarke Partnership and computer-programmed robots who now widely perform the main work of stone and glass carving. As well as anonymous labour, Hirst is associated with sculptures that are made to resemble one material but are in fact another, a trait that *Treasures* pushed to extremes. From giant clam shells, over a Mayan Calendar Stone made of bronze, to bronze statues made of resin, even the materials throughout the show acted as something they were not. An example is the displayed resin replica of *Demon with Bowl (Exhibition Enlargement)*, complete with coral shapes worked into its design, providing a tell-tale indication that it is likely the case for all the coral-covered items that they were sculpted, painted and ocean-dipped to finish them off.[11] As for the question of real coral, my reading on Indian Ocean marine biology suggests that it is within possibility that these kinds of sculptures could provide suitable substrate upon which certain coral types can live. Here is where we encounter slippages between truths, lies and possibilities, the full extent of which is beyond the scope of this chapter to examine. What I will do here is further demonstrate how elements of the *Treasures* story came to be and what truths lie in what appear to be staged postmodern mash-ups of ancient myths.

Writing the Drama

With *Treasures* operating across two venues, visitors could attend wherever they wished first. However, the guidebook determined an order beginning in Dogana, situated where the Grand Canal meets the Venetian Lagoon, upon which the show's fearsome blue bronze *Mermaid* gazed from the building's back exterior wall. Before reaching the above-mentioned entry threshold, footage of the underwater recovery operations played on a screen to the left of the entrance, as well as wall text in English, Italian and French authoritatively outlined the show's background and contents. Equivalent to the introductory text in the guidebook, this is preceded by an epigraph from *The Tempest*, cited here as displayed:

> Full fathom five thy father lies;
>   Of his bones are coral made;
> Those are pearls that were his eyes:
>   Nothing of him that doth fade,
> But doth suffer a sea-change
> Into something rich and strange.
>
> (Corry 2017, 3)

These lines are attributed to William Shakespeare as the author, but when performed in Act I Scene II (lines 400–5) of the 1611 play, they are sung by the supernatural shape-shifting sprite Ariel who was freed from enslavement by Prospero, the usurped and exiled former Duke of Milan now practising sorcery. Upon his master's command, Ariel stages a shipwreck to bring to shore Prospero's betrayers. Under a shroud of invisibility, Ariel sings the above verse to Ferdinand, convincing him that his father, Alonso the King of Naples, has died in the wreck and that his bones are already turning to coral. This is not true; the shipwreck and the deaths are staged to enable Prospero's revenge, and the subsequent actions of the marooned characters are determined by the illusions created by the island's supernatural inhabitants. Caliban and Ariel's shaping of events according to Prospero's design and command bears similarities to the work of Hirst's employees at Science. That Prospero is also a collector draws further parallels between the Shakespearean character and the artist's persona.[12] Alongside seeing the coral-encrusted sculptures being winched out of the water on the screen in the same room, the text to the screen's left indicated that things are often not as they appear, that the truth does lie between lies and truth.

The exhibition's guidebook text is attributed to Amie Corry who has been an editor, writer and head of content for Hirst and Science since 2013.[13] Corry's text goes on to explain the etymology of *apistos* and to detail the life of Amotan. It asserts that *apistos* is ancient Greek for unbelievable, but upon consulting various dictionaries it is more complex, depending on the context. It can further mean: untrustworthy, unbeliever, disbeliever, or faithless. The short definition in Henry Liddell and Robert Scott's *Greek-English Lexicon* is particularly relevant: 'not to be trusted' (1901, 173). From the term stems Apistevism, the practice of not relying on faith to know things. As reviewers such as Julia Halperin point out, 'Cif Amotan II' is an anagram for 'I am a fiction' (2018). He is alternatively referred to as Aulus Calidus Amotan (in an English transliteration of the Greek spelling, the initials would likely be A. K. A.). *Aulus* was a common Latin name meaning plausibility, while the feminine *aula* means palace and *calidus* means warm, hot, fiery, eager, or fierce. *Amotan* in Cebuano means 'to contribute'. It is a derivative of the Esperanto word *ami* meaning love. In reverse, it is the Indian Sanskrit name *Natoma*. And finally, the Latin passive future participle *amota* means 'about to be loved'. As well as providing clues regarding the exhibition's legitimacy and palatial surroundings, perhaps the name also anticipated the polarised and impassioned responses to the show.

The text claims that Amotan was from Antioch and 'lived between the mid-first and early second centuries CE' (Corry 2017, 3). Antioch was an ancient Greek city founded in 300 BCE east of the Orontes River in what was then ancient Syria and what today is near Antakya, Turkey, where some of the tourism-driven planted websites specifically claim to tour. Antioch was a western terminus for goods brought from Persia and Asia to the Mediterranean. It was annexed by Rome in 64 BCE, meaning that it was Roman when Amotan is said to have lived there. It became the third-largest city of the empire after Rome and Alexandria and was an early centre of Christianity.[14] The myth of Amotan and his folly might allegorise the west's transition away from shared, interpretative polytheisms and democracy towards patriarchal monotheisms and despotism. In the story, his greed and the lengths to which he goes to build a temple for the Mesopotamian goddess Ishtar (whose Greek and Roman equivalents are Aphrodite and Venus, respectively) could have vexed another god who took revenge – such is the likeness of his narrative to that of mythological mortals who in ancient legends anger vindictive and jealous gods.

In addition to the creative biographies, web writing and the guide text, the photography and videography, like Atlas, performed much of the exhibition's heavy lifting in writing and documenting the drama.

The -graphy suffix comes from the Greek *graphia*, meaning 'to write, describe or record'. The images appearing among and alongside the artefacts write their stories and, working in conjunction with the gallery and guide texts, invite viewers to imagine the drama of the sinking ship, informed by scenes many of us will have witnessed in all kinds of creative media, not least film culture, literature and modern history.

There is also the writing of the self to consider. The guidebook mentions the enlarged copy of a work being 'commissioned by the collector', but the identity of this collector is ambiguous (Corry 2017, 10). The exhibition highlighted at least three collectors: Amotan as the collector of the *Apistos* hoard, the bronze sculpture *The Collector with Friend* depicting a suited male figure obscured by coral, holding hands and waving with the unmistakeable shape of Mickey Mouse,[15] and *Bust of the Collector* which is a bronze likeness of Hirst. Hirst's vast art collection and his manipulation of the art market is well-documented, and with *Treasures* he has also become a collector of riches, bodies, stories and celebrity likenesses. The exhibition embodies and performs his interests in the dichotomies between science and religion, life and death. Hirst as himself in the Netflix-released film performs the Hirst brand and mythical persona, including telling a version of his artist creation myth, which is believable because it is plausible, much like the show.[16]

Treasures from the Wreck of the Unbelievable (dir. Sam Hobkinson, 2017) imagines and dramatises the types of personnel and processes central to the IEASM digs. It begins with Hirst saying that belief stems from the gaps in what we are told, followed by a range of testimonies from the salvage team that are vague enough to entice the viewer to fill in the gaps. For example, the character Peter Weiss implies that he was struggling with his doctoral thesis when he 'discovered the clip on the internet'. The film then cuts to the grainy handheld footage of a beach dated April 2008, looking like the same beach introduced minutes earlier and labelled as 'Indian Ocean, East Africa'. He claims that the clip was 'entitled "fishermen discover statue"', a real-world search for what brings up many other finds, mainly of a statue of Apollo found off the Gaza Strip.[17] In this case, it is the golden foetal monkey that was displayed in room 13 of Dogana, not so much a precious artefact than a prop. Throughout the film, associative editing links detailed but vague descriptions with enactments – I hesitate to call them re-enactments – which are intercut and crosscut with apparently observational footage from the excavations as they occurred. The amateur documentation of initial dives off the coast of the unnamed beach is shown, all of which is widescreen, with some product placement for GoPro cameras in an unnamed African diver's testimony. Just a few minutes into the film, what appears to be a polished and conventional documentary is revealed under scrutiny to be a more complex scripted showing and telling of implied rather than actual information.

The exhibition relied on an assumption that the camera does not lie, particularly when what it captures appears to be documentary in nature. Even though many people possess access to image-altering technologies such as app filters or Photoshop, general viewers still often do not seem to realise that even the most realist examples of contemporary film and television use colour-grading and computer-generated imaging. We need only read the credits – those undervalued goldmines of information – to learn the truth of production.[18] We must question why, when water tanks and image compositing are used so frequently for marine locations in popular productions, audiences can find such fakery convincing in fiction but visitors largely did not question how clear and bright the ocean-bed images are in the photography and films attached to the *Treasures* project.[19] The film is too polished, cinematic, scripted and performative to have been filmed off-the-cuff over the course of ten years, as it claims. Again, its end credits and some internet searches concerning its participants reveal another story – one in which, like in the exhibition, there exists a tangle of lies and truths presented like acts in a play, the second of which ends with a tempest and the third begins with a fresh dawn and a dramatic discovery that is key to unlocking the truth/lie, history/myth and east/west dichotomies at the crux of the exhibition.

Staging and Restaging

Around two thirds into the film, Peter urges the rest of the team to search further into an area they call the drop-off. Having scanned it before and found nothing, the rest of the team want to draw the expedition to a close. On the last day, they send a remote sub down to take one last look. Huddled around the monitor, the core team build suspense as they glimpse obscured, flickering views of faint figures in the grainy black-and-white image. Eventually, the silhouettes of what turn out to be *Kali and Hydra* become clear, and they announce that they will return for more recovery the following year.

In a way not dissimilar to the film's dramatic reveal of *Hydra and Kali*, the curation in Dogana privileged a range of reveals and spectacular views of the *Hydra and Kali* room as visitors approached. Situated in the double-height space at the venue's centre were two versions of the bronze *Hydra and Kali* sculptures and two lightbox images picturing the 'original' – not marked as such in the guidebook – underwater. The guidebook makes no claims as to the sculpture's authenticity, and the clean, unbroken version is not labelled as a replica. These large versions share the same title, and in this presentation each ought to be considered as one half of a diptych. According to the given measurements, the coral-encrusted version A is 12.5 cm taller, 9 mm longer and almost a metre narrower than its glossy counterpart. They were positioned facing in opposite directions, making comparisons awkward without the aid of photographs. As the eleventh room in the venue, it was a given by this stage that the photo lightboxes provided enough of a narrative so that no further information was needed. Exhibit C was *Hydra and Kali Discovered by Four Divers*, and D was *Hydra and Kali Beneath the Waves*, each mounted in opposing corners and capturing the eternally impending battle between two unlikely adversaries.

While *Hydra and Kali* may be no more than a postmodern mash-up, deeper probing sheds light on the sculpture's significances pertaining to the mixing and staging of ancient-world myths. In Greek mythology, the Hydra of Lerna 'was a poisonous, many-headed water-snake, with the number of its heads varying in art and literature from just a few to as many as fifty or a hundred' (March 2008, 192–93). In the Greek legends, defeating the Hydra was the second labour of the greatest of the mythological heroes, Herakles. Apart from a brief mention in the guide description of *Hydra and Kali*, neither Herakles nor his Roman counterpart, Hercules, feature in *Treasures*, which seems like a glaring omission in such a vast collection spanning a time-period in which the famed demi-god would have been a must-have inclusion. In the myths, Herakles could only the kill the Hydra with aid from his nephew, charioteer and companion, Iolaos, who seared the neck stumps to prevent the growth of new heads when Herakles chopped them off (March 2008, 194). That Kali faces the creature alone with her many arms working independently and efficiently is perhaps a tongue-in-cheek allusion to the idea that women are better multi-taskers than men, however heroic, and that her presence replaces such a canonical figure might also relate to twenty-first-century anxieties in male fandom that gender equality means the death of nostalgia.[20]

If we consider how women are written out of histories and goddesses out of religions, she is not so much substituting a male character but rather reclaiming her rightful place.

Kali is the Hindu goddess of time, death and creation. Typical depictions show Kali with black or blue skin, four arms and holding in each hand a trident, scimitar or scythe, the severed head of a man and a bowl to catch the dripping blood. She is often adorned with a garland of heads and a skirt of severed arms. Her left foot faces forward on the ground while her right rests on the chest of her white-skinned husband Shiva lying beneath her. Her bloodstained tongue protrudes; her hair is wild, showing that she is beyond external control and social norms, and that she possesses unbridled sexuality (Mohanty 2009, 9). Seema Mohanty points out that Kali's 'fame owes a great deal to European Imperialism of the eighteenth and nineteenth centuries as well as to Radical Feminism of the twentieth century'. The former used Kali's 'ghoulishness' to justify converting Indians to the conservative monotheism of Christianity, which in turn reinforced the morality or correctness of divinely decreed monarchies over democracy, the subordination of women in society and the covering up of their bodies. It is no wonder, then, that western feminists would reclaim the idea of Kali. For them, so states Mohanty, 'this defiant goddess was a manifestation of the female collective unconscious that sought liberation from male-dominated regimes' (2009, 5). There is much to discuss in her replacing of Herakles in a battle with a female water monster that can never commence.

While it seems counter-intuitive and audacious to pit the Indian goddess Kali against the Greek Hydra of Lerna, their juxtaposition in fact acknowledges demonstrable historical links between ancient Greece and India, which formed as early as the sixth century BCE (Scott 2016, 4). Looking particularly at the written accounts of Megasthenes, Greece's first official ambassador to the royal Indian court based in Pataliputra (today's Patna) at the end of the fourth century BCE, Michael Scott explains:

> Megasthenes refers to Indian legends that link the birth of their society to his own Greek gods of the Mediterranean. Dionysus, he tells us, once invaded India with an army and, having settled there, taught the Indians how to make wine, build cities and establish law and justice. Fifteen generations later, according to the same legends, the Greek hero Heracles was born among Indians and founded Pataliputra. It appeared, then, that India and Greece, far from being

disparate worlds, had been explicitly interwoven from the earliest times, sharing gods, traditions and practices in kind (2016, 4).

Although wary of the veracity of legends being discussed as history, this is just one of many examples that Scott gives to demonstrate just how interwoven east/west relations were before the common era, and, it seems, before the dominance of the Roman Empire. Considering this, the encounter on equal footing between Kali and Hydra becomes a natural arrangement, and one requiring study from many viewpoints.

There were no fewer than six repetitions of *Hydra and Kali* appearing in different media across the two venues. Table 8.1 shows their order of appearance according to the guide text and the key attributes of each version. *Hydra and Kali* epitomise the exhibition's themes of repetition

Table 8.1: Instances of *Hydra and Kali* from *Treasures from the Wreck of the Unbelievable*

Venue	Room	Exhibit	Title	Material	Size	Notable features
Punta della Dogana	11	A	Hydra and Kali	Bronze	539 x 612 x 244cm	Coral; partial swords
Punta della Dogana	11	B	Hydra and Kali	Bronze	526.5 x 611.1 x 341cm	Full swords; presented as reconstruction but not labelled as such
Punta della Dogana	11	C	Hydra and Kali Discovered by Four Divers	Powder-coated aluminium, printed polyester and acrylic lightbox	244.2 x 366.2 x 10cm	Documentation photograph by Christoph Gerigk
Punta della Dogana	11	D	Hydra and Kali Beneath the Waves	Powder-coated aluminium, printed polyester and acrylic lightbox	244.2 x 366.2 x 10cm	Documentation photograph by Christoph Gerigk
Palazzo Grassi	4	E	Hydra and Kali	Silver, paint	93.5 x 122.2 x 57.5cm	Kali's stance is different: right leg raised, hair in a long braid painted orange
Palazzo Grassi	23	A	Scale model of the Unbelievable with suggested cargo locations	Various (painted plastic)	1:32 scale of the *Apistos*	Miniature inside the scale model of the *Apistos*
Palazzo Grassi	23	L	Kali and Hydra in Battle	Graphite, pencil and silver leaf on vellum	51.5 x 64.8cm	Drawing of the scene; claimed to be Renaissance period

and multiplicity. Corry's guide text for *Hydra and Kali* states that '[t]he multiple extremities of these figures may [...] be read as an expression of movement: the woman's sword-wielding arms presented in three positions at varying heights; and the reeling heads of her foe symbolising the serpent's single thrashing body' (2017, 20). The issue with this likening to modernist impressions of movement in still images is that every sword and every serpent head is unique – a point I develop in more detail after first examining this juxtaposition of foes. Combined with the visual references to film culture throughout the exhibition, the notion of still images representing movement evokes films featuring the stop-motion animated monsters of Ray Harryhausen, specifically the Hydra in *Jason and the Argonauts* (dir. Don Chaffey, 1963) and Kali in *The Golden Voyage of Sinbad* (dir. Gordon Hessler, 1973), both films comprising remixed mythologies. The Harryhausen Hydra has seven heads animated in thrashing, snapping movements as it towers over Jason (Todd Armstrong) during their battle. The *Hydra and Kali* versions also have seven heads, but, like the Medusa heads throughout *Treasures*, each depicts a different deadly snake, including cobras and vipers found in Asia, Africa, Australia and the Americas – a globalised Hydra.

Like the Hydra's heads, the many-limbed Kali provides further pre-CGI cinematic spectacle in *The Golden Voyage of Sinbad*. Evil magician Prince Koura (Tom Baker) animates a statue resembling Kali to fight Sinbad (John Phillip Law) and crew on his behalf to allow his escape. The figure possesses six arms, each wielding a scimitar, instead of four arms each holding a different symbolic object. Such Hollywood appropriations of Kali have been derived from, and in turn have contributed to, western misunderstandings of depictions of the goddess. The extra pair of limbs and her bound hair transfer into the *Treasures* Kali, indicating that she is under the control of a male master to fight his adversaries. It follows that in the sculpture Kali replaces Herakles and the Hollywood Jason, as in the legends the Greek hero defeated the Hydra at the behest of Eurystheus and in the film it is Pelias (Douglas Wilmer) who convinces Jason to search for the golden fleece. Apart from the Hirst branding, this Kali and Hydra are abstracted and removed from servitude. Moreover, Kali's nakedness and raw sexuality are restored in the sculptures.

According to Mohanty, in representations Kali's body became increasingly covered as conservatism rose during British imperialism's civilising mission in India in the nineteenth and twentieth centuries (2009, 5). That Kali is naked, but her hair plaited (and ending in a snake head) in each

Treasures incarnation bears further significance. Mohanty explains that in Hindu traditions plaits are worn by unmarried virgins and that 'Kali is associated with all things black [...]. She defies all that a fair complexion stands for – domestication, gentleness and beauty', but that '[t]he Goddess, or Devi, sheds her dark Kali form and becomes Gauri, who is gaur or fair, only when asked to marry Shiva' (2009, 11). Not only is the miniature which appeared much later in the exhibition's second venue in silver, but Kali's braided hair is also painted a light yellowy orange, giving her a fair complexion in contrast to the black bronze of the large-scale versions. Mohanty continues that, '[a]lthough Kali is considered the consort of Shiva [...] she is also, like most other goddesses, called the virgin. The idea of being a virgin indicates that the Devi, the ultimate Goddess, is subservient to no man' (2009, 14–15). In legends and Hindu belief, Kali is a defender rather than an attacker, and she lets down her hair when called to battle (Mohanty 2009, 12), meaning that when not engaged in fighting, her hair would be braided. However, her hair is bound in every *Treasures* incarnation where she is stilled in a pensive moment before battle, as well as in *The Golden Voyage of Sinbad* while engaged in violence, indicating that, as she answers the call to battle, she maintains autonomy over her sexuality even when under the influence of patriarchal control – the men can make her fight, but they do not have sexual access to her.

The Golden Voyage of Sinbad is also significant when considering the pose or pensiveness of the frozen moment of anticipation before battle. When the Kali statue – as distinct from an invocation of the goddess – in the film first animates, it is poised in a defensive stance pointing its swords towards Sinbad for almost one minute of screen time before their weapons clash. It is not only Sinbad whom it must dispatch, but also his crew. Of course, after a tense action set-piece the eponymous hero and his gang outwit the animated, oversized statue and send it crashing to its demise. Given that Kali is also alone in facing the Hydra in *Treasures*, or at least an equivalent to Iolaos is absent, and the guide text suggests that 'the Hydra's self-regenerating heads have led to the monster's associative relationship with an endlessly repeating task' (Corry 2017, 20) – which is probably more associated with the myth of Sisyphos – the piece could also be performing the repetitiveness and seeming endlessness of tasks regarded in gender normativity as women's labour at the behest of men. With no aide to sear the neck-stumps, this Kali is doomed to eternal battle as her six arms efficiently dispatch heads, only for two more to grow back in each one's place and thereby increasing her further labour at a faster rate than the two-armed Herakles. Perhaps as occurs in feminism and similar ideological struggles for equality, as certain issues are addressed, the more other issues are revealed and need addressing. However, this epic duel only takes place in the theatre of the imagination as, cast in bronze and the slight progression in silver, Hydra and Kali are doomed to always face off, frozen in attack and defence stances, and appealing to the creativity of viewers to envisage what will happen. Contemporary film culture and mythologies offer suggestions here, particularly upon close examination of Kali's swords.

Apart from the show's introductory text explaining that 'contemporary museum copies of the recovered artefacts [...] imagine the works in their original, undamaged forms' (Corry 2017, 3), how the lost sword blades from *Hydra and Kali* A were completed in B is not explained. There is no acknowledgement that most of A's swords are partial and that the shapes of their hilts evoke broadswords with crossguards – an addition to sword hilts that emerged in Eurasia no earlier than the seventh century CE, as far as archaeologists and historians are aware (Csiky 2015). The sword in Kali's top left hand resembles no real-life sword, but an Elven Lord sabre from *The Lord of the Rings* film franchise, called Hadhafang, specifically wielded in battle by Arwen, played by Liv Tyler in *The Fellowship of the Ring* (2001).[21] While the five other swords are different variations of the broadsword, close inspection and further probing on the *Lord of the Rings* wiki fan site draws out resemblances between Kali's weapons and the Ringwraiths' swords, Glamdring, Anguirel, and Narsil. Notably, Narsil is broken near the hilt and its shards re-forged into Andúril,[22] evoking the broken swords in sculpture A, which are presented as renewed in its apparent copy. While inserting the influence of modern and contemporary mythology, the inclusion of such specific swords also references the real Anglo-Saxon practice of naming swords on which *Lord of the Rings* author J. R. R. Tolkien was an expert (Underwood 1999, 54–56). That these are specific, named swords used to defend good over evil in a modern mythology at once reinstates Kali's identity as a defender and, although continuing to westernise her, redresses misunderstandings and representations of her as a ghoulish goddess of death and destruction.

That Kali is so westernised in her appearance and weaponry could be construed as cultural appropriation, but we might also consider her as embodying the conjunction of east and west. Scott identifies Rome and China becoming dominant forces in the ancient world in the third and second centuries BCE as the period when more substantial east/west relations are first known to develop. But with growing connections came increasing conflict (2016, 104). For Mohanty, '[t]he battleground witnesses the collapse of culture and orderly conduct' (2009, 16). Kali, here, also embodies and performs the destruction that is necessary for regrowth and renewal – the labour of which repeats endlessly. Although Hydra is automatically viewed negatively due to her fearsome appearance and association as an antagonist to heroic figures, we must bear in mind my earlier observation that the array of snakes from across the globe in the *Treasures* depictions of her, together with her presence at this encounter stilled in a moment of tension before it can tip over into violence, means that both figures embody and perform mixes of cultures and are both rooted in polytheistic cultural practices, indicating that they are open to multiculturalism and plural identities (Scott 2016, 343). A message for today's real world from this mythical battle that can never begin is that cultural battles need not continue if we agree to coexist.

Changing the Narrative

With the east/west relation we return to Venice. Roger Crowley states: Venice 'lived between two worlds: the land and the sea, the east and the west, yet belonging to neither' (2011, 11). *Treasures* situated it between further tensions: tourist trade and geophysical precarity, art and show-business, culture and spectacle. As Venice's wealth was founded on trade, Hirst's was built from the commodification and trade of art, while his work continues to question what can even be considered as art and possess value as an art object. It is such questions the work asks of us, for what is theatre without an audience? The main criticisms of *Treasures* were that it was too excessive, too glitzy, too rich and too showy and that it presented an overwhelming amount of data to sift through. For users of social media, sifting through too much data to find desired content is already a daily performance. More than data collection, sorting and sifting, exhibitions like *Treasures* not only invite but audaciously dare viewers to play the detective, to act as archaeologists, to perform critical thinking, and to don the mask of data – and, therefore, cultural – analysts. With this essay, I hope to have demonstrated the necessary role of active inquiry that begins to identify not only where lies masquerade as truths, but also, importantly, where truths lie and where they may be found, should anyone choose to look for and excavate them. Everything in the fabric of *Treasures from the Wreck of the Unbelievable*, including its setting of Venice and staged myths from the past and present, facilitate the surfacing and evaluation of hidden, forgotten and erased histories that could grant us Promethean foresight for the future, should we act to change the narrative.

Notes

1. The pages emerging in searches are dated no earlier than the several months leading up to the exhibition's opening and often involve false information. I emailed the given contact for one, and the message bounced back. Examples are available at <https://travelturkeynow.wordpress.com/>, <http://romanseas.co.uk/shipwrecks/apistos_unbelievable/index.html> and <http://principate-era.com/page6/index.html> (last accessed 31 January 2019).
2. Available at <https://www.youtube.com/watch?v=K2j1UlNNYJ4> (last accessed 30 March 2020).
3. Available at <https://www.youtube.com/watch?v=oHVIVBVr0s4> (last accessed 30 January 2019).
4. Available at <https://www.youtube.com/watch?v=Kol_o1-eXjM> (last accessed 30 January 2019). The Palazzo Grassi was formerly owned by the company Fiat, which used the venue as a cultural centre exhibiting '[b]lockbuster overviews of entire cultures and epochs' (Buckley 2016, 75–76).
5. Available at <https://www.worldpressphoto.org/collection/photo/2001/science-technology/christoph-gerigk/03> and <https://www.worldpressphoto.org/collection/photo/2002/science-technology/christoph-gerigk> (last accessed 30 January 2019).
6. Available at <http://www.imarabe.org/fr/expositions/osiris> (last accessed 30 January 2019).
7. Available at <https://www.britishmuseum.org/about_us/past_exhibitions/2016/sunken_cities.aspx> (last accessed 30 January 2019).
8. But unlike Venice, London and Paris do not possess the added urgency and drama of themselves being sinking island cities with access (via the Adriatic) to the Mediterranean.
9. The myths, truths and issues around identity and the body brought together in the *Proteus* sculpture beg deeper examination in a more extensive study of *Treasures*. This can be said of much of the work.
10. My preliminary findings of investigating these claims for a larger study can be found at https://peablair.blogspot.com. The Producers Creative Partnership, Malta, website gives a sense of how staged underwater filming and photography is achieved: available at <http://www.pcpmalta.com/tanks.html> (last accessed 31 January 2019).
11. This claim is further supported by a photograph I took of what appears to be a thumbprint in the coral residue on the side of *Hermaphrodite*. That many but not all of the show's bronzes have the greenish-grey patina typical of bronze disease indicates that they were exposed to salt water for a time.
12. Quoting from *The Tempest* also evokes pre-unified Italy, implicitly acknowledging Venice's history as a city-state at the centre of a powerful and expansive empire free from Roman rule.

13. Available at <https://www.linkedin.com/in/amie-corry-69016665/?originalSubdomain=uk> (last accessed 31 January 2019).
14. Available at <https://www.britannica.com/place/Antioch-modern-and-ancient-city-south-central-Turkey> (last accessed 31 January 2019).
15. Reviewers such as Jacqui Davies (2017) identify the figure as Sergei Eisenstein (2017), while I and others believe it to be Walt Disney, as it is a copy of the copper statue *Partners* (Blaine Gibson, 1993) at Magic Kingdom Park in the Walt Disney World Resort in Florida. Upon comparative study of photographs, the coral obscures too much of the head to be conclusive, which itself adds to further myths and uncertainties in writing about the show.
16. Roger Crowley describes trade as the Venetians' 'creation myth and their justification, for which they were reviled by more terrestrial neighbours' (2011, 4), which bears parallels with Hirst's beginnings and how other artists, critics and collectors feel towards him and the ways in which he drove up commercial art prices.
17. Available at <https://www.google.com/search?q=fishermen+discover+statue&rlz=1C1JZAP_enGB826GB826&oq=fishermen+discover+statue&aqs=chrome..69i57.11051j0j7&sourceid=chrome&ie=UTF-8> (last accessed 2 February 2019).
18. Even the credits in the *Treasures* film are a work of fiction, with searches finding no trace of the given names. On the Internet Movie Database page, the cast list is sparse and awaiting verification, while the crew information includes a visual effects team of ten personnel, mainly image compositors, from UK-based post-production supplier Molinare. Available at <https://www.imdb.com/title/tt6980988/fullcredits?ref_=tt_cl_sm#cast> (last accessed 5 February 2019).
19. Although there were clues throughout the show that its premise was fake, my companion and I witnessed many other patrons believing – or suspending disbelief – in its myths, seemingly ignoring or not noticing them unravelling as the odyssey progressed.
20. I refer here to online outcries that the women-led *Ghostbusters* (dir. Paul Feig, 2016) ruined childhood memories of the 1980s film franchise of the same title.
21. I have been unable to find close enough or frontal images of Kali's face to discern for sure, but there are similarities with Tyler's face. Regardless of who the face resembles, the shape is that of a woman of recent European origin.
22. Available at <http://lotr.wikia.com> (last accessed 4 December 2018).

Owning the (Female) Experience: Theatricality, Writing and Translation in Literature, Theatre and Cinema

Agnieszka Piotrowska

Introductory Remarks

In this essay, I pose questions relating to theatricality, artificiality and spectacle. I will examine how these concepts relate to the notion of translation. In this context, I am particularly interested in how physical experience is translated into writing and ideas, on the one hand, and how ideas and complex emotions are translated into writing, on the other hand. For this process to be productive, I argue, there needs to be a disruption of the mundane and predictable mode of a discourse, which aims at creating an 'original' text. I argue that such a disruption to the mundane can be said to invoke *theatricality*. In making this argument I follow some ideas proposed by Roland Barthes, which I will present briefly later in this essay.

In his seminal work *Absorption and Theatricality: Painting and Beholder in the Age of Diderot*, Michael Fried sides with Diderot in his suspicion of theatricality in art. Fried is primarily interested in the relationship between the painting and what he refers to as 'the beholder' (see Fried 1980, 4), a relationship which can engender the beholder's absorption and concentration in the subject-matter of the painting. It is important to bear in mind that these distinctions were initially coined by Fried in his discussion of eighteenth-century French art and that our discussion of the concept today necessarily departs from Fried's original notion. Theatricality initially meant creating a theatrical moment that draws attention to the work and its author rather than the subject-matter of the work. Theatricality in Fried's terms therefore denotes a superficial relationship to the work, and to the experience thereof on the part of the exhibitor, curator, spectator, but also perhaps on the part of the artist himself: the works that 'play' to the audience and display their mechanics, so Fried claimed, are by definition false, inauthentic and, therefore, might not last. Instead, he advocated the notion of a quieter moment of full 'absorption' in which the artist's work is not on easy display, is not obvious but rather quiet and subtle, enabling the viewer's engagement with the work, and with themselves, in a reflective and contemplative way – the viewer is *absorbed*. Whilst Fried (2011) subsequently discussed some works by video artists (the discipline of the moving image had previously been deemed by him theatrical by definition and therefore not real art), theatricality remained a negative term in his assessment, a signifier of a shallow spectacle rather than deep reflection.

In Theatre Studies, theatricality has been discussed by scholars with different approaches to the word and what it denotes. It is clear that, for the theatre to exist at all, it has to be theatrical in some way– the very quality over which Fried despaired. Semioticians discuss whether any production in the theatre is in fact *a translation*, illustration, fulfilment or supplement of the dramatic text (Davis and Postlewait 2003). Theatricality therefore could be understood as a process that makes a text become 'more'. Roland Barthes famously claimed that 'theatricality is theatre minus text' (Barthes 1972, 26), referring to the system of the signs on the stage which make some productions more theatrical than others; it makes them larger than life. However, he also insisted (which is less commonly evoked) that the theatrical quality can begin at the level of the writing. In the same essay, in his discussion of Baudelaire he brings up the notion of 'artificiality' as opposed to theatricality (29). It is the former notion, artificiality, which in fact has more in common with Fried's use of the term theatricality. One could argue that Barthes, after Baudelaire, sees theatricality as denoting an authentic or original experience (xv). In particular, in his texts on writing he despairs over accepted patterns of expression that one is expected to follow, and yet, in order to be original, one must break conventions so that the attempt at true communication is noticed and registered by the recipient. He writes that . . .

> . . . in literature as in private communication, to be least 'false' I must be most 'original' [. . .]. Whoever wants to write with exactitude must therefore proceed to the frontiers of language, and it is in this that he actually writes for others [. . .]. Originality is therefore the price which must be paid for the hope of being welcomed (and not merely understood) by your reader (Barthes 1972, xvi).

For Barthes, therefore, in stark contrast to Fried, originality can indeed denote theatricality and, yes, authenticity.

In this chapter, I am interested in how some writing becomes original by being theatrical. Before I proceed, I need to clear a further possible confusion here: while a spectacle is a necessary part of theatricality, spectacle on its own, without the element of the original, could be positioned on the other side of artificiality. I will return to this in due course.

Fried's notion of absorption versus theatricality is a very particular use of the concept *out of the theatre* and denotes a moment in which Fried's viewer is outside the work, as it were. However, I argue that the interruption of the absorption could be thought of as something engendering a greater awareness of the beholder vis à vis the work.

In this chapter, therefore, I will explore the links between theatricality and its connection to writing, to truth and lies, and to the notion of translation. I argue that, in order to be truthful, the artist *must* be theatrical and thus transgress the dominant culture or genre. Theatricality thought through in this way could be considered a moment of excess which exceeds the mundane and the routine (like Barthes' example of writing a note of condolences; see Barthes 1972, xvi). This invites further consideration. In this context, I will reflect here on the writing and philosophical thinking of the Polish novelist Olga Tokarczuk, as well as on the writings of one of the most theatrical saints in the history of the Catholic Church, St Teresa of Avila, as presented by Julia Kristeva in her novel *Teresa my Love, an Imagined Life of the Saint of Avila* (2008). Finally, I will reflect briefly on my own work in an adaption of the acclaimed Zimbabwean playwright Stanley Makuwe's play *Finding Temeraire* into an experimental film. The common link between this seemingly eclectic mix of texts is their willingness to break the convention in writing and in staging, in order to experiment, to be original and theatrical at the same time.

Theatricality and Translation

In his 2004 article, 'Early, Classical and Modern Cinema: Absorption and Theatricality', Richard Rushton reviewed the initial term presented by Michael Fried in relation to cinema and film. If the difference between theatricality and absorption is that of a conscious presentation vis à vis an unconscious engagement, then, so he argues, one could compare to the notions of voyeurism and exhibitionism.[1]

Rushton, after Fried, defines theatricality as 'exaggerated and affected in manner of behaviour', or 'extravagantly or irrelevantly histrionic', 'stagy, calculated for display, spectacular' (Rushton 2004, 228). Any artwork, therefore, that openly acknowledges the moment of its creation and through that attempts to draw attention to itself can be said to be theatrical. This is a deeply significant assertion, which is the foundational assumption of this essay.

Rushton also mentions Tom Gunning and his work on the cinema of attractions, in which he says the following:

> The cinema of attractions stands at the antipode to the experience Michael Fried, in his discussion of eighteenth-century painting, calls absorption. [. . .] Early cinema totally ignores the construction of the beholder. These early films explicitly acknowledge their spectator, seeming to reach outwards and confront. Contemplative absorption is impossible here (Gunning 1989, 38; quoted in Rushton 2004, 235).

It is here, in considering theatricality outside theatre (the 'originality' that stems in part from the process of the challenging of the given work), that the notion of distancing, *'ostranenie'*, from Russian formalists, is worth mentioning. The Brechtian distancing effect, on which I have written elsewhere in relation to documentary film (Piotrowska 2014), is productive to consider. This distancing *Verfremdungseffekt* (see Weber and Beinen 2010, 32) by definition would be 'original' using Barthian definition, meaning beyond convention, deployed in order to reveal its own workings and thus to empower the spectator ('the beholder', as Fried would say). It is indeed a positioning of knowledge vis à vis pleasure.

For Brecht, famously, *Verfremdungseffekt* was a political stance designed to challenge dominant ideologies. The issue of presentation therefore is a key issue here; not just from a stylistic perspective but also from an ethical and ideological one. It is this idea of the need to look beneath the surface, which has been picked up by the philosopher Jacques Rancière (2009, 6–7). Rancière develops the idea by arguing that, on their own, images do not say enough to the spectator: in order to resist the subjectivisation of any system of power, including the power of the media, one has to challenge the image and learn what hidden messages it might be bringing with it, and some of that knowledge needs to be acquired by means other than just looking at it. Rancière (2009) further argues that any image, including a documentary image, is fiction, but of course it is a kind of fiction different from a Hollywood blockbuster. It is the fiction – in particular, the theatrical fiction belonging to the 'system of sensibilities' (*le system du partage*) of media systems – which needs to be interrogated, learnt about and challenged (Rancière 2009, 91–95).

The notion of theatricality versus spectacle versus some kind of notion of a quest for the truth, or at least knowledge, brings to mind another French thinker: Guy Debord. In *The Society of Spectacle*, Debord argues (under the influence of Foucault and Althusser) that the ubiquity of spectacle all around an individual in Western society has the effect of alienating and disempowering that individual through a separation from power. The society of the spectacle is thus a society in which an image is used as a substitution for the authentic engaged experience and thus results in a society that is ruled by negativity, passivity, repression and prohibition: 'Separation is the alpha and omega of the spectacle [. . .] The modern spectacle' – in contrast to *theatricality* – 'depicts what society *can deliver*, but within this depiction what is permitted is rigidly distinguished from what is possible' (Debord 1995, 20). More than fifty years after the publication of that seminal book, there are two points worth raising in connection with the spectacle and theatricality: one is that the spectacle of social media that we are invited to take part in is often that of conformity to the dominant discourse rather than difference from it. One could argue that the performativity of the spectacle of the images posted on Facebook, for example, which usually present a slightly better version of our lives, is the very opposite of theatricality – this spectacle, this performance often attempts to present a hetero-normative and neo-liberal ideal of life as not only desirable but perfectly attainable, therefore subliminally suggesting that the responsibility for not reaching the goals of perfect lives lies entirely with the subject rather than society. In addition, the performance/spectacle of visual attainment of the neo-liberal standards of success suggests that it is easily measurable in terms of financial rewards or recognition. As such, I suggest here that this notion of spectacle is directly opposed to theatricality as I have defined it in this essay. Theatricality becomes originality when it invites its beholders to question the dominant discourse. Through its very flamboyance and non-compliance with the demands of societal conformity, it is by definition a transgressive and subversive gesture. Spectacle is therefore very different from theatricality.[2] Lisa Plummer Crafton (2011) in her book *Transgressive Theatricality, Romanticism and Mary Wollstonecraft* focuses on this very aspect of the theatrical production of femininity on the part of the now famous feminist. Crafton draws attention to a notion of the politicisation of the theatre and the notion of the theatricalisation of culture and politics – the notion of conformity or generative and productive theatricality. It is possible that for historical reasons women have had to use various theatrical tools to fight patriarchy, in order to be noticed and have a voice of their own, never mind a room of their own. One could venture further, therefore, that theatricality has always been a tool deployed more readily by women rather than men, or perhaps, more accurately, by people who have chosen to adopt a certain theatrical femininity as a mode of relating to the world.[3]

In my own film creative work, I use theatricality to dislodge the viewer's – reader's – set of preconceived notions. In *Married to the Eiffel Tower* (2009), for example, it is the image of the women being physically close to objects that creates – or begins to create – a space in which to challenge the heteronormative standards of behaviour. In my most recent work, in Zimbabwe's post-colonial settings I have been exploring the possibility of working through post-colonial trauma through collaborative arts projects. Theatre and theatricality have been the core of this work, as well psychoanalytical paradigms. Here, I will also briefly reflect on my film *Repented* based on Stanley Makuwe's work. I will get to this project at the end of this essay, but here it is worth mentioning that at the beginning of the film the key female character changes her clothes for a more flamboyant outfit as a way of embodying theatricality. The gesture empowers her to proceed to face the man who betrayed her in the past. As she arrives in the ghetto, she cuts a curious figure with her red theatrical dress and green high-heeled shoes. All of this is designed to signal a disruption of a normal routine that will engender a transformation.

I will now turn my attention to examples of writings where theatricality is deployed to create such generative dissonances.

(Theatrical) Journeys

Olga Tokarczuk's novel essay (or essay novel), in English titled *Flights*, won the International Booker Prize in 2018. As its blurb on the back page says, *Flights* is about 'travel in the twenty-first century and human anatomy, broaching life, death, motion and migration'. The volume, very theatrical and consisting of bizarre attractions throughout, was initially written in Polish some ten years earlier. The novel was translated into English by Jennifer Croft, who shared the award with the author. As a scholar and creative person whose first language is Polish, I have to admit that I have found some of the translating solutions of the novel challenging, despite the English version's excellent voice. I have found it a curious straightening of Tokarczuk's convoluted, theatrical and ambiguous language at times. For a start, the work's Polish title *Bieguni* feels very different from *Flights*. 'Bieguni' is not a proper word in Polish, or at least not a word anybody in Poland would know (Tokarczuk explains in the novel that bieguni is the name of an ancient nomadic tribe, which may or may not be the case). Bieguni sounds as if, etymologically, it has something to do with running (*biegac*), but also with the word 'pole', as in the North Pole (*bieguny* would be the plural of pole). The title therefore immediately sounds strangely uncanny, foreign, exotic and, yes, theatrical in its evocation of travel. *Flights*, on the other hand – well! Flights just sounds like flights – has to do with a journey but of an ordinary kind, with airplanes and the airports, and maybe flights of fancy, and maybe even escapes, but the word is just an existing word and has lost the connotations of the theatricality that the original title had.

Bodies and Language

There is another concept to consider. Theatricality in the theatre is a material bodily experience. A relationship between bodily experience and speech was, of course, crucial at the outset of psychoanalysis. In *Autobiographics in Freud and Derrida* (1990), Jane Marie Todd makes a connection between a bodily symptom and an autobiographical statement, particularly linking it to the theatrical expressions of suffering by early hysterics: 'The hysterical body is a text, in fact, an autobiographical text. Every symptom tells a story about the patient's life, or rather several stories' (Todd 1990, 5). Todd further points out that the work of a psychoanalyst is really that of a translator, a translator of symptoms. Freud calls this collaboration, this task of translation, 'an analysis'. Todd further glosses that analysis is the name given to 'an autobiographical practice whose principal purpose is neither to testify nor to confess (one's sins or one's devotion), though both modes may be part of an analysis. The work of analysis is autobiographics as *cure*' (5–6).

One could take issue with the above – or many issues – one of these being Freud's at times patriarchal attitude to females which I have discussed elsewhere (Piotrowska 2019). I am putting a marker here but bracketing the discussion in order to focus on another question: if naming one's experience and thus drawing attention to it is always 'theatrical', meaning in some way a spectacle, then is translating one's experience into words always a form of creative sublimation, and therefore also therapeutic, for both the artist and her audience?

More on *Flights*

The narrator of *Flights* creates a meta-system of meaning significantly different from the obvious ways of thinking about links between experience and its physicality and the language. She does so indeed by refusing any form of absorption (borrowing Fried's term again) and instead at all times displaying flagrant originality and theatricality as a form of challenging the accepted ways of writing and of thinking about the world. Tokarczuk early on puts a curious disclaimer into her novel – which, as I have mentioned, is all about travel. Sensationally and provocatively, she believes that the translation between experience and language fails.

The English version of *Flights* is over 420 pages long, and some of its sections are almost baroque in their richness and curious phrasing, despite the translator's valiant efforts to make the language straighter. The female narrator (who incidentally is never named and has many similarities with the author, but who is not the author) questions the whole project of actually describing things through language. She bemoans: 'The truth is terrible: describing is destroying'. Then she elaborates: 'Which is why you have to be careful. It's better not to use names: avoid, conceal, take great caution in giving our addresses, so as not to encourage anyone to make their own pilgrimage. After all, what would they find there? A dead place, dust, like the dried-out core of an apple' (Tokarczuk 2018, 75). To Tokarczuk's narrator, the (intersemiotic) translation of an experience always fails.

In order to avoid this danger, therefore, in a book about travel and different places, the narrator focuses on people and stories and *not* the places where they happen. She mixes fiction and facts, and real places with made up ones. Her aim is to disturb the viewer, and maybe to inspire, but not to convey any concrete knowledge. Her stories of body parts in jars, astonishing stories of disappearances and re-appearances, horror-like accounts of bodies being stuffed, or long-lost lovers re-found only to be destroyed by curious forces, aims singularly, through its theatricality, at getting the reader to imagine at least a different form of subjectivity – outside the neo-liberal systems of Western Europe or the ultra-conservative Poland. Additionally, rather than being a nuisance, the dreaded passenger terminals most passengers would prefer to avoid in Tokarczuk's novel become mythical places where one meets extraordinary people, including philosophers, who, through bizarre theatrical performances, attempt to direct the weary traveller (and of course the reader) to a different way of thinking about the world. They fuel originality and theatricality.

One such mythical group comprises travel psychology scholars who are somewhat related to psychoanalysis ('travel psychology has not cut all ties with psychoanalysis' [Tokarczuk 2018, 81]). A certain young female lecturer attempts to interest airport passers in her lecture address, and the superiority of motion and fluidity over constancy, consistency and stability, which in any event are but an illusion related to fear. As this becomes a spontaneous airport conference, she explains that travel psychology 'studies people in transit, persons in motion, and thus situates itself in opposition to traditional psychology, which has always investigated the human being in a fixed context, in stability and stillness – for example, through the prism of his or her biological constitution, family relationships, social situations and so forth' (80), The narrator's key philosophical point is that, if a translation of the experience is bound to fail, you might just as well abandon any attempt at fidelity to it and instead have fun in creating – well, theatre and, yes, enjoyment (as in Lacanian *jouissance*; see Lacan 2006) stemming from being transgressive and theatrical, not quiet and contemplative.

In *Flights*, another lecturer – this time male – at the same *ad hoc* airport symposium offers further insights into the way in which this novel-essay or fragmentary narration is constructed. Tokarczuk makes the reader 'listen' to his presentation which insists that it is impossible to build 'a consistent cause-and-effect course of argument or a narrative' (83). He instead suggests that, in order to reflect human experience more accurately, it might be necessary 'to assemble a whole, out of pieces of more or less the same size [...]. *Constellation*, not sequencing, carries truth' (8; my emphasis).

This thought functions as a key one of the whole book – things do not come in a sequence, they come and go, feelings come and go, and impressions come and go. Life and the world are fluid – experience is transient. Even though the actual physical places might appear constant, they are far from it; they are in constant flux, which is why any attempt to describe them with words will fail miserably. The unsaid theme of the book which links it to theatricality is also its anti-establishment stance, anti-stability, anti-coupledom, anti-predictability of any kind. Its anti-description stance is indeed a stance for theatricality and against translation as an epistemological project.

There are 116 stories in the book, and they are at times over-indulgent and clearly luxuriating in the pleasure of writing, and perhaps more so in Polish than in English. The narrator of *Flights* is not exactly an unreliable narrator; she is a sort of theatrical, constellational, unnamed narrator.

The stories that Tokarczuk's narrator tells span centuries and have something important in common, namely their attention to the body. Whilst the blurb of the book speaks about anatomy, and there are indeed some gruesome stories about obtaining and preserving body parts, the main striking qualities of *Flights* are its reflections about bodily *experiences*, bodies perishing or being preserved, bodies of potential lovers being replaced or at least replaceable, bodies of unborn infants being wrenched out of the bodies of their mothers and then kept in jars with chloroform. But bodies are only vessels for spiritual adventures, for the theatrical encounters with the divine. Tokarczuk and her unnamed narrator make sure the reader does not miss that:

> Once the gods were external, unavailable, from another world, and their apparent emissaries were angels and demons. But the human ego burst forth and swept the gods up *and inside* [...]. Only in this way can the gods survive – in the dark, quiet nooks of *the human body*, in the crevices of the brain, in the empty spaces between the synapses. This fascinating phenomenon is beginning to be studied by the fledging discipline of travel psychotheology (Tokarczuk 2018, 181; my emphasis).

The sudden mention of theology in Tokarczuk's constellatory narrative is unexpected. The narrator makes a leap, and the reader is confused yet again and realises that the journey is after all not in the physical world alone. If the describing of the physical places is hopeless and impossible, language may still have a role in describing the fleeting moment of defining who we might be, on the one hand, and commenting on our clumsy communications, on the other.

St Teresa – Theatricality through Body and Language

A conversation about the body and language often becomes a conversation about God, which brings me to the psychoanalyst and philosopher Julia Kristeva's peculiar novel *Teresa my Love, an Imagined Life of the Saint of Avila* (2008), which is not a project entirely dissimilar to *Flights* in so far that it has been written by a female author; it focuses on a lone female narrator (and indeed the main protagonist is a single woman) and consists of fictional and philosophical sections. Therein the similarities end. While the unnamed narrator of Tokarczuk's novel repeatedly voices her suspicions vis à vis language and states that it must be used only as a gesture of despair, Kristeva's main notion is that St Teresa's complicated life, her suspected epilepsy, her mental health issues, her problematic relationships with others in her daily life and, finally, her deep pain and pleasure emerge only because of her writing and through it. The experience is secondary – the writing is primary. The theatricality of St Teresa's visions would have been lost forever, if not for naming it. The meaning can only come through writing. Without the description, the interpretation, the creation of the narratives, not only would Teresa of Avila have been totally forgotten *after* her lifetime, but also, and importantly here, she would have lost this precious *jouissance* in her lifetime. Her experience was not enough to make sense of her life. Indeed, without the writing, her visions would not have become 'original' or 'theatrical'. It is her writing, the description of the experience which transcends mere spectacle so as to become *more*.

Kristeva's argument, and her thesis, is therefore exactly the opposite of that of Tokarczuk: while the latter says that the experience is always superior to its narrativising, the former praises the process of writing and the process of legitimising theatricality through it:

> And so I arrived at this conclusion: Teresa's ecstasy is no more or less than a writerly effect! Spinning-weaving the fiction of these ecstasies to transmute her ill-being into a new being-in-the-world, Teresa seeks to 'convey', to 'give to understand' the link with the Other-Being as one between two living entities: a tactile link, about contact and touching, by which the divine gifts itself to the sensitive soul of a woman, rather than to the metaphysical mind of a theologian or philosopher. To sense the sense, to render meaning sensible: in Castilian, Teresa's writing and her ecstasy overlap (Kristeva 2008, 105).

Teresa of Avila, in her writings, which she began to carry out only on behest of her male confessors in order to help her soften her pain and improve her health, is also a translation of a kind. What is crucial to understand here is that St Teresa was waging a war, for *her place* in a system which did not allow for such curious women to exist. The times of St Teresa's life were brutal. This was sixteenth-century Spain, with the accusations enunciated by Luther and the Reformation against the Catholic Church, on the one hand, and the threat of the Illuminati, on the other. According to Kristeva, Teresa of Avila was lucky in so far as she had the protection of her priestly father confessors, the Jesuits. Her ecstasy could have even been seen as heresy and led to severe repercussions. However, the historical situation was complex, and the Roman Catholic Church at the time did need something different and attractive to hold on to the congregations shaken by the Reformation. This is the place Teresa was developing – not necessarily unconsciously: Kristeva suggests that this was a clever woman who, in a deliberate way, fought her demons and those of the society in which she found herself. In the misfortune of her poor health, Teresa was therefore very lucky to have met some people (male philosophers) who would support her, and it was very lucky indeed that she was able to write. In other words, she was in a position to intersemiotically *translate* her bodily and spiritual experience into words and indeed develop her own *place* in the system. The fascinating aspect of Teresa's life and work is its connection between theatricality and absorption, as uniquely in her person these two morphed into each other, and one would not exist without the other.

The Holy Inquisition took some interest in her 'theatrical' visions and her writing. Her Jesuit father confessors, well-positioned within the Church hierarchy at the time, convinced them that Teresa was no Illuminati but a legitimate visionary who could document her experiences in her writing to the benefit of the Church. The discussion of her usefulness to the Counter-Reformation is beyond the scope of this essay, but it is important to say that it was quite extraordinary how the intellectual religious elite of the time, Jesuits and Dominicans, grabbed the opportunity of the spectacle in order to attract the masses back to its fold (see, for example, Eire 2019). We will never know what happened all these centuries ago, but we know something: Teresa translates her religious faith and her deep *autoerotic* enjoyment, her *jouissance* into words, into a theatricality that was finally readable to others, and this ability saved her. The writing was her salvation, the creativity was her key to freedom and more to power within a society that did not tolerate powerful women with any degree of ease. Kristeva sees this process of translation from the bodily suffering and pleasure to *writing* as crucial. Without her writing, she would have perished – at best, she might have sunk into obscurity; at worst, she might have been imprisoned and even 'disappeared'. It was her writing that saved her – not metaphorically, but literally. And her writing was deeply 'theatrical', meaning dislodging those who knew about her visions from their comfortable and ordinary lives. Her theatricality, her *mots justes* were at the heart of her mysticism but also, indeed, at the heart of her worldly success.

> Hunting for the mots justes, for an exact image of the touching-touched body thrown open to the plenitude of Other-Being, Teresa adds to the water fiction of the Life and later works of fiction of *overlapping dwelling* places inside *a castle*: heaped, penetrable, ostensibly numbering seven but consisting of a host of doorless rooms and cellars, porous spaces separated as if by the stretches of translucent film (106; emphasis in original).

Finding Temeraire and *Repented*

If St Teresa in Kristeva's book could inhabit one of the stories told in *Flights*, then so too could Primrose, the main character of Stanley Makuwe's play *Finding Temeraire*, which premiered first at the Harare International Festival of the Arts in May 2017 (and which I directed). The play was then performed in New Zealand where the Zimbabwean author now lives (although this time I did not direct). I then adapted it to the screen as a medium-length experimental film entitled *Repented* (2019). Here the issues have been plentiful, for a male Zimbabwean author wrote a strong female character and asked a European female director to direct it. Makuwe wrote a very powerful female voice and asked me to direct the play in order, so he said originally, to give the play the right emotional engagement with the material. There have been very many works on cinema and adaptation (for example, Andrew 1984, Cohen 1979, Corrigan 1999, Stam 2004), but here I am trying to focus in particular on the process of describing and naming what adaptation might mean in terms of theatricality and originality. I am also interested in the ability of writing to describe physical experience as an enabling procedure – not only enabling knowledge, but also facilitating deep enjoyment, or psychoanalytical *jouissance*. The case-study of my own work which I am using here is but one example, but the questions raised above have broader significance, also in terms of establishing the relationship between the experience and the description of that experience. Here, the particular translation occurs between the two, between author (and therefore the reader and the viewer) and the experience described.

Finding Temeraire and then *Repented* was an inter-cultural collaboration, the examples of which I have given before (Piotrowska 2017). Here, the play was written in English, and not in the local language Shona, the initial process of translation taking place in the writer's mind – as the characters lived in colonial times, it is possible that English was indeed their main shared tongue. Nonetheless, in my experience of Zimbabwe in contemporary times, people would mostly speak Shona to each other in intimate circumstances, despite English being one of the legal languages. Stanley Makuwe takes pleasure in his mastery of the English language, writing a voice for a subaltern woman (that is, inter-gender, inter-lingual translation), and asked a European woman director to translate it for the stage and the film (intersemiotic translation). I was slightly anxious, but I considered the situation and was seduced by the beauty and strength of Makuwe's work, so I put other doubts aside. Between us, we managed to subvert and circumvent the inter-gender and inter-lingual issue of the female voice being written by a man.

Finding Temeraire takes place in a former mining village called Mashava. The play is a two-hander, consisting of a woman visiting an ex-lover for revenge. Primrose carries on long monologues about the past, before actually revealing her own identity as that of Temeraire's former lover and the mother of his son who, faced with his coldness and the indifference of the world, has a psychotic breakdown, murdering her baby soon after his birth. The play's construction works in a way that in part is indeed similar to Tokarczuk's 'constellation', in so far as the main character re-tells a number of short stories of their life in pre-independence Mashava. It is interesting to consider that the process of finding her voice, rather like with St Teresa in Kristeva's essay novel, makes it possible for Primrose to find a different place for herself: through the words spoken at last, she shifts from a crazy vengeful woman to a place of forgiveness. Makuwe lets his character create a space in which the words at last become an important speech act. Here, theatricality creates a performance for the lover who never listened to Primrose when they were lovers. Now there is a demand that she must be heard, and she is, finally, although in order to achieve this, she carries out a certain amount of violence, including gagging her former lover.

The play, like *Flights*, opens with a description of loneliness which leads into a story. The arrival of the woman is an intrusion, an unwanted visitor – on the surface, but in another way, this is a deeply yearned-for interruption of the loneliness. Temeraire, who remains silent for most of the play, begins it this way: 'I am Temeraire, once the plumber of Mashava. It is like this. I am killing cockroaches when this woman comes to my house. At that time the afternoon sun is hot but not too hot' (Makuwe, *Finding Temeraire* unpublished manuscript).

The stage direction after the first short introduction is 'a crumbling house', and the very first words uttered by Primrose relate to the settlement's state of decay, the Compound, as she calls it, now infested by cockroaches. I will come back to the presence of cockroaches in the play, but for now let us just consider the character of Primrose and her long monologues, both before she physically overwhelms Temeraire and afterwards. Her stated plan is revenge. Once she has tied and gagged him, she appears to be preparing to hurt him further. 'She circles him, like she wants to tear him apart'. She enjoys taunting him, too: 'Tell me, Temeraire. Are you afraid to die? Are you afraid of death? Do you fear hell?' Yet, she also appears to still consider whether torture might not be enough. 'Not so fast. Your type dies better in a slow cooker'. And then: 'Temeraire, I am not here to kill you. I'm here to piss in your face' (Makuwe 2017, 11, 13).

Crucially, before any of her torture can take place, she demands that he talk to her – for it appears he never really talked to her in the past:

Primrose: You don't want to talk.
She sharpens the knife.
Primrose: Ooh, today you will talk. I swear, you will talk (14).

The story that Primrose tells Temeraire (as well as the audience) is that of a subaltern woman not only not being listened to by anybody but also really not knowing how to *translate* any of her experiences or emotions into words. In the past, as a very young woman, as she describes, she never learnt how to find pleasure in talking (never mind writing). This is reminiscent of the (post)colonial melancholy, as Ranjana Khanna would say, and its metaphorisation – that is, the ability to describe emotions, the negative ones, which will lead to violence (on this point, see Piotrowska 2017). Psychoanalytically, we know that, in order to develop a place for one's subjectivity, it is necessary to use words, to talk, or to write – there is no other way. However, the only *jouissance* that Primrose knew in her youth was a simple bodily pleasure – which, when corrupted, turned into a full psychotic episode and physical violence. There is nowhere to go, and when she is abandoned by all with her unwanted baby son, she first strangles him with a scarf that she shows Temeraire and then drowns him in the white men's sewage pond.

Through her long speeches, Primrose is able to develop her own place, which does not depend on violence – not even on her body this time, but on language. This is the journey of describing, for the first time, her emotions and her suffering. She is able to arrive at a point when she can move beyond her despair and her fury – and eventually forgive Temeraire. Despite Makuwe's mistrust of descriptions and naming – emotions as much as places – the naming does work. When Primrose leads Temeraire to the sewage pond to look for their son buried there twenty-five years ago, clearly a metaphorical gesture of despair, she demands that he name him. Naming is crucial after all, for without naming the experience is meaningless and does not last. Words do matter: 'Do you have a name for your son, Temeraire? . . . Name him. Name him now so that we call him by name'. She waits. He says nothing. 'When you call someone, you call them by name. You can't just say, "hey you, hey you", as if you are one of those white people whose shit swallowed your son's dead body. There has to be a name, Temeraire. This is your son, not your garden boy. You are the father. Name him' (Makuwe 2017, 22).

In Makuwe's play, Temeraire, who by now has totally lost the power of speech, fails to name their dead son, and the word he eventually enunciates is the one word which by now really matters to him: her name, 'Primrose'. For our film, we decided that he would not speak at all, and he only begins to narrate the experience once some time has elapsed.

In his classic work on adaptation, Robert Stam defines adaptation as 'less a resuscitation of an originary word than a turn in an ongoing dialogical process. Intertextual dialogism, then, helps us transcend the aporias of "fidelity"' (Stam 2004, 24). Later in the volume, in his discussion of *Robinson Crusoe*, Stam quotes author Salman Rushdie, who celebrates 'hybridity, impurity, intermingling, the transformation that comes of new and unexpected combinations of human beings, ideas, politics, movies, songs' (Rushdie; in Stam 2004, 362). He concludes by writing that 'artistic innovation [...] occurs on the transnational borders of cultures and communities and discourses', and 'it is only in the eyes of another medium [...] that a medium reveals itself fully and profoundly' (Stam 2004, 364–65). It is beyond the scope of this chapter to review critiques of Stam's view, and my case is very different – it was a collaboration with a Zimbabwean writer, which in some ways was simple and respectful to the original. In other ways, particularly in the screen version, my work did take Makuwe's play into a slightly different direction, without, I hope, changing the spirit of his work.

My main innovation regarding the theatre production of *Finding Temeraire* was nothing out of the ordinary regarding the writer/director collaboration. Among other things, I lowered the ages of the main characters for reasons of my own – the actors Charmaine Mujeri and Eddi Sandifolo are my trusted collaborators, and I had confidence that they could pull off the difficult parts. I also thought that it was possible to imagine the characters from twenty or twenty-five years ago as young rather than already middle-aged then – and I, in fact, questioned in any event the initial suggestions of their ages as written by Makuwe. My vision was that Primrose would have been a very young woman indeed, naïve in her infatuation with Temeraire.

The key issue of the adaption of Makuwe's play was indeed the issue of the translation of the sense of theatricality of the piece without making it too much like a theatrical performance. To this end, I decided to deploy an additional level of intertextuality – and that was through the use of black-and-white archive footage not necessarily directly linked to the proceedings, or rather linked thematically and conceptually to the emotions of Primrose. This seems a very simple idea now and almost obvious, but it was neither of these two things when I first presented it as a plan to the film's editor Anna Dobrowodzka. We then experimented with introducing split screens to the film, again making it even more distancing and theatrical, both in order to offer different perspectives onto the narrative and to translate the historicity of it onto the screen, at times alongside the live action of the drama between the two main characters. All of the footage we used would have been shot during colonial times in Rhodesia and South Africa, by those who were either supporting the oppressive regime or directly hired by representatives of it. All of it was shot by men. We reclaimed the footage in order to give Primrose more power. The final element of this discussion of this particular theatricality is the notion of ethics and fidelity regarding using the archive as found footage. In his essay on 'The Ethics of Appropriation', Thomas Elsaesser reminds us that 'the origins of found footage films, as opposed to compilation films, are usually located within the Marcel Duchamp tradition of Dada and conceptual art, of Surrealism and the *objet trouvé*, the 'found object'. He continues: 'The point of such a stranded object, left behind by the tide of time, is that it is made beautiful and special by the combination of a recent loss of practical use and its perishable or fragile materiality' (Elsaesser 2015, 32).

The situation here is both different and similar: different because the archive and the split screens have a direct role to play in the film, which is not to do with beauty, but rather with truth and knowledge – and indeed the writing and the describing of what life may have been like in the past. However, this appears to be only a part of the story: the characters of the play *Finding Temeraire* remember *the place* of Mashava as a good place. True, it is to do with them being young at the time, but there is also a certain ambivalent and ambiguous nostalgia which they both seem to evoke and which Makuwe has captured in his play. The nostalgia might be indeed for the rigid, predictable and fixed, as opposed to the independence which has brought with it cockroaches – a most bizarre image in Makuwe's play, which resonates uncomfortably with the known colonial insults towards the local population. Now, they stand for a dirty mess and lack of order – even as the order of the past was a denigrating and, in the end, hated order. In our appropriation of the archival footage, we also wanted to convey what it is that was being missed – as it was not just the profound injustice and oppressiveness of the place, but also parties and dances and fun, almost as a gesture of defiance, as well as, painfully, a re-enactment of the systematic inequality.

The split screens and the archive clearly spoil a spectator's absorption in the film, but they also add to the sense of theatricality and, along with that, so I would add, to the film's authenticity and originality.

(Tentative) Concluding Thought

In this chapter, I have suggested that theatricality can be close to the term 'originality' as proposed by Roland Barthes, not only in theatre and film, but also in literature and writing. I have tried to take issue with Fried's assertion that theatricality is a harbinger of superficiality on the part of artist and beholder alike, and that instead it can be thought of as something that creates a productive disruption, not only on the part of the artist, but also very much on the part of the person who receives the work. I have suggested that, in the creation of any form of theatricality in the sense of distancing, a process of translation takes place: the translation from experience to a public presentation. The notion of an interruption of the mundane seems quite an important concept to interrogate further – in different iterations of cultural creations as well as in society at large.

Notes

1. Similarly, Metz (1982) compared voyeurism to '*histoire*' and exhibitionism to 'discourse'.
2. See also Rushton (2001) on the spectacle in *Gladiator* as the harbinger of the end of times.
3. The seminal essay on femininity as masquerade by the psychoanalyst Joan Riviere (1986) would perhaps demand a discussion of a certain form of theatricality, but this is outside the scope of this short paper.

10

Performance, Photography, Theatricality and Citationality: Theatricality as a Mode of Performing Citation in the Still Photographic Image

Allan S. Taylor

Photography's inherent theatricality has been evident since its origins, when Hippolyte Bayard first posed in protest against the endorsement of the Daguerrotype in his work *Self-Portrait as a Drowned Man* (1839). Pauli (2006, 13–15) refers to Bayard as an actor, storyteller and photographer, and the idea of posing for camera has become ingrained in our cultural consciousness. Initially this was due to the technical limitations of exposure times requiring a pose to be struck and held in order to create a successful photograph, but more latterly has become an intentional tool used in both domestic and professional photography so as to produce a certain effect. The tension that arises in photography as a medium in particular is what Barthes originally described as the specific claims that it makes on presence and the spectator's perceived desire for that realism that has given theatricality such a problematic position in photography (Barthes, 2000, 5–6).

Theatricality has, historically, been disparaged particularly by Fried (1998b, 17, 164), who states that its presence in artwork is somewhat soporific and encourages passivity in the spectator,[1] arguing that such theatrical works project their presence onto the viewer and anticipate the role of cinema in contemporary practice. Taylor dismisses this anti-theatrical approach, suggesting that the constructedness of performance signals its artificiality to reveal an anti-theatrical prejudice which in more complex readings recognizes the constructed as coterminous with the real (Taylor 2003, 6). She states that it is possible for performance to be 'real' in whatever terms it is understood. This is confluent with Rancière's notion that drama is *necessary* in imagery, if there is to be any action (Rancière 2009, 87).[2]

Henry also supports this positive view of theatricality by describing the gesture specifically in relation to postmodern photography, as that which 'knows itself to be appearance' – a self-reflexive 'mirror' revealing the nature of contemporary representation and that theatricality has historically (and perhaps wrongly) earned itself a bad name (Henry 2006, 113). She admits that, while early-twenty-first century photography 'makes no effort' to deny the spectator constructed fictions, what underlies this is an invitation for the viewer to 'participate in an imaginative engagement with representation itself and with the state of affairs in general' (154). In turn, she illustrates that the blurring between theatricality and photography is not caused by the fictions it creates *per se*, but by the way in which it can visually create situations and scenarios through which spectators can identify contemporary culture and their relationship to it.

Therefore, the shift of perceiving the presence of performance and its associated theatricality in photographic works is not a matter of using performance as a form of dramatic metaphor, and neither are these images intended to be fictitious pictorial narratives created for the camera. Although narrative may happen in the spectator's individual enactment of the photograph, these acts are meant to be viewed as staged actions that call upon the practice of citationality as a way to disrupt, deconstruct and analyse performative utterances generated through performance. It is only through the intentional performance of such citations that are then captured and displayed as photographs that we can deconstruct, analyse and consider the role of such citations in contemporary culture.

In this chapter, I examine the idea of employing theatricality as an intentional tool in photographic practice – particularly in instances of performance to camera – as a way of calling upon the power of citation as a way of 're-presenting' culture to the spectator. As an intentional mode of delayed performance, this kind of practice allows the spectator the *différance* (or simultaneous distance and deferral, from Derrida 1988) to consider such citations within a wider structural unconsciousness. Using Auslander's arguments on the performativity of performance documentation and borrowing his example of Yves Klein's *Leap into the Void* (1960) and its subsequent appropriations by Yasumasa Morimura (2010) and Ciprian Muresan (2004), I will illustrate that, beyond being used as a tool to proliferate and disseminate performance, photography that involves such performed and theatrical moments has a wider political, social and cultural function when viewed as a means of presenting and representing citation.

Différance and the Image: Photography as Deferred Performance

Employing the term citation signals an awareness of the way in which the present gesture is always an iteration or repetition of preceding acts. It therefore points to a wider collective dimension of speech and action. Derrida would argue that there is no such thing as a performance that is not a repetition, since iterability is a structural characteristic of every mark (Derrida 1988, 15). For him, it is impossible to distinguish between citational statements, on one hand, and singular, original statements, on the other. This is because an intention to say or do anything can never be entirely present to itself; there is always at work what he calls a 'structural unconsciousness' (18). The distinction is useful for thinking about different art practices and the aims associated with them. The term *performative* in relation to performance-to-camera then could be reserved for those putting into play repetition and the iterative character of the citation.

Engaging with theatricality through the medium of photography requires a switch in temporal register; as a consequence, one might view the reason for employing photography in performance practices through the lens of Derrida's concept of *différance* (1988, 7). Derrida describes speech and thought as having a much more simultaneous relationship, albeit that there is still a delay between these two modes. Writing, however, takes place at a point much further away from the original thought, inviting a gap that he calls *différance* or 'difference/deferral'.

In the same way, we could look at performed citations and their photographic transcription as having the same relationship between presence and a kind of 'transcribed presence' (*énoncément* and *énoncé*, in Derrida's terms) in writing. There is a much more simultaneous relationship between thought and performed act, but when the shutter on the camera closes, the performed act is instantaneously removed from a linear temporal structure.

Hence, the camera shutter becomes a surgical knife that causes the caesura and splits the performance in two: one part of the performance continues to exist in the physical realm, the other is captured by the photograph. If we think of performance like a cell, the shutter on the camera separates the original cell into two halves. They contain the same raw material, but as they become separate parts of the same whole, they divide, multiply and propagate independently. Thus, the photograph has the 'life' of performance because it comes from the same original cell as the performance and contains the same building blocks of the performance's life. The performance captured by the camera, severed by the shutter, becomes the initiation of a performative utterance embodied in photographic form and starts the citation.

I use the term citation within Judith Butler's model of performativity (see Butler 2011, 1999). By the Butlerian definition of performativity, any radical break with conventions must fail – that is, singular expressive acts considered to be outside of existing citations are not possible. In this case, everything becomes referential, but simultaneously evolving through the individual performance of a particular act. Every act is unique, and yet it calls upon the repetition of an unknown cultural source.

Re-performance could also be considered as re-enactment, and Schneider discusses the implications of re-enactment by asking what remains of performance and the body after an act is over (Schneider 2007, 2011). She uses the term 'interinanimation' to describe how performance can give life to other objects. Using sculpture as an example, the pose is given life in the first instance by the body, then is enacted and re-enacted over time, playing out a recursive loop. This word has proven to be a useful addition to the vocabulary of explaining how documents could be seen to perform, and the context outlined illustrates in the example of photography how it occurs. Schneider also describes the 'temporal drag' in which live artists are stuck and implies that a document of performance could have the same citational quality as performativity in that the act is repeated:

> If a pose or a gesture or a move happens across time, what pulse of multiple time might a pose or a gesture or a move contain? Can a trace take the form of a living foot – or only in the form of a footprint? What time is a live act when a live act is reiterative? An action repeated again and again [...] has its own kind of staying power (Schneider 2011, 37).

Rather than considering the performance as having happened in the photograph as an indexical access point to the past, one could instead see that – through the reconstruction of the photograph as event – the photographic performance anticipates all time scales. It predicates a series of future 'nows' in which the photograph might be seen to exist on all temporal levels:

in the past, present and future. Taken collectively, these ideas then explain how Barthes's concept of the *studium* becomes an enactment of the photographic performance.³ The *punctum* acts as a catalyst, puncturing and injuring the viewer, and the *stadium* becomes a process through which the imagination heals that wound, allowing the respective spectators to animate the photograph, incorporate it within their subjective cultural understandings, experience it as a moment that has co-temporal presence and then respond accordingly to its performative provocation.

Différance also infers distance, and it must be recognized that not only are we working with time, but also how distance affects the way in which a given artefact is viewed by its audience. In the case of the photograph, it becomes its own singularity in time and space: it breaks with the constant disappearance of performance and isolates an individual moment. However, as I have previously explained, if we accept the Butlerian conventions of performativity and pair it with Schneider's idea of looping, then this moment embodies a convention of live art – repetition with difference, same gesture, same moment, but with differing results enacted in the imagination of its audience.

Therefore, we can conclude here that, when an artist chooses to use photography as a medium for theatricality, they are intentionally dealing with the dimensions of time, distance and *différance* in order to defer the performance. This mode of deferred performance outlined provides its own contribution to the performative effect of photography. Photographing theatrical acts then becomes the method through which writing (or transcribing) performance as a photograph engages with the idea of citational gestures and speech acts in order to become a provocation or utterance the spectator then enacts. Beyond performing or having a 'performic' quality, performance's transcription and visual reception as a still image uses citational gesture(s) to place the artist back into a wider social and cultural map that the artist hopes will provoke a response from the spectator, who in turn configures it within their experience and understanding.

Leaping into Citation

Auslander (2006) makes this point in his discussion of performance documentation using Yves Klein's *A Leap into the Void* (1960) – which Klein himself described as a 'performance' – to infer that in phenomenological terms a photograph can give the impression of a live act occurring, even though this particular photograph was produced using montage and studio compositing techniques.⁴ Auslander poses the question of the difference between the likes of performance documentation of live art and that of Klein's intentionally constructed photography, answering:

> If we are concerned with the historical constitution of these events as performances, it makes no difference at all. [...] We cannot dismiss studio fabrications of one sort or another from the category of performance art because they were not performed for a physically present audience. My suggestion that performance art is constituted as such through the performativity of its documentation is equally true (Auslander 2006, 8).

Furthermore, Auslander asserts the idea that documentation does not serve merely as a reminder, instead supposing that a photograph could be seen as performative. He writes that the power, presence and authenticity of these pieces do not derive from looking at the photograph as an indexical access point to a past event – nor from seeing performance as just a live medium – but instead 'from perceiving the document itself as a performance that directly reflects an artist's aesthetic project or sensibility and for which we are the present audience' (9).

For Auslander, phenomenology is the primary condition of the performative nature of the photographic document. However, a final consideration comes from Butler who distinguishes between *performance* and *performativity*. She argues that performativity is a reiteration of norms that precede, constrain and exceed the performer and cannot be taken as the performer's will and choice (Butler 2011, 95). In this manner, Butler describes how the performer can perform, but what the performative action *is performative of* will be something that is beyond what they have intentionally acted, as the performance act leads to an iteration that the performer cannot control and sometimes does not recognize within themselves as performer.

What we are then interrogating is how the theatrical and intentional performance of such actions embody a sense of the *performative* on its transcription to a photographic still image – that is to say, how writing (or transcribing) a performance in a theatrical manner as a photograph engages with the idea of citational gestures and speech acts in order to become a provocation or utterance which the spectator then enacts.

Changing the perspective of Klein's image to fit the idea that it is a theatrical performance of a citation to be photographed and received at a later point in time, the performance itself might then be viewed as an act that is calling upon a relationship or citation of the engagement between the body and the physical laws of the world; one which is universally and mutually understood by both the subject of the photograph and the photographic spectator. Klein employs a playfully fatalistic mode of performance to show the image of a solo falling man attempting to resist those physical laws. On its transcription to a photograph, the performance does not reach its conclusion, and so it employs the deferral available in the image to suspend his fate, allowing the spectator to consider whether this resistance is a success or failure. But it is the solitary nature of this theatrical, staged falling that takes on profound significance.

Lepecki writes about this as a form of solipsism – a method through which artists can cite performatives of the body through a seemingly solitary performance. He argues that, instead of the subject of the work being pictured as a passive slave of these performative commands, the artwork instead plays out the rules of a game that purposefully activates a will that aims to destroy or re-analyse existing performatives. He writes:

> Choreographic solipsism is a way to dismantle modernity's subjectivisation as a mode of idiotic, self-propelled, autonomous solitude from within. Solipsism becomes a critical and choreographic counter-methodology, a mode to intensify critically and physically the hegemonic conditions of subjectivisation and to explode them in improbable directions (Lepecki 2006, 39).

Lepecki especially emphasises that this choreographic practice is a way of critiquing what he calls the 'modernist male' (white, middle-class, heterosexual, cisgender male). As the photographic iteration of the performance keeps presenting the solitude of this falling, Klein offers his body as a form of critique, comedy and absurdity that isolates his actions from an everyday context to place them under greater scrutiny, allowing distance to criticise concepts of embodiment and what these citations provoke.

Klein's role is both comical and critical, and Kreider and O' Leary refer to this role as the 'slapstick body' through which we both understand and emasculate the world:

> The slapstick body…
>
> > …appears/disappears through the repetition of gesture and effect
> > …defies gravity
> > …jerks and pulses

    …is laughter and pain in a paradoxical twist
    …is existentially at odds with the world
    …is the surest way to undermine authority (Kreider and O'Leary, 2015; abridged, 47–56).

Klein similarly has found the medium of photography as a way to defy the physical laws of gravity and, in this semi-ridiculous suspension of those natural laws, brings into question whether it is possible to evade what might be perceived as 'inevitable' through the perceived temporal delay that photography affords.

Re-Enacting the Fall

Returning to the idea of the solipsistic questioning of hegemony, Yasumasa Morimura replicates Klein's act in *A Requiem: Theater of Creativity/Self-Portrait as Yves Klein* (2010) as a way of relocating a body within the work. Allen argues that calling upon these citational acts is exactly that: that citation presupposes and searches for a 'lost body' – there is someone always assumed to be gone, and the reinsertion of the body is a way of locating the totality of the work (Allen 2005, 179). What is even more interesting is that Allen writes specifically about photographing such acts of citation and describes a process of double alienation, because as the biological body is replaced by the mechanical reproduction of the photographic image, 'the actor's presence becomes superfluous, the audience becomes the missing body that is endlessly reproduced and interchangeable, across time and space' (200). Allen then claims that, as the script shifts from actors to spectators, interpretation is no longer about authenticity but reception. She poses that 'the question is not "is this reenactment true to the past?" but "is this reenactment true to the present?"' (201). Thus, the reinsertion of oneself into the frame, further utilises the tool of *différance*. When the body is put back into the work, it becomes lost on its transcription and asks the spectator to find that body within the present and consider its relevance. This reinsertion not only calls upon the provocation of the 'now' but also upon the spectator to use their unconscious knowledge as a form of agency with which to recollect and reinscribe.

    In re-enacting Klein's leap, Morimura not only critiques the place of the body, but asks the spectator to reconsider the original image in light of the information that his new body brings to the image. Removing it from a predominantly Western context, he asks how we reconfigure the image and its role in visual culture now that it has been re-cited in an Asian context. What new meanings does it accrue as a result of this action? The spectator enters a state of doubled disorientation: not only are they experiencing the phenomenon of suspension and delay from the subject's fate, but a reconfiguration of the image's place in the structural unconsciousness.

Ahmed explores the idea of disorientation in *Queer Phenomenology*, explaining why a phenomenology of orientation might be perceived in these images. She suggests that, beyond a term to describe sexuality, orientation is a word that we use to mean 'directed towards', so when we discuss orientation, we are not only talking of sexual preference, but of finding our way, of registering our proximity to objects and to others. 'Being oriented' is a normative state: a state we often do not notice because it is our usual way of being. In becoming oriented we must first be disoriented, and it is in this disorientation that the space begins to be queered. Being upright conforms to normative expectations of the world. As soon as the subject slips from a sense of being upright, both Klein and Masimura cite a dissatisfaction with the world's involvement (or lack thereof) with their bodies. Ahmed writes:

> The 'upright' body is involved in the world and acts on the world, insofar as it is already involved. The weakening of this involvement is what causes the body to collapse, and to become an object alongside other objects. In simple terms, disorientation involves becoming an object [. . .] Disorientation is unevenly distributed: some bodies more than others have their involvement called into crisis. This shows us how the world itself is more 'involved' in some bodies than it is in others, as it takes such bodies as the contours of ordinary experience (Ahmed 2006, 159).

Ahmed defines disorientation as a slip between the proximity of body and object – literally slipping away – and through these photographs, a sense of social disorientation is performed. This vague definition of 'social' is based on the fragile and tense performatives which we unwittingly rehearse and to which we conform. The subjects literally form the normative dialogue between body and object to produce another equally fragile situation at the point of collapse, questioning at what point the performatives on which we have based our daily lives on also fall down. In falling, the shared sense of bodily disorientation in performer and spectator both demands to be restored to a sense of orientation. Morimura layers the disorientation of cultural context in order for the spectator to locate themselves within the various cultural relationships portrayed in the image and orient themselves accordingly.

Images of the Falling Man

It is difficult to discuss falling and the male body in contemporary visual culture without thinking of *The Falling Man* – the famous image captured by Associated Press photographer Richard Drew of a man falling from the North Tower of the World Trade Centre on 11 September 2001.[5] There has been a significant shift in contemporary imagery since the events of 9/11, and now the image of a falling male body is overshadowed by – and becomes representative of – the crisis of the West itself. It may, metaphorically, be seen as a huge leap, but so powerful has the image become in relation to our understanding of present-day culture that both Phelan and Taylor discuss this event in relation to the documentation of its 'event'.[6] More specifically, Walsh picks up on the crisis specifically relating to how the male body can perform such conditions, asking us to read the male body as a 'social synecdoche' that marks the limits of hegemonic norms. He writes that 'the turning of the 21st century has coincided with great anxiety in the West, marked by increased concerns over the penetrability and violability of masculine Euro-American borders' (Walsh 2010, 11–12).

Morimura and Klein play with the idea of suspension, which gives the photograph the sense of an event. Derrida argues that the 'event' as the work of art is often presumed to be the result of unforeseeable conditions, that only an event worthy of its name does not announce itself in advance (Derrida 2007, 349, 360–61). But in a post-9/11 world where *The Falling Man* has entered our collective visual consciousness, Ciprian Muresan's *Leap into the Void, After Three Seconds* (2004) removes the sense of event in order to confront the perceived shortcomings of the predominantly white, Western capitalist patriarchy. Muresan took this iconic image and transported the scene to a similar-looking street near the historic centre of Cluj-Napoca, a city in the northwest of his native Romania, a site not far from that of the Romanian revolution, during which President Nicolae Ceausescu's communist regime was overthrown in 1989. By revising and resituating an iconic image from the canon of Western European art, Muresan's photograph reflects on the changing status and precarious

Fig. 10.1: Ciprian Muresan, *Leap into the Void, After three Seconds,* 2004.

situation of post-communist Romania. In this way, Muresan's image resonates with the artist's experience of failure and the post-communist condition.

While Klein questions the efficacy of the male body against the physical laws of nature, Muresan presents the conclusions of postmodernism: that both Western capitalism and Eastern communism are fallible and imperfect.

All three images rely on a mutual understanding between spectator and artist on previous understandings of the act. In Klein's case, the spectator merely needs to know the phenomenological experience of falling. But as soon as it enters the structural unconsciousness, the license for appropriation and re-enactment is given. It is only through the intentional theatrical performance and re-performance of such acts captured by the photograph that the artist makes the fleeting moment visible and brings it into question, thereby initiating a conversation with contemporary culture.

Borrowing from Azoulay, we might use the concept of civil imagination to explain how the ontology of the photograph arises from the possibilities that performance can provoke (see Azoulay 2012). In order for change to be possible, citizens have always had to have the ability to imagine an order that was radically different from the one that was in power at the time. She therefore states that, although not a physical quality, the photograph is dependent on imagination in order to access something not available to the immediate senses so as to provoke change:

> Imagination enables us to create an image on the basis of something that is not accessible to the senses [. . .] However material the images that we produce in our mind's eye might be, they remain disembodied and do not enjoy independent presence in the world except for that presence which is contingent upon our imagination (Azoulay 2012, 4).

She continues by arguing that photography holds the same power to initiate the beginnings of change. Applying it to theatricality in photographic practice, we could say that a level of 'staging' is required because the artist is trying to render an alternative idea, or some deconstruction of a citation, into the civil imagination, and this will not exist if they do not *make it happen*. In order to instil in the spectator the possibility of a situation or performative changing, then the artist has to *be the change* and realise it through an intentional act of performance. In this sense, staged acts are required on the part of the artist to provoke the spectator to move towards the change in their own imagination.

Therefore, although the performance that happens through the photograph is imagined, it does not make it any less powerful. The performative incitement behind the photographic performance is intended to use the mind's eye to envision something beyond the frame. The imagination is the stimulation for change: the performativity of the still image says that, if one can imagine it happening, then it portrays the effect that it can happen or has already happened, provoking the recipient of the utterance to respond to that possibility.

The more poignant and significant point of these images that play with the theme of falling – falling men, falling masculinity – is that it points towards 'the problem with reference', as Caruth has described it (see Caruth 1996). When the apple fell on his head, Isaac Newton realised that we are all falling all the time with the force of gravity pulling us towards the Earth's core. So perhaps the 'queer' notion of spatial disorientation that happens in capturing these images, as I have outlined, is illustrative of a special case of something that is always happening – perhaps a truth that is too traumatic for us to recognize, to be reminded of and of which to be conscious. When we sit on a chair, we fall towards it. The rendering of falling into the civil imagination has gained so many negative connotations that to contemplate the idea that we are in a constant mode of falling may be too much for the psyche to take. The related problem, so Caruth speculates, is not simply confronting the science behind falling but confronting the fact that there are, perhaps, no words to refer to such a moment. Granted, many of us survive our perpetual moments of falling perfectly well. But the figure of the falling man illustrates, so argues Caruth, 'an example of the occurrence of difference: the difference between living and dying – which resists being generalised into a conceptual figure or law' (Caruth 1996, 89).

The deconstruction of the act of falling into a singular frame allows the spectator to map the falling man back into a series of historical and social contexts in which we might imagine falling, failing, saving, delaying – in both our personal lives and our collective cultural consciousness. When the transition between moments is *withdrawn* in the still image, the performance of the instantaneous becomes performative, because it slows movement down to a single frame in order to confront the trauma of the everyday experience of gravity. We are always falling within a framework, and that framework is defined both by the physical laws of gravity and by the cultural rules that govern our use of objects. By queering the normative usage of objects and appearing to defy gravity in the photographic image, both performer and spectator are disorientated, and the state of disorientation demands to be restored through enactment.

Photographic Citation as Performative Provocation

Bringing together these points, photographic works engaging with theatricality do not necessarily use the ambiguity of the photographic medium as a device to deceive the spectator. Nor is it solely meant to evoke a fictitious narrative. Even though the actions are arguably theatrical in execution, in each case it does not discount the fact that there was a *doing* before the camera that actually occurred to express the performative utterance. Nor does it negate that behind these theatrical actions there is an intention to engage the spectator in wider social, political and cultural provocations. What I am attempting to illustrate here is that theatricality in photography does not necessarily mean a 'staged scenario to produce narrative', more a 'staged action to produce provocation'.

If it can be surmised that, when performers know they are playing with the *différance* of photography, they are actively thinking of how the gesture is received in such a manner. In the examples here, the images all play with the varying modes of delay and expectation of falling in the still image. Because this mode of photographic presentation relies on the spectator's *past* understandings and the *différance* of the photograph is geared towards being received in the future, the visual reception of the act in the present deconstructs those past meanings as the act of enacting, and the image ushers it forth into the present. Therefore, on each presentation of this statement, the spectator recalls and compares the refracted logic of the photographic image to the comparative reasoning of their own comprehension of the cultural memory that it encapsulates, asking themselves if it could be possible *in this moment*.

Subsequently, the idea of engaging with theatricality is read in relation to performativity in photography as an intentionally performed act happening in time rather than an act intended to be witnessed in a sculptural or painterly tradition of 'posed stillness' (for instance, through the use of tableau or meticulously staged portraiture). Fried's recent work perhaps explains this view more clearly when he shifts his usage to the term of picture (see Fried 2008b, 35, 50, 59, 91). Although he emphasises his views on art soliciting its viewers in a theatrical manner have not shifted in substance over the years, his preferred term becomes more generic, encompassing a range of pictorial arts. He thereby disavows in advance any strong (or narrow) conception of medium-specificity. As a result, we might understand these pictures existing in any medium, and what Fried disparages is a notion of theatrical pictorialism. In contrast, what I propose is that it is temporality that demarcates the specificity of the theatrical in photography, not pictorialism.

Theatricality as a photographic mode allows the distance from a performed act in order to pose possibilities – and herein lies its impact. As Lütticken (2010: 130) writes, '[w]e live in a culture of performance [...] To act is to step beyond the now; to perform is to extend the now, to prolong the present. But this need not be a static opposition. What is a failed performance if not an act, whether intentional or not?' (Lütticken 2010, 130).

Citational practice that plays with these possibilities in performance to camera becomes performative by allowing the spectator to turn and return to moments in popular culture. Kartsaki discusses how returning to an event again and again in memory or writing is a process that attempts to restore or repair experience, to resist the ephemeral, to enable us to feel the sorrow of what is gone, or to come to terms with what resists appropriation (see Kartsaki 2016, 196, 206–7). This process may not have a singular end; yet sometimes we may be in search of a feeling of closure. Ultimately, however, endings escape from us, forming an experience that is *not quite yet*. In the same way, our search for finitude in such photography leads the loop to be played repeatedly, and in so doing continually unpicks the *différance* between what we thought we knew and what we now understand; a process that in itself has no definitive conclusion.

Notes

1. The term 'spectator' comes directly from Rancière's definition of 'the emancipated spectator' in his eponymous 2009 book. Rancière theorises the spectator as an active interpreter rather than a passive observer of the 'spectacle' of the image (Rancière 2009, 22).
2. See the chapter 'The Intolerable Image' (Rancière 2009, 83–105), in which he declares: 'Thus, we need images of action, images of the true reality or images that can immediately be inverted into their true reality, in order to show us that the mere fact of being a spectator, the mere fact of viewing images, is a bad thing. Action is presented as the only answer to the evil of the image and the guilt of the spectator' (87). Rather than being 'immersive' and 'soporific', images require theatricality, or 'drama' in his terms, to provoke the spectator to take action.
3. Barthes describes the punctum as 'a sting, speck, a cut hole [...] that accident which pricks me (but also bruises me, is poignant to me)' (Barthes 2000, 27). He also describes it as having a latency effect – that we can only identify the punctum after the fact (53). The deferred performance and the immediacy of the performative act could be behind some aspect of the punctum that causes this injury, as latency seems similar to Derrida's ideas of *différance*. He also writes that '[t]he *studium* is of the order of liking, not of loving; it mobilizes a half desire, a demi-volition; it is the same sort of vague, slippery, irresponsible interest one takes in the people, the entertainments, the books, the clothes one finds "all right". To recognize the *studium* is inevitably to encounter the photographer's intentions, to enter into harmony with [them]' (Barthes 2000, 26).
4. This is detailed by Jones, who writes that Klein had no audience apart from 'close friends and photographers' when he jumped (which he did several times, 'attempting to get the desired transcendent expression on his face'). Klein used a protective net that does not appear in the photograph, which is actually a composite of two different shots unified in the darkroom. Jones points out that Klein deliberately exposed the theatricality of his image by publishing two different versions of it (see Jones 1994, 554).
5. The photograph initially appeared in newspapers around the world, including on page 7 of *The New York Times* on 12 September 2001.
6. Taylor argues that, for those who failed to fit comfortably into the position of hero or victim in the official 9/11 narrative popularised on TV and in the press, taking photographs offered an opportunity to 'do something' (Taylor 2003, 243–44). Phelan refers to the beautiful and consoling nature of the photograph, claiming it 'reframes his life [...] simultaneously haunting and recuperating' (Phelan 2010, 60–61).

11

Music, Miles Davis and Theatricality

Nicholas Gebhardt and Richard Rushton

American comedian George Crater once quipped: 'What does a Miles Davis doll do when you wind it up? It turns its back on you' (cited in Szwed 2002, 190). What can be made of Miles Davis's gesture, at certain times, of playing with his back to the audience? In truth, Davis rarely played with his back to the audience, although he often played during the 1970s and 1980s with his horn pointed downwards towards the stage floor instead of being projected forward towards the audience. Davis certainly had a tendency to ignore the audience, especially when other members of his band were soloing. He would often wander to the back of the stage or even off stage into the wings. During the 1950s and 1960s, Davis could be counted among the most important band leaders and jazz trumpeters in the world; hence, to turn his back on audiences would seem to be a fairly explicit gesture of some sort. A musician or performer will most often be expected to play out or 'up' to an audience. Indeed, surely that is what we expect from a musical performer: to 'play' to the audience; to face and explicitly address that audience; to appeal to and gesture towards the members of the audience. A stage of jazz musicians, especially in a small combo of five or six players, will typically be set up to foreground the musicians' direct frontal addressing of the audience. A pianist may well be side-on, or even slightly pointed away from the audience so that his or her hands and the piano's keyboard become visible, but a horn player, bassist, guitarist, or drummer would be expected to be pointed directly towards the audience. Similar formations will be seen in an orchestra: all the musicians will more or less face the audience. Of course, the orchestra's conductor will conduct with his or her back to the audience, and so, too, typically will the leader of a jazz big band be expected to face his band's players in order to conduct them. But a small jazz combo will be different, suffused with notions of freedom, independence, collaboration and improvisation. Here, then, there will be no need for band leaders to face and conduct the group; rather, they will face the audience. Why, therefore, might Davis on occasion have been known to turn his back on his audience?

Davis himself gives a first hint of what is at stake. He claimed:

> [W]ell, they say I'm rude, and that I turn my back on the audience, and that I don't like white people. And that I don't like the audience. But the thing is, I never think about an audience. I just think about the band. And if the band is all right, I know the audience is pleased. I don't have to hold the audience's hand (Taylor 1993, 18).

There is a complex mix of propositions here. One is that to turn one's back on an audience is rude and implies that the person turning their back does not like the audience. But Davis follows this up by defending such actions: a performer should not be expected to hold the audience's hand, and, even more emphatically, this performer never even thinks about an audience. He declared on another occasion: 'I can't be concerned with talking and bullshitting with the audience while I'm playing because the music is talking to them when everything is right'. Furthermore, he claimed: 'That's what I'm doing when I have my back to the audience' (Davis and Troupe 1989, 346).

We want to argue that Davis's gesture of turning his back on his audience can be taken as a prime example of what, in the history of art, Michael Fried has called *absorption*. Of course, we are writing about a musical performer, whereas Fried is most often writing about paintings and then most often about the ways in which figures, especially human figures, are depicted in those paintings. And yet, the gestures that Fried describes, those actions of being absorbed in an activity, so absorbed that one becomes unaware that one is being seen (or that one could be seen), are ones that surely pertain to musical performances, or indeed to performances of any kind. In short, these are performers who are absorbed in their performance. Fried, as is well known, argued that opposed to gestures of absorption are gestures that could be called *theatrical*. Such gestures are ones performed in an overt way, in ways designed to attract attention; that is, they explicitly appeal to an audience.

In the history of art, beginning in the mid-eighteenth century, Fried identified many instances of what he calls states of absorption, and one version of such a state consists of figures in paintings who are depicted from behind. A famous early example for Fried is that of Jean-Baptiste Siméon Chardin's *Young Student Drawing* of 1738 (see Fried 1980, 13–15). The most striking depictions are those of Caspar David Friedrich (1774–1840) in what are known as *Rückenfiguren*, with the *Woman Rising Before the Sun* (1818) and *The Wanderer above the Sea of Fog* (1818) providing perhaps the most famous examples. *The Wanderer* features a figure – a man; we see only his back – perched on a very high hill or mountain surveying the grandeur of the vista stretched out beneath and before him. The gist of Fried's reading of the painting is that Friedrich is trying to paint a figure who does not know he is in a painting; that is, a figure who is not explicitly posing to and for the beholder of the painting, as would typically be expected in a portrait. Friedrich's attempt to paint a figure who is absorbed in the activity that he is pursuing – viewing a landscape – continues a tradition of absorptive, anti-theatrical painting that originates (at least) with Chardin (1699–1779) in mid-eighteenth-century France and which is expressed most fervently in the contemporary art criticism of Denis Diderot (1713–84). Fried condenses such points in a piece written on Friedrich, arguing that the aim of such moves in painting pertains to questions of 'how to make paintings that, by one means or another, manage somehow to establish the supreme fiction or ontological illusion that they are not made to be beheld' (Fried 2014, 117). That is, Friedrich's habit of having the figures in his painting turn their backs to the beholder – and thus to be absorbed in whatever activity they are engaged in – is one way of trying to formulate the 'supreme fiction' that the painting itself is unaware that it has been made in order to be to be looked at.

Our initial hypothesis, therefore, as an attempt to figure out why Miles Davis might turn his back on his audiences, concerns absorption. That is, during these moments of turning away from his audience, Davis might be said to be so engrossed in the music he is playing that any sense of an audience is deemed superfluous for him: it no longer matters. In short, we will argue that Davis's gestures are absorptive, and to that degree, they are also, as Fried would say, anti-theatrical.

We want to call Davis's gesture anti-theatrical. But what does that mean? Fried, in discussions of various artists over many years, has elaborated the stakes of this 'supreme fiction', as he calls it, that is central to the anti-theatrical tradition. At stake for absorption and anti-theatricality in painting was the question of, as we have already stated, the supreme fiction that what was on the canvas was not explicitly meant to be viewed. The fiction of a painting that is not supposed to be looked at is one thing – and we are probably familiar with the fiction of 'looking in on a private world' that many paintings deliver – but for Davis we are dealing with music that is made to be heard. We cannot even have a fiction, surely, of a kind of music that is made so as to *not* be heard.[1] Therefore, if we are calling Davis's gestures anti-theatrical, then that anti-theatricality cannot pertain to the music as such. Or can it? (We shall try to answer this question.) At any rate, it cannot do so in the direct terms that Fried uses; that is, of music made under the pretence that it not be heard. Thus, we will surmise that the stakes of absorption and anti-theatricality, for our analysis of Davis, must be matters of the way in which the music is created, of the ways in which it is performed and made. It is here that we can begin to sketch a vision of the ways in which a musician performing may be considered to be in a state of absorption – that is, of being so caught up in the activity of playing the music that all consideration of playing to an audience is elided.

For a painter to capture such moments – or instants – of absorption is one thing, but for such absorption to unfold over a period of time, such as occurs with playing music, is another. Fried has considered such possibilities, however; to some degree, the play between the instant and duration is central to the themes which he has pursued over many years. Yet, Fried has also considered works that do unfold in time, especially films. In a discussion of Douglas Gordon and Philippe Parreno's 2006 film, *Zidane: A 21st Century Portrait*, Fried comments at length on the absorptive demeanour of the film's subject, football player Zinedine Zidane. 'Zidane himself', writes Fried, 'is depicted as wholly absorbed throughout almost the entire film', as he plays in a football match (Fried 2008b, 228). Fried goes on to state that, for Zidane, this absorption 'requires the keenest imaginable attention from start to finish and in addition calls forth the most intense and concentrated physical effort on his part' (ibid.). Zidane is doing all this in front of a vast audience, some 80,000 spectators inside the stadium and vastly more via the game's television coverage. Fried therefore highlights the tension in the film that arises from Zidane's absorption in the match and the knowledge or awareness that he is being watched. Fried will go so far as to claim that 'the film lays bare a hitherto unthematised relationship between absorption and beholding – more precisely between the persuasive representation of absorption and the apparent consciousness of being beheld' (Fried 2008a, 230). The relationship is one between being absorbed in activity, on the one hand – activities such as reading, doing work on a computer, cooking, painting, knitting, or simply reflecting (and many other things) – and, on the other hand, knowing that one is being observed. We might surmise, for example, that most of the time when we are reading, we will not be observed. Rather, we will be absorbed in what we read and be more or less oblivious to our surroundings. In such situations we are alone, unobserved and absorbed. But Fried tries to claim here that, for the kind of performance delivered by Zidane, the stakes are somewhat different: Zidane is thoroughly absorbed in his activity, even as he knows that he is being watched by a vast number of people in the stadium as well as by film and television cameras. Therefore, what is at stake is the relationship between being absorbed in an activity, and thus being oblivious to an audience, and yet at the same time knowing that you are being observed by an audience. This is precisely what is dramatised by *Zidane*, according to Fried.

Issues such as these are intensified when Fried begins to discuss a musician – a jazz musician, no less: the saxophonist known as Moondoc – as depicted in Anri Sala's 2005 short film *Long Sorrow*. Fried is clear: 'The first thing that struck me about *Long Sorrow* [...] was the saxophonist's seemingly total absorption in his playing' (Fried 2011, 38). In doing this, the film and Moondoc's playing evinced precisely the same tension as that exhibited in *Zidane*: '[I]t made the dual issue of absorption and to-be-seenness immediately palpable' (ibid.). In other words, Moondoc is completely absorbed in his playing, while at the same time he is aware that he is being filmed and, thus, being beheld. But Fried then links this with another point: Moondoc's absorption is also an indicator of the *authenticity* of his playing. 'There was', Fried writes, 'no question as to the authenticity of the saxophonist's engagement in what he was doing: it seemed inconceivable that he was mugging for the camera, or that the sounds I was hearing could have issued from any other source than his efforts' (38–39). Fried thus foregrounds an opposition here. Moondoc's absorption in his playing is an indicator of authenticity. The opposite of authenticity would be something called 'mugging for the camera', and one assumes that such actions are inauthentic or fake, or as Fried would have it, they are *theatrical* rather than *absorptive*.

There is one other point in relation to Sala's *Long Sorrow*: the *presentness* of Moondoc's playing. By this – presentness – Fried means the sense that this music is unfolding in the present. This is not a document that is capturing a past event. Rather, the urgency of this playing – its absorption – as well as various strategies of depiction used by Sala, are all geared towards the portrayal of action-in-the present. Fried goes so far as to write that 'it is the project of improvisation' – for Moondoc is indeed improvising here – 'that underwrites the moment-to-moment intensity – the sustained effect of present-tense motivatedness – that marks Sala's video from first to last' (45–46).

We want to take up these two key points. First of all, Fried stresses the interplay between *absorption* and *being beheld*. Secondly, he emphasises the sense of *presentness*, of being 'in the moment'. We want to investigate these two points in relation to Davis's gesture of turning his back on the audience.

We have already indicated that there is surely a major difference between the visual arts – something made to be seen – and the musical arts – something made to be heard. Thus, the dialectic between absorption and to-be-seenness may well function for the visual arts, but it is difficult to work out how there can be an equivalent dialectic for music. Zidane, for example, is playing football, and it need not matter if those acts are being seen by anyone. Well, of course, his actions must be seen by the other members of his team, and the opposing team, too. Perhaps not for the whole game, but certainly for the periods of the game when Zidane is closely involved – dribbling the ball, passing, making an attack and so on – both his teammates and the opposing players will be watching him. There is a process of watching that is internal to the game: the players will watch each other. Therefore, this process of players watching the other players is internal to the game. The watching that occurs in this way is allied with absorption. Indeed, part of Zidane's absorption in the game is his watching what other players are doing and, conversely, involves other absorbed players watching Zidane.

This process of absorption that is internal to the game – an absorption that involves watching intensely and being watched intensely, with great concentration (with great concentration, that is, if one is a good player) – is very different from any one player's relationship to the audience that is merely watching the game. The audience is not playing the game: they are there to behold it. And so it will come to pass that, at many moments of the game, Zidane and other players will turn their backs on their audience. Indeed, we could go so far as to say that this will be a normal way of playing. A player must concentrate on the game, not on pleasing the audience. We surely know that this is the case by virtue of its inverse demonstration: when a player scores a goal, he (or she) will most likely run to the edge of the pitch so as to cheer, gesticulate and celebrate in front of the fans who are watching the game. The game effectively stops, and all absorption in the game can be abandoned so that instead a fully theatrical – performed – celebration can occur. Often nowadays such celebrations for the fans will be rehearsed – a specific cartwheel or a pose for the fans – as though the player is declaring: 'Look at me! Look how great I am! And how great that goal was!' Significantly, as though wanting to emphasise his anti-theatricality, Zidane's response is somewhat muted for each of the two goals that his team scores in this match – even after the first of these results from a fairly extraordinary cross-kick delivered by Zidane – and the one moment of the film which he apparently did not like was when he dropped his absorptive concentration to share a joke with teammate Roberto Carlos (see Fried 2014, 229).

* * *

There are striking parallels between Fried's description above of Zidane's and Moondoc's total absorption in their respective performances, and accounts of Davis's anti-theatrical method while playing live. As an example, we want to explore several performances of the song 'My Funny Valentine', especially those performed at the Plugged Nickel Club in Chicago by the Miles Davis Quintet (known as the second great quintet), which featured Davis on trumpet, Herbie Hancock on piano, Wayne Shorter on saxophone, Ron Carter on bass and Tony Williams on drums. In late December 1965, Davis and his band flew to Chicago following a series of shows at major North American jazz clubs: the Village Vanguard in New York, the Showboat in Philadelphia, the Grand Lounge in Detroit and the Bohemian Caverns in Washington DC. Davis had been unable to play for almost eight months prior to this tour because of two serious hip operations, and the Plugged Nickel gigs were the first time that the full quintet had been together since the early part of the year, when they had recorded *E. S. P.*, the group's first studio album (Carr 1998, 204–5).

'My Funny Valentine' was originally written for the Broadway musical comedy, the 1937 coming-of-age comedy *Babes in Arms* by Richard Rogers and Lorenz Hart. By the mid-1950s, the song had become established as a standard among jazz musicians, and there were many influential recordings available, including versions by Charlie Parker, Stan Kenton,

Sarah Vaughan, Ben Webster, Artie Shaw, Chet Baker and Frank Sinatra. Davis had first recorded it in the studio in 1956, for the LP *Cookin' with the Miles Davis Quintet*, and over the next decade the song featured frequently in his live performances, alongside other well-known jazz standards such as 'If I Were a Bell', 'Stella by Starlight', 'Autumn Leaves', 'Yesterdays' and 'When I Fall in Love'. Through a series of live recordings, which began with *Jazz at the Plaza* in 1958 and ended with the 1965 Plugged Nickel Performances, we want to suggest that Davis pursued a conscious strategy of anti-theatricality via these standards, many of which were composed for Broadway musicals and defined by their theatricality. Moreover, what is of particular importance about these recordings is the way in which they demonstrate the challenges that he faced in continuing this strategy. Audiences came to hear his band because of these standards; yet, by the late 1950s, there was a growing dissatisfaction among the musicians in these bands with these songs as the primary medium for improvisation.

We can go through each of these performances one at a time, for they give an excellent indication of the changes that took place in Davis's playing, and in the aspirations of his bands, over the period from 1956 to 1965. The 1956 studio recordings were part of a famous series of sessions that Davis put together in order to fulfil his contractual obligations to the Prestige label. He was keen to move to the Columbia label and so ran through a range of numbers with his quintet of the time – John Coltrane on tenor saxophone, Red Garland on piano, Paul Chambers on double bass and Philly Joe Jones on drums – with the result of producing enough music for four albums (*Workin'*, *Steamin'*, *Relaxin'* and *Cookin' with the Miles Davis Quintet*) and therefore bring his Prestige years to an end.[2] 'My Funny Valentine' was one of the last of these numbers recorded. It features a series of moves that would be repeated in subsequent performances. There is, for example, a sweet piano opening. This opening is played with a gentle underlying rhythm, accompanied by the rest of the band, except Coltrane: in this version, there is no saxophone at all. Davis's trumpet is muted, and during his solo the rhythm moves back and forward between the 4/4 ballad tempo and double time. The double time continues when Garland begins a solo, and then the tune returns to the slower, balladic tempo for Davis to come back in with the melody. He only plays the barest outlines of the melody, however, still muted; a series of piano trills, echoing the opening of the track, sees the tune through to its completion.

The next performance is a live one from The Plaza Hotel in New York, recorded on 28 July 1958, with Bill Evans replacing Red Garland, Jimmy Cobb now on drums and Julian 'Cannonball' Adderley replacing John Coltrane on saxophone. As with the 1956 recording, the piano opens the number. Evans's chords are slow and contemplative, and more or less out of time. The bass and drums then enter with a slow swing tempo, followed by Davis's muted trumpet, which introduces the melody. Davis bends and stretches the tune here, rather than directly stating it. The tempo remains much the same – there is no shift into double time – through to Evans's solo, which keeps things rather dark, contemplative and 'balladic'. After Evans, Chambers solos on the bass, while the rest of the band sits out. Again, there is no saxophone. To end the tune, Davis comes back in, muted again, all at a slow tempo.

The next recording of 'My Funny Valentine' is from the famous 12 February 1964 NAACP benefit concert at the Lincoln Center's Philharmonic Hall in New York – Lincoln's birthday, no less. The concert would lead to two albums, the first being named after the first tune on the bill, *My Funny Valentine*, while another was called *'Four' and More*. (The band were not entirely happy to do a benefit concert, which meant that they would not be paid. They figured this was fine for Davis, who was making a lot of money by this point. The new, young band members were, by contrast, still struggling musicians.) The version of 'Valentine' here begins, as had become typical for Davis's bands, with a solo piano introduction. These are very slow, contemplative chords, played by Herbie Hancock, joined here by Ron Carter on double bass, Tony Williams on drums and George Coleman on tenor saxophone. Hancock plays a series of chords, then effectively stops playing to allow Davis to introduce the key notes of the head – those that would usually be sung as 'My Funny Valentine' – and these six opening notes will become crucial ones for future performances. Davis is no longer using a mute here, so his tone is more open and, all in all, larger. Our feeling is that this tone more effectively mimics the human voice, and we both also feel as though Davis is in some way trying to replicate the voice of Frank Sinatra: bold, stark, yet fragile and introspective, too. A tempo is introduced part-way through the head by Carter's bass, then soft brushes come in on the drums; the piano plays chords to accentuate the tempo; Williams flirts with introducing sticks on the drum kit, but very quietly and sparingly. On the back of all this, Davis delivers a punchy solo. As Davis's solo progresses, Williams finds a place to double the tempo on the ride cymbal and bring in the full drum kit, while Carter adds a walking bass line. The double time replicates that of the 1956 recording, but it is held for longer here, and it has greater rhythmic intensity. By this point, the tune has begun to lose its ballad feel, and we have a medium-tempo jazz beat. At around four minutes in, Davis fluffs a note quite badly and boldly, but he continues on, seemingly unflustered (it was not the first or last time that he would do such a thing). In general, the tempo remains fairly standard here, although towards the end the band switch briefly into double time and then back to the regular swing rhythm. Significantly, Coleman, with his sweet tenor saxophone tone, takes a solo here (as noted, neither Coltrane nor Adderley took solos on the earlier recordings). It is an excellent solo that expands on many of the melodic and rhythmic motifs established by Davis. Again, there are brief shifts between the double and regular swing rhythm, and towards the end the drums drop out, the tempo fades, and a balladic sensibility returns. Then comes the piano solo. It begins simply as piano and bass. The tempo has more or less dropped out here, and the band enters a kind of free-form improvisation that will be accentuated in later performances. Needless to say, Hancock's solo is exceptional. Williams tries to find his way back in by tapping on his snare at various points (with the snare wires removed), but he backs off. Carter eventually re-finds the tempo: we return to medium rhythm now, but the drums stay out. Davis then comes back in as the tempo shifts from double time back to the single time of a ballad. Davis sketches the edges of the melody as the tempo seems to get even slower. He ends with a glorious evocation of the final words of the chorus, 'Each day is Valentine's day', in ways that aim to replicate Sinatra's 1953 recording on his album *Songs for Young Lovers*.

A second recording from 1964 is taken from a live performance at Tokyo's Kohseinenkin Hall on 14 July. It is the same band as the New York performance, although Sam Rivers has replaced Coleman on tenor saxophone. Hancock's piano again sets things underway, but this time with what can only be described as almost impossibly melancholic chords. Then he stops completely for Davis's entry – those six key notes – which receives some applause from the audience. Midway through the head, Carter introduces the semblance of a rhythm on the bass: a very slow ballad tempo. Williams flirts with brushes on the snare drum and marks several beats with sticks on his cymbal, but he backs off. Davis's solo continues without drums, and with a pulse rather than a clear tempo, until finally a clear beat is found, and Williams marks it out on the ride cymbal. Williams continues with the cymbal and marks out some extraordinary moments of emphasis and climax: Davis is in stunning form here. Towards the end of the solo, the tempo drops out, only to come back for another climax for the solo's conclusion. This kind of to-ing and fro-ing of tempi and intensity will reach its apogee at the Plugged Nickel performances. Rivers then comes in for his saxophone solo. The tempo remains a medium-tempo swing rhythm, shifts briefly into double time, goes back to swing before folding back to a single time ballad feel. It has to be admitted that the band has difficulty finding where to go now. Rivers's solo seems a little directionless, so Hancock takes over. By this point the drums have dropped out, and then the bass also drops out, so that most evidence of rhythm has been lost. Davis comes back in for a final, very truncated chorus, and the tune comes to an end. Davis's solo might be one of the best he ever recorded, and it is as though the rest of the band could not quite work out what do to after Davis had finished.

Not long after this performance, and just prior to a tour of Europe in 1964, Davis replaced Rivers with tenor saxophonist Wayne Shorter. This change of personnel had a profound effect on the group, as Davis notes:

> Wayne had been known as a free-form player, but playing with [drummer] Art Blakey for those years and being the band's musical director had brought him back in somewhat. He wanted to play freer than he could in Art's band, but he didn't want to be all the way out, either. Wayne has always been someone who experimented *with* form instead of someone who did it *without* form. That's why I thought he was perfect for where I wanted to see the music I played go (Davis and Troupe 1989, 263).

More and more, the musicians began to openly question the standard repertoire (see the recording of the band performing 'My Funny Valentine' for Italian television at the Teatro Dell'Arte in Milan on 11 October 1964), while also working on a set of new compositions by Shorter. By the time they arrived in Chicago, things had reached a critical point. In his autobiography, Hancock talks about the problems that they were having with their live set.

> By now [1965] Miles, Ron, Tony, Wayne, and I had been performing in the quintet for more than a year, and we'd gotten so cohesive as a band that it had become easy to play together. We had figured

out a formula for making it work, but of course playing by formula was exactly the opposite of what we wanted to do. We needed to put the challenge back in, to figure out ways to take more risks. I had noticed that our playing had gotten a little too comfortable, but on the flight to Chicago it was Tony who started the conversation. 'I've got an idea', he said. 'Let's play some anti-music'. He wanted us to promise that during our sets at the Plugged Nickel, whatever anybody in the band expected us to play, we would play the opposite (Hancock and Dickey 2014, 92–93).

There are two versions of 'My Funny Valentine' from the band's two nights at the Plugged Nickel. It is the first track of the second set of the first night, 22 December, then it is the third track of the second set on the following night, 23 December. The first of these features an opening very much like the 1964 versions: a soft piano introduction, with unmuted Davis coming in with the six key notes. This time, however, he does so with almost impossibly large spaces between the first set of notes ('My fun-ny val-en-tine'), and those which follow ('Sweet comic valentine / You make me smile . . . with your heart'). To us, this is a fine example of the ways in which Davis's band here tries to stretch the tunes they play towards the limits of their expressibility. It is almost as though Davis stops playing as he waits – we presume – for just the right moment to introduce the next notes. One could feel that he makes a mistake here, or that he has forgotten which notes to play. But we would prefer to believe that Davis is experimenting at the limit. He is pulling this tune to pieces, note by note. He is also exploring a mood, for, as we shall see, the mood of this performance is markedly different from that which occurs the following night. We are tempted to say that Davis feels lost here, and he searches for notes, almost as though he is trying to find himself, to work out what to play, to work out how he can express himself. As though trying to help Davis, Williams scratches out a tempo with brushes on the snare, so the looseness of the opening sections of the 1964 recordings is negated here. Davis very much economises, and there continue to be large gaps between his sets of notes, almost as though he might have left the stage. Williams eventually comes in with his ride cymbal at double tempo, which echoes the medium swing mood of the first 1964 recording (the NAACP concert). After a while, Davis seems to get into his stride. There is a very open dimension to his playing here, as though nothing at all is planned and the tune really could go anywhere. Williams tries to push the tempo in a different direction, as though trying to shake up the band to see where things might go. All of this creates moments of play, emphasis and climax. At certain points Davis seems to drop out completely, then comes back in, searching. There is no real shape to Davis's solo; any pre-rehearsed licks are now gone, and the solo comes to an end without really coming to an end. Rather, Shorter steps in and takes over, while the rest of the band maintains its tempo and intensity. Early in Shorter's solo, the tempo then comes to a halt: the drums stop; the bass stops walking. Then Williams comes back in with the tempo, while Carter jumps around rhythmically, playing a beat here and there, but with no consistency. With this, Shorter begins to find direction: a series of jagged, staccato notes. This then inspires Carter to take up a walking bass line, and Williams intensifies his rhythmic pulse and Shorter begins to play out, louder and harder. Shorter also brings back bits of the melody to remind us of the tune. As if responding to the return of the tune, Williams slows down to a single-time ballad tempo as that Shorter can round things off with the notes that sing to 'Each day is Valentine's Day'.

Next up, Carter takes a solo (we hear a telephone ring) – the tune has been going for over twelve minutes now (by comparison, the *whole* 1956 recording of the song is a mere five minutes and fifty-nine seconds). Williams taps out a rhythm on the brushes, and Hancock embellishes on piano. Davis soon comes back in with a very brief reiteration of the tune, but he leaves large gaps – again – until every member of the band pretty much drops out: there is no rhythm here. Davis noodles around the melody, until the double rhythm again emerges, led by Williams, and off they go again (the tune has been going for sixteen minutes now). Davis gets to the notes for 'Each day . . .', and then the song fizzles out. The tune does not really get to the end before William starts pounding out the drum introduction to the next number, 'Four'. Neither Davis nor the other members of the band are waiting for applause.

On the following night, the band, in their second set, had played 'All of You' and were now coming to the end of their second tune, 'Agitation'. They just about get to the end of that tune when Davis comes in with the crucial six notes: 'My fun-ny val-en-tine'. There is no time for applause after 'Agitation' comes to an end: we are on to the next number. This means that there is no piano introduction here, as we might have come to expect. Suffice to say that this is completely different from the previous night's opening. Williams and Carter fiddle in the background, trying to work out where the tune is going to go, and Davis finally finds the space to run with the tune. None of the huge gaps that had characterised the previous night's performance are here. In fact, this is a much happier, less introspective rendition of 'My Funny Valentine'. It is a different mood: last night's performance is no longer relevant. Williams brings in a pulsing rhythm, and Davis blows hard. His solo is completely different from the one that had taken place just twenty-four hours before: strong, loud, confident. We can probably call it medium-tempo jazz, full of explosive climaxes, with a brief reference to the previous night's mood in the middle.

Shorter comes in as the tempo and intensity remain the same. But fairly soon things begin to become jagged, with pulsating tenor saxophone stabs. Williams drops out – a repetition of the night before – and the tempo grinds to a halt. The band has now gone into ballad mode, and that is pretty much the first time that it has done so in this version. It is just saxophone and bass for a while: we are over six minutes in. Then Williams eventually comes back in at double time on the ride cymbal, Carter walks the bass, and we are back on medium-tempo jazz terrain. That ground is ever-shifting, with piano stabs here and there, oblique references to the melody by Shorter, or Williams will jump to the hi-hats to play triplets. Each member of the band searches for something new, something different. Hancock begins a solo, and Williams taps out a sort of marching band rhythm on the snare drum. But all tempo soon fades. Hancock now plays dark, melancholy chords: the happy mood of Davis's solo is here reversed, and we have returned to full ballad mode. (We are eleven minutes in, and we hear a telephone ring in the background.) Williams brings back the swing, and Hancock starts to play more notes. Carter sets up a walking bass line, and suddenly a medium tempo re-emerges. Hancock goes down a number of potential avenues, but none of them really leads anywhere, so Davis butts in and takes up the tune. He does so, again, with a relatively 'happy' tone. He even gives us a proper ending: 'Each day is Valentine's Day', as though deliberately undoing the non-ending of the night before.

What can be made of these different versions? The fairly uncontroversial claim – as we see it – that we want to make is that, over the years from 1956 to 1965, the Davis bands effectively dismantle the 'standard' nature of 'My Funny Valentine'. This dismantling has something to do with dismantling a typical or expected relationship between what a musician is playing, on the one hand, and what an audience is expecting to hear, on the other. All of this introduces another dimension of arguments related to absorption and theatricality: that the conditions or expectations of absorption will change over time, so that what might have been called absorptive in 1956 will no longer seem so by 1965. Rather, what had once been absorptive may increasingly seem to veer towards theatricality. As we suggest above, whereas from the late 1920s until the mid-1950s jazz standards were the primary medium for jazz improvisation, by the late 1950s, for many musicians, they had come to feel stale and restrictive. As Robert Pippin notes in a significant commentary on Fried, 'Las Vegas lounge singers theatricalise jazz standards, even soul and blues songs, by fitting phrasing and expression into extremely predictable, narrow conventions' (Pippin 2021, 113). There is no reason why the Davis group could not have played the same arrangements over and over, so that each night would be much like the night before, and the next night the same again. Therefore, we are forced to ask: why did the Davis group of this period take their music in such a direction, one that insisted that each night was as different as it could be? One reason – and again here we invoke the writings of Pippin – is to suggest that the stakes pertain to questions of what 'art' is; that is, to questions of what makes art important and to questions of why human beings are drawn towards artistic expressions of one sort or another. Here, some sense of the historical situatedness of artistic expression is key – we are not concerned with questions of art's essence, or the essence of jazz, nor even issues of good versus bad art or music. Rather, what Pippin wants to emphasise is, as he puts it, 'the simple, sweeping question of what it means that human beings make art, how it is that this activity is so significant to them, how it could be that this sense of its significance could change, often radically, and still be identified as the making of significant art' (Pippin 2014, 71). We want to suggest that the Davis group is doing something like this for music and/or jazz: the musicians are asking the question of what makes music meaningful, or what, at this particular moment in time, will make jazz music meaningful?

We need to draw these elements together. We want to emphasise the three key points that have emerged in our discussion.

- the interplay between *absorption* and *being beheld* (or *being heard*);
- the sense of *presentness*, of being 'in the moment';
- the historical question of what it means for human beings to make art.

Absorption and being beheld. To return to the football analogy and Fried's discussion of *Zidane*, we can surely affirm that the members of the Davis band are absorbed in what they are playing, and a function of that playing is to listen intensely to what the other members of the band are playing, to the sounds they are making. This is a mode of playing that is not directed towards an audience – at any rate, it does not seem that it is *primarily* directed towards an audience – but is instead directed inwards, to the stage and the other musicians. And so, too, with football: the footballer's primary address will be towards the ball and the other players in the match. Only secondarily will the footballer be concerned about or interested in the spectators watching the match.

Davis seems fairly explicit about this point: the music is primary; an audience is secondary. In an interview with novelist Alex Haley in 1962, he explained what this strategy meant for jazz musicians, alongside the difficulties it entailed:

> Look, man, all I am is a trumpet player... I ain't no entertainer, and I ain't trying to be one... The reason I don't announce numbers is because it's not until the last instant I decide what's maybe the best thing to play next. Besides, if people don't recognise a number when we play it, what difference does it make?... Why I sometimes walk off the stand is because when it's somebody else's turn to solo, I ain't going to just stand up there and be distracting from him. What am I going to stand up there for? I ain't no model, and I don't sing or dance, and I damn sure ain't no Uncle Tom just to be up there grinning. Sometimes I go over by the piano or the drums and listen to what they're doing. But if I don't want to do that, I go in the wings and listen to the whole band until it's the next turn for my horn... Then they claim that I ignore the audience while I'm playing. Man, when I'm working, I know the people are out there. But when I'm playing, I'm worrying about making my horn sound right... When I'm working I'm concentrating (Haley 2002 [1962], 199–200).

Davis's claims chime directly with the kinds of claims that Fried makes for painters and painting. Fried argues that the aim for painters in the anti-theatrical tradition was to 'depict [...] figures so engrossed or [...] *absorbed* in what they were doing, thinking, and feeling that they appeared oblivious of everything else, including, crucially, the beholder standing before the painting' (Fried 1998a, 48). Opposed to absorption in such paintings were strategies he calls theatrical. 'The antithesis of absorption', Fried writes, 'was theatricality, playing to an audience, which quickly emerged as the worst of artistic faults' (48). Likewise, for Davis, 'playing to an audience' becomes the worst thing a jazz musician can do. (Think of the Bebop musicians' rejection of Louis Armstrong's 'clowning': in Davis's case, one must assume issues of race are clearly at stake here, whereby theatricality becomes a matter of pandering to white audiences. This is not a criticism of Armstrong, merely an acknowledgement of what was at stake for African-American jazz musicians in these decades).

The sense of *presentness*. The famous (*infamous?*) final sentence of Fried's landmark article, 'Art and Objecthood', is 'Presentness is grace' (1998b, 168). For Miles Davis, grace is not an issue. But presentness surely is. Fried rather enigmatically argued that presentness – and absorption – were freed from duration. That can be the case for paintings or sculptures, but not for music. And yet, lack of duration – that is, a work that does not unfold in time – is only part of what Fried means. As he puts it right near the end of 'Art and Objecthood', this lack of duration is, in fact, a matter of the way in which '*at every moment the work itself is wholly manifest*' (167). He then goes on to write that what this adds up to is the work's 'perpetual creation of itself, that one experiences', so he argues, 'as a kind of *instantaneousness*' (ibid.). We have already alluded to the ways in which Fried takes up these points in his discussion of Moondoc's moment-to-moment intensity in Anri Sala's *Long Sorrow*, and we think we are correct to argue that this is an important aspect of what Davis's band during the 1960s was trying to achieve: to make the music new at each and every moment. This is not quite free jazz, for Davis insists on playing standard tunes here, as we have already pointed out. It is instead a matter of making each note count; to play the tune in a way in which it had not been played before; to play each note as though it was the first time you had played it. As Hancock points out, when the band took the stage at the Plugged Nickel, . . .

> I started focusing on how I could play against expectation. Whenever a song would build up, getting to a natural peak, the natural inclination would be to push it over the top – but instead I would suddenly bring it down with one quiet note. Tony did the same, building up his playing in volume and intensity, and then, instead of hitting the bass drum, he'd gently tap the cymbal. We did the opposite, too, suddenly ratcheting up the intensity just as a tune was winding down. . . We knew we were using the audience as guinea pigs for our experiment, but this was a way to break the habits we had formed – by destroying the structure, then picking up the pieces and building something new (Hancock and Dickey 2014, 92–93).

Finally, there is the historical question of what it means for human beings to make art – in this case, to make music. Pippin, in a commentary on Fried, takes up the latter's claims on Édouard Manet (in *Manet's Modernism*). Why did Manet invent a new kind of painting in the 1860s and 1870s? He did so because the old style of painting did not work or no longer made sense (see Pippin 2018, 51; cf. Fried 1996, 64). Transposing those arguments to jazz music, we might therefore say that Davis makes a new kind of music, a new kind of jazz, with his band of the mid-1960s because the old ways of playing jazz were no longer meaningful in the same way; they had lost their 'intensity and honesty', as Hancock notes (2014, 93). Hence Williams's desire to make anti-music: an entirely new kind of music was at stake. And Davis certainly did not end his quest for a new kind of music there. He went on in the late 1960s, with a new band, to pretty much abandon jazz standards altogether. And he also abandoned most of the numbers that the 1950s and 1960s bands had made famous, tunes such as 'So What', 'Footprints', 'Joshua' and others. The shared intelligibility that had sustained jazz performances since the 1920s and 1930s, that had brought a sense of conviction for performers and audiences alike in the aesthetic and existential possibilities of the music, was increasingly being challenged, both within and outside of the jazz world. Davis's emphasis on being absorbed in the music above all else, his refusal to play to the audience, was thus all about navigating this challenge and creating a meaningful space for his art in this context. As he said towards the end of his life, '[w]hen people come up to me and ask me to play "My Funny Valentine" . . . I tell them to go buy the record. *I'm* not there in that place any longer and I have to live for what is best for me and not what's best for them' (Davis and Troupe 1989, 384).

Recordings Mentioned

The Miles Davis Quintet (1957), *Cookin'*. Prestige CD.
The Miles Davis Sextet (1973), *Live at the Plaza*. Volume 1. Columbia CD.
Miles Davis Quintet (2007), *Milan 1964*. Improv-Jazz DVD.
Davis, M. (1965), *My Funny Valentine*. Columbia CD.
Davis, M. (2005), *Miles in Tokyo*. Columbia CD.
Davis, M. (1995), *The Complete Live at the Plugged Nickel 1965*. Columbia CD.
Sinatra, F. (1954), *Songs for Young Lovers*. Capitol CD.

Notes

1. We will acknowledge John Cage's 4'33" (1952) as the exception that proves the rule – and yet, of course, Cage's piece is one that is made in order to be heard, so it is also not as much of an exception as it might at first appear.
2. The sessions occurred on 11 May and 26 October 1956. An additional, earlier session took place on 11 November 1956 and led to *The New Miles Davis Quintet*. All sessions were recorded at Rudy Van Gelder's legendary studio of the 1950s (located in his parents' living room!).

Part 4

Theatre and Cinema

12

Metaphoric Theatricality: Theatricality as a Weapon of Resistance: The Production of *Our Grand Circus* in 1973 Greece

Michaela Antoniou

In an interview conducted in 1999, Greek playwright Iakovos Kambanellis stated: 'There existed political conditions in Greece during which the audience who had just followed a performance was ready to start a demonstration. It occurred during the Dictatorship. I certainly believe that art plays some part in politics. The production of *Our Grand Circus* was the reason that Karezi, Kazakos and I were persecuted during the dictatorship' (Kambanellis 1999, 46). On 22 June 1973, at the Atheneon Theatre in the centre of Athens, just a few blocks from the Athens Polytechnic that harboured the 1973 November student upheaval, premiered the production of *Our Grand Circus*.[1] It was a production that cast famous and popular protagonists of the Greek stage and collaborated with emblematic figures of the field of music and the Greek shadow theatre (*Karaghiozis*). The play was written by Iakovos Kambanellis, one of the most important playwrights of twentieth-century Greece. The success was instant, and the Athenians filled the large theatre because the play and the production shaped and projected a concealed protest against the totalitarian regime. During a period when censorship was implemented in almost every aspect of public expression, this company of artists employed theatrical means in order to communicate with their audience.

This chapter will focus on how this production, which appeared to be an innocent and inoffensive narrative of Greek history, united the audience and, by appropriating theatricality, cultivated opposition to the Dictatorship of the Colonels. The historic conditions of 1973 Greece, the force of the regime of the Colonels and the position of the company within the theatre field of the period will be discussed in relation to the production. The concept of *metaphoric theatricality* will be explored, and a succinct outline that explains the links of this kind of theatricality to the stage will reveal the power that the production and the play had on the Greek people of the period. The analysis of the play and, most importantly, of the production will show how metaphoric theatricality helped communicate with an audience that was craving a public exchange of ideas, aspirations and hopes, as well as the need to put aside their fears and protest against an oppressive and illegal government.

A Theatricality of the Stage

In *The Cambridge Introduction to Theatre Directing*, Maria Shevtsova introduces the notion of 'metaphoric theatricality' (Innes and Shevtsova 2013, 111). Theatricality has embodied a wide range of meanings through the ages (see Davis and Postlewait 2003, 1). Metaphoric theatricality, however, is an aspect of theatricality which pertains primarily to theatre performance. It defines a theatricality that invents a new theatrical language, a kind of code, with which a theatre company or production can communicate in a covert manner with its audience. Shevtsova describes a theatricality which was developed initially by Arianne Mnouchkine and later utilised by directors of Eastern Europe who were part of the Soviet bloc. While in France Mnouchkine did not have to fight against censorship and the power of a totalitarian regime, directors of the Soviet Republics were accustomed to finding ways to fool Big Brother's eye. Thus, this theatricality, so write Innes and Shevtsova, is 'linked to the principle of showing one thing and meaning another so that what is shown both hides and reveals its inner content' (Innes and Shevtsova 2013, 111).

This hiding and revealing presupposes a recipient, a spectator who will be able to grasp the meaning of what is going on onstage, but it also suggests the establishment of an interaction. Willmar Sauter, who explores the function of theatricality onstage, points out, after discussing the various connotations that theatricality has acquired over time by numerous theoreticians, that 'only Josette Féral underlines the necessity of the physical presence of both performer and spectator as a prerequisite of theatricality' (Sauter 2000, 53). In his own attempt to describe a theatricality pertaining to the stage, he argues that 'theatricality is not something which is produced by the performer alone, but is established through the interplay between performer and spectator' (57). The prefix 'inter' defines the ceaseless give-and-take, the communication, which takes place between the performer and the spectator.

In the case of metaphoric theatricality, this interplay is definitely a prerequisite. The performance does not have a function if it is not received, perceived and interpreted by the spectator, who ceases solely to spectate and becomes a part of the performance, as she is the one who will decode the meanings of the actions on stage. This process can be called the spectator's complicity with the performance presented. Thus acting, directing and set-design – in short, all elements that comprise a performance – follow a covert complicity: a 'metaphoric theatricality' which becomes a 'weapon of resistance' (Innes and Shevtsova 2013, 111), because the code that is established between the stage and the auditorium can provide spectators with a form of common conscience that will, in turn, result in the formation of a common viewpoint which will lead to resistance, as will be explained in the course of this chapter.

The concept of an act of resistance was, indeed, what defined the production of *Our Grand Circus*. During that dark period of Greek history, the play aimed to invent a metaphor, a cryptic language, in its text as well as its scenic presentation, in order to not only establish a form of concealed communication with its spectators and to awaken them, but also to reassure them that they were not alone in this fight against the unjust regime. Thus, resistance became a creative process, and as such it refuelled a theatricality that had a social and political objective.

This theatricality derives from the work of directors such as Vsevolod Meyerhold and Jacques Copeau, who, according to Postlewait and Davis, 'created a new theatricalism in the architectural components of the *mise-en-scéne*' and who were inherently connected with the styles and ideas that defined modernism (Postlewait and Davis 2003, 12). Their creations opposed the restrictions of realism and searched for an alternate way to approach performing and directing. Those two important directors, who acknowledged that 'theatre as a social art and a social act', as Milling and Ley (2001, 55) put it, shaped twentieth-century notions of theatricality and were Mnouchkine's 'book-masters' (Innes and Shevtsova 2013, 97). As Meyerhold states, '[n]o man (no actor) has ever been apolitical, a-social; man is always a product of the forces of his environment' (Braun 1998, 168).

It is important to note that the social function of theatre was connected to the new manifestation of the actor on the stage. The quest to avoid realism and to return to popular forms of theatre, such as *commedia dell'arte*, or to search for inspiration and guidance in the techniques of the theatre of the East, was in line with the aim to create a theatre that included the spectator: a new form of popular theatre that focused on the art of the actor, who created pure theatrical codes that spoke to and addressed the audience. Those codes evoked existing sociocultural conventions. Thus, the spectators, always aware of the fact that they were following a theatrical act, did not hide in the dark auditorium trying to immerse themselves in a detached, completed, finished and different chronotopical environment, but partook in the scenic creation, sharing ideas and emotions. This performing process and presentation resulted in what I would call theatricality.

Mnouchkine's metaphoric theatricality can be linked to Meyerhold, whose 'influence on Mnouchkine', so write Innes and Shevtsova, 'is much more a matter of "dust" settling on her in another time, place and sociocultural and political space', and it shows primarily in her notion of *théâtralité* (theatricality), which, for her, is synonymous with 'non-realism' (Innes and Shevtsova 2013, 97).

The eclectic affinity between Mnouchkine and Meyerhold characterises Mnouchkine's theatricality, and it is evident in the ways in which the French director not only stages her productions, but also characterises her political and social awareness. Theatricality, its opposition to realism, as well as theatre's social function, compose the amalgam that defines it. The line 'This is one way to recount history; we have chosen another' – from Mnouchkine's *1789, la révolution doit s'arrêter à la perfection du bonheur* – which delineates the narrative of 1789 and stresses the aspect of theatricality of the performance, characterises the aim of the Théâtre du Soleil's production (see Bradby 1991, 200). Following the events of the May 1968 upheaval, the company wanted to narrate the history of the people who are not always part of History and to enable their fellow citizens to retrospect on the events that had occurred a couple of years earlier.

The director of *Our Grand Circus*, Kostas Kazakos, and the leading lady, Jenny Karezi, had seen the Théâtre du Soleil's production in Paris (Kazakos 2017). Inspired by *1789*, the Greek company utilised a similar technique to address issues that concerned a nation tyrannised by an oppressive government. The affinity between the two plays rests in their thematic and their narrative technique – namely, focusing on historic events narrated by the people. *Our Grand Circus* did not concentrate on one particular event but presented an overview of Greek history;

however, they both aimed to tell the 'small history', as Kambanellis calls it, a history told by everyday human beings, rather than by the officials. Kambanellis claimed that *Our Grand Circus* narrates the history of the unprivileged, the people who have been muted by the history of the powerful (Kambanellis 1975, 8).

A Production for a Wide Audience

On 21 April 1967, a group of Army Officers assumed power of the Greek State and proclaimed a Military Junta. Democracy was abolished, and the constitution was suspended. During the seven years that the Junta remained in power, dissidents were muted, threatened, terrorised, arrested, imprisoned, tortured and exiled, and censorship spread in all forms of public expression (press, television, radio, theatre, song-writing and so on). There existed a Censorship Committee to which all material that was to be performed, sung or composed had to be submitted, and the committee modified all of this material according to its will and preference (Georgakaki 2015, 24–25). Theatre, during that period, was one of the few forms of public gathering permitted by the regime, and thus it became a platform from which a form of resistance was encouraged in a concealed manner. The mere attendance of a production that addressed everyday life's problems was acknowledged by the attendants as a form of political action (Mavromoustakos 2005, 138).

A number of small and unknown theatre groups produced new Greek plays during that period, as well as productions of famous Greek or foreign plays with political innuendoes. It was not, however, until the production of *Our Grand Circus* that a communication with a wider public was established, resulting in turmoil. There are three main parameters that caused this reaction: the first is related to the position and composition of the company, the second to the play, and the last to the performance. As these parameters are intrinsically connected and created a dynamic composition, it is impossible and misleading to analyse them separately. Thus, this text will leap from the one aspect to the other, in an attempt to provide a complete spectrum of this theatrical event and its meta-theatrical connotations.

The Karezi-Kazakos Company was what can be classified as a leading actors' company – that is, a company which earns its success due to the appreciation of an audience, 'which regarded theatregoing as [...]

part of the ritual of bourgeois life' (Mavromoustakos 2005, 91). It was a commercial company which had, to use Pierre Bourdieu's words, 'the consecration bestowed by the choice of ordinary consumers' (Bourdieu 1993, 51). Both Karezi and Kazakos had been famous for their participation in popular films of the Greek screen. Karezi, being the more popular of the two, was acknowledged as one of the two female stars of Greek Cinema, starring in romantic comedies or dramas as the beautiful, attractive, delicate or audacious, rich or poor, witty or daring young lass. She met the slightly less famous Kazakos in 1967, and they married the following year. Kazakos was left-wing and later became a member of the Greek Parliament for the Greek Communist Party. Together, they starred in films and were the type of actors who featured on the covers of magazines, having a wide audience empathise with the birth of their son or their public appearances.

In 1968, during the Junta, Karezi formed a company with her politically-oriented husband Kazakos. She abandoned light comedies and turned to plays with social concerns, such as *Viva Aspasia* by Kambanellis and *Madame Sans-Gene* by Victorien Sardou and Emile Moreau. In 1973, they presented the politically-oriented *Our Grand Circus*. The change that Karezi underwent – namely, her transformation from a politically and socially aloof, beautiful, popular icon to a citizen concerned with and aware of contemporary social and political issues – was on its own a paradigm for citizens who had not been involved in actions against the oppressive regime. The 'Dear Jenny' of the bourgeois spectators leapt forward and protested against the Junta, becoming an example to the mass audience that followed her and showing them that they had to react to what was happening to their country.

The entire company consisted of famous and iconic figures of the Greek artistic field, who joined their forces against the regime and became an example for the public. The older, extremely popular and exceptionally talented character actor Dioneses Papagiannopoulos, who was a co-star in many of Karezis's movies, had a right-wing orientation. His widely known political standing affected a large number of conservative spectators. Moreover, there was Nikos Xelouris, a young Cretan singer who was worshipped by the public and who had become synonymous with Cretan vigour and integrity. There was also the successful and talented composer Stavros Xarhakos, who also had a right-wing orientation; the shadow theatre player Evgenios Spatharis, who was the emblem of the neo-Greek tradition of Karaghiozis; and, of course, the important playwright

Kambanellis. Their involvement in the production raised strong metatheatric connotations and disseminated effectively and widely the political aspect of the production, because making the production attractive for a wide range of spectators required a recognizable reference point, and, as Erickson claims, 'democratic political change cannot take place without the support of a broad audience' (Erickson 2003, 180). Accordingly, these artists reached out to the public and put forward their intention to oppose the oppressive Dictatorship of the Generals, thereby creating a political production that had a dynamic impact on the people.

A Play about 'Small' History

Our Grand Circus was written by Kambanellis for the Karezi-Kazakos Company, following long discussions during which the three of them examined ways to attack the oppressive regime (Kazakos 2017; Pefanis 2005b, 59). The amalgamation of their ideas, artistic aims and staging possibilities resulted in a novel and powerful production, where the mixture of genres concentrated their political aims in a play about the essence of Greece. When artists are in contact with socio-political conditions and feel the need to act upon them, such a collaboration during the creative process is necessary. The necessity for a dramatist and the actors to work together when composing a production has been a desideratum in Meyerhold as well as Copeau (Milling and Ley 2001, 57). It also characterised the Soleil's creative process; even though the *Circus* was not a collective creation as such, Kambanellis wrote it in close collaboration with both Kazakos and Karezi, aiming to create a piece that would simultaneously address and project the conditions surrounding the events of the specific time and place.

The printed play, which was published in 1975, after the fall of the Junta, records the script of the first production, while the stage directions refer to and describe the *mise-en-scène*. The title – as most of Kambanellis's titles – is a 'brief, compact sentence that encapsulates [. . .] the meaning of the text [. . .] in a satiric way' (Pefanis 2000, 121).[2] However, it goes beyond satire introducing the metaphor which characterises the entire piece and the production. There is an inherent ambiguity in both the words 'grand' and 'circus': 'grand' has an ironic nuance that juxtaposes not only the long and significant Greek history with the petty, pitiful and mean period that Greece was undergoing, but also the artistic, social and political significance of the endeavour within the restricted and uninspired world of the censorship imposed by the regime. Circus, besides the ironic hint which related Greece to a circus, refers directly to the kind of show that will be presented, a production that utilises popular means of entertainment, a circus, or a fair where ordinary people are gathered in order to communicate. The notion of communication and interchange is linked to the aim of engaging the public and of the political awaking of the audience, thus sustaining the theatrical metaphor.

The play consisted of episodes from Greek history, from the mythological birth of the Greek race until the German Occupation during the Second World War. It narrated, as already mentioned, the small history of everyday people. It consisted of independent episodes, using the familiar structure of revues; however, its classification as a revue limits its political intentions and theatrical value.[3] The episodes were connected, explained and critiqued by Romios and Romiaki – played by Kazakos and Karezi, respectively. Romios, which is the common root of both names, means 'Greek', but it is a word used to characterise the Greek people under the Roman, Byzantine and Ottoman Empires. There exists, therefore, a diminishing nuance that becomes an analogue to the current situation in Greece. The ending -aki refers to something that is smaller or younger. Those two vagabonds essentially became representatives of the Greek people by their very names, which defined their origin, as well as by their inherent connection to the history that they narrated. As characters, Romios was a lunatic, but also a savant who knew how things operated in the world, while Romiaki was an ignorant, naïve, but kind-hearted girl who gained knowledge and was transformed in the course of the play. This transformation is also a transformation that Karezi herself underwent as an artist, as has been indicated above, and this identification between the role and the actress ultimately strengthens the influence that the production exercised on the spectators on a meta-theatrical level. The parts of Romios and Romiaki were additionally linked to Karaghiozis and the character of Kollitiri (Pefanis 2005b, 57), the young son of Karaghiozis, the traditional shadow theatre figure, which appeared in the opening of the second act of the play, to be analysed in due course.

The production was presented in an old open-air cinema that was converted into a theatre venue and became one of the most popular summer theatre venues in Athens for the following three decades (unfortunately, the theatre was demolished in 2019). Kambanellis favoured the idea of an open-air theatre, which had always been very popular in Greece during the summer, claiming that it mirrored Greek mentality and the need for a theatre that would 'speak openly' (Kambanellis 1990, 43–44). Kambanellis alluded to the function of the theatre in ancient Greece and its link to the *demos* – namely, the citizens of the city. This allusion strengthened even further the impact of the production; however, more practical reasons forced the Karezi-Kazakos company to perform that summer, such as the fact that they wanted to mount a production for that summer period (Kazakos 2017).

The choice of this venue, as it was not originally built as a theatre venue, gave the company the ability to reconstruct the entire edifice. For this particular production, the large front of the theatre was decorated with multi-coloured strings of triangle flags and lightbulbs. In the foyer, large pictures of shadow theatre figures hung from the walls, a juggler performed tricks, interacting with the audience, and music was heard from a barrel organ, a popular instrument that toured Greek fairs and brought to mind a successful film in which Karezi had starred, which featured her as touring fairs with a couple of vagabonds playing the barrel organ. The entire space of the open-air theatre in the centre of Athens brought to mind a local fair. As can be detected, the use of space was transformed to become inherently connected to the thematic of the play. This practice of extending the action beyond the stage also brings to mind Mnouchkine's practice, as it was established at La Cartoucherie.

The aim was to create this alternative space of the circus/fair in order to: first, show the audience the tools that the production utilised, tools which were familiar to them and triggered memories from their common tradition – such as the shadow theatre of Karaghiozis; second, present from the beginning the image of Greece as a place where everything was possible – oppression and revolt – strengthening the metaphor of a Bakhtinian carnivalesque environment where everything is reversed; and third, and most importantly, masquerade the real intentions of the production. The playful, joyous, carefree ambience that was projected by the bright, shining lights and the smiling faces in the foyer was the perfect hideout for a political production that aimed to awaken the minds and hearts of the oppressed, muted spectators.

The stage was also constructed to serve the production, which was presented on polytopic stages that consisted of the main, frontal, conventional stage on the one side of the auditorium, a small central stage in the middle, and a medium stage on the other side. The three performance spaces were joined by corridors (Kambanellis 1990, 43). The spatial configuration of the acting space aided the historical journey through the periods of Greek history and also provided the two commentators, Romios and Romiaki, with a way to interact with the audience. Moreover, this is one more influence of Mnouchkine's *1789* production with its five stages and linking corridors.

The Complicity of the Production

The idea that interconnected the episodes of the play and provided its main thematic was of the Titan Chronus, who swallowed his own children in order to retain his power. This was an idea that tormented Kambanellis and reminded him of the political and social conditions of his era (Kambanellis 1975, 9). This metaphor was apparent in the text, as Kambanellis, according to Puchner, 'embodies in the speech of the written text his own concept of the performance' (Puchner 2010, 23; cf. Felopoulou 2006, 392). The episodes commenced by narrating the history of the Greek Hellenistic period continued to the Byzantine era, recounted incidents of the 1821 revolution and concluded with the occupation during the Second World War. As E. D. Karampetsos argues, 'history and myth become one recurring nightmare of momentary glory subverted by treachery and transformed into defeat and subjugation'. However, he adds, instead of Zeus, who would save the world from Chronus, 'there are brave people willing to sacrifice themselves in a foredoomed insurrection against oppression' (Karambetsos 1979, 211). These were the everyday people who constructed a 'small' history. They were, in turn, the spectators who followed the production during the Junta.

The production commenced with a dialogue between Romios and Romiaki who were looking for the stage and addressed the audience, as if they were members of an Aristophanian Parabasis. Romiaki asked the spectators if they had any idea where the stage was, while Romios responded: 'I don't really care where it is. I will say what I have to say from wherever I am' (Kambanellis 1975, 8). These opening lines achieved the two primary goals of the production: on the one hand, they established a connection with the spectators, making them accomplices of the events that occurred within the theatre venue; on the other hand, they assumed that the stage would not be limited to one specific place – if you have something to say, you can say it from wherever you are, thus expanding the performance space and the meanings of the production beyond the confined environment of the stage, the theatre venue, or the city of Athens, including the whole of Greece. In that manner, the everyday people who were part of history could act and react in their everyday life, in the way in which they inhabited their lives.

The episodes were linked and commented upon with songs sung by Xelouris, the popular Cretan singer, who was wearing the traditional costume of Crete – black shirt, khaki trousers, black boots and a black kerchief tied around the top of his head. This traditional costume referred to revolt, resistance and strength – characteristics that described the Cretans, were commonly acknowledged by all Greek people and created one more metaphor within the performance. These songs had been composed by Xarhakos and the lyrics written by Kambanellis. They were closely connected with the episodes commenting on the action, supporting or providing antitheses to what was being said on the stage. They were ample with epic and agonistic references, of varied structure and representative of different genres, such as reminiscent of Greek popular songs (δημοτικά τραγούδια – demotic songs) or blank verse (Pefanis 2005a, 258–59). Kambanellis claimed that the reason why there were so many songs included in the production was because 'a song has the density of a cry or of laughter or of a proverb or of myth [. . . These songs] are like bridges of experience, which help us cross from one episode to the next' (259). All the songs led to the last, which was a direct call to arms:

> People don't bend your head anymore,
> don't have fear by your bedside,
> the fights you've given are not worthy
> if the blood that has been seeded isn't rewarded.
> People don't bend your head anymore,
> fear inscribes the black doom of the coward
> joy to the one who aims for freedom (Kambanellis 1975, 95).

It is important to note that this call to arms was disguised, hidden even, in the playful ambience of the circus metaphor. There was, intentionally, no indication of it nor of the last speech of the performance, where the spectators were directly addressed to think and react.

The play and the production were a metaphor, starting from the title and the configuration of the entire theatre venue and ending with the two narrators and the independent episodes. I will elucidate some indicative moments of the power of metaphoric theatricality within the performance.

The first is related to the episode of the statue of the great Greek independence fighter of the 1821 revolution, Theodoros Kolokotronis. Kolokotronis was a chieftain who during his lifetime was imprisoned and undermined because his beliefs and his influence on the common people did not always coincide with the interests of the rulers of Greece. His name was restored for future generations, and Greeks acknowledged him as one of the most important figures of Greek liberation from the Turks. In the episode of the performance, his statue, which was played by Papagiannopoulos, came alive and learned about everything that had happened in Greece in recent decades. His fury and opposition were evident. The production gave an alternate meaning to this figure of the 1821 revolution, making him an image that united contemporary Greeks. This was necessary because the appropriation of the 1821 fighters was used by the regime of the Colonels as the icon and symbol of a solid Greek tradition, serving their interests. It was related to issues of ethnicity, continuity and authenticity regarding history, supporting the regime and their intentions. This image, however, backfired and became the representation of a fighter against oppression, for freedom and independence.

The second indicative moment was established in the episode of the guillotine and through the speech of the president of the village, who welcomed this instrument of death in the Greek state. Spiros Konstantopoulos, who performed the part of the president, imitated the intonations and tone of voice of the Head of the Dictatorship, Georgios Papadopoulos, alluding to the madness and cruelty of the oppressive government.

Finally, it is worth commenting on two incidents that defined the power of the production's theatricality. First, because of the episodic structure of the play, Kambanellis and the company submitted to the Censorship Committee the various episodes of the play in a random order and included some episodes that were overtly opposing the regime, which they knew were going to be censored. However, as the committee did not have a complete overview of the text of the production, they requested to follow the general rehearsal. The company was terrified, but Kazakos instructed his actors to perform the whole production at an extremely fast pace (Kazakos 2017). The piece lasted one hour and ten minutes, while it normally took over three hours, and the committee did not grasp the connotations of the play, which needed real acting and the complicity of the audience in order to convey its true meaning. Second, when the Censorship Committee ordered the company to exclude certain lines because they were offending the Junta, actors conducted the action without words, while referring to the fact that these lines had been forcefully excluded. This resulted in a pantomime, which, on an external level, obeyed the rules that had been imposed by the regime. It also constructed, however, a silent interlocution between the stage and the spectators, imbued in hidden meanings that enabled a complicit communication. This is, ultimately, the epitome of metaphoric theatricality.

The Use of a Popular Theatre Form: *Karaghiozis*

The second part of the production opened with a segment of Karaghiozis. As has already been noted, the decoration of the theatre space used elements from Karaghiozis's shadow theatre. Such elements were also used in the set-design of the production. There were two gigantic snakes which covered the front of the proscenium arch. Those snake figures were borrowed from the Greek shadow theatre and instantly identifiable by the audience as characters of the extremely popular Greek shadow theatre fable titled *Alexander the Great and the Cursed Snake*. This shadow theatre play had been inspired by a popular legend from the mythological past, by combining contemporary Greek-Orthodox religion, referring to the dragon slayed by St George, and the tradition of idolatry myths (Damianakos 2011, 10). This amalgam described a Greek culture that was strongly linked to Christianity as well as the past of Classical Greece.

The use of Karaghiozis and his company of friends was a practice followed by a few of the author's contemporaries.[4] It is important to clarify the significance of Karaghiozis to the Greek people. Theodoros Hadjipantazis explains:

> Karaghiozis did not come from Turkey in the same manner that Italian opera and American jazz have come to Greece. Turkish shadow theatre was part of the artistic tradition of the mixed peoples of the Ottoman Empire, one of which happened to be Greeks. This means that within the framework of that diverse society, from a certain point on, Karaghiozis stopped being exclusively Turkish and became trans-national and multilingual (Hadjipantazis 1976, 18).

Furthermore, Hadjipantazis adds, for many years 'the shadow theatre was recognized by the Greek masses as the only true mirror of their social and cultural situation' (ibid.), and the character of Karaghiozis 'no doubt reflects the experiences of a large segment of the Greek population during the end of the nineteenth and the beginning of the twentieth centuries' (26).

What is true of the beginning of the twentieth century is also true of the period in question. Karaghiozis expressed the Greek condition. He was the eternally hungry, but resourceful Greek who would undertake any endeavour in order to survive. This was also the director's opinion (Kazakos 2017). Karaghiozis was not a rebel; he was a rayah, a slave, who spoke up, but also hid behind linguistic ambiguities and the inability of his interlocutors to understand the real meaning of his words. Thus, he became the perfect conveyor of metaphoric theatricality, saying one thing and meaning another, while the audience was always aware of this constant hide-and-seek, as it has been a part of the Greek tradition of shadow theatre.

As a genre, Karaghiozis was always linked to contemporary political and historical events (Spatharis 1992, 49). His plays were used to encourage soldiers during wartime (61) and civilians under the German Occupation (153), and they determined the vote results of municipal elections (114). The apotheosis (αποθέωση) – namely, the practice in historic Karaghiozis plays to abandon the shadow figures and to play the last, heroic scene of the play with live actors in front of the berdes (μπερντές), the drape – gave an alternate dimension to the sequence presented by the company of *Our Grand Circus* on the stage of the Athenian theatre (130).

Like an apotheosis, the section of Karaghiozis was presented on the frontal, central stage of the theatre, following the conventions of shadow theatre. Thus, the actors performed in profile and in rows, one next to the other, although there was a plasticity in their movement as they did not imitate the staccato moves of the shadow figures. Karaghiozis was acted by Papagiannopoulos who, as the most popular actor of the period's Greek theatre, undertook both emblematic figures of the production, Kolokotronis and Karaghiozis. The other shadow theatre characters of the episode were the traditional figures of this genre: Hadjiavatis, Karaghiozis's friend, who had compromised and collaborated with governmental forces; Barba-Giorgos, the uneducated peasant who was strong and ready to physically oppose his enemies; Nionios, the short but brave man from the Ionian Islands, who did not give in; Stavrakas, the marginal and straightforward character who had no problem speaking his mind; and, Morfonios, the ugly, well-bred figure who was ultimately afraid to act. In short, those characters were indicative of types of individuals and became symbols of everyday people. The shadow theatre, with its characters and conventions, gave the Greek people during the dark period of the Junta the freedom of mind to make deductions and thus activated their mental mechanisms to think and react.

Conclusion

It should be stressed, once more, that audience attendance was enormous, as the theatre was packed every single night. It is not wrong to claim that the massive and general impact of the production played some part in the Polytechnic uprising the November of 1973, the massive student uprising during which university students occupied the building of the Athens Polytechnic on Patision Street in order to express their opposition to the practices of the Dictatorship. The occupation lasted for three days; on the eve of the fourth day, a tank crashed the main gate of the Polytechnic, killing the students that hung on the metal fence. Indicative of this connection could be the fact that, three days after the fall of the Polytechnic, first Karezi and, a few days later, Kazakos, were arrested and imprisoned. However, when they were released, they continued their performances in a winter venue. Meta-theatric and meta-dramatic allusions enabled the audience to empathise and identify with what they saw. As Walter Puchner argues, . . .

> During the Dictatorship, plays and plots happened to unexpectedly take alternate, evocative dimensions, or the Censorship Committee missed the real meaning of the texts that were submitted for approval. That was the case of *Our Grand Circus* [. . .] However, when the play was performed, all the innuendoes became apparent because of the audience's response. The police waited for a chance to intervene. Following the Polytechnic events Kazakos and Karezi were arrested (Puchner 2010, 46).

Notes

1. The production was reprised on 23 July 1974, with some alterations to cast and text. This play is the only text written during the dictatorship that was performed in a later period (see Puchner 2010, 29, 453).
2. See also Puchner 2010, 860–71, especially 865: '*Our Grand Circus* is a misleading title solely in relation to the satiric aims and the hidden political propaganda.

The presentation of history as a circus that includes multiple spectacles is a common metaphor in international literature and, as such, it conveys no suspicion. The hidden edge derives from the characterisation of the current affairs as a circus'.

3. Theodoros Hadjipantazis claims that Kambanellis's play 'introduced the particular genre of Historic Revue' (2006, 247). Walter Puchner, in his book on Kambanellis, explains that the author used the familiar structure of the revue (2010, 253). Konstantza Georgakaki includes the play in her book of twentieth-century revue history in Greece (2015, 162–63). This classification should be regarded with caution.

4. Indicatively, during that same period Karolos Koun's Theatro Technis (Arts Theatre) was presenting George Skourtis *Karaghiozis Almost Vizier* and in 1975 George Michalidis's political play *The Battle of Athens*, which incorporated in its structure scenes from Karaghiozis. Furthermore, Kambanellis's next play, *The Broad Bean and the Chickpea*, also performed by the Karezi-Kazakos Company, used figures and scripts inspired by Karaghiozis's shadow theatre.

13

Theatricalising Sci-Fi: Theatre and the Multiverse in *Mouse: The Persistence of an Unlikely Thought* (Daniel Kitson, 2016) and *Constellations* (Nick Payne, 2012)

Anna Wilson

Introduction

All too often, theatre exploring philosophical or scientific ideas relies on content-driven drama, seen within the 'theatre of ideas' or the 'thesis play', where a full theatrical experience is compromised in favour of communicating ideas through dialogue-driven drama. Two performances challenge this assumption: Daniel Kitson's *Mouse: The Persistence of an Unlikely Thought* (2016) and Nick Payne's *Constellations* (2012). Both performances explore the concept of the multiverse, a subject more commonly found in cinema or television, and the sci-fi genre they accommodate so well. The skilful translation of genre and subject-matter to the medium of theatre within these performances informs part of the inquiry here: what are the challenges of presenting science fiction on stage? My response to this question is outlined in relation to the broader context of sci-fi theatre, underpinned by the discussions of Willingham, Farnell and Callow on this ever-expanding terrain. The multiverse, a wide-ranging concept originating in quantum physics in the 1950s, is examined through the lens of Hugh Everett's (1957) Many Worlds Interpretation (MWI). There are many conflicting definitions of theatricality circulating, to which the chapters in this book testify. It is not my intention to examine the myriad ways in which the term might be used but, rather, to focus on a selection of perspectives characterised in relation to theatre aesthetics, specifically. Michael Fried's concept of audience/performer materiality (1980, 1998a);

Fiebach's 'ostentatious presentation of creative human skills', 'intelligent timing of activities' and 'the making of specific spaces' (2002, 17); the relationship of stylisation/symbolism to Rancière's notion of a 'poetic labour of translation' (2009, 10), and Loiselle and Maron's self-reflexivity (2012) are the key perspectives in question.

This chapter examines the ways in which the two performances exhibit, nurture, embrace, or develop these attributes of theatricality in relation to the subject-matter being explored. It considers how theatrical affect is generated through a sensitivity to and development of the theatrical medium. In this sense, my definition shifts from one of taxonomy to one of value. It is probably also worth pointing out that the collected theories upon which I base my definition of theatre aesthetics do not necessarily originate from neutral sources. For instance, Fried's theory infers a negative attitude to the definition of theatricality that he outlines. Conversely, Fiebach specifically articulates his thinking in relation to 'theatre's aesthetic pleasure', using value-laden adjectives such as 'intelligent' and 'attraction' to couple value with definition. It is not my intention to instrumentalise here – that is, to align generic value or success within formulaic prescriptions of theatre form, but rather to assess the ways in which individual theatre pieces respond to or cultivate the essential qualities that I perceive to be characteristic of the theatrical medium.

My aim is not, as Auslander puts it, to 'yield a reductive binary opposition of the live and the mediatised' (Auslander 1999, 3); on the contrary, the two performances in question were chosen because of their ambitious fusion of cinematic and theatrical form and their ability to challenge academic notions of theatre ontology. It is also worth noting that, while my focus is on the theatrical presentation of the two performances (in terms of live theatre aesthetics) I do, on occasion, resort to the inclusion of Payne's play text to ensure accuracy when recounting the dialogue. This study will finish by briefly considering the value in both cinematic and theatrical depictions of the multiverse in relation to wider notions of choice, consequence, possibility and responsibility.

The Subject of Sci-Fi

The concept of the multiverse is, usually, a subject more commonly found in the medium of film/television and the sci-fi genre that they accommodate so well. One only has to think of the following few obvious examples from an extensive lineage. In film, there are *Interstellar* (Christopher Nolan, 2014), *Coherence* (James Ward Byrkit, 2013), *The Family Man* (Brett Ratner, 2000), *Sliding Doors* (Peter Howitt, 1998) and *Source Code* (Duncan Jones, 2011). In television, one can find *Bandersnatch* (Charlie Brooker, 2019), *The Man in the High Castle* (Frank Spotnitz, 2015–19), *Parallels* (Christopher Leonne, 2015), *Quantum Leap* (Donald P. Bellisario, 1989–93), *Star Trek* (Gene Roddenberry, 1966–67) and *The Twilight Zone* (Rod Serling, 1959–64). As Andrew Haydon, writing for the *Guardian*, suggests, . . .

> Sci-fi so rarely makes it onto the stage. As well as being regarded with a certain warmth, there's also a sense of mistrust around the genre. Writers fear that it's somehow a bit uncool – a bit 70s – and so we get interminable plays about Urgent Contemporary Issues rather than coolly speculative projections (Haydon 2008).

Haydon's suggestion that theatrical sci-fi is somehow 'uncool' potentially relates to perceptions of the form, which maintain that, as one writer puts it, 'the theatrical act should be subservient to the scientific fact' (Djerassi; in Farnell 2019, 6). Academic and playwright Carl Djerassi develops these sentiments by suggesting that such 'facts' should be 'channeled through a purposefully didactic method' (ibid.). While Djerassi is keen to make a separation between what he terms 'science-in-theatre' and 'science-fiction theatre', Farnell foregrounds the shortcomings in Djerassi's taxonomical division. He suggests that the distinction that Djerassi uses to differentiate 'science-in-theatre' from that of 'sci-fi theatre', is a nebulous one, refuting Djerassi's claim that 'science-in-theatre' can be identified by theatrical representations of science smuggled through fiction, which are either 'impeccably accurate or at least plausible' (2002, 193). It is not my intention, here, to analyse the semantic issues that arise when attempting to define science-fiction theatre, but rather to endorse Farnell's supposition that 'the wider academic view of science fiction [. . .] has long been established as a genre of the plausible' (Farnell 2019, 6).

Haydon's notion that science-fiction 'so rarely makes it onto the stage' is, increasingly, a common misconception. The organiser of Talos, the first ever science-fiction theatre festival in London, Christos Callow Jr is keen to point out that 'we are approaching a "golden age" of science-fiction theatre' (Gray 2017, 11). Callow Jr's claim is endorsed by an accompanying archive to the festival, providing an extensive list of science-fiction theatre works from the twenty-first century. This ever-expanding database is testament to the growing popularity of the field, even if questions of definition (and quality) remain. The following are a few examples included in or in addition to the rather broad repertoire of theatrical sci-fi: *Future Bodies* (Rash Dash and Unlimited Theatre, 2018), *X* (Alistair McDowell, 2016), *Heisenberg: The Uncertainty Principle* (Simon Stephens, 2015), *Zero Hour* (imitating the dog, 2013), *Tangle* (Unlimited Theatre, 2008), *The Ethics of Progress* (John Spooner, 2007), *Infinities* (John Barrow, 2002), *QED* (Peter Parnell, 2001), *Moving Bodies* (Arthur Giron, 2000), *A Brief History of Time* (Vanishing point, 2000), *Copenhagen* (Michael Frayn 1998), *Schrodinger's Box* (Reckless Sleepers, 1998), *Possible Worlds* (John Mighton, 1990), *Doctor Who: The Ultimate Adventure* (Terrance Dicks, 1989) and *The Blue Flame* (Hobart and Willard, 1920).

However, the *multiverse* – a scientific concept that will be unpacked shortly – is an idea less commonly spotted on stage, I suspect, as a result of its perceived suitability to cinema and screen. In narrative terms, this could relate to the temporality of film and its ability to create simultaneity – the phenomenon of actions occurring at the same time – or multiplicity – multiple versions of the same phenomena. Within this medium, the present moment can be immortalised: recorded, repeated and/or multiplied many times over, with relative ease. As André Bazin suggests, 'the photographic image is [...] freed from the conditions of time and space that govern it' (1967, 14). Simultaneity is evident in the split-screen convention utilised within shows such as *Russian Doll* (Lyonne, Headland & Poehler, 2019), or the multi-screen set up within films such as *Time Code* (Mike Figgis, 2000). The classic editing technique of cross-cutting also facilitates ease of movement between different locations, alternating 'shots of events in one location with shots of events in other places [...] ty[ing] together the different lines of action' and 'bringing out a temporal simultaneity' (Bordwell and Thompson 2013, 246).

In contrast, live theatre is always moving forward in time: as in life, each moment is already 'dead' before it can be thought of. For Kagarlitski, theatre is a 'conditional art [...] whose power derives from the sense that the events on stage are happening now, at the moment of presentation' (in Murphy 1992, 198). Achieving the effect of multiple simultaneity on stage, then, is a theatrical challenge for any theatre-maker. Many live productions respond to this challenge through a use of mediatised versions of bodies or locations in multi-media presentations.[1] Yet, the question remains as to how you might stage simultaneous multiplicity without relying on recorded footage. The use of body doubles and/or duplicated sets could be one answer: presenting the same (but different) characters and locations at the same time. However, this can be hard to achieve, particularly in the register of realism where suspension of disbelief is continually compromised by the live practicalities of the medium. The tradition of multi-roling within the theatre also potentially obfuscates the task of trying to signify that different actors are, in fact, the same person. While such an approach can and has been successfully achieved on stage,[2] it is often through an embracing of the playful duplicity of theatrical form and not through an attempt at theatrical realism. In a similar manner, Ralph Willingham, in *Scenic Realism and Science-Fiction Theatre*, suggests that 'the theatre can create the fantastic worlds of science fiction [. . .] but it must do so within the conventions of theatre not within those of the motion picture' (1991, 75).

Many Worlds Theory

Hugh Everett's Many Worlds theory (MW) made a lasting, if highly contested (and largely unproven), contribution to the expanding scientific field of the multiverse. An MW's interpretation of the multiverse depicts a world in which infinite worlds exist, involving illimitable permutations or possibilities of existence. However, due to our existence within just one of these permutations (or 'branches', as Everett describes them), it is impossible for us to see or measure any of these alternative permutations. As Everett suggests, 'no observer would ever be aware of any "branching", which is alien to our experience' (Everett 1957). Everett's theory was a response to what is described within quantum physics as the 'measurement problem'. To simplify, the measurement problem refers to the idea that an object (or particle) occupies multiple qualities simultaneously, but that these simultaneous qualities cannot be measured through objective (classical) observation. This is because, upon observation, these multiple qualities collapse and are reduced to a single value, a result of something known as 'quantum supposition'. This is described by the Copenhagen physicists as 'wave function collapse'.[3] In contrast, Everett suggests that, rather than the wave function collapsing to a single value (or outcome), it would split, along with the observer, each time both come into contact with the other (or, at the quantum-level, each time sub-atomic particles interacted with each other), resulting in multiple possible outcomes.

In Everett's formulation, the classical separation between object and observer was now 'entangled' within an inseparable whole system. When considered at the non-molecular level, similar interactions in everyday life involving decisions that embody a probability of outcome also produce a similar splitting. We can only experience one outcome of the decision we make, but in the multiverse there are infinite versions of alternative outcomes playing out. Every time there is a situation involving choice, the universe splits, so that each outcome can be realised. As Everett explains, '[e]ach time an individual splits he is unaware of it, and any single individual is at all times unaware of his "other selves" with which he has no interaction from the time of splitting' (Everett 1957).

The Performances

It is this supposition of Everett's that I see playing out in Daniel Kitson's 2016 theatre performance *Mouse: The Persistence of an Unlikely Thought*. The show features a lonely writer, William Booth, who receives a mysterious telephone call from someone called Bill. We later discover that Bill is another version of William, calling from an alternative, parallel universe. This conceit utilises a degree of artistic licence in terms of scientific accuracy: somehow, Bill has managed to penetrate the membranes of time and space by ringing his lost mobile in one universe and inadvertently ringing William's landline in another. The connection between these two characters is slowly realised throughout the ninety-minute telephone conversation, in which we see William speaking to Bill on speakerphone and where the fictional time of the two characters extends to include the entire night. Despite a shaky start – Bill believes that William has, in fact, stolen his phone – both discover that they have more in common than they initially thought, including their names, where they went to university, the fact that they are both writers and their uncannily similar tone of voice. As rapport builds between the two characters, William tests out on Bill convoluted ideas for a story on which he has been working, about a woman who believes that she can communicate with a mouse, the notes and timelines of which are scribbled across the numerous whiteboards that line the back wall of the shipping container in which William works. At one point, Bill introduces William to Rachel, his wife, and we learn of their new baby, Dot, named after Bill's grandmother. Bizarrely, William's grandmother is also called Dorothy, another seeming coincidence in the strange unfolding of the characters' relationship.

This telephonic two-way duologue is interrupted with sharp shifts in sound and lighting: electrical-type surges which jolt us into the present moment where Kitson addresses the audience as 'himself'. In this new space, wryly described by Kitson within the show as 'audaciously dismantling the fourth wall', we are introduced to another writer: that of Kitson himself and his process of putting together William's back-story. Kitson shares this process with the audience in between playfully berating certain spectators for yawning or looking at their phones. It is here that we eventually learn of a crucial moment in William's past: a moment of seemingly insignificant – or even unconscious – decision-making, which we discover to have changed the course of his life. Upon stopping off in a car park one day to use the toilet, William exchanged glances with a rather attractive woman talking to a squirrel. Torn between the decision of continuing his mission to find the toilet and striking up a conversation with the woman, William decides on the former course of action, igniting a split in his universe, which results in the current timeline in which William finds himself. We discover that the woman talking to the squirrel was, in fact, Rachel, Bill's wife, and that William could, in fact, be living the life of Bill, had he chosen the latter course of action. Instead, we see William, a single, thirty-nine-year-old unknown writer working out of a somewhat lonely shipping container.

In contrast, *Constellations* by Nick Payne presents innumerable permutations on the lives of two characters, Marianne and Roland. In these permutations, the characters meet different versions of each other, as opposed to different versions of themselves, more accurately upholding Everett's theory. Marianne is a young theoretical physicist who meets Roland, an apiarist, at a barbeque. It is the barbeque which opens the play where the audience is introduced to the two characters, through Marianne's various attempts to make contact with Roland. These numerous (and largely failed) attempts to attract Roland's romantic interest are presented in short bursts of almost identical interaction. Eventually, we hit upon a scene (or multiverse) where the couple 'hit it off'. The play then focuses on the multiple possibilities of their relationship: one sees the couple staying together, and Marianne develops a brain tumour; in others, both Roland and Marianne commit adultery, with each one leaving the other.

Theatricality and the Productions

Among a plethora of contesting definitions, Davis and Postlewait, in the introduction to their book *Theatricality*, suggest that 'the quintessence of theatre' is often cited as a way to understand the term (2003, 1). It is this definition on which I draw here, examining the essential qualities of the *medium* of theatre and proceeding from what Fischer-Lichte might describe as an aesthetic concept of theatre, 'based on the narrow concept of theatre as an artform only' (1995, 87). To cultivate a concept of theatricality engendered through theatre aesthetics, an articulation of how I am defining 'theatrical medium' is necessary. Theatrical medium inevitably relates to conceptions of theatre itself. However, the polymorphic nature of the term 'theatre' as an ever-changing notion which is both historically and culturally contingent – referring to a theatre building itself at various moments in time, the performance of which takes place within it or as a mode of perception – problematises ease of definition. Michael Kirby goes some way in diverting from the nuances and complexities of such definitions by offering the notion of 'intent' as a key definer of the term. He suggests:

> Theatre does not occur in nature. It is not accidental [...] Intent is a necessary and crucial element. People make something that develops and changes in time – a performance – with the intent of having it affect an audience [...] It is the intent and not the event itself or its impact on us that makes something theatre (Kirby 1987, x–xi).

The notion of intent eliminates definitions pertaining to 'modes of perception' by locating the term in relation to an intention to 'show the performance at some time to an audience' (xi). It is the notion of intention to affect an audience which is key to my developing definition of theatricality. Josette Féral sums up a position similar to Kirby's: 'Theatricality cannot be, it must be for someone. In other words, it is for the Other' (in Gran and Oatley 2002, 178).

Willingham outlines two aesthetic approaches which, he believes, nurture the theatrical medium and which can help in the staging of science fiction theatre. The first of these is Minimalism, which relies on the imagination to visualise the fantastic. He suggests that 'the most important convention on which science fiction theatre can rely is audience imagination' (Willingham 1991, 75). Here, there is a willingness on the part of the audience 'to imagine what cannot be staged', while 'making judicious use of realistic staging conventions when they are necessary' (ibid.). As Ray Bradbury suggests, '[w]hen in doubt strip away' (Bradbury, in Willingham 1991, 76). In a similar manner, but more generally and somewhat pejoratively, Michael Fried talks about theatricality in relation to minimalist sculpture (which he describes as 'literalist' art). In 'Art and Objecthood', Fried suggests that modernist art 'degenerates as it approaches the condition of theatre' (Fried 1998b, 164). Locating the term in opposition to the idea of absorption – something that he seems to value far more – Fried dislikes theatricality in this context, because it prevents the spectator from escaping the present moment and from the ability of the artwork to be complete or autonomous:

> Literalist sensibility is theatrical because, to begin with, it is concerned with the actual circumstances in which the beholder encounters literalist work. [. . . T]he experience of literalist art is of an object in a *situation* – one that, virtually by definition, *includes the beholder* (Fried 1998b, 153).

It seems that, for Fried, the 'awareness of one's body in a situation' (Ridout 2006, 8) is too close to the experience of everyday life, contravening Modernist art's claim of being able to sit outside of or above it.

Minimalism could be seen to occur within *Mouse* in the following ways: the single, unchanging room makes 'judicious use of realistic staging' presented as something familiar or recognizable to the contemporary world. The provision of scenographic detail is enabled by the lack of any scene changes, enabling all movement to take place within the one hermetically sealed world. Willingham describes how in 'live theatre [. . .] scene-shifting distracts from the narrative' whose 'visual deceptions can never be as spectacular as film' (Willingham 1991, 64). Setting the production in the one space therefore avoids, as Nicholas Ridout once described it, 'the rattle and clatter of unseemly machinery in the wings' (2006, 9), allowing for more economy and fluidity in the throughline of the material. Designing the staging in such a way enabled Kitson to negotiate the theatrical challenge of simultaneity and multiplicity by focusing on just two versions of the multiverse, one which was communicated aurally and the other being a fully realised world maintained on stage throughout: that of William Booth's dingy green shipping container office, modestly decorated with potted plants.

Willingham's second aesthetic approach is that of estrangement. This technique treats 'the familiar as strange and the strange as familiar', where fantastical science fiction worlds can be created without the 'benefit of gadgetry indigenous to science fiction literature' (Willingham 1991, 72). What heightens the fantastic is the treatment of everyday objects as something strange and unfamiliar, such as an apple sitting inside a glass globe, eliciting fear and scientific scrutiny from the characters involved.

It is in the coupling of the ordinary recognizable world of William Booth and that of his alternate self, calling from another dimension, that the estrangement effect can be felt most profoundly. The slow discovery that William is, in fact, talking to himself, is slowly unravelled throughout the course of the production, creating an uncanny kind of effect without recourse to science-fiction gadgetry. Of course, there is reliance on recorded footage here: William speaks to a pre-recorded voice, allowing for a simultaneous conversation with himself to take place. However, there is something in the fact that the recording is audio rather than visual, which allows for an extended use of the imagination to take place. It is, as Willingham suggests, in what we cannot see that the fantastic can be imagined. The fact that the intergalactic conversation also takes place on an old-fashioned landline phone (complete with the United Kingdom's 1471 answer phone technology) adds an additional element of estrangement to the proceedings. As an almost obsolete piece of technology, we are asked to imagine that William's landline telephone has embodied cross-dimensional capabilities, a humorous, antiquarian gag involving the re-claiming of a defunct piece of machinery that once played an important role in many people's lives.

In addition to minimalism and estrangement, Joachim Fiebach proffers the following aspects of theatre aesthetics that constitute the medium's appeal:

> Our attraction to theater rests on the ostentatious presentation of creative human skills, the demonstration of physical abilities, the intelligent timing of activities and the making of specific spaces [. . .] The staging of such abilities is the necessary-perhaps even primary-source of theater's aesthetic pleasure (Fiebach 2002, 17).

The emphasis on 'ostentatious creative human skills' potentially links to Kirby's notion of intention to affect an audience alongside the corporeality of the theatrical medium. For instance, the coupling of ostentation, understood in terms of a deliberate act of 'showing', and *human* skill – as that which is less machinic than, for example, recorded forms of performance – suggests an attraction to skills which are happening (largely) unaided, in real time and space, and with the sole aim of affecting an audience. This could involve witnessing a high level of physical ability, either in terms of the general stamina or energy required of performers within theatre works which take place in real time and space, or more specifically in terms of their skilled use of the body within the three-dimensionality of the performance space. Of course, the 'demonstration of physical abilities' is not necessarily exclusive to the medium of theatre. Physical ability has for a long time in Hollywood cinema constituted credible or Oscar-worthy performances. This occurs, for instance, when performers commit to physically changing their bodies to render the character as realistically as possible, as is seen in many Method performances. I would argue that the difference with theatre is related to the level of risk involved in terms of the physical ability presented, conditioned by the live situation and the prospect that the performance could 'go wrong' at any minute. Ridout goes so far as to suggest that theatre's potential failure is actually a constitutive part of the essential experience of theatre, something he refers to as 'ontological queasiness' (2006, 3).

What Fiebach calls the 'intelligent timing of activities' relates to the temporality of theatre: the live unfolding of a performance in real time. As Fried suggests, 'the sense which, at bottom, theater addresses, is a sense of temporality, of time both passing and to come, *simultaneously approaching and receding*' (1998b, 167). Timing is perhaps most commonly associated with stand-up comedians and their ability to perfectly pitch punchlines in accordance with the reciprocal rhythm of an audience. Again, it is the presence of the audience that necessitates good comic timing: without them, live standup could not exist. We can, however, talk more generally about theatre's relation to the 'intelligent timing of activities'. For instance, I would argue that, on the whole, it is the sole responsibility of theatre performers to ensure the appropriate delivery of pace, rhythm and energy required within a live performance. In screen work, a director can intercept and re-shoot a scene/shot. The editing also plays a major role in determining the overall rhythm/pace of a film. In contrast, theatre performers must ensure that each scene/act/moment delivers the appropriate pace and rhythm of the performance, every time it is performed.

Kitson presented the 'intelligent timing of activities' through his ability to pull off a seemingly natural conversation with, essentially, a machine.

While on the one hand conversing with a machine could help secure and regulate the timing of the live action, responding to a fixed and unchanging recording can be challenging for an actor, leaving, as it does, little room for spontaneity or 'swing' (to borrow a musical phrase). Interacting with a recording can quickly feel mechanical and stale, due to the rigid precision needed to keep in time. It was to Kitson's credit that he was able to keep this duologue energised and engaging for an audience. At ninety minutes, the solo show also evidenced the 'ostentatious presentation of creative human skills' with all of the material written and performed by Kitson himself.

The 'ostentatious presentation of creative human skills' and 'intelligent timing of activities' is also evident with *Constellations*. The performers seem to glide effortlessly through their changeable universes, sustaining believable and compelling encounters throughout. In a piece which not only jumps forwards and backwards along a singular timeline but also laterally across a multiplicity of trajectories, an actor has to, arguably, understand, remember and navigate the varying given circumstances of those multiple situations to motivate their performances. For instance, at the start we see five alternating versions of the barbeque scene, followed by a scene occurring much later in one timeline, where Marianne talks about leaving work due to her illness. The material then jumps back to four consecutive, alternating scenes in which the couple deliberates spending the night together after a first date.

The linear and lateral, forward and backward traversing is, surely, a feat for any actor, but particularly so within a theatre piece such as this, where there are no second takes or 'off set' moments to collect one's thoughts and prepare for the particular scene being shot or staged, as is common within the disjointed process of film production. Indeed, the two performers are on stage throughout the duration of the performance, continually navigating their way through the often fast-paced and seemingly instantaneous shifting of alternating worlds. In addition to this, for many actors, line-learning is particularly challenging when sections of text appear similar. Scenes that contain similar adjectives or turns of phrase often present difficulty when learning lines in the abstract. This is taken to the extreme in *Constellations*, where the repetition of slightly varying scenes is woven into the choreographic structure and rhythm of the piece.

Additionally, Fiebach's making and staging of specific spaces (2002, 17) can also be applied to the two performances in question. It is key for me that Fiebach uses the term *space* here rather than *place*. Traditional terms such as 'setting' or 'location' are more commonly associated with Naturalistic works which aim to place a fictional world in a specific time and place. While originating in the theatre, Naturalism has, arguably, found a more suitable home within film and television where the task of suspending one's disbelief is, arguably, a far easier job. As Bazin suggests, cinema has satisfied 'once and for all and in its very essence, our obsession with realism' (1967, 12). The 'making and staging of specific spaces', then, seems to allude to the three-dimensionality of theatrical space, a space which can be utilised in a manner similar to the minimalist sculpture discussed by Fried, where the beholder becomes integral to the overall meaning of the work. Abstraction, stylisation and/or symbolism are, therefore, often evident with theatrical staging and hence theatricality, due to the three-dimensionality of the medium which is often treated with imaginative freedom to present and/or stage in ways that do not simply attempt to represent reality.

In a production at the Lowry Theatre, Manchester, on 10 June 2015, directed by Michael Longhurst, designed by Tom Scutt and featuring Louise Brealey as Marianne and Joe Armstrong as Roland, *Constellations* confronted the theatrical challenge of multiplicity through a rejection of realism within its staging design and seamless execution of transitions between worlds. This almost simultaneous fluidity between worlds was created through lighting, sound and the movement of the actors, a fluidity not compromised by an attempt to create 'realistic' depictions of the multiverse on stage (if such a thing is possible). The performance was staged on a floor of black, hexagonal tiles, around which floated clouds of giant white balloons and spherical lights. Seemingly infinite colour combinations of light were projected onto these balloons, indicating the shifts in multiverse as they were occurring. These shifts were also helped by a short screeching audio cue each time Marianne and Roland found themselves in an alternate reality.

While the individual performances were committed to believable, life-like interactions, the use of stylisation in the staging removed any overall sense of realism from the piece, inviting the audience to engage with the varying and multi-layered metaphors in play. For instance, the function of the balloons appeared multifarious, indicating their celebratory aspect in one world – when seen at the engagement barbeque at the beginning of the play – and as a symbol of condolence, when seen in the context of a dying loved one. This is reflected in a conversation between Marianne and Roland towards the end of the play, when Marianne, in one world, suffering from a brain tumour, remarks:

> *Marianne*: There was a photograph of a woman with God knows how many tubes hanging out of her and she was surrounded by these garish fucking balloons.
> *Roland*: Some people like to give people balloons.
> *Marianne*: If you give me a balloon, I will fucking garrotte you.
> (Payne 2012, 65).

As well as prosaic signification, the staging of the balloons appeared both cosmic – as a vast infinitude of space populated with celestial spheres – and molecular: an atomic carpet covering the stage and dwarfing the characters. Again, connections between symbolism in the staging and the thematic of the narrative are reflected in the text. In an early encounter with Roland, Marianne tries to explain to him the nature of her work:

> *Marianne*: Most of my time is spent sitting in front of a computer.
> *Roland*: Right.
> *Marianne*: Inputting data.
> *Roland*: Right.
> *Marianne*: Cosmic microwave background readings.
> *Roland*: Okay.
> *Marianne*: Radiation left over from the big bang.
> *Roland*: Right.
> *Marianne*: Cosmology. Theoretical early universe cosmology.
> (Payne 2012: 24–25).

The audience is invited to read the work metaphorically, connecting ideas in the text to the visual presentation on stage, opening up a space for active spectatorship and cultivation of the imagination. I use the term active spectatorship here, not in the sense of physical participation, but rather in terms alluding to Willingham's 'imagination' or Rancière's 'poetic labour of translation' (2009, 10), where 'the spectator [. . .] acts [. . .] observes, selects, compares, interprets' (Rancière 2009, 13) that which s/he sees. Rather than presenting the material realistically, *Constellations* presents an abstracted scenography, emphasising the key thematic and conceptualisation at the heart of the play through 'imaginative remove'

(Farnell 2019, 7). On a symbolic level, the denial of a realistic representation honours the scientific supposition that the multiverse is actually *beyond comprehension*: beyond the knowable world. Subsequently, all we have to visualise and conceive of such phenomena is our imagination.

The final notion of theatricality which will end this discussion is the notion of self-reflexivity. Described by Loiselle and Maron in the introduction to their *Stages of Reality: Theatricality in Cinema* as that which 'refers broadly to all representations that call attention to their own representationality' (2012, 4), self-reflexivity often references the actuality of the theatre event itself, either in terms of audience interaction or through conscious deconstruction of the process of making the performance. Kitson cultivates both definitions through finely tuned audience involvement and a layer of self-reflexivity in which the process of writing William's fictional life is thrown into sharp relief against that of Kitson's own. Within this section, Kitson reflects on many things, some directly connected to that of William's life, some more tangentially so. Indeed, at one point in the show, Kitson declares 'sad is the man who has no time to wonder', and it is with such sentiment that Kitson considers and shares with his audience ideas related to conversations with strangers; the nature of friendship; memory foam pillows; and the wider cosmos. As an audience, we too are 'invited to wonder' with Kitson and to reflect on the relative connections of the material to that of our own lives and the theatrical situation we share.

Consequence, Responsibility, Possibility and Choice

The two theatrical explorations of the multiverse present interesting ideas related to notions of consequence, responsibility, possibility and choice. In *Mouse*, the particularities of individual choice and consequence seem emphasised: it is the result of William's decision not to look at the woman that seems to be the focus of the show. As an audience, we are invited to lament on the virtues of individual courage and action, in a 'fortune favours the brave' type of morality tale. This is, of course, if you aspire to the more conventional life lived by Bill as opposed to that lived by William – which I am in no way suggesting is a given. However, whether this was the intention or not, I left *Mouse* with the sense that it is the individual who is responsible for a given course of action or outcome: that it is the individual who *creates* that outcome as opposed to every outcome being possible 'in an unimaginably vast ensemble of parallel universes' (Payne 2012, 27).

This is in contrast to *Constellations* where, as Marianne suggests at one point, '[i]n none of our equations do we see any sign whatsoever of any evidence of free will' (Payne 2012, 28). She elaborates:

> You, me, everyone, we might think that we have some say in – we might think that the choices we make will have some say in the – [...] We're just particles governed by a series of very particular laws being knocked the fuck around all over the place (Payne 2012, 28).

The presentation of the material seems to honour this supposition in a show where we are subjected to multiple inevitabilities, as opposed to just two alternatives which seem effected by conscious volition.

What is interesting is what presentations of the multiverse might offer audiences in terms of how they see their lives and their individual roles/choices within them. For instance, if free will is perceived to be compromised, as we see within *Constellations*, responsibility for one's actions could also be perceived to be diluted in some way. A similar notion was identified by Payne during the process of writing *Constellations*. He describes how his opinion on the subject of the multiverse changed throughout the process of writing the play after speaking to a cosmologist at the University of Sussex. He explains how the cosmologist felt that the idea of the multiverse 'could remove the idea of consequence' from human action (see Costa 2012) – for example, killing someone in one universe but knowing that in another universe they will live (ibid.). Similarly, the consequences to the characters' actions within *Constellations* seem irrelevant, caught, as they appear to be, in a web of infinite possibilities which are outside of their making.

Coda

I hope to have shown the ways in which innovation and imaginative sensitivity to the theatrical medium can render 'scientific notions anew, interpreting them [...] through dialogue [...] physical action or image on stage with the implementation of set design, lighting and movement' (Campos 2013, 298–99). However, while I have argued that presentations of the multiverse might affect symbolic meaning for an audience, meaning related to consequence, responsibility, possibility and choice is not necessarily confined to theatrical treatments of the subject. For instance, screen portrayals of the multiverse may also induce similar resonances for audience members. Although I do not necessarily agree with Bazin that theatrical experience is 'more uplifting [...] nobler [...] more moral' (1967, 98) than that of cinema, and with the potential implication that theatrical experience may hold more value than that of cinema, I might be inclined towards his notion that theatre 'excites' (99): a potential by-product of its 'ontological queasiness', as foregrounded in the discussion here (see Ridout 2006, 3). In this sense, ideas explored within shows where 'staging and inherent liveness' is 'equal to their scientific underpinning' seem more absorbing and vital; a result, I suspect, of a fuller, theatrical experience (see Farnell 2019, 8). The ability of the two shows to explore such ambitious ideas in an arresting and effective way, through skilful and creative treatment of simultaneity/multiplicity and an astute understanding of the theatrical medium in which they were working, induced a similar excitement within me, motivating me to write about the work, in an attempt to preserve its ephemerality in written form.

Notes

1. Seen in productions such as *Kellerman* (imitating the dog, 2008), *Mare's Nest* (Station House Opera, 2006), or *The Doors of Serenity* (The Chameleons Group, 2002).
2. See the recent performance of *Scala* by Yoann Bourgois (2019), where he utilised a similar technique whereby multiple versions of the same character were signified through identical costume, similar body shape/physicality and relatively low lighting.
3. The Copenhagen Physicists consisted mainly of Niels and Margaret Bohr and Werner Heisenberg. Responsible for progressing the field of Quantum Mechanics through theories such as the Uncertainty Principle, the research of these physicists played a crucial role in the development of atomic energy.

14

The Interconnectedness between Melodrama and Theatricality in Pedro Almodóvar's *The Skin I Live In* (2011) and Nelson Rodrigues' *Woman without Sin* (1941)

Isadora Grevan

In the Introduction to the collection of essays titled *Theatricality as Medium*, Samuel Weber begins to un-weave the concept of theatricality by exploring Plato's Allegory of the Cave (from *The Republic*). His clever play with the idea that the theatrical is associated with the idea of confinement to an artificially created world takes Weber on a loop back to theatre as a means to mirror this confinement back to the spectator. The cave of theatre is both self-referential and freeing, a theatre of theatres, as in the following passage:

> Theater is thus, from the very beginnings of what, for convenience, we continue to call 'Western' thought, considered to be a place not just of dissimulation and delusion but, worse, self-dissimulation and self-delusion. It is a place of fixity and unfreedom, but also of fascination and desire. A prison, to be sure, but one that confines through assent and consensus rather than through constraint and oppression. Theater, in short, is that which challenges the 'self' of self-presence and self-identity by reduplicating it in a seductive movement that never seems to come full circle (Weber 2004, 9).

This theatrical mode of self-referentiality through allegories of fences, cages and cave-like spaces is a means by which we enter both works by Brazilian playwright Nelson Rodrigues (1912–80) and Spanish director

Pedro Almodóvar (1949–). Both authors use literal references to captivity and confinement in order to comment on the theatricality of both stage/cinema and the characters' gendered bodies in and outside the scene.

The space of the theatrical in *The Skin I Live In* starts with the idea of prison in defining a theatrical space, while using the style of melodrama for one of the narrative tones throughout. In fact, the first two scenes of the movie set the stage for what is about to be told and seen by providing a contrast between a long shot of the city of Toledo, Spain, followed by a close-up of the iron gates that bar the entrance to the 'El Cigarral' mansion enclosure. Although the origins of the meaning of *cigarral* estates are not completely known, their immediate connotation is related to the word *cigarra*, or *cicada*, which are insects known for shedding their skin after a two-to-seventeen-month cycle. This is the first reference the movie makes of skin as both enclosure and something that can be shed or exchanged. In the case of *Woman without Sin*, the space is also defined by the confinement of the house, the extremely brief time-period in which the story is set, which is one day, and melodrama as a theatrical tone. Melodrama is used as theatrical tone in both works, as a means to cause a double effect of both recognition and pathos while at the same time inciting a feeling of strangeness and anxiety in the spectators, fractioning the typical melodramatic response. In fact, Almodóvar immediately confuses the spectator by showing Vera, wearing a second skin, watching on television a yoga programme in which the instructor warns not to confuse form (*asana*) with depth. Thus, from the start of the movie, the director makes it clear that appearance and skin are deceiving.

In what concerns melodrama, both works make use of typical melodramatic narratives as described by Mark Allinson. He writes: 'Melodramatic plots involve omniscient narration, twists and reversals, chance events and encounters, and secrets. Flashbacks are another common feature, a result of the need for dramatic action without the sense of progression that characterizes other more dynamic genres' (Allinson 2009, 142). Allinson describes Almodóvar's cinema as having a tendency to complicate the 'simplistic division between tragic theater as high art and melodramatic cinema as popular art' (143). This same effacement of clear boundaries between high and popular art is also present in the theatre of Nelson Rodrigues. In the case of Rodrigues, for example, during the period when he wrote his first play, he was responsible for bridging the gap between what was considered classical theatre (high art) and theatre as entertainment (a lower, commercial type of theatre), due to his use of colloquial language and the exploration of what were considered marginal characters on stage.[1] Brenda Austin-Smith also describes a few characteristics of the style of melodrama present in American films of the 1930s, which add to this analysis by exploring the presence of female victimisation, by depicting romance, domestic relationships and child-rearing. She writes: 'It was, though, the emotional suffering of the melodramatic heroine that made these films popular with their female audiences, and gave rise to the pejorative term "weepie" used to describe them' (Austin-Smith 2012, 102). Another important feature of these particular types of melodrama, which we will see in both authors, are the use of an '"aesthetics of astonishment", extreme emotional states of grief and rage, and of plots that stir the hearts of viewers through their depiction of victimization and injustice' (Allinson 2009, 219). The two authors analysed make use of this type of aesthetics and characters in order to deconstruct preconceived notions about them.

Woman without Sin was the first play written by Nelson Rodrigues, one of the precursors of modern Brazilian theatre, in 1941. The play is divided into three acts. According to the author's stage directions, the *mise-en-scène* is very simple, comprised of grey curtains and stairs. Olegario's imagination is put on display in the first scene and throughout the play, where we see a little girl walking by, to describe a figment of his imagination. In fact, this staging of fantasy becomes a common feature of Nelson Rodrigues's theatre. Appearance is also confusing here, on Rodrigues's stage, since oftentimes spectators are not made aware of the clear separations between what is happening in reality and what is happening in Olegario's imagination.

The plot revolves around Olegário, the patriarch of the family, who is confined to his wheelchair and his own fantasies. He is Lídia's husband, and throughout the play he reveals a pathological jealousy towards his wife. He is visited by the ghosts of three women in his life: his mother who, despite being alive, spends her days twisting a piece of cloth while confined to a chair, in a dark room, looking catatonic (an eerie presence); his wife as a little girl (a figment of his imagination); and his dead former wife whose voice he constantly hears. Lídia's mother and her step-brother live with them, as well as the maid Inézia and the driver Umberto. Olegario has Inézia and Umberto monitoring Lídia's every move, culminating in a jealousy towards every man in the house, even against her own thoughts, as he says: 'You look at me with the eyes of a martyr! Like now. In this instance, this minute, you could be remembering a friend, someone you have known or not known. Even a passer-by. You could be desiring an adventure. The life of an honest woman is so empty! I know that! I really do!' (Rodrigues 2003, 540).[2]

It is not completely clear throughout the play whether Lídia has or has not been faithful to Olegario, although it is assumed in the end that he comes to a favourable conclusion, after years of monitoring and psychological torture. In the end, Olegario finally decides to end the charade of needing to be confined to a wheelchair in order to test Lídia's faithfulness. Indeed, he comes to the realisation that Lídia is the only faithful woman he will ever meet (in his own words), at which point she escapes with Umberto, the driver.

The fact that it remains ambiguous whether Lídia has been faithful creates a much more complex theatrical narrative than we would expect at first. It is Olegario's acting that is put on display, as well as society's conflicting expectations of women, not the judgment of Lídia's character in relation to this morality based on the traditional patriarchal family's values. In his worrying, his obsession with purity and faithfulness, his trying to inscribe his wife into the saint-and-whore duality, we learn that he used to be a man who never paid attention to his wife sexually and most likely had lovers of his own in the past, completely ignoring his own moral stance towards Lídia. Lídia is stereotypically seen by him as someone from a poor background and judged for being promiscuous just because of her upbringing. She dresses provocatively, wears kimonos, enjoys feeling sexy, as we would expect of a woman her age (in her twenties), nothing as aberrant as Olegario's own imagination, as he himself proclaims and admits: 'No one is completely faithful to anyone. Each woman hides an infidelity, past, present and future one' (Rodrigues 2003, 567). If we follow the logical consequences of the narrative, it appears that his own madness drives his wife to leave him and cheat, but that is also not obvious if we look closely at the text. She is driven to leave him, because he cannot have a relationship with her, neither of friendship nor of mutual sexual desire. Through flashbacks we know that Olegario, throughout the first years of marriage, has paid more attention to his work and lovers, at her expense. Lídia even says that 'my friends tell me things, and I get shocked, very shocked. I am a wife that knows nothing, or almost... In boarding school, I learned more than in marriage!' (Rodrigues 2003, 589).

Subsequently, feeling his wife losing interest in trying to connect with him both sexually and personally, he feigns a disability and constructs an entire charade in order to catch her in the act. We also slowly find out that

Olegario believes that his wife should be treated as a saint, and sex should only be performed with women outside marriage. Rodrigues exaggerates the Catholic guilt instilled by society, creating a hypocritical relationship between man and woman in the home. The absurdity of it is put on display as farcical by Olegario's own words: 'The consequence of my state is that we are a couple, contrary to most, that has remained completely chaste to one another' (567).

Petra Ramalho Souto in her book *As Mulheres de Nelson* observes through other critics of Rodrigues's work that the playwright explores 'the dichotomous vision of women in Brazilian society (whore/saint)' (Souto 2004, 29). Souto concludes (focusing on Aurora and Silene in *The Seven Kittens* [1957]) by interpreting the behaviour of a number of female characters in Rodrigues's oeuvre as essentially having two different facets, or dichotomous selves. The first fits perfectly with Lídia's character:

> [O]ne, from whom is expected righteousness (read righteousness, virginity and purity, according to the precepts of the time) but who wants to surrender to the pleasures of sex and, the other, 'woman who sells her body' (in Portuguese, the literal translation of an expression to denote prostitution is 'that does life', 'from life'), but who deep inside want to get married and be a mother and wife (79).

The problematics of this dichotomous position in which the women are placed is that they might not fit into either of them, or they might be forced to, not just morally, but legally. Divorce, for example, only became legal in Brazil in 1976, and many of the women's civil rights depended on the approval of the husband until more substantial changes in legislation occurred in 1988. Moreover, when it came to adultery, for example, the courts tended to side with husbands who kill for being dishonoured, proving that Lídia's escape, adulterous behaviour and (possibly) divorce could lead to her death.

> Jurists and the general public also continued to argue over whether cuckolded men who 'washed their honor in blood' should be forgiven. Since the 1940 code stipulated that 'intense passion' no longer abrogated 'criminal responsibility', lawyers invented the 'legitimate defense of honor' strategy, arguing that killing to defend one's honor was an act of self-defense (*legítima defesa* is analogous to 'self-defense' in Anglo-American law). Debates over the issue were

reinvigorated, but the defense survived for another half century. As late as 1975, São Paulo appeals court judge and law professor Edgard Bittencourt wrote that husbands who assaulted and battered adulterous wives were acquitted 'in most trials', while murderous husbands received reduced sentences, a state of affairs the author and most other jurists found legally sound (Caulfield 2000, 193).

The passion of Lídia's plight as a victim in this situation is certainly intensified by this fact, considering the year when the play was written, although the ironic tone of the play with its absurd and often comic innuendos attenuates the impact of Lídia's choice.

Olegario learns that Inézia has entered Umberto's room during the night, and so he threatens to fire him for indecency. In a twist of roles, Umberto acts to Olegario as someone who has been castrated so that he will not seem like a menace to him (as all other men are), and also as a defence, so that he will not get fired. As Umberto gains confidence by pretending to have been castrated, he pursues Lídia and convinces her to run away with him. He seems to have become fearless, since he is less afraid of being caught by Olegario during this period. In the process, we learn that Lídia, as opposed to acting pure, has always wanted to have sexual contact with her husband and is excited when the driver goes after her in a very animalistic and sexual way. Whereas for Olegario the symbol of the woman he would like to possess is a representation of chaste love, Lídia has a different picture of love, one that is neither pure nor chaste.

The plot of Almodóvar's *The Skin I Live In* is essentially divided into three parts: the present tense of the narrative, the change of direction through flashbacks, and Vera's new position in the house as 'free' in the concluding part. We learn from the start of the film that Dr Robert Ledgard (Antonio Banderas) is a very successful scientist and a plastic surgeon who runs an underground lab, where he conducts experiments on transgenesis and cloning. He develops a fire-resistant skin through the use of pig's blood and other experiments, which we find out only later; he is motivated by a deeply personal set of traumatic personal events in his own life. Vera (Elena Araya), as we see her in the beginning of the film wearing a second skin and doing yoga poses, manages to stay sane while imprisoned, by making art, writing, doing yoga and playing with scraps of material that resemble skin, in a manner that recalls Louise Bourgeois's famous hominoids. From the beginning, we see what we, the spectators, think to be a woman, reversing the theatrical expectations of her gender, by using the dresses and make-up she receives to make art, as opposed to actually wearing them. As the movie advances, we find out through a series of flashbacks and dream imagery that Vera used to be Vicente. Vicente used to work in his mother's dress shop. One day he went to a wedding party and met Norma, Ledgard's daughter. They both walked outside of the wedding venue and started to kiss. Norma was under the influence of psychiatric drugs, while Vicente was under the influence of illegal recreational drugs. Norma suddenly heard a song that her mother used to sing to her and, as a result, began to experience a panic attack. This led Vicente to slap her, causing her to faint. This episode triggered Norma's descent into mental illness and suicide. It remains uncertain whether Vicente raped Norma, although such an act is implied. Ledgard then catches Vicente riding away on a motorcycle, tracks him down and eventually performs a vaginoplasty and skin transplant so that he comes to look more and more like his deceased wife. Ledgard uses Vicente's body-turned-into-Vera as a means to avenge his daughter's suicide and as a substitute for his wife following her suicide.

Furthermore, as we move forward to the present, there are a series of surveillance cameras throughout Ledgard's house, as a way to reference the act of filming as oppressive and theatrical, another type of reference to the camera and the captor's gaze; that is, the gaze of the male protagonist on the female protagonist. At one point in the story, Vicente-turned-Vera realises that, by owning her skin, as a masquerade of femininity and love, she can possibly find a way of escaping from her captor. Just like Umberto in *Woman without Sin*, it is the consciousness of performance that helps Vera manipulate her captive situation to her benefit. In fact, as time goes by, Vera realises that she is unable to escape from Ledgard's house, as well as from her new body as a woman. She thus decides to use this in her favour, by pretending that she feels at home in her new skin. She slowly becomes more feminine in the way in which she dresses and more docile towards Ledgard, as a way to gain his trust.

Marilia confides in Vera after Vera is raped by Ledgard's half-brother Zeca (Roberto Álamo), due to the fact that she resembles Ledgard's former wife Gal (who happened to be his half-brother's lover). Zeca, like all the characters in the story, also hides a secret and a skin underneath his tiger costume. Marilia's son by a different man, Zeca, grew up in Brazil and has become a robber and smuggler. Marilia's two sons are criminals who exhibit psychopathic tendencies, although they are separated by playing their different social roles, roles that are ascribed to different social classes.

This is the most melodramatic part of the story, when through flashbacks and voice-over narration we learn of the suicides of Ledgard's wife and daughter, while Marilia and Vera watch Zeca's remains being burnt. We learn through flashbacks that his daughter Norma was apparently raped by Vicente when they went to a party, while she was still in treatment, but again it is not completely clear if it really was rape or a misunderstanding. Vicente even affirms that he has not raped her. The different memories that compose the story are made subjective due to the spectator's lack of reference. They are made even more subjective by the fact that Ledgard becomes a monster and Vicente an innocent victim. During the time when Ledgard is disposing of Zeca's body, Marilia recounts to Vera how she conceived both Zeca and Ledgard from different men, information that she had not revealed to any of them in the past. Ledgard was adopted by the couple who had employed Marilia for most of her life. Zeca ended up on the streets, as a drug dealer, whereas Ledgard became a prominent plastic surgeon, marrying a woman named Gal. Gal ended up falling in love with Zeca when he returned from Brazil; while trying to escape together, they suffered a car accident, which left Gal badly burnt. Ledgard took in Gal, in an effort to heal her skin, preventing her from seeing her burnt skin in any mirror reflection. One day, she accidentally saw her disfigured face reflected in the window glass, and the trauma led her to jump out of the window to her death.

Clearly, Ledgard is convinced that Vicente raped Norma, and he takes revenge on him by transforming him via complex medical procedures and plastic surgery into Vera in ways that resemble his former wife, Gal. Contrary to traditional melodramatic plots, where real events might take centre stage to tell the victim's story, here it is the mind of the protagonist that determines the story's fate. As in *Woman without Sin*, the protagonist is positioned as a controlling figure who has an easier time possessing rather than relating to the female characters. In the present, after his story is told, Vera promises Ledgard that she will never leave him; in exchange, he promises: 'No more locked doors'.

Ledgard ends up announcing that he will give up his practice and that he looks forward to life with Vera, but this is all a performance of extreme femininity that never takes place in Vicente's mind. The act is never consummated, and the final resolution for the lack of both daughter and wife, which was never present in the first place, is never resolved. As is also true for Rodrigues's play, the story only ends favourably for the captive character when he or she finally realises the theatre in which they are inserted. Once they become aware of the character that they are expected to play, they can use that knowledge to escape. Finally, Vera escapes and is reunited with her mother (who has tirelessly looked for Vicente), after killing both Marilia and Ledgard. In the last scene, Vera tells her mother who she is. Vicente, affirming who he is, male despite the skin he lives in, sums up what has happened to him.

A feature that is also common in melodramatic narratives, which we see here as a means to questions patriarchy, is melancholia. Both male protagonists, Olegario and Ledgard, experience loss as a type of 'ego loss' that threatens their sanity. Allinson argues:

> One of the ways that Freud describes the psychic mechanism of melancholia is as an 'object-loss' (as in normal mourning) that in melancholia becomes incorporated as an 'ego-loss' (249). The ego incorporates the lost object into itself, thus 'regressing' from object choice to an ambivalent narcissism that feels perpetually 'slighted, neglected, or disappointed' (251) (Allinson 2008, 168).

To make up for his inability to prevent the suicides of both his wife and daughter, Ledgard neglects all ethical standards of his profession and becomes blind to the difference between appearance and reality. It is also important to point out that the chronological order of facts does not serve to explain Ledgard's action, since his character of the patriarch feeling anguish about possessing the women in his life appears to be part of the larger structural problem of the family to begin with. Marilia (Marisa Paredes) herself is the victim of a system that might have engendered Ledgard's narcissism in the first place (her lower social position, her submissive position as a woman, the secret she did not feel free to divulge – that is, that he had been adopted by her employers). In turn, in *Woman without Sin*, Olegario's set of tragic events that led to his melancholia does not acquit him either, revealing misunderstandings between the different expectations ascribed to 'womanhood' as more structural than causal when looked at from the perspectives of the two narratives. As is aptly explained by Allinson, melodramatic modes of narratives have interested feminist critics in many ways:

> What interested Mulvey and other feminist critics was the extent to which melodrama might be understood as conservative, as educating women to accept the constraints of the patriarchal order,

or conversely, the extent to which it might be understood as more subversive, as exposing and exploding the myths of patriarchy (Allinson 2008, 146).

Rodrigues's theatre is known for characters that, in an effort to combat their own fear of solitude, aim to possess others, either by feigning madness, or by performing other types of acts in order to find out a secret about the other with whom they are obsessed. This hidden, prison-like treasure hunt for the innermost parts of another's soul always proves futile, a theatrical pursuit, consciously orchestrated as theatre by the author, as is especially true in *Woman without Sin*. Olegario's acting as someone suffering from a disability due to an accident, compounded by his constant vigilance of his wife's every move, is put on a display as mental ill health and society's gender-based madness. His numerous conversations with Lídia, himself and other characters show a man intent on moulding Lídia to become a perfect wife. This perfection is something that has to be proven on a superficial level (by testing her faithfulness), as opposed to the level of an actual mutual relationship. Psychologically speaking, we know that Olegario is overly anxious and melancholic due to his first wife's death, compounded by the fact that Lídia is much younger and from a class lower than his. Paradoxically, his sense of superiority towards Lídia also becomes a source of insecurity for him. In fact, the fragile patriarchal family dynamics of Brazilian society is put on display here.

In turn, Pedro Almodóvar's cinema has featured a number of characters who, in an effort to deal with loss and pain, also feign madness. They hide and create a separate world of fantasy behind closed doors, using theatricality as melodrama by exploring its intersections with aesthetic art. In *The Skin I Live In*, the hidden treasure search is achieved through the skin of someone's body, to possibly reinsert the woman as masquerade as a possession of the male protagonist. For André Loiselle and Jeremy Maron, . . .

> . . . cinematic theatricality refers to film representations that call attention to their own artifice, foregrounding their rhetorical purposes, functioning as self-conscious interruptions within realist discourses to undermine their seeming naturalness. On film, theatricality becomes a means to fracture the impression of reality and transparency that cinema projects; it is a way for cinema to reflect upon itself through the eyes of its older sibling, theatre (Loiselle and Maron 2012, 112).

In this movie, Almodóvar is constantly undermining naturalness, by showing references to art as constructions of gender norms throughout. Ledgard's own profession is explored as a form of artistic mimesis since Ledgard's main goal is to do the impossible: transform Vicente into his former's wife own image. As we see his beautiful Frankenstein, Vera, we are also bombarded by a series of paintings, tableaus and sculptures that explore women's bodies and love in different ways. Ledgard's choice of artworks shows a predilection for women's bodies in reclining poses. We see copies of two large paintings of Venus by Titian on the walls of Ledgard's mansion, the *Venus of Urbino* (1534) and *Venus and Musician* (1550). The images of these paintings are followed by the framed surveillance video of Vera, in a similar pose. At first, although Vera seems asexual and strangely dressed, Ledgard looks at her with erotic, obsessive eyes. Ledgard seems content to use art solely for his aesthetic pleasure, without any concern for depth. The juxtaposition of the different art objects – from those that seem to endorse a classical female beauty aesthetic, over a more contemporary view of love in Guillermo Pérez Villalta's *Dionisios encuentra a Ariadna en Naxos* (2008), which shows figures without faces (but Ariadne still in the typical reclining nude pose), to Louise Bourgeois's more critical depiction of female gender roles – help to create this counterpoint between Ledgard and Vera/Vicente. Thus, there is a clear contrast between the art objects chosen by Ledgard and those chosen by Vera, as well as how they function in each other's lives. Vera's art is visceral, paralleling Bourgeois's quote that 'art is a guarantee of sanity', something Vera scribbles on the wall. Ledgard's art, as a plastic surgeon, leads him to extreme *hubris*, whereas Vera's art is a form of self-reflection which helps to keep her alive and motivated.

As with Rodrigues's plays, gender is also deconstructed by exploring the masculine's completely tenuous position as a traditional patriarchal father. This position holds a power that needs to be constantly affirmed and constructed in fantasy. Moreover, the most intriguing and theatrical aspect of this gender theatre put on display by Almodóvar is that a man (Vicente) becomes a means by which women's captivity is discussed, especially through direct references to Louise Bourgeois to which Vera-Vicente feels particular affinity. The drawings that Vera-Vicente makes of Bourgeois's *Femme Maison* series (1994) are particularly poignant in discussing her trapped-gendered body. As a prisoner, she is trapped, but also as a woman she is confined to a position in the house, as lover, wife, mother, a from which she desires to escape. As Allinson emphasises, '[i]n Almodóvar, the self-conscious foregrounding of gender and other signs of identity forms part of a more generally self-conscious mode of representation that lays bare the constructed or performative nature of all art and all identity' (Allinson 2008, 151).

We cannot help but conclude that gender is both construction/form and depth in Almodóvar's cinema. He goes beyond those lines by showing that womanhood is masquerade and confinement. However, there is a depth of gender identification that cannot be changed through skin and form, since Vicente never changes his masculine identity, despite his appearance as female. He thus realises, as Kaja Silverman points out, that '[d]ress is one of the most important cultural implements for articulating and territorialising human corporeality – for mapping its erotogenic zones and for affixing a sexual identity' (Silverman 1986, 146). This realisation is the key for his escape, as has already been pointed out. In fact, Vicente had been a tailor before he was captured, working at his mother's boutique.

Moreover, both authors put on display melodramatic oppositions, clearly defined social structures and family values, to quickly break them as the plot unfolds. Both Olegario and Ledgard display an intense curiosity about their wives' hidden minds and bodies. This is done through performances of madness, body dysmorphia and masquerade. Using Joan Riviere's article, 'Womanliness as Masquerade', we can also investigate how women's faces figure prominently in the two works as tropes for questioning cultural constructions of gender and explorations of the mind's many borders, through the use of melodrama as a form of theatricality.

In a conversation about melodrama, French filmmaker Georges Franju replies:

> The concept of melodrama is purely affective. It is sentimental, emotional. That is its sole basis. But I refuse to believe that melodrama aims at our better feelings, as they're called. I don't believe in the better feelings. I might believe in purity, but never in innocence. If I show you Fleur de Misere and you feel an urge to protect her, it's because she's pretty, isn't it? You wouldn't want to protect her if she were ugly. That's melodrama – the pretty, soft, sweet, weak victim. [. . .] Our desire to protect the victim conceals another desire-to possess her. And this urge to possess her isn't just sentimental, it's sexual. And that's the hypocrisy of melodrama (Conrad and Franju 1981, 35).

In the case of Almodóvar and Rodrigues, in what concerns the voyeuristic aspect of melodrama, both play with the idea of woman as mask to convey this desire for possession of both the protagonists and the spectators. The heroines are both beautiful and sensual, shown in aesthetically pleasing ways to excite spectators, or at least to make us reflect upon this process, as is certainly true with Almodóvar. However, because of the strangeness of the two women behind their masks, and the juxtaposition of art objects in Almodóvar's case, this desire to protect is always complexified. As Franju points out, in a disturbing way, . . .

> We also ignore the fact that there are two supposedly impure notions that enter into every bond of love or erotic attraction throughout all literature, sentimental or not: money and notoriety. We're not supposed to talk about them. Yet money is erotic. Notoriety is erotic. One doesn't talk about the eroticism in sentiment. But it's all bound up together. And melodrama is made of all this (Conrad and Franju 1981, 43).

Indeed, in the two works studied, the idea of eroticism and power, marriage and money, women and masks of femininity are all intertwined. Both Lídia (in the present of the narrative) and Gal (in the past) are implicated in a system where they are captive because of their social circumstances. Their husbands have power, notoriety and money, which probably had been a reason behind their desire to marry them. As time went on, the controlling nature of both husbands, because of their inflated sense of self, also determined their desire to be sexually involved with men from a lower class, but who showed an animalistic desire towards them, which they had been missing from their husbands. In the case of Gal, she escapes with Ledgard's half-brother from the same mother, who was Ledgard's family's maid (a secret which had been kept from him, until his brother's death). Gal kills herself when she sees her burnt face in the reflection on her bedroom window, the horror of seeing her mask of femininity missing, after a failed attempt to escape.

The patriarchal figure of Olegario in *Woman without Sin* is staging and controlling his life and that of others throughout almost the entire play, and he is not as comfortable in his position as we might detect at first. His anxiety to possess requires theatricality of himself and his life within the play. Through the theatrical both characters want to prove the point of love, faithfulness and femininity. Since both are the parts that they play, they themselves become theatrical props, not just for the author/director but also manipulated by the 'women' or skin that they are trying to contain, since in the end these women look back at them and manage to escape.

The patriarch's underlying narrative is that they might be madly fantasising possession of the object in order to find the solace of pure love, innocence and beauty, triggered by the impact of trauma and family drama in their lives or their inability to contain the feminine within their desired fences. This drama is told through a melodramatic lens, such as in the scene where Ledgard's mother tells the story of how Gal escaped with Ledgard's half-brother (although neither of them knows that they are brothers) and how her face was disfigured by the fire from the car's impact. After the accident, Ledgard, to keep his wife from seeing her face in any mirror or reflection and for healing purposes, kept the house in complete darkness. One day, while his daughter Norma was singing a Portuguese song about love, her mother woke up from her stupor and once again started feeling emotions. When she opened the window to see her daughter singing down below, she briefly saw her face reflected in the window glass, at which point she screamed and jumped out of the window in desperation. Upon seeing her mother's tragic suicide, Norma developed psychological disturbances of her own. We can conclude that it is Ledgard's extreme anxiety about the truth and keeping secrets that effectively killed Gal. Both Olegario and Ledgard appear to be acting in an insane manner. Ledgard's mother suggests that he inherited her craziness, since both brothers from different fathers are crazy. Olegario has visions of his wife as a little girl and also hears voices. He says absurd things, such as: 'How obscene is a face! Why do they permit a naked face?' (Rodrigues 2003, 567), or 'a woman could be a lesbian lover of her own self' (574), revealing his complete uneasiness with his wife's mere existence as a woman.

Ledgard goes into an obsessive sadistic search to transform Vicente into his dead wife's body by using a type of skin that he has invented. Ledgard performs the role of a respected doctor, with visionary and creative genius, while at the same time eliciting ethical suspicions from his colleagues. Olegario orchestrates the whole scenario of not being able to walk while slowly the performance starts gaining a life of its own, and the characters he is directing start performing their own unique roles; roles of which he is not aware. Whereas he wants to use his performance and orchestration of his wife's every move to prove that his wife is faithful and pure, in the process his wife revolts against him and leaves. They both use their femininity, be it skin deep or not, to trap the men and escape.

One riddle of Riviere's seminal article on masquerade is that the text itself becomes a type of mask that never stops being uncovered. At first view, Riviere posits the position of this particular woman in regard to her femininity insofar as it equates the way in which Freud and Ernest Jones look at homosexual women. That type of woman is described as an exception. As the text unfolds, the concept of womanliness-as-mask – as a type of theatrical performance, consciously and unconsciously performed by different types of women to come to terms with their own position as castrated – is revealed to be the same for every woman, not an exception to the rule. When the mask is effaced, there is nothingness, no essence. From the moment the woman is aware of her femininity, she is motivated to wear this mask (see Riviere 1986).

What is interesting to point out in Riviere's work, when looking at the two characters Vera and Lídia in melodramatic theatricalities, is that in the case of the two works the womanliness as masquerade is a mask of which they are both consciously aware and which they eventually want to maintain in order to not be annihilated by masculinity. In Riviere's article, it is the woman, holding a position of lecturer and speaker, who projects the mask in order to abate her fear of subjugation by men. When this happens, such a woman immediately wears the mask of the innocent woman. In the case of Vera, when she asserts the masculine power to escape, she is always caught or saved. In Riviere's article, the woman's desire for masculinity is what engenders the mask of femininity and represents a type of agency and power, as opposed to a form of subjugation. In the two films in question, the masks of femininity are superficial, hiding an essence, a theatrical pursuit, as well as the reality of material presence and identification of both Lídia and Vera-Vicente as existential figures wearing the only masks they might know how at the moment.

Although the types of theatricality as melodrama that both director and playwright explore point us towards a question of mask versus essence, we can see that none of them are concerned with ready-made answers. The oppositions are there, as a type of reflection on life and theatricality, to help us reflect on the ways in which gender not only imprisons us but can also be used for creating subjects and rethinking life in more creative ways. The crux that binds both authors together is their unusual use of melodrama, presenting a level of intense emotion through an overly exaggerated theatrical distancing, an exploration of the body as aesthetic object to be created and manipulated and art as life itself.

Notes

1. Many consider Nelson Rodrigues the father of Modern Brazilian Theatre, almost solely responsible for bringing Brazilian national theatre into the twentieth century. Before him, most of the theatre being performed in the country was comprised of boulevard-type comedies, European plays put on by foreign acting companies and *chanchadas*. By bringing Brazilian characters with issues of local concern to the stage, he gave rise to a theatre that was mostly focused on Brazilian marginal figures. Furthermore, he introduced novelties in stage-set design and narrative style, in addition to deliberately incorporating colloquial language and characters representative of the different social classes, belonging to very specific but heretofore ignored milieux in Brazilian society.
2. Translations from the original Portuguese text into English are mine.

15

Popular Theatricality in Spike Lee

Angelos Koutsourakis

Introduction

A commonplace argument among film critics and scholars alike is that Spike Lee's films do not conform to the principles of classical Hollywood narrative. Critics complain that at times his films are characterised by structural disjointedness and dramatic incoherence. Even commentators positively predisposed towards his overall oeuvre, such as Roger Ebert and Adrian Martin, criticise this aspect of his films. In his positive review of *School Daze* (1988), Ebert admits that the film 'has big structural problems and leaves a lot of loose ends' (1988). Similarly, Adrian Martin's review of *Jungle Fever* (1991) suggests that Lee's 'films are not dramatically well-constructed in the conventional sense, and nor have they ever wished to be. They come out of another cultural tradition – one that is loud, boastful, erratic, performative, obsessed with surface glitz on the one hand, and the Big Statement on the other' (Martin 1991). Along similar lines, Jason P. Vest states that 'Lee's juxtaposed style, as such, will appear jumbled, incoherent, and inartistic to audiences schooled in classical Hollywood filmmaking' (Vest 2014, xxx). All the same, Todd McGowan acknowledges that incoherence is a central feature of Lee's movies. As he says, many positive and negative reviews of *Jungle Fever* drew the same conclusion – that is, the film looks like 'a series of disparate narratives edited together' (McGowan 2014, 56). Lee himself has not denied the fact that loose storylines and interpretive ambiguity are part and parcel of his aesthetic. As he says, 'I don't believe in Hollywood script structure' (cited in Aftab 2005, 298). Yet, at the same time, the discontinuity of the narrative aside, his films successfully merge entertainment with political critique. Narrative is not negated in Lee's cinema but rendered loose, and this can be understood as a re-appropriation of forms of popular theatricality that were influential, not only in modernist theatre, but also in the early days of the medium. In what follows, I will discuss the popular theatricality of Lee's cinema in reference to four films: *School Daze, Do the Right Thing* (1989), *Bamboozled* (2000) and *Chi-Raq* (2015). I suggest that a discussion of tropes of theatricality in his films can offer a better understanding of the interconnection between aesthetics and politics in his work. But before moving on to the discussion of the case-studies, a series of comments on cinema and popular theatricality are in order.

Some Notes on Cinema and Theatricality

My deployment of the term popular theatricality is indebted to Noël Burch's non-evolutionary/archaeological approach to cinema history. Burch argues that the development of narrative cinema as premised on dramatic rather than popular theatrical principles was simply one of the possible roads taken by an imperfect medium and not an inevitable, teleological development. Burch explains that the early cinema between 1895 and 1912 made use of tropes associated with what he names 'popular theatricality', which originated from folk art such as the circus, vaudeville theatre, cabaret and magic-lantern shows. This 'primitive mode of representation' was at odds with what followed, which was cinema's embracement of literary and naturalist theatre conventions of linearity, psychological characterisation and the three-act narrative structure. What differentiates the cinema of popular theatricality from what Burch idiosyncratically calls 'the theatricality of "the grown-ups", of the bourgeois theatre' is that it addressed a working-class audience (Burch 1978, 98). Its key characteristics were the independence of each tableau/frame, the acentric aspect of the image, the absence of psychological camera direction and the lack of narrative closure. Put simply, the primitive cinema was a cinema of self-consciousness whose primary interest was not simply the capturing of dramatic actions; instead, dramatic actions were captured in such a way that the formal qualities of representation were not subordinated to the storyline but powerfully emphasised.

For Burch, cinema's change from a medium reliant on tropes of popular theatricality to one that embraced the textual dramaturgy of naturalist theatre – psychological characterisation, the three-act structure, mimetic acting and narrative closure – was one of the ways in which the film industry could expand beyond an urban working-class audience and become popular with the upper classes, who tended to look down on the new medium. Similarly, Raymond Williams suggests that the early cinema was characterised by a working-class theatricality. In the following passage, Williams chides many scholars and students who seem to...

> ...know surprisingly little about the popular theatre on which, in that phase, it [cinema] drew so heavily. Some people still compare the new medium with such older forms as the bourgeois novel or academic painting, when they ought really to be looking at the direct precedents, with the same urban audiences of melodrama and theatrical spectacle (Williams 2006, 110).

Sabine Hake has also written extensively on how the upper classes used to despise cinema, considering it as a form of crass entertainment. What these early writers found threatening in the new medium was its reliance on technologies of reproduction and the emphasis on actions that could be portrayed without the aid of language. In their view, this aspect of the medium reduced its narratives to 'sensationalist stories and lurid effects' (1993, 77). But the most important anxiety had to do with the fact that cinema's replacement of a predominant textual dramaturgy with a visual one would signal 'the death of the individual as eternalized on the bourgeois stage' (77). This fear was a symptom of early cinema's debt to spectacular theatrical traditions that preceded it, which were at odds with the text-based dramaturgy concerned with the inner life of characters. Burch notes:

> *Uncle Tom's Cabin*, according to the historians of linearity, is a 'retrograde' film. And the montage model it presents is indeed the first and the most elementary produced by the cinema (around 1896): a succession of tableaux without continuity links, either spatial or temporal, undoubtedly 'modelled' on the theatre, but – and the qualification is important – the popular theatre: we are a long way from the 'three unities' which the bourgeois theatre borrowed from the classical breviary. And one has to be completely blinded by 'the ideology of progress' in the cinema not to realise that within the framework fixed by this model, no matter how elementary,

remarkable films were produced: Haggar's *The Life of Charles Peace* (1904), for instance, or Billy Bitzer's *Kentucky Feud* (1905), not to mention films which have, admittedly been more universally recognized, like Zecca's *L'Histoire d'un crime* or Melies' *Le Voyage dans la Lune* (1902). These films, deriving from popular entertainments and bearing no real relationship to the theatre of Shaw, Feydeau, Antoine or Belasco, constitute a cinematic 'specificity' whose legitimacy we should, after Warhol, after Godard, be in a position to recognize. We can, in other words, no longer impugn the plebeian origins of the cinema, taxed with 'theatricality', as a sort of original sin expiated by the 'great Griffith'. In fact Griffith and his more innovatory contemporaries were to endow the cinema with the essential characteristics of another theatricality – that of 'the grown-ups', of the bourgeois theatre – through a number of contributions which were undoubtedly constituent of a second 'specificity' (Burch 1978, 98).

Burch's diagnosis invites a reconsideration of the connection between the two different types of theatricality and the institution of cinema. For his point that the replacement of popular theatricality by the bourgeois text-based theatricality associated with naturalist theatre coincides with the institutionalisation of cinema has its predecessors in other critiques of textual dramaturgy in the art of theatre. The theatre practitioner Vsevolod Meyerhold, whose work was extremely influential on Soviet cinema, criticised naturalist theatre's prioritisation of words over movement, gestures and plasticity. Meyerhold starts from the premise that there is a connection between the establishment of a literary dramaturgy that replaced past theatrical forms rooted in the people and the institutionalisation and de-radicalisation of theatre. He thus proposed a type of theatre that made use of popular folk art forms which would not be subservient to the primacy of the text, but would ensure that 'speech and plasticity are each subordinated to their own separate rhythms and the two do not necessarily coincide' (Meyerhold 2016, 65). Meyerhold thought that theatre needed to return to its roots and create productions that would be characterised by stylisation which would render representation more complex, by serving not dramatic continuity but the production of associations. This stylised theatre was characterised by self-consciousness in acting and *mise-en-scène*, and its ultimate aim was to avoid dramatic closure and produce gaps that necessitated spectatorial collaboration. The spectator, therefore, becomes a collaborator; unlike naturalist productions, the show is not reduced to a 'mere illustration of the author's words' (34).

Importantly, Meyerhold's critique of institutionalised theatre and his call for a re-theatricalisation of the medium finds deep resonances in the cinema of Sergei Eisenstein, whose work has had a significant impact on Lee's oeuvre. Eisenstein was schooled next to Meyerhold and was influenced by the latter's preference for an episodic style, stylised acting and typage over psychological characterisation. Like Meyerhold, Eisenstein acknowledged his cinema's debt not only to popular art forms such as the circus and the music hall, but also to a broader 'typage tendency' that had its roots in the theatre and enabled a filmmaker to produce a series of associations out of the combination of semi-independent episodes. This theatrical typage designates an aesthetic that goes beyond character portrayal and describes 'a specific approach to the events embraced by the content of the film' (Eisenstein 1977, 9). This type of dramaturgy is not consistent with the three-act structure of naturalist theatre. Instead, it brings the acting, the plastic elements and the *mise-en-scène* to the fore. As such, film form is not subordinated to content and the script, but all the compositional elements are manipulated to produce the key idea which is integral to the subject-matter. This is perhaps best captured in Eisenstein's remark regarding the effective use of *mise-en-scène*, which 'should unfold on stage the entire process' and not only 'the scripted piece of "information"' (Eisenstein 2014, 6). The expressive quality of the visual and the acoustic materials and the acting become means of discovering information and material not predetermined by the script.

Another index of the roots of Eisenstein's cinema in popular theatricality is his labelling of his work as 'a cinema of attractions', a term that has been associated with early cinema's roots in a non-literary dramaturgy that prioritised an aesthetic of showing/exhibiting rather than telling, as Tom Gunning's seminal study has also demonstrated. It is Eisenstein's own teacher, Meyerhold, who has brilliantly demonstrated the Soviet filmmaker's indebtedness to this form of popular theatricality. Significantly, Meyerhold identifies connections between Eisenstein and Charlie Chaplin, precisely because both deployed a rhythmic representational form in which each episode does not simply anticipate what is about to follow. As Meyerhold comments, ...

> When we come to examine Eisenstein's pronouncements we shall see how he divides up everything into 'attractions' – that is, into

episodes, each with an unfailingly effective conclusion. He constructs these episodes according to musical principles, not with the conventional aim of advancing the narrative. This may sound rather abstruse unless we understand the nature of rhythm. Rhythm occurs as the result of a picture having a rigid, harmonious overall plan. Eisenstein constructs a picture rhythmically, and it is by examining this aspect of his work that we discover his creative qualities. Eisenstein achieves something on the screen beyond the bounds of story and plot, something beyond the action (which is vital to the theatre but dispensable in the cinema); he achieves it on the basis of laws unique to the cinema. I fear I may be misinterpreted when I say 'something beyond the action which is vital to the theatre but dispensable in the cinema' (Meyerhold 2016, 396).

Meyerhold explains that he employs a similar technique in his theatre work, aiming to produce meaning out of multiple fragments, so as to activate the audience's critical faculties and imagination. Yet, this radicalisation of representation is not the product of a desire to do away with narrative, but the outcome of a re-theatricalisation of representation rooted in popular theatrical forms. This can be seen as part of a larger history of re-appropriation of popular tropes on the part of modernism and the avant-garde, something that has also been observed by Tom Gunning in his discussion of the cinema of attractions (Gunning 1990, 59), as well as by the theatre and film director Peter Brook, who explains that the attempts by modernist theatre practitioners to revitalise the theatre were predicated on going back to popular theatricality: Meyerhold to the circus, Brecht to the cabaret, and Artaud to the origins of the theatre in collective rituals (see Brook 1990, 76).

As evidenced in the above comments, film theatricality is a far more complex term that cannot be merely reduced to theatrical forms based on textual dramaturgy. André Bazin has also highlighted the connection between popular theatricality and cinema. Bazin rightly points out that theatre's influence on the film medium extends beyond the popular genre of the filmed theatre and expands even to films that we tend to consider as cinematic. As he explains, early cinema was very much a continuation of theatrical forms, and Georges Méliès himself saw his work as 'refinement of the marvels of the theater' (Bazin 1967, 78). This is also important because in Méliès's work the episode is more important than the whole. As he says, '[c]ontrary to what is usually done, my procedure for constructing this sort of film [fantasy, magical films] consisted in coming up with the details before the whole; the whole being nothing other than the "scenario"' (cited in Gaudreault 1987, 114). The theatrical in Méliès's case seems to be at the antipodes to the dramatic – that is, the mere reproduction of a story. In Bazin's view, such a theatricalised excess extends beyond the early days of the medium and can be identified in subsequent films. He suggests that the majority of American and French comedies have their roots in popular theatrical forms. One of his key examples is Charlie Chaplin, whose work is very much indebted to the English mime tradition as well as the music hall. Furthermore, as he explains, comedians such as Max Linder, Buster Keaton, and Laurel and Hardy extended a comic tradition the origins of which are to be found in the Commedia dell'arte and theatre farce. What bears noting when it comes to these popular theatrical forms is the deployment of type characters and the repertoire of stock themes and motifs. In a way, the stories of Commedia dell'arte were variations of pre-existing motifs and storylines, and something similar takes place in the film comedies produced in the first two decades of the twentieth century.

Significantly, Bazin cautions against the proponents of 'pure cinema' who consider the medium to be in opposition to its predecessor and concludes that knowledge of the theatre is a precondition of the mastery of 'the language of cinematography' (Bazin 1967, 116). Similarly, Susan Sontag questions the evolutionary approach to dramatic arts according to which cinema is a developed version of the theatre medium, since it replaces the static aspect of the theatre with a fluid type of representation not constrained by spatial stasis. Sontag challenges Erwin Panofsky's idea that the key criterion for appraising a film is 'its freedom from the impurities of theatricality' (Sontag 1966, 24). Her critique of Panofsky starts from the premise that his understanding of theatricality is limited because he confuses it with 'dramatized literature, texts, words', which he opposes to the visual qualities of the film medium (27). Against such an evolutionary understanding of cinema, Sontag explains that historically cinema and theatre are in dialogue with each other and that there is room for thinking about theatricality as an aesthetic which goes beyond the primacy of the text. Posing the question of film theatricality, she suggests that it refers to an aesthetic of 'self-consciousness' that highlights the artificiality of representation (27).

From the prolegomena, we can deduce that theatricality describes a process that is not to be confused with the reproduction of fixed dramatic content; it refers instead to a representational strategy that departs from a literary dramaturgy and a script-based way of thinking. This is why it is a concept that extends far beyond the theatre medium and is relevant when considering other artistic media, including film. The understanding of theatricality as something that exceeds literary dramaturgy chimes neatly with one of the most influential definitions of the term by Roland Barthes. Reflecting on Baudelaire's theatre, Barthes asks:

> What is theatricality? It is theater-minus-text, it is a density of signs and sensations built up on stage starting from the written argument; it is that ecumenical perception of sensuous artifice-gesture, tone, distance, substance, light – which submerges the text beneath the profusion of its external language. Of course theatricality must be present in the first written germ of a work, it is a datum of creation not of production. There is no great theater without a devouring theatricality – in Aeschylus, in Shakespeare, in Brecht, the written text is from the first carried along by the externality of bodies, of objects, of situations; the utterance immediately explodes into substances (Barthes 1972, 26).

Silvija Jestrovic cogently explains that Barthes's definition stresses the materials of representation that go beyond the dramatic text and corresponds to modernist conceptions of theatricality – for example, by Antonin Artaud and Nikolai Evreinov who understood it as this representational property that cannot be expressed solely by means of 'words and dialogue' (Jestrovic 2002, 43). In these terms, theatricality counters the understanding of representation as a process of imitation of reality that seeks to efface the media of its own articulation. Instead, theatricality intends to connect to the real by highlighting the artificiality of its own enunciation and the process over the finished product. It transforms the real by estranging it, so as to highlight social mediations that elude our routine relationships and behaviours. Theatricality, thus, produces a sense of representational excess that seeks to render the familiar strange. In highlighting the process over dramatic finality, it produces representational gaps and goes beyond the understanding of representation as the illustration/staging of a pre-existing play – or script when it comes to the art of cinema.

Theatricality is therefore intimately tied to a representational approach that invites us to see things out of their normal context and in keeping with the Russian formalist concept of *Остранение* (*Ostranenie*): it makes things visible by making them strange. The prerequisite for this is an expressive style of representation. Eisenstein was one of the key examples of this approach since he distinguished between the expressive (figuration) and the superficially representational *mise-en-scène*. The aim of the former was to produce sensual and affective effects so as to lead to a revitalisation of one's intellectual understanding of social phenomena (see Kessler 2014, 40–41). It is, however, important to emphasise that this transformative capacity of popular forms of theatricality has been also an element that permeates more commercial films. Tim Burton's work is a particular case in point where carnivalistic theatricality and cinematic excess invite the audience to question canonical binaries associated with the genres he manipulates – for instance, the superhero film. One needs to consider *Batman Returns* (1992) where theatrical masquerade and grotesque *mise-en-scène* turn into a commentary on the duality of the characters beyond the binaries of good and evil; as the filmmaker states, in the film 'the line between the villain and the hero is blurred', and such an approach problematises questions of normality and abnormality, making one rethink the hazy aspect of such dichotomies (Burton 2008). As such, excessive theatricality renders the familiar strange by producing audiovisual materials not wholly organised by narrative logic.

Spike Lee: Scenes as Self-Sufficient Units, Productive Editing and Separation of Elements

In both Eisenstein's and Burton's cases, the scene operates as part of a broader narrative, but it simultaneously functions as a self-sufficient unit. The transition from scene to scene is neither transparent nor clearly motivated by smooth continuity but is subject to the logic of cinematic attractions, emphasising concurrently the power of the gaze within the narrative – the exaggerated manner with which the characters interact with each other – as well as in the ways in which it communicates its materials to the audience by means of abrupt cutting. Something similar occurs in Spike Lee's cinema, since the narrative organisation of his films is relatively disjointed and the connection between the scenes is somewhat loose. Many of his films reanimate the aesthetic of cinematic attractions, not in the sense of the predominance of spectacle over narrative as per the post-classical Hollywood, but in the Eisensteinian dialectical fashion, according to which the collision of antithetical materials produces an extra-diegetic commentary on something that transcends the limits of the story.

To begin with, it is important to note that the majority of Lee's films start *in medias res*. Consider, for instance, the opening of School Daze, a film focusing on the political divisions among black students within a historically black college. Following a title card that states that it is a Friday homecoming weekend in Mission College, the camera immediately registers Dap (Lawrence Fishburne) leading a demonstration opposing the university's investments in South Africa. A sound-bridge provides off-screen acoustic information of a group of men led by Julian (Giancarlo Esposito) shouting slogans for a fraternity group, and the camera suddenly cuts to a crowd parading in a semi-militaristic way and interrupting the political meeting against Apartheid. The scene is structured in such a way that it creates a chorus effect. Eventually, the two groups come face to face with each other and start arguing. When a representative of the university comes to separate them, the scene concludes with the group of fraternity men doing a military-style drill and shouting pro-Gamma (fraternity group) songs. These men are chained on leashes and move in a choreographed manner, and we soon realise that their performance is also part of a hazing ritual to which all newly pledged members are subjected. The sequence concludes with the university president McPherson (Joe Seneca) and Virgil (Gregg Burge) silently looking through their window at the crowd dispersing. While this opening sequence introduces us to the key antagonisms within the college community, it also produces a sense of cinematic excess that aggressively seeks to attract the audience's attention to the material on screen. The transition to the next sequence is abrupt and has little connection to the preceding one. Now we are in a campus room where the newly pledged members of the Gamma Fraternity perform humiliating acts in front of the senior ones.

David Sterritt accurately observes that the tensions within the African-American community of the college are 'sketched out with hyperbole and tendentiousness rather than realism or objectivity in mind' (Sterritt 2013, 28). This hyperbolic style is communicated by means of an expressive *mise-en-scène*. The opening of the film certainly serves the aim of familiarising the viewer with the key antagonisms in the campus community, but in such a way that these antagonisms are portrayed as collective rather than individual ones. On the one hand, there is the group of politically sensitive students, while, on the other hand, the apolitical ones are concerned more with the traditional hierarchies of fraternities and sororities. But the arrangement of the material is done in a manner that has an entertaining/sensual effect which produces narrative information and functions concurrently as a social commentary.

Something analogous takes place in the opening of *Do the Right Thing*, a film about racial tensions in Brooklyn. The film's loose continuity is so persistent that, following thirty minutes of screen time, it is difficult to identify the connective diegetic element in what seems to look like autonomous scenes taking place in a Brooklyn neighbourhood. The film opens with a close-up of the radio presenter Señor Love Daddy (Samuel Jackson) framed in an angular perspective that registers parts of his face and his lips. The character speaks in a highly theatricalised manner, as if addressing the imaginary diegetic radio audience, but the expressive camera angle and the acting add another dimension, as if the character's performance were directed to an extra-diegetic addressee. Throughout the film, Señor Love Daddy functions as a narrator who comments on the story. Following this introductory sequence, the camera cuts to a room where an old man, Da Mayor (Ossie Davis), wakes up and complains about the weather. Meanwhile Da Mayor's turned-on radio provides a sound-bridge that enables the audience to continue listening to Love Daddy speaking. The scene that follows registers Smiley (Roger Guenveur Smith) who is framed from a low-angled shot and introduces himself by showing the pictures of Martin Luther King and Malcolm X which he sells to passers-by. Again, the transition from the previous passage to this one is not subject to the principles of smooth continuity, while the framing of the character and his direct address to the camera look as if he were addressing the audience and not the characters in the diegetic universe. Smiley forcefully seeks to attract the audience's attention, while the rapid shift from one dramatis persona to another looks stagey.

As the film progresses, we are introduced to the other characters in the narrative, such as Mookie (Spike Lee), the pizzeria owner Sal (Danny Aiello), his sons Pino (John Turturro) and Vito (Richard Edson), and Radio Raheem (Billy Dunn). But the sequences follow one another frantically, and we see the characters participating in situations that have a semi-independent status within the narrative. For instance, we are introduced to Sal and his sons by means of a family squabble between the three of them, stemming from Pino's aversion to the neighbourhood. When this scene culminates, the camera cuts to a high-angle shot of Ella (Christ Rivers) looking at the camera and arguing with her three friends. Their conversation is interrupted by the sudden appearance of Radio Raheem, who is mocked by Ella and her friends. The camera captures brief episodic conversations/arguments that offer a miniature-painting of the characters. Similarly, the first appearance of Buggin' Out (Giancarlo Esposito) in Sal's pizzeria turns into an argument regarding the latter's disrespect towards the black community. The sequence is fundamental in the progression of the narrative, but the argument erupts abruptly and has little connection to the preceding scene. The narrative organisation is not fluid, and the film looks like a collection of happenings succeeding one another.

This can well be considered in light of what Jacques Aumont describes as the difference between 'productive' and 'transparent' editing. According to Aumont, cinema history consists of films that choose between these two different approaches to editing. The first one aims at foregrounding editing's capacity to produce sensual and shock effects, while the latter one is committed to attenuating editing's 'sensational value' so as to suture together the images in a causal narrative chain (Aumont 2014, 10). Developing Aumont's point, we can stress the connections between productive editing and an aesthetics of theatricality. In the first category belong films from the early cinema of attractions, as well as the Soviet montage tradition and the late cinematic modernism of Resnais and Godard. Drawing on the definitions of theatricality in the previous section of this essay, we can see that theatricality produces a kind of interruptive/shock effect, since it aspires to solicit aggressively the viewer's attention to the material on screen. Furthermore, the productive editing assigns equal importance to the instant as well as to the dramatic whole, given that each episode has some sense of autonomy. It serves the narrative, but at the same time allows the succession of episodes to produce gaps. Instead, the transparent editing is committed to an aesthetic of smooth continuity and narrative flow that aspires to conceal any gaps between the succeeding scenes.

Consider another example from the opening of *Bamboozled* (2000). Inspired by Elia Kazan's *Face in the Crowd* (1957) and Sidney Lumet's *Network* (1976), the film addresses questions of power relations and structural racism in the American film and television industry. It focuses on Pierre Delacroix (Damon Wayans), a television network executive who, dissatisfied with his boss's (Michael Rapaport) condescending attitude, decides to put forward a proposal for a series tiled the New Millennium Minstrel Show, whose lead characters will be performing in blackface. He hires two impoverished street performers, Manray (Savion Glover) and Womack (Tommy Davidson), to star in the show. Delacroix hopes that the obviously demeaning character of the series will provoke negative reactions from the TV executives and that the audience that will get him fired and enable him to skip his contract. But the show becomes an unexpected hit with the audiences and the *casus belli* for a militant underground black group, the Maus Maus.

The film opens *in medias res*, with the protagonist brushing his teeth and quoting a definition of satire: 'Satire 1a: a literary work in which human vice or folly is ridiculed or attacked scornfully; 1b the branch of literature that composes such work. 2. Irony, derision or caustic wit used to attack or expose folly, vice, or stupidity'. It then cuts abruptly to a close-up of Pierre who introduces himself in a direct address to the camera and informs the audience about his work as a television executive for the CNS network. This scene is shot in the typical Lee signature shot, in which the actor and the camera are placed on dollies making the character appear dissociated from the background. There is a double theatricality in this passage. On the one hand, Delacroix's intentionally phony French accent raises questions regarding the character's performing a role to become accepted in the corporate environment. On the other hand, this performative mode of address is equally directed at the viewer. The character's performance blurs the boundary between the diegetic and the extra-diegetic address since Pierre retains this accent throughout the film.

Pierre's introduction is followed by a quick cut to a dilapidated building where two poor men, Manray and Womack, prepare to go and earn some money on the street. The transition to this shot is extremely abrupt, as is also the case with the following one that captures Manray performing an exceptionally elaborate tap-dance for the passers-by while his companion collects the money. Again, the sequence is shot in a particularly theatricalised manner. Close-ups of Manray's feet alternate with medium shots capturing both Manray and Womack performing for the crowd, followed by minor sequences shot in anamorphic lenses that imbue the scene with a sense of representational excess. Of interest here is that the capturing of the duo's performance is not merely an introduction to the characters, but also an intentional exposition of their virtuosity. When they encounter Pierre in the following sequence, the camera intentionally connects the two different worlds – Pierre's corporate working environment and their own deprived status by means of a sound-bridge offering a dialectical clash of opposites. In all these sequences, the editing is not structured around a seamless construction but the transition from shot to shot produces deliberate clefts. The sequences can be understood as self-sufficient because their succession is not based on match-on action editing. In doing so, the director stresses the material in each sequence aiming to force us to look at each separate passage in the film as if it were unique. In effect, the narrative organisation becomes extremely fragmented, because the prerequisite for smooth continuity is the simple subordination of certain sequences to narrative imperatives. Instead, Lee potently organises the material to attract the audience's gaze, while the power of the gaze is also accentuated within the diegetic environment by means of the highly stagey manner in which the characters address each other.

This aesthetic approach chimes neatly with Josette Féral's idea that theatricality describes an intense process of linking an onlooker with the performed material. According to Féral, theatricality designates representational schemas that acknowledge the inability to produce absolute meaning. At the heart of this argument is the idea that theatricality does not produce narrative harmony, but what Féral names 'cleavages', and it is by means of these cleavages that artists aim to re-establish communication with their audience, to make them see familiar things in a different light. The ultimate aim of this approach is to establish a more dynamic form of interaction between those who look at the performed material and those who are being looked at.

> If the notion of theatricality goes beyond the theater, it is because it is not a 'property' belonging to the subjects/things that are its vehicles. It belongs neither to the objects, the space, nor to the actor himself, although each can become its vehicle. Rather, theatricality is the result of a perceptual dynamics linking the onlooker with someone or something that is looked at (Féral 2002, 105).

In a similar manner, Lee constantly seeks to solicit the audience's attention so as to make the ordinary look extraordinary, through an audiovisual style that is equally concerned with the portrayed actions as well as with the foregrounding of the significance of style itself. Emblematic in this respect are the film's passages capturing Manray and Womack performing their roles in the Minstrel show. Episodic satirical sequences follow one another, and while they are part of the narrative, they also serve a role which is extraneous to the logic of the narrative. They act as an extra-diegetic commentary on the persistence of structural racism in the entertainment industry that tends to relegate African-American actors to roles of buffoonery.

Yet, the material becomes even more complex because Mantan's (Manray's minstrel role) and Sleep'n'Eat's (Womack's minstrel role) performances are very skilful, and they motivate the audience (both the TV audience in the diegetic world and the extra-diegetic spectators) to enjoy them. The aesthetics of exaggeration serves an entertaining function, while it also offers political critique. Provocatively, their acts are funny in spite of their racist implications. Commenting on this aspect of the film, Lee suggests that this was a contradiction that the film intended to explore. Historically, many of the performances of buffoonery were funny, despite the hate behind them. As he says, 'that's the irony – that these artists [the performers playing in minstrel shows in the past] were so great that they could take a dehumanising form and still make it somewhat humanistic' (Crowdus et al. 2001, 6).[1] But one is also immediately urged to ask whether the film's critique of racist stereotypes also participates in the perpetuation of buffoonery. The key precept here is that it is by means of the film's loose dramaturgy that thematic complexity arises, something that corresponds with Féral's point that theatricality produces a sense of formal discontinuity that leads to interpretative ambiguity and complexity.[2]

The film's politics are directly interconnected with its aesthetics, since the loose dramaturgy and the preference for episodic satirical sequences manipulate the very reality of the minstrel shows, whose racial stereotyping – albeit in a much more refined form – is still identifiable in the film and television industry. This contrast between a sombre subject-matter and comic excess produces a sense of incompleteness that echoes past practices and theoretical perspectives on the political implications of farcical comedy. Eisenstein, for instance, suggests that the radical aspects of comedy are founded upon its capacity to negate things that one takes for granted. Drawing on the philosophy of Kant and Bergson, Eisenstein suggests that comedy is characterised by a sense of irrationality which enables one to comment on aspects of reality that appear to be self-evident (see Eisenstein 2014, 31). This prompts me to add that film comedy, as per Bazin's above-mentioned assessment, makes use of forms of theatricality, because it is by means of its manipulation of excess and irrational situations that it vigorously connects the observer with the material to be observed.

The key contradiction posed by *Bamboozled* is that, in trying to expose a history and culture of racial stereotypes, one might unwillingly and unconsciously perpetuate it. Lee's self-reflexively acknowledges this, and nobody escapes from his critique, not even the radical gangsta rap group Maus Maus, who react against the show by kidnapping Manray and executing him live on the internet. As W. J. T. Mitchell convincingly suggests, despite the filmmaker's conviction that the film can depict a reality hidden behind the biased stereotypes of the film and television industry, *Bamboozled* instead demonstrates 'how difficult it is to find this critical standpoint, to achieve a "just estimation" of images that transcends distortion and madness' (Mitchell 2005, 311).

This sustained engagement with stereotypes is something that characterises Lee's entire oeuvre. In most of his films he resorts to a theatrical typage – à la Eisenstein – that invites one to consider how characters might be imprisoned in the stereotypical roles projected on them. A case in point is the racial slur sequence in *Do the Right Thing*, where a representative of each ethnic group shown in the film directly addresses the camera, throwing insults to an off-screen invisible addressee. The sequence starts unexpectedly, following a conversation between Mookie and Pino regarding the latter's constant denigration of black people. This is followed by a medium shot of Mookie looking at the camera and mocking Italian-Americans. It then zooms from a medium shot to Pino's face in the pizzeria, insulting African-Americans. Cut to another medium shot of a young Puerto Rican, Stevie (Luis Antonio Ramos), insulting Koreans. It then captures a policeman (Rick Aiello) mocking the Puerto Ricans and then a Korean grocer, Sonny (Steve Park), who concludes his own slur with some anti-Semitic comments. The sequence culminates with a stationary shot of Señor Love Daddy, who rolls towards the camera and urges an invisible audience to calm down. With this sequence Lee intensifies an aesthetic of excess that characterises the film as a whole. The difference here, however, is that this passage does not serve narrative progression, given that none of the characters addresses any person in particular. As such, the whole sequence functions as an assault on the audience, which highlights the divisions between ethnic minorities. It also points to the fact that, despite the racial/ethnic stereotyping to which they have been subjected, vulnerable minorities are ready to do the same and typecast people belonging to an ethnic background different from their own.

The self-sufficiency of this unit is much more self-evident than the other passages in the film, which, despite their semi-independent status, are loosely connected to the broader story. In this case, however, the scenes succeed one another frantically and produce dialectical clashes. Marilyn Fabe makes a strong case that this and other, less forceful passages in the film recall Eisenstein's *modus operandi*, according to which a series of attractions are placed alongside each other, with the view to producing gaps that need to be filled by the audience (see Fabe 2004, 194). It is noteworthy that, like Eisenstein, Lee resorts to popular culture tropes – including the frequent use of slang – in his structuring of these dialectical clashes. Todd McGowan observes that 'these instances of direct cinematic address remove us from the conventions of narrative cinema and return us to cinema's origins, a time in which spectacle and enjoyment took precedence over the pleasures of narrative continuity' (McGowan 2014, 123). Yet, spectacle and entertainment are part and parcel of a representational approach that sees artificiality and audio-visual excess as means to the end of transforming perception – an idea that corresponds with the twentieth-century advocates of theatricality, such as Meyerhold, Brecht and Artaud. The racial slur sequence in particular is unambiguously stagey, as if asking the viewer to 'look and listen to this'; the invisible addressee is none other than the audience itself, whose subjection to an audio-visual assault by the blinkered characters questions their own complicity in the perpetuation of stereotypes.

In other cases, Lee manipulates the motif of the self-sufficient unit that exceeds narrative motivations when he employs a Brechtian separation of elements.[3] The musical passages in a play or film, according to Brecht, should be arranged in such a way that they would compellingly assert their independent status in the narrative. Along with Hanns Eisler and Theodor W. Adorno, Brecht reacts against the use of unobtrusive film music that serves mere illustrative purposes. He argues instead for the production of musical sequences that step outside the narrative and offer commentary on the situations encountered by the characters, so as to connect them with real contradictions in the extra-diegetic world. As Eisler (Brecht's musical collaborator) and Adorno explain, the productive use of music does not aim to neutralise, but to intensify the material on screen. Music in this way is used as a dialectical counterpoint that connects the particular with the general and directs the audience's attention 'back from the sphere of privacy to the major social issue' (Adorno and Eisler 2007, 6). In these terms, the musical sequences are part of a broader aesthetics of theatricalisation that intends to highlight rather than neutralise the audio-visual means of expression.

Importantly, Brecht and Eisler were very keen on using popular music as a pedagogical tool that could connect the fictional with the extra-fictional reality. I want to consider two passages from *School Daze* and *Chi-Raq* in which Lee makes use of this Brechtian separation of elements with the aid of popular music. In *School Daze*, there is a musical sequence titled 'Good and Bad Hair', which follows an argument between the Jigaboos (a pejorative term for black women with dark skin) and the Wannabes (an insulting term for black women with light skin). The sequence starts unexpectedly. Initially, we see the two groups arguing in a campus room and throwing insults at each other. Then, following the generic tradition of musicals, the film cuts to an imaginary sequence in a beauty salon where the two groups sing and dance. It is by means of the choreography and the songs that the filmmaker highlights the antagonism between the two groups. The sequence is structured in the form of argument and counter-argument, since a member of each group comes to the forefront and insults a member from the other group about their 'nappy' or 'straight' hair. This is followed by the two groups singing in chorus. Although Lee manipulates generic conventions, he pushes them further to allow for an exploration of the divisions within the black community. Lee himself states: 'What we did was use a historically black college as a microcosm of black America, hoping to highlight the so-called differences that I feel are petty, that keep blacks from being a unified people, class, skin color, hair type, that type of stuff' (cited in Aftab 2005, 57). The collective in the sequences, therefore, is far from being a fused group. McGowan, for instance, notes that the sequence's setting in a beauty parlour is an intertextual reference to *Grease* (1978). However, the contrast is that, whereas in *Grease* and generally in musicals the song and dance sequences aspire to flatten any differences and conflicts between the characters, Lee intensifies them (see McGowan 2014, 101). He does not unify the two opposing groups in a utopian way, but instead highlights their separation. This is also put forward through *mise-en-scène* choices. For example, the dark-skinned girls are dressed in red and the light-skinned ones in silver, thus further intensifying the rift between them.

This tactic of manipulating generic conventions with the view to politicising mainstream genres is also evident in *Chi-Raq* (2015); a loose adaptation of Aristophanes's *Lysistrata*, *Chi-Raq* tells the story of a group of black women who go on a sex strike to protest against gang violence on the south side of Chicago. The film draws on the genres of musical, comedy and hip-hop gangsta film, a genre that Lee despised for its glamorisation of nihilistic violence and its caricature of black people.[4] *Chi-raq* has an episodic quality which is strengthened by the inclusion of a narrator, Dolmedes (Samuel Jackson), and the interruption of the action by hip-hop/rap sequences that operate as political commentary. The film's opening shows a map of the USA visualised on screen followed by Nick Cannon's – Chi-Raq's protagonist – song 'Pray 4 my City'. The song here has a polemical, agit-prop function that articulates the problem of gang violence; the lyrics appear in red text on the screen and introduce the audience to the film's key thesis, which is that gang-violence divides an oppressed community and maintains conditions of structural racism.

Thus, the opening song has a pedagogical function, which is also reinforced by the excessive theatricality – that is, its desire to bring the spectator face to face with the material on screen. After this opening sequence, the film cuts to a night club, where a rowdy crowd rhythmically sings the name of rap singer Chi-Raq (Nick Cannon). The background of the crowd suddenly freezes, and Dolmedes introduces the film's subject, making references to Aristophanes' *Lysistrata*. Then, Chi-Raq appears on stage and starts singing a rap gangsta song. During his performance, the lyrics appear in the form of Whatsapp messages on screen: 'If I see Dem Boys in Orange Then its 'Bout to be Some Trouble. My Hood on my Back. I swear all niggas love me. If I Need a Job Done Dey Gonna Kill a Nigga for Me'. The camera alternates between the rappers on stage and the crowd dancing rhythmically as a unified group. The musical sequence here is prominent and makes a mockery of the gangsta hip-hop culture. At the same time, it is impressive and builds on the pleasures of hip-hop culture, only to criticise the gangsta culture from within.[5] The scene concludes with a violent shooting that interrupts the concert and makes the crowd disperse. Here, the musical passage is not a plot accessory but acts as a self-sufficient unit that merges entrainment with political critique. One is invited to question the machismo and violence of the underground hip-hop culture and the negative effect of the gangster culture on the community. As such, the music and the lyrics exceed the diegetic boundaries and palpably address an extra-diegetic addressee, a motif that can be identified in Lee's entire oeuvre as already discussed above.

In conclusion, in all these examples and many other passages from Spike Lee's films one discovers a form of theatricality that hovers between representation and communication, constantly playing on this duality of fiction and reality. One crucial feature of this aesthetic approach is the conscious deployment of autonomous sequences that connect loosely with the broader dramaturgy. Many of these sequences deliberately manipulate popular culture tropes that challenge dramaturgical consistency and invoke cinematic strategies that were prevalent in the early days of the medium. From this perspective, we can understand the dramaturgical inconsistency of Lee's cinema as a reanimation of the popular theatricality that is opposed to the dominant script-based dramaturgy and the tradition of the well-made script. Acknowledging this type of theatricality that deliberately blurs the boundaries between diegetic and extra-diegetic address can offer a productive prism through which to understand the connection between aesthetics and politics in Spike Lee's cinema. In his review of the 25th Hour (2002), Adrian Martin unwittingly captured this facet of Lee's aesthetic, arguing that 'perhaps Lee wishes he was making movies in the silent era, when a loose genre called the city symphony freely mixed fragments of documentary and fiction' (Martin 2003). While the connection between Lee and the city-symphony is debatable, Martin's point that his films evoke the early days of the medium and merge fictional and extra-fictional material holds true, especially if we consider the filmmaker's aesthetic that emphasises the power of the gaze in such an exaggerated manner as if trying to break the barrier separating the observer and the material on screen.

Notes

1. Interestingly, a film reviewer – Stuart Klawans – identified this dual property of the film. As he says, 'Spike Lee has applied his erudition to this American [minstrel] tradition and discovered not just how it wounds but also how it entertains' (cited in Rogin 2001, 14).
2. Although Todd McGowan does not see theatricality as a medium in Lee's films, he cogently argues that his films are permeated by cinematic excess (not only in terms of form, but also in terms of the characters' portrayal and behaviour) that complicates interpretation. Commenting on *Bamboozled*, he points out: 'For the spectator of *Bamboozled*, there is no place safe from the onslaught of excess. It occurs most prominently through the television program that features characters in blackface, a setting in a watermelon patch, a musical group known as the Alabama Porch Monkeys, and an emcee whose tagline is "Niggers is a beautiful thing". At every turn, there is much more overt racism than spectators typically see. The excess permeates throughout the film, from those involved with the program to those militantly opposed to it' (2014, 128).
3. Carl Platinga has recently published an article linking Lee to Brecht from a cognitive approach (see Platinga 2019).

4. While making *Clockers* (1995), Lee explained that 'I really wanted to talk about the violence. We wanted to deglamorize the violence that still exists today in hip-hop and this whole gangsta stuff. We wanted to show what these bullets and knives really did to your body' (Ibid., 190).
5. Jonathan Munby asserts that something analogous is the case in films from the gangsta genre pointing at 'gangsta's entry into the (inter)national language not as something that confirms or reifies the existing racializing of the social order, but as something that disturbs the mainstream from within (2011, 180).

Bibliography

Abel, L. (2003) *Tragedy and Metatheatre: Essays on Dramatic Form*, New York: Holmes & Meier.
Adorno, T. W., and Eisler, H. (2007) *Composing for the Films*, New York: Bloomsbury.
Aftab, K. (2005) *Spike Lee: That's My Story and I'm Sticking to It*, London: Faber and Faber.
Agamben, G. (1993) 'In Playland', in *Infancy and History*, London: Verso, 67–87.
Ahmed, S. (2006) *Queer Phenomenology*, Durham, NC: Duke University Press.
Åkervall, L. (2015) 'Die Wahrheit von Auto-Tune: Stimmodulationen in digitalen Medienökologien', *Navigationen: Zeitschrift für Medien und Kulturwissenschaften*, 2: 77–98.
Åkervall, L. (2020) 'Post-Cinematic Unframing', in J. Murphy and L. Rascaroli (eds), *Theorizing Film Through Contemporary Art: Expanding Film*, Amsterdam: Amsterdam University Press, 255–76.
Albacan, A. I. (2016) *Intermediality and Spectatorship in the Theatre Work of Robert Lepage: The Solo Shows*, Cambridge: Cambridge Scholars Publishing.
Allen, J. (2005) 'Einmal ist keinmal: Observations on Re-Enactment', in S. Lütticken (ed.), *Life, Once More: Forms of Re-Enactment in Contemporary Art*, Rotterdam: Witte de With Centre for Contemporary Art, 179–201.
Allinson, M. (2008) *A Spanish Labyrinth: The Films of Pedro Almodóvar*, London: Tauris, 2008.
Alston, A. (2016) *Beyond Immersive Experience: Aesthetics, Politics and Productive Participation*, London: Palgrave Macmillan.
Andrew, D. (1984) 'Adaptation', in *Concepts in Film Theory*, New York: Oxford University Press, 96–106.
Artaud, A. (1976) *Collected Works: Volume Four*, London: John Calder.
Aumont, J. (2014) *Montage*, trans. T. Barnard, Montreal: Caboose.
Auslander, P. (1999) *Liveness*, London: Routledge.
Auslander, P. (2006) 'The Performativity of Performance Documentation', *PAJ: A Journal of Performance and Art* 28: 3, 1–10.
Austin-Smith, Brenda (2012) 'The Ethics of Murder: Trial as Performance in the Maternal Melodrama', in André Loiselle and Jeremy Maron (eds), *Stages of Reality: Theatricality in Cinema*, University of Toronto Press, 102–15.

Azoulay, A. (2012) *A Civil Imagination: A Political Ontology of Photography*, London: Verso.
Bailes, S. J. (2011) *Performance Theatre and the Poetics of Failure: Forced Entertainment, Goat Island, Elevator Repair Service*, London: Routledge.
Balme, C. (2007) *Pacific Performances: Theatricality and Cross-Cultural Encounter in the South Seas*, Basingstoke: Palgrave.
Balsom, E. (2017) *After Uniqueness: A History of Film and Video Art in Circulation*, New York: Columbia University Press.
Barish, J. (1981) *The Antitheatrical Prejudice*, Berkeley and Los Angeles: The University of California Press.
Barthes, R. (1972) *Roland Barthes: Critical Essays*, trans. R. Howard, Evanston: Northwestern University Press.
Barthes, R. (2000 [1980]) *Camera Lucida*, trans. R. Howard, London: Vintage.
Bazin, A. (1967) *What is Cinema, Volume 1*, Los Angeles: University of California Press.
Benveniste, É. (1971) 'The Nature of Pronouns', in *Problems in General Linguistics*, trans. M. E. Meek, Miami: University of Miami Press, 217–22.
Berry, D. M. (2014) *Critical Theory and the Digital*, New York: Bloomsbury.
Berry, D. M., and Dieter, M. (eds) (2015) *Postdigital Aesthetics: Art, Computation and Design*, Basingstoke: Palgrave Macmillan.
Bishop, C. (2004) 'Antagonism and Relational Aesthetics', *October* 110, 51–79.
Blas, Z., and Gaboury, J. (2016) 'Biometrics and Opacity: A Conversation', *Camera Obscura: Feminism, Culture, and Media Studies* 31: 2, 155–65.
Blau, H. (1990) *The Audience*, Baltimore: Johns Hopkins University Press.
Bolter, J. D., and Grusin, R. (2003) *Remediation: Understanding New Media*, Cambridge, MA: MIT Press.
Bordwell, D., and Thompson, K. (2013) *Film Art: An Introduction*, New York: McGraw-Hill.
Bourdieu, P. (1993) *The Field of Cultural Production*, Cambridge: Polity Press.
Boyle, M. (2016) 'Additive Theories of Rationality: A Critique', *European Journal of Philosophy* 24: 3, 527–55.
Bradby, D. (1991) *Modern French Drama 1940–1990*, Cambridge: Cambridge University Press.
Braidotti, R. (2013) *The Posthuman*, Cambridge: Polity Press.
Braun, E. (1998) *Meyerhold on Theatre*, London: Methuen.
Brook, P. (1972) *The Empty Space*, London: Penguin.
Brooks, P. (1976) *The Melodramatic Imagination: Balzac, Henry James, Melodrama, and the Mode of Excess*, New Haven: Yale University Press.
Buckley, J. (2016) *The Rough Guide to Venice and the Veneto*, London: Rough Guides.
Burch, N. (1978) 'Porter, or Ambivalence', *Screen* 19: 4, 91–106.
Burgess, M. (2018) *What is GDPR? The Summary Guide to GDPR Compliance in the UK*, WIRED UK, http://www.wired.co.uk/article/what-is-gdpr-uk-eu-legislation-compliance-summary-fines-2018. Accessed 29 May 2018.
Burns, E. (1972) *Theatricality: A Study of Convention in the Theatre and in Social Life*, London: Longman.
Burrington, I. (2015) 'A Journey into the Heart of Facebook', *The Atlantic*, http://www.theatlantic.com/technology/archive/2015/12/facebook-data-center-tk/418683/. Accessed 22 January 2016.
Burton, T. (2008) *Burton on Burton*, ed. M. Salisbury, London: Faber and Faber.

Butler, J. (1999) *Gender Trouble: Feminism and the Subversion of Identity*, New York: Routledge.
Butler, J. (2011 [1993]) *Bodies That Matter: On the Discursive Limits of 'Sex'*. London: Routledge Classics.
Byers, J., and Waits, L. (2006) 'Good Genes: Sexual Selection in Nature', *Proceedings of the National Academy of Sciences of the United States of America* 103: 44, 16343–45.
Cadwalladr, C. (2019) 'A Digital Gangster Destroying Democracy: The Damning Verdict on Facebook', *The Guardian*, 18 February, https://www.theguardian.com/technology/2019/feb/18/a-digital-gangster-destroying-democracy-the-damning-verdict-on-facebook. Accessed 18 February 2019.
Campos, L. (2013) 'Science in Contemporary British Theatre: A Conceptual Approach', *Interdisciplinary Science Reviews* 38: 4, 295–305.
Carlson, M. A. (2002) 'The Resistance to Theatricality', *SubStance: A Review of Theory and Literary Criticism* 31, 238–50.
Carr, I. (1998) *Miles Davis: The Definitive Biography*, London: Harper Collins.
Caruth, C. (1996) *Unclaimed Experience: Trauma, Narrative, and History*, Baltimore: Johns Hopkins University Press.
Caulfield, S. (2018) *In Defense of Honor: Sexual Morality, Modernity, and Nation in Early-Twentieth Century Brazil*, Durham, NC: Duke University Press.
Cavell, S. (1967) 'The Avoidance of Love: A Reading of *King Lear*', in *Must We Mean What We Say?*, Cambridge: Cambridge University Press, 246–325.
Chan, J. (2014) 'Notes on Post-Internet', in O. Kholeif (ed.), *You are Here: Art After the Internet*, Manchester: Cornerhouse Publications, 106–23.
Chapple, F., and Kattenbelt, C. (2006) *Intermediality in Theatre and Performance*, Amsterdam: Rodopi.
Chun, W. H. K. (2016) *Updating to Remain the Same: Habitual New Media*, Cambridge, MA, and London: MIT Press.
Cohen, K. (1979) *Film and Fiction: The Dynamics of Exchange*, New Haven: Yale University Press.
Conrad, R., and Franju, G. (1981) 'Mystery and Melodrama: A Conversation with Georges Franju', *Film Quarterly* 35: 2, 31–42.
Corrigan, T. (1999) *Film and Literature: An Introduction and Reader*, Upper Saddle River: Prentice-Hall.
Corry, A. (2017), *Treasures from the Wreck of the Unbelievable: Damien Hirst*, Venice: François Pinault Foundation.
Costa, M. (2012) 'Playwright Nick Payne: Master of the Multiverse', *The Guardian*, 2 November, https://www.theguardian.com/stage/2012/nov/02/nick-payne-playwright-constellations. Accessed 14 February 2019.
Crowdus, G., and Georgakas, D. (2001) 'Thinking About the Power of Images: An Interview with Spike Lee', *Cineaste* 26: 2, 5–9.
Crowley, R. (2011) *City of Fortune: How Venice Won and Lost a Naval Empire*, London: Faber & Faber.
Csiky, G. (2015) *Avar-Age Polearms and Edged Weapons: Classification, Typology, Chronology and Technology*, Leiden: Brill.
Damianakos, S. (2011) «Εισαγωγή» [Introduction], in *Θέατρο Σκιών. Παράδοση και Νεωτερικότητα* [*Shadow Theatre: Tradition and Modernism*], Athens: Plethron Publications, 9–20.
Darwin, C. (2004) *The Descent of Man, and Selection in Relation to Sex*, London: Penguin.

Davies, J. (2017) 'Damien Hirst's Treasures from the Wreck of the Unbelievable: Anatomy of a Blockbuster', *Sight & Sound*, 3 August, https://www.bfi.org.uk/news-opinion/sight-sound-magazine/comment/festivals/damien-hirst-s-treasures-wreck-unbelievable-anatomy-blockbuster. Accessed 31 January 2019.

Davies, S. (2012) *The Artful Species: Aesthetics, Art, and Evolution*, Oxford: Oxford University Press.

Davis, M., with Troupe, Q. (1989) *Miles: The Autobiography*. London: Macmillan.

Davis, T. C. (2003) 'Theatricality in Civil Society', in T. C. Davis and T. Postlewait (eds), *Theatricality*, Cambridge: Cambridge University Press, 127–55.

Davis, T. C., and Postlewait, T. (2003) *Theatricality*, New York: Cambridge University Press.

Dawkins, R. (1989) *The Extended Phenotype*, Oxford: Oxford University Press.

Debord, G. (1995 [1967]) *The Society of the Spectacle*, trans. D. Nicholson-Smith, New York: Zone Books.

Den Oever, A. (ed.) (2010) *Ostrannenie*. Amsterdam: Amsterdam University Press.

Denson, S., and Leyda J. (eds) (2016) *Post-Cinema: Theorizing 21st Century Film*, Falmer: Reframe.

Derrida, J. (1978) 'The Theatre of Cruelty and the Closure of Representation', in *Writing and Difference*, trans. A. Bass, London: Routledge, 292–316.

Derrida, J. (1981) 'The Double Session', in *Dissemination*, London: Athlone, 173–286.

Derrida, J. (1988) *Limited Inc*. Evanston: Northwestern University Press.

Derrida, J. (2007) *Psyche: Inventions of the Other, Volume 1*, ed. P. Kamuf and E. Rottenberg, Palo Alto: Stanford University Press.

Djerassi, C. (2002) 'Contemporary "Science-in-Theatre": A Rare Genre', *Interdisciplinary Science Reviews*, 27: 3, 193–201.

Dutton, D. (2009) *The Art Instinct: Beauty, Pleasure, and Human Evolution*, Oxford: Oxford University Press.

Ebert, R. (1988) 'School Daze', RogerEvert.com, https://www.rogerebert.com/reviews/school-daze-1988. Accessed 11 February 2019.

Eire, C. (2019) *The Life of Saint Teresa of Avila: A Biography*. Princeton: Princeton University Press.

Eisenstein, S. (1977) *Film Form: Essays in Film Theory*, ed. and trans. J. Leyda, London: Houghton Mifflin Harcourt.

Eisenstein, S. (2014) *Mise en jeu and mise en geste*, trans. S. Levchin, Montreal: Caboose.

Elsaesser, T. (2015) 'The Ethics of Appropriation: Found Footage between Archive and Internet', *Found Footage Magazine* 1, 30–37.

Erickson, J. (2003) 'Defining Political Performance with Foucault and Habermas: Strategic and Communicative Action', in T. Postlewait and T. C. Davis (eds), *Theatricality*, Cambridge: Cambridge University Press, 156–85.

Everett, H. 'The Amoeba Metaphor: Early Draft of Everett's Doctoral Dissertation', PBS.org, http://www.pbs.org/wgbh/nova/manyworlds/orig-01.html. Accessed 14 February 2019.

Everett, H. (1957) 'Everett's Letter to Bryce DeWitt of May 31, 1957', PBS.org, https://www.pbs.org/wgbh/nova/manyworlds/orig-02.html. Accessed 14 February 2019.

Fabe, M. (2004) *Closely Watched Films: An Introduction to the Art of Narrative Film Technique*, Berkeley: University of California Press.

Farnell, I. (2019) 'Science, Science Fiction, and Nick Payne's *Elegy*: A Conceptual Third Way', *Studies in Theatre and Performance*, 29: 2, 206–23.

Felopoulou, S. (2006) «Η Τεχνική της Θεατρικότητας στον Ιάκωβο Καμπανέλλη» [The Technique of Theatricality in Iakovos Kambanellis], in *Πρακτικά Πανελλήνιου Συνεδρίου προς τιμήν του Ιάκωβου Καμπανέλλη* [*Proceedings of Panhellenic Conference in Honour of Iakovos Kambanellis*], Patras: Patras University, 391–400.

Féral, J. (1982) 'Performance and Theatricality: The Subject De-Mystified', *Modern Drama* 25: 1, 170–81.

Féral, J. (2002a) 'Foreword', *SubStance: A Review of Theory and Literary Criticism* 31: 2/3, 3–13.

Féral, J. (2002b) 'Theatricality: The Specificity of Theatrical Language', *SubStance: A Review of Theory and Literary Criticism* 31: 2/3, 94–108.

Fiebach, J. (2002) 'Theatricality: From Oral Traditions to Televised "Realities"', *SubStance: A Review of Theory and Literary Criticism* 31: 2/3, 17–41.

Fischer-Lichte, E. (1995) 'Introduction: Theatricality: A Key Concept in Theatre and Cultural Studies', *Theatre Research International* 20: 2, 85–89.

Foster, S. L. (2002) 'Walking and Other Choreographic Tactics: Danced Inventions of Theatricality and Performativity', *SubStance: A Review of Theory and Literary Criticism* 31: 2/3, 125–46.

Fried, M. (1980) *Absorption and Theatricality: Painting and Beholder in the Age of Diderot*, Chicago: University of Chicago Press.

Fried, M. (1996) *Manet's Modernism, or, The Face of Painting in the 1860s*, Chicago: University of Chicago Press.

Fried, M. (1998a) 'An Introduction to My Art Criticism', in *Art and Objecthood: Essays and Reviews*, Chicago: University of Chicago Press, 1–74.

Fried, M. (1998b) 'Art and Objecthood [1967]', in *Art and Objecthood: Essays and Reviews*, Chicago: University of Chicago Press, 148–72.

Fried, M. (2008a) 'Portraits by Thomas Struth, Rineke Dijkstra, Patrick Faigenbaum, Luc Delahaye, and Roland Fischer; Douglas Gordon and Philippe Parreno's *Zidane*', in *Why Photography Matters as Art as Never Before*, New Haven: Yale University Press, 191–233.

Fried, M. (2008b) *Why Photography Matters as Art as Never Before*. London: Yale University Press.

Fried, M. (2011) 'Presentness: Anri Sala', in *Four Honest Outlaws: Sala, Ray, Marioni, Gordon*, New Haven: Yale University Press, 29–66.

Fried, M. (2014) 'Orientation in Painting: Caspar David Friedrich', in *Another Light: Jacques-Louis David to Thomas Demand*, New Haven: Yale University Press, 111–49.

Gadamer, H.-G. (2013) *Truth and Method*, trans. J. Weinsheimer and D. G. Marshall, London: Bloomsbury.

Galloway, A. R. (2012) *The Interface Effect*, Cambridge: Polity.

Gaudreault, A. (1987) 'Theatricality, Narrativity, and Trickality: Reevaluating the Cinema of Georges Méliès', *Journal of Popular Film and Television*, 15: 3, 110–19.

Georgakaki, K. (2015) *Βίος και Πολιτεία μιας Γηραιάς Κυρίας στην Επταετία. Επιθεώρηση και Δικτατορία* [*Life and State of an Old Lady during the Junta: Revue and Dictatorship*], Athens: Ziti Publications.

Giddens, S., and Jones, S. (2009) 'De-Second Naturing: Word Unbecoming Flesh in the Work of Bodies in Flight', in S. Broadhurst and J. Machon (eds), *Sensualities/Textualities and Technologies: Writings of the Body in 21st Century Performance*, Basingstoke: Palgrave Macmillan, 38–49.

Goffman, E. (1959) *The Presentation of Self in Everyday Life*. New York: Anchor Books.

Gordon, M. (1987) *Dada Performance*, New York: PAJ Publications.
Gran, A. G. and Oatley, D. (2002) 'The Fall of Theatricality in the Age of Modernity', *SubStance*, 31: 98/99, 251–64.
Gray, S. (2017) 'Guest Editorial', *Foundation: The International Review of Science Fiction*, 43: 117, 11–12.
Groys, B. (2012) *Under Suspicion. A Phenomenology of Media*. New York: Columbia University Press.
Gunning, T. (1989) 'An Aesthetic of Astonishment: Early Film and the (In)credulous Spectator', *Art & Text* 34: 31–45.
Gunning, T. (1990) 'The Cinema of Attraction[s]: Early Film, Its Spectator and the Avant-Garde', in T. Elsaesser et al. (eds), *Early Cinema: Space, Frame, Narrative*, London: BFI, 56–62.
Hadjipantazis, T. (1976) «Ο ανεπίσημος νεοελληνικός πολιτισμός» (The Unofficial Greek Civilisation) in *Ο Κόσμος του Καραγκιόζη. Φιγούρες* (*The World of Karaghiozis: Figures*), Athens: Ermis Rublication, 10–38.
Hadjipantazis, T. (2006) *Το Ελληνικό Ιστορικό Δράμα. Από το 19° στον 20° αιώνα* [*The Greek Historic Drama: From the Nineteenth to the Twentieth Century*], Heraklion: Cretan University Publications.
Hagener, M., Hediger, V., and Strohmaier, A. (eds) (2017) *The State of Post-Cinema: Tracing the Moving Image in the Age of Digital Dissemination*, Basingstoke: Palgrave Macmillan.
Hake, S. (1993) *The Cinema's Third Machine: Writing on Film in Germany, 1907–1933*, Lincoln: University of Nebraska Press.
Haley A. (2002 [1962]) 'The Playboy Interview', in G. Early (ed.), *Miles Davis and American Culture*, Saint Louis: Missouri Historical Society Press, 199-207.
Hall, S. (1988) 'Popular-Democratic vs Authoritarian Populism: Two Ways of "Taking Democracy Seriously"', in *The Hard Road to Renewal: Thatcherism and the Crisis of the Left*, London: Verso, 123–49.
Halperin, J. (2018) 'Damien Hirst Created a Fake Documentary About His Fake Venice Show – and Now You Can See It on Netflix', *Artnet News*, 5 January, https://news.artnet.com/art-world/damien-hirst-created-fake-documentary-venice-show-can-see-netflix-1192922. Accessed 31 January 2019.
Hancock, H., with Dickey, L. (2014) *Possibilities*, New York: Penguin Books.
Hansen, M. (1999) 'The Mass Production of the Senses: Classical Cinema as Vernacular Modernism', *Modernism/Modernity* 6: 2, 59–77.
Haraway, D. (1988) 'Situated Knowledges: The Science Question in Feminism and the Privilege of Partial Perspective', *Feminist Studies* 14: 575–99.
Haraway, D. J. (2016) *Staying with the Trouble: Making Kin in the Chthulucene*, Durham, NC: Duke University Press.
Harvie, J. (2013) *Fair Play: Art, Performance and Neoliberalism*, Basingstoke: Palgrave Macmillan.
Haydon, A. (2008) 'Is Theatre Sci-fi's Final Frontier?' *The Guardian: Theatre Blog*, https://www.theguardian.com/stage/theatreblog/2008/apr/01/istheatrescifis-finalfrontier. Accessed 14 February 2019.
Hayles, N. K. (1999) *How We Became Posthuman: Virtual Bodies in Cybernetics, Literature and Informatics*, Chicago: University of Chicago Press.
Hazou, R. T. (2011) 'Hypermediacy and Credibility in Documentary Theatre: The Craft of Make-Believe in Théâtre Du Soleil's Le Dernier Caravansérail (2005)', *Studies in Theatre and Performance* 31: 3, 293–304.

Hediger, V., and De Rosa, M. (eds) (2016) 'Special Issue: Post-What? Post-When? Thinking Moving Images beyond the Post-Medium/Post-Cinema Condition', *Cinéma & Cie* 26/27.
Heidegger, M. (1962) *Being and Time*, trans. J. Macquarrie and E. Robinson, London: Camelot Press.
Heidegger, M. (1978 [1936]) 'The Origin of the Work of Art', in D. F. Krell (ed.), *Basic Writings*, London: Routledge, Kegan & Paul.
Heidegger, M. (1995) *The Fundamental Concepts of Metaphysics: World, Finitude, Solitude*, trans. W. McNeill and N. Walker, Bloomington and Indianapolis: Indiana University Press.
Heidegger, M. (2006) *Mindfulness*, trans. P. Emad and T. Kalary. London: Continuum.
Henry, K. (2006) 'The Artful Disposition: Theatricality, Cinema and Social Context in Contemporary Photography', in L. Pauli (ed.), *Acting the Part: Photography as Theatre*, New York: Merrell, 106–21.
Holl, U. (2002) *Kino, Trance & Kybernetik*, Berlin: Brinkmann & Bose, 137–58.
Husserl, E. (1964) *The Idea of Phenomenology*, trans. W. P. Alston and G. Nakhnikian, The Hague: Martinus Nijhoff.
Innes, C., and Shevtsova, M. (2013) *The Cambridge Introduction to Theatre Directing*, Cambridge: Cambridge University Press.
Jenkins, H., Ford, S., and Green, J. (2013) *Spreadable Media: Creating Value and Meaning in a Networked Culture*, New York: New York University Press.
Jones, A. (1994) 'Dis/playing the Phallus: Male Artists Perform their Masculinities', *Art History* 17: 4, 546–84.
Jones, A. (2006) *Self-Image: Technology, Representation, and the Contemporary Subject*, Arlington: Routledge.
Jones, A. G., and Ratterman, N. L. (2009) 'Mate Choice and Sexual Selection: What Have We Learned since Darwin?', *Proceedings of the National Academy of Sciences*, 106: 1, 10001–8.
Jones, S. (2018) 'The Future Perfect of the Archive: Re-Thinking Performance in the Age of Third Nature', in P. Clarke, S. Jones, N. Kaye and J. Linsley (eds), *Artists in the Archive*, London: Routledge, 301–322.
Joselit, D. (2012) *After Art*, Princeton: Princeton University Press.
Jurgenson, N. (2011) *Defending and Clarifying the Term Augmented Reality*, TheSociety Pages.org, https://thesocietypages.org/cyborgology/2011/04/29/defending-and-clarifying-the-term-augmented-reality/. Accessed 10 January 2017.
Kambanellis, I. (1975) *Το Μεγάλο μας Τσίρκο* [*Our Grande Circus*], Athens: Ermias.
Kambanellis, I. (1990) *Από Σκηνής και από Πλατείας* [*From the Stage and from the Auditorium*], Athens: Kastaniotis Publications.
Kambanellis, I. (1999) «Ιάκωβος Καμπανελλης» [Iakovos Kambanellis], Interview with Giorgos Papadakis, Περίτεχνον [*Peritechnon*] 2, 42–46.
Kant, I. (2000) *Critique of the Power of Judgment*, trans. P. Guyer and E. Matthews, New York: Cambridge University Press.
Kaprow, A. (1993) *Essays on the Blurring of Art and Life*, Berkeley: University of California Press.
Karambetsos, E. D. (1979) 'Tyranny and Myth in the Plays of Four Contemporary Greek Dramatists', *World Literature Today* 53: 2, 210–14.
Kartsaki, E. (2016) 'Farewell to Farewell: Impossible Endings and Unfinished Finitudes', in E. Kartsaki (ed.), *On Repetition: Writing, Performance and Art*, Bristol, UK: Intellect, 199–207.

Kazakos, K. (2017) Interview with Michaela Antoniou.
Kern, A., and Moll, H. (2017) 'On the Transformative Character of Collective Intentionality and the Uniqueness of the Human', *Philosophical Psychology* 30: 3, 315–33.
Kessler, F. (2014) *Mise-en-scène*, Montreal: Caboose.
Kirby, M. (1987) *A Formalist Theatre*, Pittsburgh: University of Pennsylvania Press.
Krämer, S. (1998) 'Das Medium als Spur und als Apparat', in S. Krämer (ed.), *Medien, Computer, Realität: Wirklichkeitsvorstellungen und Neue Medien*, Frankfurt am Main: Suhrkamp, 73-94.
Kramnick, J. (2011) 'Against Literary Darwinism', *Critical Inquiry* 37: 2, 315–47.
Krauss, R. (1987) 'Theories of Art after Minimalism and Pop', in H. Foster (ed.), *Discussions in Contemporary Culture* 1, 56–87.
Kreider, K., and O' Leary, J. (2015) *Falling*, London and Ventnor: Copy Press.
Kristeva, J. (2008) *Teresa My Love: An Imagined Life of the Saint of Avila*, trans. L. S. Fox, New York: Columbia University Press.
Lacan, J. (2006) *Écrits*, trans. B. Fink. New York: Norton.
Lavender, A. (2006) 'Mise En Scene, Hypermediacy, and the Sensorium', in F. Chapple and C. Kattenbelt (eds), *Intermediality in Theatre and Performance*, Amsterdam: Rodopi, 55–66.
Lavender, A. (2012) 'Viewing and Acting (and Points in Between): The Trouble with Spectating after Rancière', *Contemporary Theatre Review* 22:3, 307–26.
Lehmann, H.-T. (1999) *Postdramatisches Theater*, Frankfurt am Main: Verlag der Autoren.
Lehmann, H.-T. (2006) *Post-Dramatic Theatre*, trans. K. Jüers-Munby, London: Routledge.
Lepecki, A. (2006) *Exhausting Dance: Performance and the Politics of Movement*, London: Routledge.
Levinas, E. (1998) *Otherwise than Being*, trans. by A. Lingis, Pittsburgh: Duquesne University Press.
Liddell, H., and Scott, R. (1901) *A Greek-English Lexicon*, 8th edition, Oxford: Clarendon.
Loiselle, A., and Maron, J. (2012) *Stages of Reality: Theatricality in Cinema*, Toronto: University of Toronto Press.
Lütticken, S. (2010) 'Acts in the Age of Virtuoso Performance', *Texte Zur Kunst* 79, 124–33.
Lyotard, J.-F. (1973) *Des Dispositifs Pulsionnels*, Paris: Union Général d'Editions.
Macbeth, D. (2014) *Realizing Reason: A Narrative of Truth and Knowing*, Oxford: Oxford University Press.
Machon, J. (2013) *Immersive Theatre: Intimacy and Immediacy in Contemporary Performance*, Basingstoke: Palgrave Macmillan.
MacIvor, D., and Bolt, C. (1993) *Never Swim Alone & This Is A Play: Two Plays*, 1st edition, Toronto: Playwrights Canada Press.
Mackenzie, J. (2001) *Perform or Else: From Discipline to Performance*, London: Routledge.
Madrigal, A. C. (2018) 'The Most Important Exchange of the Zuckerberg Hearing', *The Atlantic*, https://www.theatlantic.com/technology/archive/2018/04/the-most-important-exchange-of-the-zuckerberg-hearing/557795/. Accessed 29 May 2018.
March, J. (2008) *The Penguin Book of Classical Myths*, London: Penguin.
Muelder Eaton, M. (2004) 'Art and the Aesthetic', in P. Kivy (ed.), *The Blackwell Guide to Aesthetics*, Oxford: Blackwell, 63–77.

Marciniak, P. (2007) 'Byzantine Teatron: A Place of Performance?' in M. Grünbart (ed.), *Teatron*, Berlin: de Gruyter, 277–286.
Martin, A. (1991) 'Jungle Fever', FilmCritic.com, http://www.filmcritic.com.au/reviews/j/jungle_fever.html. Accessed 10 February 2019.
Martin, A. (2003) '25th Hour', FilmCritic.com, http://www.filmcritic.com.au/reviews/t/25thhour.html. Accessed 10 February 2019.
Mavromoustakos, P. (2005) *Το Θέατρο στην Ελλάδα 1940-2000. Μια Επισκόπηση* [*The Theatre in Greece 1940–2000: An Overview*], Athens: Kastaniotis Publications.
McGillivray, G. (2009) 'The Discursive Formation of Theatricality as a Critical Concept', *metaphorik* 17, 100–14, http://www.metaphorik.de/sites/www.metaphorik.de/files/journal-pdf/17_2009_mcgillivray.pdf. Accessed 16 August 2023.
McGowan, T. (2014) *Spike Lee*, Chicago, Springfield and Urbana: Illinois University Press.
Mejias, U. A. (2013) *Off the Network: Disrupting the Digital World*, London and Minnesota: University of Minnesota Press.
Melville, H. (2006) *The Confidence-Man: His Masquerade*, ed. H. Parker and M. Niemeyer, New York: Norton.
Merleau-Ponty, M. (1968) *The Visible and the Invisible, Followed by Working Notes*, ed. C. Lefort, transl. A. Lingis, Evanston: Northwestern University Press.
Metz, C. (1982) 'Story/Discourse (A Note on Two Types of Voyeurism)', in *Psychoanalysis and Cinema: The Imaginary Signifier*, London: Macmillan, 89–98.
Meyerhold, V. (2016) *Meyerhold on Theatre*, trans. and ed. E. Braun, London: Bloomsbury.
Miller, G. (2001a) 'Aesthetic Fitness: How Sexual Selection Shaped Artistic Virtuosity as a Fitness Indicator and Aesthetic Preferences as Mate Choice Criteria', *Bulletin of Psychology and the Arts* 2: 1, 20–25.
Miller, G. (2001b) *The Mating Mind: How Sexual Choice Shaped the Evolution of Human Nature*, New York: Anchor Books.
Miller, G. (2008) 'Kindness, Fidelity, and Other Sexually Selected Virtues', in W. Sinnott-Armstrong (ed.), *Moral Psychology, Volume 1: The Evolution of Morality: Adaptations and Innateness*, Cambridge, MA: MIT Press, 209–44.
Milling, J., and Graham, L. (2001) *Modern Theories of Performance: From Stanislavski to Boal*, New York: Palgrave Macmillan.
Mitchell, W. J. T. (1994) *Picture Theory: Essays on Verbal and Visual Representation*, Chicago: Chicago University Press.
Mitchell, W. J. T. (2005) *What Do Pictures Want? The Lives and Loves of Images*, Chicago and London: University of Chicago Press.
Mohanty, S. (2009) *The Book of Kali*, New Delhi: Penguin Books.
Montelle, Y.-P. (2009) *Paleoperformance: The Emergence of Theatricality as Social Practice*, London: Seagull Books.
Moran, R. (2018) 'Formalism and the Appearance of Nature', in M. Abbot (ed.), *Michael Fried and Philosophy: Modernism, Intention, and Theatricality*, London: Routledge, 117–28.
Mulhall, S. (1996) *Heidegger and Being and Time*. London: Routledge.
Mulvey, L. (1989a) 'Visual Pleasure and Narrative Cinema', in *Visual and Other Pleasures*, London: Macmillan, 14–26.
Mulvey, L. (1989b) 'Film, Feminism and the Avant-Garde', in *Visual and Other Pleasures*, London: Macmillan, 111–26.

Munby, J. (2011) *Under a Bad Sign: Criminal Self-Representation in African American Popular Culture*, Chicago and London: University of Chicago Press.

Münz, R. (1998) *Theatralität und Theater: Zur Historiografie von Theatralitätsgefügen*, Berlin: Schwarzkopf und Schwarzkopf.

Murphy, P. (1992) *Staging the Impossible: The Fantastic Mode of Modern Drama*, Westport, CT: Greenwood Press.

Nicholson, H. (2013) 'Participation as Performance Sells', in T. Noorani, C. Blencowe and J. Brigstocke (eds), *Problems of Participation*, Lewes: Arn Press.

Nield, S. (2014) 'Speeches That Draw Tears: Theatricality, Commemoration and Social History', *Social History* 39: 4, 547–56.

Pauli, L. (2006) *Acting the Part: Photography as Theatre*, New York: Merrell.

Pavis, P. (2018) *The State of Current Theatre Research*, citeseerx.ist.psu.edu. Accessed 13 June 2018.

Payne, N. (2012) *Constellations*, London: Faber & Faber.

Pefanis, G. P. (2000) Ιάκωβος Καμπανέλλης. Διαδρομές σε Μεγάλη Χώρα [*Iakovos Kambanellis: Paths in a Vast Counrty*], Athens: Kedros Publications.

Pefanis, G. P. (2005a) «Τα θεατρικά τραγούδια του Ιάκωβου Καμπανέλλη» [Iakovos Kambanellis's Songs for the Theatre], in F. Ar. Dimitrakopoulos (ed.), *Επιστημονική Επετηρίς της Φιλοσοφικής Σχολής Πανεπιστημίου Αθηνών* [*Scientific Yearbook of the School of Philosophy of the University of Athens*], Athens: University of Athens.

Pefanis, G. P. (2005b) «Η Ιστορική Διάσταση στην Πολιτική Τριλογία του Ιάκωβου Καμπανέλλη: *Το Μεγάλο μας Τσίρκο, Το Κουκί και το Ρεβύθι, Ο Εχθρός Λαός*» [The Historical Dimensions in the Political Trilogy: *Our Grand Circus, The Broad Bean and the Chickpea, Enemy People*], *Θέματα Λογοτεχνίας* [*Literature Subjects*] 30, 58–101.

Phelan, P. (2003) *Unmarked: The Politics of Performance*, London: Routledge.

Phelan, P. (2005) 'Reconstructing Love: *King Lear* and Theatre Architecture', in B. Hodgdon and W. B. Worthen (eds), *A Companion to Shakespeare and Performance*, Oxford: Blackwell, 13–35.

Phelan, P. (2010) 'Haunted Stages: Performance and the Photographic Effect', in *Haunted: Contemporary Photography/Video/Performance*, New York: Guggenheim Museum, 50–87.

Pickford, J. (2015) 'British Museum Throws Light on Egypt's Lost Worlds', 30 November, https://www.ft.com/content/a88d0a00-976e-11e5-9228-87e603d47bdc. Accessed 27 September 2017.

Pine, B. J., and Gilmore, J. H. (1999) *The Experience Economy: Work is Theater and Every Business a Stage*, Boston: Harvard Business School Press.

Pinkard, T. (2012) *Hegel's Naturalism: Mind, Nature, and the Final Ends of Life*, New York: Oxford University Press.

Pinkard, T. (2017) *Does History Make Sense? Hegel on the Historical Shapes of Justice*, Cambridge, MA: Harvard University Press.

Piotrowska, A. (2014) *Psychoanalysis and Ethics in Documentary Film*, London: Routledge.

Piotrowska, A. (2017) *Black and White: Cinema, Politics and the Arts in Zimbabwe*, London: Routledge.

Piotrowska, A. (2019) *The Nasty Woman and the Neo Femme Fatale in Contemporary Cinema*, London and New York: Routledge.

Pippin, R. B. (2014) *After the Beautiful: Hegel and the Philosophy of Pictorial Modernism*, Chicago: Chicago University Press.

Pippin, R. B. (2018) 'Why Does Photography Matter as Art *Now*, as Never Before? On Fried and Intention', in M. Abbott (ed.), *Michael Fried and Philosophy: Modernism, Intention, and Theatricality*, New York: Routledge, 48–63.

Pippin, R. B. (2021) *Philosophy by Other Means: The Arts in Philosophy and Philosophy in the Arts*, Chicago: University of Chicago Press.

Platinga, C. (2019) 'Brecht, Emotion, and the Reflective Spectator: The Case of 'BlacKkKlansman'', *NECSUS: European Journal of Media Studies* 8:1, https://necsus-ejms.org/brecht-emotion-and-the-reflective-spectator-the-case-of-blackkklansman/. Accessed 28 April 2020.

Plummer Crafton. L. (2011) *Transgressive Theatricality, Romanticism and Mary Wollstonecraft*. Farnham: Ashgate.

Postlewait, T. (2003) 'Theatricality and Antitheatricality in Renaissance London', in T. C. Davis and T. Postlewait (eds), *Theatricality*, Cambridge: Cambridge University Press, 90–126.

Povoledo, E. (2008) 'Filmmaker Adds a Cinematic Scope to a Storied Painting', *New York Times*, 2 July.

Prensky, M. (2001) 'Digital Natives, Digital Immigrants', *On the Horizon* 9: 5, 1–6.

Prokop, Z., et al. (2012) 'Meta-Analysis Suggests Choosy Females Get Sexy Sons More Than "Good Genes"', *Evolution* 66, 2665–73.

Prum, R. O. (2012) 'Aesthetic Evolution by Mate Choice: Darwin's Really Dangerous Idea', *Philosophical Transactions of the Royal Society* 367, 2253–65.

Prum, R. O. (2013) 'Coevolutionary Aesthetics in Human and Biotic Artworlds', *Biology & Philosophy* 28: 5, 811–32.

Prum, R. O. (2017) *The Evolution of Beauty: How Darwin's Forgotten Theory of Mate Choice Shapes the Animal World – and Us*, New York: Anchor Books.

Puchner, W. (2010) *Τόποι Ψυχής και Μύθοι Πολιτείας. Το θεατρικό σύμπαν του Ιάκωβου Καμπανέλλη* [*Psychic Locus and City Legends: The Theatrical Universe of Iakovos Kambanellis*], Athens: Papazisis Publications.

Quick, A. (2007) *The Wooster Group Workbook*, London: Routledge.

Quinn, A. (2010) 'Nightwatching (18)', *The Independent*, 26 March.

Rampley, M. (2017) *The Seductions of Darwin: Art, Evolution, Neuroscience*, Pittsburgh: Pennsylvania State University Press.

Rancière, J. (2004) *The Politics of Aesthetics*, New York and London: Continuum.

Rancière, J. (2007) 'Painting in the Text', in *The Future of the Image*, trans. G. Elliot, London: Verson, 69–90.

Rancière, J. (2009) *The Emancipated Spectator*, trans. G. Elliot, London: Verso.

Rancière, J. (2011) 'The Gay Science of Bertolt Brecht', in *The Politics of Literature*, trans. J. Rose, Cambridge: Polity, 99–127.

Reed, P. (2012) 'Co-Autonomous Ethics and the Production of Misunderstanding', *Fillip* 16, https://fillip.ca/content/co-autonomous-ethics-and-the-production-of-misunderstanding. Accessed 16 August 2023.

Ridout, N. (2006) *Stage Fright, Animals and Other Theatrical Problems*, Cambridge: Cambridge University Press.

Riviere, J. (1986) 'Womanliness as a Masquerade (1929)', in V. Burgin (ed.), *Formations of Fantasy*, London: Methuen, 35–59.

Rodowick, D. N. (1994) *The Crisis of Political Modernism: Criticism and Ideology in Contemporary Film Theory*, Berkeley: University of California Press.

Rodrigues, N. (2003) *Teatro completo de Nelson Rodrigues*, Rio de Janeiro: Editora Nova Aguilar.

Rogin, M. (2001) 'Nowhere Left to Stand: The Burnt Cork Roots of Popular Culture', *Cineaste*, 26: 14–15.

Röttger, K. (2010) '"What Do I See?" The Order of Looking in Lessing's "Emilia Galotti"', *Art History* 33: 2, 378–87.

Röttger, K. (2013) 'The Mystery of the In-Between: A Methodological Approach to Intermedial Performance Analysis', *Forum Modernes Theater* 28: 2, 105–16.

Rushton, R. (2001) 'Narrative and Spectacle in *Gladiator*', *CineAction* 51, 34–43.

Rushton, R. (2004) 'Early, Classical and Modern Cinema: Absorption and Theatricality', *Screen* 45: 3, 226–44.

Rushton, R. (2007) 'Absorption and Theatricality in the Cinema: Some Thoughts on Narrative and Spectacle', *Screen*, 48: 1, 109–12.

Russell, L. (2012) 'Digital Dualism and The Glitch Feminism Manifesto', *Cyborgology*, https://thesocietypages.org/cyborgology/2012/12/10/digital-dualism-and-the-glitch-feminism-manifesto/. Accessed 2 December 2016.

Russell, L. (2020) *Glitch Feminism: A Manifesto*, New York: Verso Books.

Said, E. (1978) *Orientalism*, London: Penguin.

Saltz, D. Z. (2001) 'Live Media: Interactive Technology and Theatre', *Theatre Topics* 11: 2, 107–30.

Sauter, W. (2000) *The Theatrical Event: Dynamics of Performance and Perception*, Iowa City: University of Iowa Press.

Schneider, R. (2007) 'Cut, Click, Shudder: The "Document Performance"', in M. Vason and D. Johnson (eds), *Encounters*, Bristol: Arnolfini, 34–36.

Schneider, R. (2011) *Performing Remains: Art and War in Times of Theatrical Re-enactment*, London: Routledge.

Schramm, H. (1996) *Karneval des Denkens: Theatralität im Spiegel philosophischer Texte des 16. und 17. Jahrhunderts*, Berlin: Akademie Verlag.

Schramm, H. (2017) 'Einleitung: Das offene Buch der Alchemie und die stumme Sprache des Theaters', *Spuren der Avantgarde: Theatrum alchemicum: Frühe Neuzeit und Moderne im Kulturvergleich*, in H. Schramm, M. Lorber and J. Lazardzig (eds.), Berlin: De Gruyter, pp. xiii–xxxiv.

Scott, M. (2016) *Ancient Worlds: An Epic History of East and West*, London: Hutchinson.

Shakespeare, W. (1997) 'The Tempest', in S. Greenblatt, W. Cohen, J. E. Howard and K. Eisaman Maus (eds), *The Norton Shakespeare*, New York and London: W. W. Norton & Company, 3055–107.

Shaviro, S. (2010) *Post-Cinematic Affect*, Winchester: Zero Books.

Silverman, K. (1986) 'Fragments for a Fashionable Discourse', in T. Modleski (ed.), *Studies in Entertainment: Approaches to Mass Culture*, Bloomington: University of Indiana Press, 139–52.

Simler, K., and Hanson, R. (2018) *The Elephant in the Brain: Hidden Motives in Everyday Life*, New York: Oxford University Press.

Sontag, S. (1966) 'Film and Theatre', *The Tulane Drama Review* 11: 1, 24–37.

Sooke, A. (2016) 'Sunken Cities: The Man Who Found Atlantis', *The Telegraph*, 29 April, https://www.telegraph.co.uk/art/what-to-see/sunken-cities-the-man-who-found-atlantis/. Accessed 30 January 2019.

Souto, P. R. (2004) *As Mulheres De Nelson: Representações Sociais Das Mulheres Em Os Sete Gatinhos De Nelson Rodrigues*, João Pessoa: Editora Idéia.

Spatharis, S. (1992 [1960]) *Αυτοβιογραφία και η Τέχνη του Καραγκιόζη* [*Autobiography and the Art of Karaghiozis*], Athens: Agra Publications.

Stam, R. T. (2004) *Literature Through Film: Realism, Magic, and the Art of Adaptation*, Malden, MA: Blackwell.
Stein, G. (1988 [1935]) *Lectures in America*, London: Virago Press.
Stephenson, J. (2017) 'Theatre of the Real in the Age of Post-Reality', *Upsurges of the Real: A Performance Research Blog*, 18 January, https://realtheatre.blog/2017/01/18/theatre-of-the-real-in-the-age-of-post-reality. Accessed 16 August 2023.
Sterritt, D. (2013) *Spike Lee's America*, Cambridge: Polity.
Stone, J. (2018) 'Mark Zuckerberg to Face Public Grilling at European Parliament after Rejecting UK Parliament's Invitation', *The Independent*, 21 May, http://www.independent.co.uk/news/uk/politics/mark-zuckerberg-eu-parliament-house-commons-uk-hearing-facebook-data-a8361066.html. Accessed 29 May 2018.
Stoppard, T. (1967) *Rosencrantz and Guildenstern Are Dead*, London: Faber.
Strathern, M. (2004) *Partial Connections*, updated edition, Oxford: AltaMira Press.
Szondi, P. (1987) *Theory of The Modern Drama*, Cambridge: Cambridge University Press.
Szwed, J. (2003) *So What: The Life of Miles Davis*, London: Arrow Books.
Taussig, M. (1993) *Mimesis and Alterity: A Particular History of the Senses*, London and New York: Routledge.
Taylor, A. (1993) *Notes and Tones: Musician-to-Musician Interviews*, New York: Da Capo Press.
Taylor, D. (2003) *The Archive and the Repertoire: Performing Cultural Memory in the Americas*, Durham, NC: Duke University Press
Tegmark, M. (2017) *Life 3.0*, London: Allen Lane.
The Lord of the Rings Fandom website, http://lotr.wikia.com/wiki/Main_Page. Accessed 4 December 2018.
Todd, J. M. (1990) *Autobiographics in Freud and Derrida*, New York: Garland.
Tokarczuk, O. (2018 [2007]) *Flights*, trans. J. Crofts, London: Fitzcarraldo Editions.
Tolkien, J. R. R. (1954) *The Lord of the Rings*, London: George Allen & Unwin.
Tomasello, M. (1999) 'The Human Adaptation for Culture', *The Annual Review of Anthropology* 28, 509–29.
Treasures from the Wreck of the Unbelievable: Damien Hirst, exhibition curated by Elena Geuna, Venice: François Pinault Foundation, 2017.
Tsing, A. L. (2011) *Friction: An Ethnography of Global Connection*, Princeton: Princeton University Press.
Underwood, R. (1999) *Anglo-Saxon Weapons and Warfare*, Stroud: Tempus.
Vest, J. P. (2014) *Spike Lee: Finding the Story and Forcing the Issue*, Santa Barbara: Praeger.
Veyne, P. (1988) *Did the Greeks Believe in Their Myths? An Essay on the Constitutive Imagination*, trans. P. Wissing, Chicago: Chicago University Press.
Walsh, F. (2010) *Male Trouble: Masculinity and the Performance of Crisis*, Basingstoke: Palgrave Macmillan.
Warhol, A. (2007) *The Philosophy of Andy Warhol: From A to B and Back Again*, London: Penguin.
Weber, B. N., and Beinen, H. (2010) *Bertolt Brecht: Political Theory and Literary Practice*, Athens: University of Georgia Press.
Weber, S. (2004) *Theatricality as Medium*, New York: Fordham University Press.
Whitaker, B. (2000) 'Ancient Egypt Yields Its Underwater Secrets', *The Guardian*, 5 June, https://www.theguardian.com/world/2000/jun/05/brianwhitaker. Accessed 30 January 2019.

Williams, K. (2001) 'Anti-Theatricality and the Limits of Naturalism', *Modern Drama* 44: 3, 284–99.
Williams, R. (2006) *Politics of Modernism: Against the New Conformists*, London: Verso.
Willingham, R. (1991) 'Scenic Realism and Science Fiction Theatre', *Foundation* 64, 64–78.
Wilson, C. (2016) 'Another Darwinian Aesthetics', *The Journal of Aesthetics and Art Criticism* 74: 3, 237–52.
Witt, M. A. F. (2014) *Metatheater and Modernity: Baroque and Neobaroque*, Vancouver: Fairleigh Dickinson University Press.
Wittgenstein, L. (2009) *Philosophical Investigations*, trans. G. E. M. Anscombe et al., Oxford: Wiley-Blackwell.
Zahavi, A. (1975) 'Mate Selection: A Selection for a Handicap', *Journal of Theoretical Biology*, 53: 1, 205–14.
Zahavi, A., and Zahavi, Z. (1997) *The Handicap Principle: A Missing Piece of Darwin's Puzzle*, New York: Oxford University Press.
Žižek, S. (2017) *The Courage of Hopelessness: Chronicles of a Year of Acting Dangerously*, London: Allen Lane.
Zola, E. (1893) *The Experimental Novel and Other Essays*, New York: The Cassell Publishing Company.

Index

Abel, Lionel, 74–5
acting, 4–7, 16, 31, 72, 81, 122, 123, 130, 135, 137, 225, 232, 234, 259, 261, 265, 269, 274, 275–6, 282
adaptation, 19, 78, 179, 182, 289
Adderley, Julian 'Cannonball', 209, 210
Adorno, Theodor W., 288
Aeschylus, 279
Agamben, Giorgio, 13
Ahmed, Sara, 194
Aiello, Danny, 282
Aiello, Rick, 287
Akerman, Chantal, 3
Åkervall, Lisa, 17, 42, 46, 56n
Álamo, Roberto, 262
Allen, Jennifer, 193
Allinson, Mark, 257, 258, 264–5, 266–7
Almodóvar, Pedro, 20, 256–7, 261, 265–8
Alston, Adam, 105, 114
Althusser, Louis, 38, 39, 171
Araya, Elena, 261
Aristophanes, 232, 289, 290
Armstrong, Louis, 217
Artaud, Antonin, 7, 10, 11, 14, 15, 116, 118, 277, 279, 288
Aumont, Jacques, 283

Auslander, Philip, 187, 190–1, 240
Austin-Smith, Brenda, 258
Azoulay, Ariella Aïsha, 196–7

Badiou, Alain, 131
Balsom, Erika, 53
Bamboozled (2000), 21, 273, 283–4, 286–7, 291
Banderas, Antonio, 261
Barish, Jonas, 29, 128
Barthes, Roland, 167, 168–9, 184, 186, 190, 200n, 279
Batman Returns (1992), 280
Baudelaire, Charles, 168, 279
Baudry, Jean-Louis, 44
Bayard, Hyppolite, 186
Bayliss, Sarah, 65
Bazin, André, 242, 251, 255, 277–8, 286
Bergson, Henri, 286
Bethenod, Martin, 148, 149
Big Swallow, The (1901), 45, 47
Bishop, Claire, 105
Blair Witch Project, The, 50–4
Blakey, Art, 211
Blau, Herbert, 121
Bohn Pedersen, Ninna, 65
Bolt, Carol, 71, 75
Bolter, Jay, 74, 79
Bourdieu, Pierre, 228

Bourgeois, Louise, 261, 266
Bourriaud, Nicolas, 105
Bradbury, Ray, 247
Braidotti, Rosi, 2013
Brecht, Bertolt, 6, 7, 10, 11, 14, 15, 19, 47, 76, 170, 277, 279, 288–9, 291
Brook, Peter, 277
Brooks, Daniel, 71
Buñuel, Luis, 146
Burch, Noël, 21, 273–5
Burge, Gregg, 281
Burns, Elizabeth, 31, 61, 132
Burr, Raymond, 3
Burton, Tim, 280
Butler, Judith, 113, 189, 190, 191

Campos, Liliane, 254
Cannon, Nick, 290
Carlson, Marvin, 59, 61
Carr, Ian, 207
Carter, Ron, 207, 209, 210, 213, 214
Caruth, Cathy, 197–8
Cavell, Stanley, 19, 134–7, 141
Ceausescu, Nicolae, 195
Chambers, Paul, 208, 209
Chaplin, Charlie, 276, 278
Chapple, Freda, 73
Chardin, Jean-Baptiste Siméon, 10, 43, 96, 103, 203
Chekov, Anton, 16
Chi-Raq (2015), 21, 273, 289–90
Clockers (1995), 292n
Coleman, George, 209, 210
Coltrane, John, 208, 209, 210
Constellations (2012), 20, 239, 245, 250–2, 254
Copeau, Jacques, 225, 229
Corry, Amie, 152, 154–5, 156, 161, 162–3
Crowley, Roger, 145, 164, 166n

Dada, 14, 184
Darwin, Charles, 88, 89–90, 93, 94, 95, 97, 104n
Davidson, Tommy, 283

Davies, Stephen, 87, 92, 93, 97
Davis, Miles, 20, 201–19
Davis, Ossie, 282
Davis, Tracy C., 28, 29, 59, 61, 62–3, 68, 69, 125, 126, 129–30, 133, 168, 224, 225, 246
Dawkins, Richard, 91
Debord, Guy, 19, 74, 107, 171
Derrida, Jacques, 11, 19, 116, 173, 187, 188, 195, 200
Diderot, Denis, 17, 29, 40n, 96–7, 103, 167, 203
Différance, 19, 187, 188, 190, 193, 198–9, 200
digital media, 58, 59, 72
Do the Right Thing (1989), 21, 282, 287
Dobrowodzka, Anna, 183
Documents of the Future, 57, 58, 61, 64, 66, 67
Drew, Richard, 195
Duchamp, Marcel, 184
Dunn, Billy, 282
Dutton, Denis, 87–92, 94, 98, 99, 102, 103

Edson, Richard, 282
Eisenstein, Sergei, 21, 166n, 276–7, 280, 286, 287, 288
Eisler, Hans, 288–9
Elsaesser, Thomas, 184
Erickson, Jon, 229
Esposito, Giancarlo, 281, 283
Evans, Bill, 209
Everett, Hugh, 20, 239, 243–5
Evreinov, Nikolai, 279

Fabe, Marilyn, 288
Féral, Josette, 28, 31, 59, 61, 130, 132–3, 140, 224, 246, 285, 286
Fiebach, Joachim, 240, 248, 249, 250–1
Fischer-Lichte, Erika, 132, 140, 246
Fishburne, Lawrence, 281
Fitch, Lizzie, 42, 47–9
Forced Entertainment, 18, 106, 122

Foucault, Michel, 113, 171
Franju, Georges, 267–8
Freeman, Martin, 35
Freud, Sigmund, 173, 174, 264, 270
Fried, Michael, 8–11, 17, 18, 21n, 29, 30, 39, 40, 42–4, 56, 88, 96–7, 103, 125, 132, 167–70, 174, 184, 186, 199, 202–7, 215–18, 239, 240, 247, 249, 251
Friedrich, Caspar David, 203

Galileo, 7, 13
Garland, Red, 208, 209
George, Aaron, 72, 79–82
Gerigk, Christoph, 149, 151–3, 160
Geuna, Elena, 147–8, 149
Glover, Savion, 283
Godard, Jean-Luc, 40n, 45, 47, 56, 275, 283
Goddio, Franck, 149, 151
Golden Voyage of Sinbad, The (1973), 161
Goldrich, Alex, 72, 79–82
Goncourt, Edmond de and Jules de, 10–11, 21
Gordon, Douglas, 204
Greenaway, Peter, 17, 25–8, 32, 34–5, 39–40
Greuze, Jean-Baptist, 10, 21, 96
Groys, Boris, 27
Grusin, Richard, 74, 79
Guenveur Smith, Roger, 282
Gunning, Tom, 42, 44, 170, 276, 277

Hake, Sabine, 274
Hall, Stuart, 131–2
Hamlet (Shakespeare), 74, 123
Hancock, Herbie, 207, 209–14, 217, 218
Hansen, Miriam, 44
Hanson, Robin, 98
Haraway, Donna, 59
Hardy, Oliver, 278
Harryhausen, Ray, 152, 161
Harvie, Jen, 105, 114

Hayles, N. Katherine, 108
Hazou, Rand, 76
Hegel, G. W. F., 89, 99, 100, 103
Heidegger, Martin, 18, 100, 105, 109–24
Hesiod, 147
Hirst, Damien, 19, 145–65, 166n
Hitchcock, Alfred, 3
Hixson, Paula Jean, 72, 73, 78–82
Hobkinson, Sam, 156
Hollow Tongues ([Play]ground-less), 57, 61, 64, 66, 67, 70
Homer, 147
Husserl, Edmund, 110

intermedial, intermediality, 18, 27, 33–6, 63, 71–6, 81–3

Jackson, Samuel L., 282, 290
Jason and the Argonauts (1963), 161
Jeanne Dielman, 23 quai du Commerce, 1080 Bruxelles (1975), 3
Jenkins, Henry, 54
Jones, Amelia, 113, 200n
Jones, Ernest, 270
Jones, Philly Joe, 208
Joselit, David, 46, 48, 49
Jungle Fever (1991), 272
Jurgenson, Nathan, 66

Kambanellis, Iakovos, 223, 227–34, 238n
Kandinsky, Wassily, 11
Kant, Immanuel, 18, 88, 94–5, 97–9, 101–2, 286
Kapoor, Anish, 7–8
Karaghiozis, 223, 228, 230, 231, 235–6, 238n
Kardashian, Kim, 46, 48
Karezi, Jenny, 223, 226–31, 237, 238n
Katsaki, Eirini, 199
Kattenbelt, Chiel, 73
Kazakos, 226, 228–31, 234, 236, 237, 238n
Kazan, Elia, 283

Keaton, Buster, 278
Kelly, Grace, 3
King Lear (Shakespeare), 19, 129, 134–41
King, Rodney, 53
Kirby, Michael, 246, 248
Kitson, Daniel, 20, 239, 244–50, 253
Klein, Yves, 20, 187, 190–6, 200
Koloktronis, Theodorus, 234, 236
Krauss, Rosalind, 126, 132
Kreider, Kirsten, 192–3
Kristeva, Julia, 19, 169, 177–80

Lacan, Jacques, 133, 175
Lam, Nikki, 67
Laurel, Stan, 278
Lavender, Andy, 4–5, 7, 8, 9, 11, 74, 76
LeCompte, Elizabeth, 15
Lee, Kevin B., 46, 56
Lee, Spike, 21, 272–3, 276, 280–91
Lehmann, Hans-Thies, 30, 137, 138
Lepecki, Andre, 192
Linder, Max, 278
Loiselle, André, 240, 253, 265
Longhurst, Michael, 251
Lord of the Rings, The (2001–3), 74, 163
Lord of the Rings, The (Tolkien), 163
Lumet, Sidney, 283
Lütticken, Sven, 199
Lynch, David, 152
Lyotard, Jean-François, 11

Machon, Josephine, 106, 115
MacIvor, David, 18, 71, 75–6, 81
MacKenzie, Jon, 115
Madero, María Angélica, 65
Makuwe, Stanley, 19, 169, 172, 179–84
Malevich, Kazmir, 11
Manet, Édouard, 218
March, Jenny, 147, 158
Marey, Etienne-Jules, 44
Maron, Jeremy, 240, 253, 265
Married to the Eiffel Tower (2009), 172
Martin, Adrian, 272, 291

Masson-Bergoff, Aurelia, 150
McGowan, Todd, 272, 288, 289, 291n
McPherson, Hannah, 42, 49, 51
media, 15, 17, 27, 30, 32, 33, 37, 38, 40, 41, 42–56, 74, 76, 77, 82, 107, 118, 121, 151, 156, 160, 170, 171, 279; *see also* multimedia, social media, digital media
mediated, mediation, 58–61, 63–5, 67–9, 71, 72, 74, 76, 78–82, 120, 137–9, 141
mediatised, 240, 242
Mejias, Ulises A., 59, 63
Méliès, Georges, 277–8
Melville, Herman, 9–10
Mendes, Sam, 134–5, 141
Merleau-Ponty, Maurice, 32, 36
Metz, Christian, 44, 185
Meyerhold, Vsevolod, 21, 225, 226, 229, 275–7, 288
Mill, John Stuart, 95
Miller, Geoffrey, 90–1, 92, 98, 99, 101
Minimalism, 42–3, 246–7, 248, 251
Mnouchkine, Arianne, 76, 224, 225, 226, 231, 232
Mohanty, Seema, 159, 161–2, 164
Morimura, Yasamusa, 20, 187, 193, 195
Mouse: The Persistence of an Unlikely Thought (2016), 20, 239, 244–5, 247–8, 253
Mitchell, W. J. T., 27, 32, 33, 38–40, 287
Mujeri, Charmaine, 183
multimedia, 28, 82, 242
multiverse, 20, 239, 240, 242, 243–4, 245, 247, 251, 253–5
Mulvey, Laura, 2–4, 44, 264
Munby, Jonathan, 292n
Münsterberg, Hugo, 44
Muybridge, Edweard, 44
'My Funny Valentine' (Richard Rogers and Lorenz Hart), 20, 207–14, 218

Naturalism, 13, 98–9, 129, 102, 103, 251
Never Swim Alone (1991), 18, 71–83
Newton, Isaac, 197
Nield, Sophie, 133

O'Leary, James, 192–3
Our Grand Circus, 20, 223–37

Paine, Katie, 67
Panofsky, Erwin, 38, 39, 278
Papagiannopoulos, Dioneses, 228, 234, 236
Papdopoulos, Georgias, 234
Paredes, Marisa, 264
Park, Steve, 287
Parreno, Philippe, 204
Pavis, Patrice, 73
Payne, Nick, 20, 239, 240, 245, 252–4
Pefanis, G. P., 229, 230, 233
Peláez, Juan Sebastian, 49
Phelan, Peggy, 77, 135, 195, 200n
Pickford, James, 150
Pinkard, Terry, 88, 99, 100
Piotrowska, Agnieszka, 170, 174, 180, 182
Pippin, Robert B., 101, 103, 215, 218
Plato, 128, 256
Plummer Crafton, Lisa, 171–2
Pollock, Jackson, 11
postcinema, 42, 45–7, 49, 51, 52, 55
Postlewait, Thomas, 28, 29, 59, 125, 129, 168, 224, 225, 246
Prensky, Mark, 109
Prum, Richard, 92, 93, 94, 104n
Puchner, Walter, 232, 237, 238n

Ramos, Luis Antonio, 287
Rancière, Jacques, 4–7, 10–12, 17, 19, 21, 69, 170, 171, 187, 200, 240, 252
Rapaport, Michael, 283
Real Magic (2017), 18, 106, 122–4
real-time, 51–3
real-world, 151, 156

real, the, 1–3, 8–12, 14–16, 18, 44, 54–5, 65, 76–7, 79–80, 94–5, 97, 101, 129–33, 138, 140, 152, 163–4, 168, 174, 187, 249, 263, 279, 288
realism, 13, 41, 48, 129, 186, 225–6, 243, 251, 281
Rear Window (1954), 3
Reed, Patricia, 114–15
Rembrandt van Rijn, 17, 25–7, 35–40
remediation, 50, 73, 74, 77
Resnais, Alain, 283
Ridout, Nicholas, 247, 249, 255
Rihanna, 49, 151
ritual, 12, 13, 75, 77, 81, 228, 277, 281
Rivers, Christ, 282
Riviere, Joan, 185n, 267, 270
Robinson Crusoe (Defoe), 182
Rodowick, D. N., 45
Rodrigues, Nelson, 20, 256, 257–60, 263, 265, 266, 268–9, 271n
Rushdie, Salman, 182
Rushton, Richard, 42–3, 170, 185n
Russett, Andrea, 51, 53, 54–5

Said, Edward, 136
Saint Teresa, 169, 177–8, 179, 180
Sala, Anri, 205–6, 217
Saltz, David, 73, 79, 80–1
Sandifolo, Eddi, 183
Sauter, Willmar, 224
Schechner, Richard, 12
Schneider, Rebecca, 189, 190
School Daze (1988), 21, 281, 289
Schramm, Helmar, 28, 31
Scott, Michael, 147, 159–60, 163–4
Seneca, Joe, 281
Seyrig, Delphine, 3
Shakespeare, William, 19, 129, 138, 139, 154, 279
Shaviro, Steven, 42, 45
She She Pop, 19, 137–40, 142
Shevtsova, Maria, 224, 225, 226
Shorter, Wayne, 207, 211, 213, 214
Silverman, Kaja, 267

Simler, Kevin, 98
Sinatra, Frank, 208, 209, 210, 218
Sinders, Caroline, 67
Skin I Live In, The (2011), 257, 261–9
Smith, Tony, 9
social media, 48, 51–3, 66, 67, 112, 164
Sontag, Susan, 278
Sopranos, The (HBO), 41–2, 44, 45, 47
Souto, Petra Ramalho, 260
Spatharis, Evgenios, 228, 236
spectacle, 10, 13, 19, 41, 44, 48, 59, 60, 68, 74, 82, 107, 161, 164, 167–9, 171, 174, 177, 178, 185n, 200n, 238n, 274, 280, 288
spectator, 3, 6, 13, 16, 29, 59–60, 62–4, 68–9, 95, 119, 122, 126, 127, 129, 130, 132, 133, 187, 190–200, 224–6, 256, 257, 275, 290, 291
  active, 5, 133
  and Artaud, 14, 15
  and Brecht, 15
  and cinema, 43–4
  and Féral, 31, 133
  and Fried, 167, 170, 186, 247
  and photography, 187, 190–200
  and Rancière, 4, 10, 12, 252
Spielberg, Steven, 152
Stam, Robert, 179, 182–3
Stein, Gertrude, 59, 64
Stephenson, Jenn, 77, 81
Sterritt, David, 281
Stewart, James, 3
Stoppard, Tom, 74
Szwed, John, 201

Taussig, Michael, 133
Taylor, Diana, 186–7, 195, 200n
Tegmark, Max, 108
Tempest, The (Shakespeare), 154
Testament (2010), 137–42
Third Nature, 105–9, 112–13, 115–17, 124

Titian, 266
Todd, Jane Marie, 173
Tokarczuk, Olgo, 19, 169, 172–7, 180
Trecartin, Ryan, 42, 47–9
Trump, Donald, 19, 130–6
Tsing, Anna Lowenhaupt, 59–60
Turturro, John, 282
  25th Hour (2002), 291
Tyler, Liv, 163, 166n

Uncle Josh at the Picture Show (1902), 44, 45, 47
unconscious, 14, 159, 178, 187, 188, 193, 194, 196, 245, 270

Vawter, Ron, 15–16
Veblen, Thorstein, 102
Vest, Jason P., 272
Veyne, Paul, 147
Villalta, Guillermo Pérez, 266

Walsh, Fintan, 195
Wayans, Damon, 283
Weber, Samuel, 73, 77, 128, 134, 141, 256
Whitaker, Brian, 151
Williams, Pharrell, 152
Williams, Raymond, 274
Williams, Tony, 207, 209–14, 218
Willingham, Ralph, 239, 243, 246, 247–8, 252
Wilson, Catherine, 90, 91
Witt, Mary Ann Frese, 71
Woman Without Sin (1941), 256, 257, 258–62, 264–5, 268–9, 270
Wooster Group, The, 15–16

Xarhakos, Stavros, 228, 231
Xelouris, Nikos, 228, 233

Zahera, Belén, 65
Zidane, Zinedine, 204–5, 206–7, 215
Žižek, Slavoj, 130–1, 136, 140
Zola, Émile, 13–14
Zuckerberg, Mark, 68

EU representative:
Easy Access System Europe
Mustamäe tee 50, 10621 Tallinn, Estonia
Gpsr.requests@easproject.com

www.ingramcontent.com/pod-product-compliance
Lightning Source LLC
Chambersburg PA
CBHW052052230426
43671CB00011B/1884